Seven Metaphysical Poets

Seven Metaphysical Poets

A Structural Study of
the Unchanging Self

ROBERT ELLRODT

OXFORD
UNIVERSITY PRESS

OXFORD

UNIVERSITY PRESS

Great Clarendon Street, Oxford OX2 6DP

Oxford University Press is a department of the University of Oxford.
It furthers the University's objective of excellence in research, scholarship,
and education by publishing worldwide in

Oxford New York

Athens Auckland Bangkok Bogotá Buenos Aires Calcutta
Cape Town Chennai Dar es Salaam Delhi Florence Hong Kong Istanbul
Karachi Kuala Lumpur Madrid Melbourne Mexico City Mumbai
Nairobi Paris São Paulo Singapore Taipei Tokyo Toronto Warsaw

and associated companies in Berlin Ibadan

Oxford is a registered trade mark of Oxford University Press
in the UK and certain other countries

Published in the United States
by Oxford University Press Inc., New York

British Library Cataloguing in Publication Data

Data available

Library of Congress Cataloging in Publication Data

Ellrodt, Robert.
Seven metaphysical poets: a structural study of the unchanging self/Robert Ellrodt.
p. cm.
1. English poetry—Early modern, 1500–1700—History and criticism. 2. Metaphysics in
literature. 3. Self in literature. I. Title.
PR545.M4 E43 2000   821'.309384—dc21   99–086586
ISBN 0-19-811738-8

1 3 5 7 9 10 8 6 4 2

Typeset in Sabon by
Cambrian Typesetters, Frimley, Surrey
Printed in Great Britain
on acid-free paper by
Biddles Ltd,
Guildford and King's Lynn

Preface and Acknowledgements

The three volumes of my doctoral thesis *Les poètes méta-physiques anglais*, which appeared in 1960, were designed to be a complete study of the characteristics and origins of the so-called Metaphysical poetry. Their very exhaustiveness may have partly obscured what I have come to consider as the main inter-est of my exploration after forty years of controversy over theory. At a time when French structuralism was in its heyday, I had sought to trace structures within the mind of each poet from an entirely different point of view. My emphasis was on the self of the author, whose 'death' was to be proclaimed by Roland Barthes shortly afterwards. For many years deconstruc-tion and other postmodernist currents have reduced personality to the 'subject of the enunciation' or 'the subjectivity effect'. The wheel of theory keeps turning, yet the neohistoricist method is still characterized by a tendency to look upon the self as a fiction or mere role-playing. My approach towards the problem forty years ago may therefore deserve attention from the new perspective of the turn of the century. Though my book was kindly reviewed as a literary study of the Metaphysicals, there has been so far no discussion of my contention that there is a permanent structural network of interrelations in the ways of thinking, feeling, and imagining of each author.

From the first two volumes of the earlier work I have extracted only what was essential for a demonstration of the coherence of a 'formal' personality. I have changed the architec-ture of the book, altered many details, and focused attention on the main argument. Several chapters on 'historical landmarks' have been added to trace the emergence of new trends and perceptions in the late sixteenth or early seventeenth century, and yet show that transformations in the environment did not determine individual choices but only made some of them possi-ble. The long Introduction is meant to provide theoretical grounds for my position.

Since 1960 hundreds of books and articles, many of them

brilliant, have been written on the Metaphysicals and their period. I have tried to take them into account whenever they either confirmed or contradicted my own views. Yet, with the exception of the Introduction and some chapters, I thought it best to confine these references or brief discussions to the notes. When the ideas I had expressed long ago had been—knowingly or unknowingly—restated and often enriched, it was the only way to show that I was not dressed in borrowed robes in the present volume.

I am thankful to the Librairie José Corti for the right to make extensive use of material borrowed from: *L'esprit du temps et l'inspiration personnelle chez les poètes métaphysiques anglais*, 3 vols. (Paris, 1960; vols. 1 and 2 reprinted 1973); and my essay 'De Platon à Traherne: L'intuition de l'instant chez les poètes métaphysiques anglais', in *Mouvements Premiers: Etudes critiques offertes à Georges Poulet* (Paris, 1972), 9–25.

Parts of the Introduction and of Chapters 4 and 17 are revised versions of my articles: 'Unchanging Forms of Identity in Literary Expression', *European Review*, Interdisciplinary Journal of the Academia Europaea (published by Cambridge University Press), 7 (1999), 113–26; 'Marvell's Mind and Mystery', in *Approaches to Marvell*, ed. C. A. Patrides (Routledge, 1978), 216–33; 'Espace et poésie de Donne à Traherne', *Espaces et représentations dans le monde anglo-américain*, Publications de la Société d'études anglo-américaines des 17e et 18e siècles (Presses de l'Université Paris-Sorbonne, 1981).

Some stray sentences are borrowed from my contribution to the Sphere History of English Literature: 'George Herbert and the Religious Lyric', in *English Poetry and Prose 1540–1674*, ed. Christopher Ricks (Sphere Books, 1970).

R.E.

Contents

Editions and References

CRASHAW, RICHARD

The Poems, English, Latin and Greek, ed. L. C. Martin (Oxford, 1927).
The Complete Poetry, ed. G. W. Williams (Garden City, NY, 1970).

DONNE, JOHN

Verse
Donne. Poetical Works, ed. H. J. C. Grierson (Oxford, 1929, repr. 1990).
NB: References are given to this edition (almost identical with the original 1912 edition) for the sake of clarity since the Elegies and the 'Holy Sonnets' are variously numbered in other editions.
The Divine Poems, ed. Helen Gardner (2nd edn., Oxford, 1978).
The Elegies and the Songs and Sonnets, ed. Helen Gardner (Oxford 1965).
The Epithalamions, Anniversaries and Epicedes, ed. W. Milgate (Oxford, 1978).
The Satires, Epigrams and Verse Letters, ed. W. Milgate (Oxford, 1967).

Verse and Prose
John Donne, ed. John Carey (Oxford, 1990).
John Donne. Complete Poetry and Selected Prose, ed. John Hayward (London, 1945).

Prose
Biathanatos, ed. Ernest W. Sullivan (Newark, NJ, 1987).
Devotions Upon Emergent Occasions, ed. Anthony Raspa (Oxford, 1987).
Essays in Divinity, ed. Evelyn M. Simpson (Oxford, 1952).
Paradoxes and Problems, ed. Helen Peters (Oxford, 1980).
The Sermons of John Donne, ed. George R. Potter and Evelyn M. Simpson, 10 vols. (Berkeley and Los Angeles, 1953–62).
In the absence of a complete modern edition Donne's Letters are usually quoted from Hayward or from:
The Life and Letters of John Donne, ed. Edmund Gosse, 2 vols. (London, 1899).

HERBERT, GEORGE

The Works of George Herbert, ed. F. E. Hutchinson (Oxford, 1941).

HERBERT OF CHERBURY, EDWARD, LORD

The Poems English & Latin, ed. G. C. Moore Smith (Oxford, 1923).
De Veritate, trans. and ed. Meyrick H. Carré (Bristol, 1937).

MARVELL, ANDREW

The Complete Works in Prose and Verse, ed. A. B. Grosart, 4 vols.
   (London, 1872–5).
The Poems and Letters, ed. H. M. Margoliouth, rev. P. Legouis and
   E. E. Duncan-Jones, 2 vols. (Oxford, 1971).

TRAHERNE, THOMAS

Centuries, Poems, and Thanksgivings, ed. H. M. Margoliouth, 2 vols.
   (Oxford, 1958).
Christian Ethicks, ed. Carol. L. Marks and George Robert Guffey
   (Ithaca, NY, 1968).
Commentaries of Heaven. The Poems, ed. D. D. C. Chambers
   (Salzburg, 1989).
Select Meditations, ed. Julia Smith (Manchester, 1997).

VAUGHAN, HENRY

The Works of Henry Vaughan, ed. L. C. Martin, 2 vols. (Oxford,
   1914).
NB: I occasionally cite *The Complete Poems*, ed. A. Rudrum
(Harmondsworth, 1976; New Haven, 1981).

In all references to poems I give only the title or the first line (sometimes shortened) without page reference since various readers will use different editions and the titles or first lines may be found in the tables or indexes of the editions mentioned.

For any other work or edition cited, including other prose works of Donne, Lord Herbert, and Marvell, as well as for all critical studies, full bibliographical indications are given in the footnotes *at the first occurrence in each chapter*. Thereafter surname and shortened title only are mentioned.

Not to puzzle the reader only the more common abbreviations are used for *periodicals* with the exception of *GHJ* for the *George Herbert Journal*, *JDJ* for the *John Donne Journal*.

Abbreviations

EA	*Etudes Anglaises*
ELH	*A Journal of English Literary History*
ELR	*English Literary Review*
GHJ	*George Herbert Journal*
JDJ	*John Donne Journal*
JHI	*Journal of the History of Ideas*
MLN	*Modern Language Notes*
MP	*Modern Philology*
NLH	*New Literary History*
PMLA	*Publications of the Modern Language Association of America*
RQ	*Renaissance Quarterly*
SEL 1500–1900	*Studies in English Literature 1500–1900* [Rice University]
SP	*Studies in Philology*
TSLL	*Texas Studies in Literature and Language*
UTQ	*University of Toronto Quarterly*

Introduction: The Singularity of the Self and its Revelation

The human psyche is part of the observed data of science.

Harold J. Morowitz in *The Mind's I*[1]

That a literary work, or a work of art, can be the expression of personality, bear the imprint of an individual self, has been considered an obsolete assumption for several decades by a large number of thinkers and critics, nowadays loosely labelled 'postmodernists'. Roland Barthes claimed that 'the author is never more than the instance writing, just as *I* is nothing other than the instance saying *I*'. Derrida maintained that 'there is nothing outside of the text'. Foucault denied the existence of 'an originating subject', and only admitted that the 'author' was a notion which allowed a 'limitation of the cancerous and dangerous proliferation of significations'. Though their perspective and methods are different, neohistoricists often concur with these views: Stephen Greenblatt concluded his brilliant study of several Renaissance authors with the assertion that he had not discovered 'an epiphany of identity freely chosen but a cultural artifact'.[2]

One should not forget that the questioning of personal identity started long before the twentieth century. It has even been claimed that the 'project of radically impersonalising discourse has obvious precedents in the mimetic tradition' and 'admits very little distinction from the inspirational tradition of Classical, Patristic

---

[1] Ed. D. R. Hofstadter and D. C. Dennett (Harmondsworth, 1981).
[2] Barthes, 'The Death of the Author' (1968), in Seán Burke's *Authorship: From Plato to the Postmodern* (Edinburgh, 1995), 127; see Burke's previous book: *The Death & Return of the Author* (Edinburgh, 1992). J. Derrida, *Of Grammatology* (1967), trans. G. C. Spivak (Baltimore, 1976), 158. M. Foucault, 'What is an Author?', in *Literary Criticism and Theory*, ed. C. Davis and L. Finke (Longman, 1989), 730. S. Greenblatt, *Renaissance Self-Fashioning from More to Shakespeare* (Chicago, 1980), 256.

and Medieval theory'.[3] There is, however, a major difference
between the unselfconscious objectivity prevailing in ancient and
medieval literature and the deliberate and insistently argued
denial of subjectivity—or its reduction to a 'subjectivity effect'—
in our own age. I have suggested that this denial was the last stage
in the development of an ever more intense reflexive consciousness from Montaigne to Amiel, Valéry, and Jean-Paul Sartre, and
must refer the reader to earlier studies of this evolution.[4]

Hume was first responsible for the philosophical negation of
any identity in the mind, though his observation of the disorderly flow of perceptions had been anticipated by Montaigne:

The mind is a kind of theatre, where several perceptions successively
make their appearance; pass, repass, glide away and mingle in an infinite variety of postures and situations. There is properly no *simplicity*
in it at one time nor identity in different . . .[5]

With the Romantics, however, the belief in the unifying power
of the imagination magnified the self. In Browning's youthful
poem *Pauline*, the Cartesian *cogito* became a rapturous intuition of individuality:

> I am made up of an intensest life,
> Of a most clear idea of consciousness
> Of self—distinct from all its qualities,
> From all affections, passions, feelings, powers . . .
> This is myself . . .

But this intuition could divest the self of all particularities,
allowing it to 'be all, have, see, know, taste, feel all'. A mind
given (unlike Browning's) to constant introspection would only
discover in its 'pure subjectivity' what Henri Frédéric Amiel
descried as 'a negation of negation, a reflection which is
reflected like two mirrors placed in opposition to each other',[6]

---

[3] Burke, *Authorship*, p. xvi. See also John Carey's 'Afterword 1990', *John
Donne: Life, Mind and Art* (rev. edn., London, 1990).

[4] See *Genèse de la conscience moderne*, ed. R. Ellrodt (Paris, 1983).

[5] *A Treatise of Human Nature*, I. iv. 6; on Montaigne see R. Ellrodt,
'L'interrogation sur l'identité de Montaigne à Donne', in *Renaissances européennes
et Renaissance française*, ed. G. Gadoffre (Montpellier, 1995).

[6] Amiel, *Journal intime*, 19 April 1876; ed. Gagnebin (Lausanne, 1987), X.
681. Amiel saw himself 'comme boîte à phénomènes, comme lieu de vision et de
perception, comme personne impersonnelle, comme sujet sans individualité déter-
minée, comme déterminabilité et formabilité pures' (8 March 1868; VII. 13).

a clear anticipation of the later descriptions of consciousness as trapped between parallel mirrors in the introspection of Valéry and the ontology of Sartre.[7]

In a different way, closer to Hume's and to late eighteenth-century sensationalism, nineteenth-century scientific thought reduced the self to 'the sum of the mutable sensations produced in an organism', claiming that it was 'always incomplete and never identical with itself', which made a 'total metamorphosis of the individual possible', as suggested by pathological cases of split personality.[8] In literature, however, two different tendencies produced different kinds of impersonality. The objective novelist could absent himself from his work, like Flaubert, and still bestow a definite identity on each of his characters. On the other hand the stream of consciousness novel brought individuality to the forefront only to dissolve it. For Virginia Woolf as for David Hume 'the mind receives a myriad impressions . . . an incessant shower of atoms'. The self is not denied: 'Perhaps there's "I" at the middle of it, she thought; a knot, a centre . . .'. But individuality is obscure and diffuse; it is not experienced as a reflexive ego, only as a 'wedge-shaped core of darkness' or 'the unseen part of us which spreads wide'. In later novels identity becomes soluble; the self and the world, or the self and the other merge: 'I am not one person; I am many people; I do not altogether know what I am'; 'Am I all of them? Am I one and distinct? I do not know.'[9]

The negation of identity was not carried further when Barthes spoke of a 'dispersion' and 'diffraction' of the self. Nor did he say anything Montaigne had not already observed when he saw mere pretence in the 'distinctive features of personality', even from the point of view of intellectual allegiance: 'you discover that you are at once (or in succession) obsession-ridden, hysterical, paranoiac and furthermore perverse, . . . or

---

[7] J.-P. Sartre, *L'être et le néant* (Paris, 1943), 118. E. Gaède points out a parallel between Valéry (in *Variété I*, 189) and Nietzsche: *Nietzsche et Valéry* (Paris, 1962), 469.

[8] Jean Starobinski, 'Sur quelques formes de critique de la notion d'identité', *Identität*, ed. O. Marquard and K. Stierle (Munich, 1979), 644–53. These theories have been revived by modern biologists and critics.

[9] V. Woolf, *The Common Reader* (London, 1925), 189; *The Years* (London, 1937), 395; *To the Lighthouse* (London, 1927), 99; *Mrs Dalloway* (London, 1925), 232; *The Waves* (London, 1931), 196, 205; cf. *The Years*, 150.

that you add up all decadent philosophies: epicureanism, eude-
monism, asianism, manicheism, pyrrhonism'.[10] The structuralist or postmodernist view of the self is only original when it rests
on the assumption that 'it is language which speaks, not the
author'.[11]

My own conviction has always been that the author does
speak and, when the writing is not purely imitative, does reveal
some characteristics of his identity. Besides, through the study of
a number of poets I was led to think that some unchanging
structures of the individual mind were discernible in literary
works. This was not at all a plea for biographical criticism: long
before Barthes, Montaigne already knew that, in some respects,
'it is the work which affects the life, not the life which affects
the work',[12] which does not imply that the work is unaffected
by the author's individual ways of thinking, imagining, and feeling. Barthes asserted that even in autobiography an author was
'dispossessed of himself' by the text and could only assume
different *personae*.[13] Seeing 'a mere plurality' in the author, he
maintained that the very invention of a language results in 'the
destruction of the subject'. When he described Loyola, Sade, or
Fourier as 'founders of language', he did not seek particular
idiosyncratic characteristics in their style (with an exception for
Fourier): his interest lay only in what lends itself to a decompo-
sition since structuralist criticism looks upon a literary work as
'a system of functions'.[14]

One may choose to privilege the flavour of individual speech
or style (which need not imply the discarding of function);

---

[10] *Roland Barthes par Roland Barthes* (Paris, 1973), 146–7; cf. Montaigne,
Essais II. i and III. ii.

[11] Barthes, 'The Death of the Author', in Burke, *Authorship*, 126.

[12] Barthes, 'Image-Music-Text', in *Literary Criticism and Theory*, ed. R. C.
Davies (London, 1989), 717; cf. Montaigne, *Essays*, III. ix: 'I finde this unexpected
profit by the publication of my maners, that . . . I am sometimes surprised with this
consideration, not to betray the history of my life' (Everyman, III. 225). The *Essays*
are quoted in English from Everyman's edition of Florio's translation (3 vols.,
London, 1965); in French, from the Pléiade edition (Paris, 1950).

[13] *Roland Barthes par Roland Barthes*, 6. Seán Burke is right when he claims
that Barthes, however, finally turned the author into 'an object of biographical pleasure' (*Death & Return*, 47). His scattered 'biographemes' may even remind us of
Montaigne's 'essays'; yet, unlike Montaigne, Barthes never said that his book was
the faithful reflection of his 'forme essentielle': *Essais*, III. iii; Pléiade, 920.

[14] Roland Barthes, *Sade, Fourier, Loyola* (Paris, 1971), 14; *Essais critiques*
(Paris, 1964), 251.

witness the words of a later Jesuit, the true creator of his own 'language' in poetry, Gerard Manley Hopkins:

. . . I consider my selfbeing, my consciousness and feeling of myself, of *I* and *me* above and in all things, which is more distinctive than the taste of ale or alum, more distinctive than the smell of walnut leaf or camphor, and is incommunicable by any means to another man (as when I was a child I used to ask myself: What must it be to be some-one else?). Nothing else in nature comes near this unspeakable stress of pitch, distinctiveness, and selving, this selfbeing of my own. Nothing explains it or resembles it, except so far as this, that other men to themselves have the same feeling. But this only multiplies the phenomena to be explained so far as the cases are like and do resemble. But to me there is no resemblance: searching nature I taste self but at one tankard, that of my own being.[15]

The inner sense of personal identity is here apprehended as a savour and a smell: this is a sensation, not a metaphor. One might think of Sartre's perception of the body as a 'goût fade' in *La Nausée*, but with Hopkins it is a flavour particular to each individual. In one of his poems sound becomes the revelator of identity and singularity:

> each tucked string tells, each hung bell's
> Bow swung finds tongue to fling out broad its name;
> Each mortal thing does one thing and the same:
> Deals out that being indoors each one dwells;
> Selves—goes itself; *myself* it speaks and spells;
> Crying *What I do is me: for that I came.*

> ('As kingfishers catch fire, dragon flies draw flames')

Here the poet only reveals his own subjective reaction to sense impressions. But is it not true that the sound of a voice enables us to recognize someone unseen? Psychoanalysts agree that style is not merely the product of a culture at a given moment, but an individual mode of expression. According to Janine Chasseguet-Smirgel 'any fragment of a work by Rembrandt or Bonnard, a single sentence of Proust or Chateaubriand, a line of Mozart or Debussy, are—at least virtually—recognizable, just as a fragment of bone allows a naturalist to discern the animal it belongs

[15] 'On St Ignatius's Spiritual Exercises', in *A Hopkins Reader*, ed. J. Pick (Oxford, 1953), 297.

to, just as a graphologist can identify a scriptor from one stroke of the pen'.[16] No individual creates his language *ab ovo*, but the social instrument of communication does acquire in the thinking mind and the speaking mouth particular turns, tones, and sounds whenever it is not limited to psittacism or tautology, or used for parody. *Oratio imago animi* was a commonplace, expanded by Ben Jonson: 'Language most shows a man: Speak that I may see thee. It springs out of the most retired and inmost parts of us, and is the image of the parent of it, the mind. No glass renders a man's form or likeness so true as his speech.'[17]

It may be objected that this assumption rests on unverifiable impressions. Is there an objective basis for the singularity of the self and its revelation in creative writing? One may look for it in biology, in psychoanalysis, and in personality studies.

The existence of an 'immunological' or 'biological self', based on a genetic profile, is undisputed.[18] Whether human cloning, if ever practised, would make several individuals perfectly alike is a question as yet unanswered;[19] but, if it did, we would have a reduplication of a single identity whose unique character would not be destroyed. Besides, in all likelihood, each cloned human being, through varied experiences, would develop particular reactions to stimuli, feel particular emotions, form particular thoughts, and thus become an identifiable self, which some may choose to call a soul. This might realize Keats's dream of a soul originally deprived of identity and achieving it through its life in the 'vale of soul-making'.[20]

The genetic 'identity card' of each individual, however, results from processes which are not conscious. Despite its 'capacity for distinguishing the *self* from the *non-self*', the immune system is not a 'subject'; it cannot give origin to the

[16] *Pour une psychanalyse de l'art et de la créativité* (Paris, 1971), 46.

[17] *Discoveries*, in *Ben Jonson*, ed. C. H. Herford, Percy Simpson, and Evelyn Simpson (Oxford, 1925–52), VIII. 625.

[18] In *Le cerveau et la liberté* (Paris, 1995), 74–88, Pierre Karli offers a clear exposition of this identity and its limitations. The existence of the biological self is acknowledged by psychoanalysts: see Wolf H. Friedman, 'La connaissance de soi biologique', in *L'inconscient et la science*, ed. R. Dorey (Paris, 1991).

[19] Changeux, however, confidently assumes that 'aucun individu n'est identique à son voisin, fût-il un clone': J. P. Changeux and Paul Ricœur, *La nature et la règle* (Paris, 1998), 206.

[20] *Letters*, To George and Georgiana Keats, 3 May 1819.

intuition of personal identity.[21] Between the genetic profile of an individual and its psychic profile there may be relations but, as C. J. F. Williams observed, it is neither possible nor even intelligible to assert there is any identity between phenomena that may be physically and chemically described and the states of mind apprehended and described by a subject.[22]

When it steers clear of Lacanian myths,[23] psychoanalysis can shed light on the development of personal identity. Castoriadis, disinclined to follow 'the Lacan/Barthes/Derrida line', refused 'to resorb the human subject in language'. Admitting that Freud has described the psyche as a multiplicity rather than a subject by distinguishing and opposing various instances (the id, the ego, and the superego), he nevertheless assumed that the human subject tends to unity. He showed how, through the interplay of various instances and the process of sublimation, a 'social individual' emerges, whose 'unity/identity' is not due only to his social condition, but to values and motivations which make his behaviour largely—though not always—predictable. Yet he acknowledged that this social artefact, which hides the contradictions of the psyche, cannot be the human subject. This subject is the Freudian *Ich*, the conscious *I*, which cannot be reduced to a reasoning and calculating performance found in animals as well. Its distinctive feature is the self-reflexivity which turns the very activity of the subject into an object, by position though not by nature. The conscious subject alone can say 'je m'agis comme activité agissante'. Castoriadis thought that this possibility was 'very rarely realized' in the various societies known in history and even among individuals of our own society.[24] It is the historical emergence of this self-consciousness and its consequences that I have sought to trace in literature.[25]

---

[21] Cornélius Castoriadis, 'L'état du sujet aujourd'hui', *Topique. Revue Freudienne*, 38 (Nov. 1986), 13, 26.

[22] *Being, Identity, and Truth* (Oxford, 1992); cf. Changeux and Ricœur, *La nature et la règle*, 188.

[23] Yves Lebeaux rejects 'Lacan's sharp opposition of an essentially unconscious subject, determined by the symbolic, and an essentially conscious I, caught in the illusion of the imaginary': 'Je, Sujet et identification', *Topique*, 37 (Mar. 1986), 77–92.   [24] *Topique*, 38 (1986) 13, 19–24, 26–7.

[25] In *Genèse de la conscience moderne*.

While retaining several levels—biological, psychical, social—
Castoriadis ascribed a complex unity to each human being, a
unity which may suffer change:

There is, no doubt, a certain unity of each individual psyche, at least
as a common origin and binding coexistence of forces waging a long
war in the same theatre of operations. There is, in a way, the more or
less stable unity imposed upon the individual by society. Beyond it,
there is a unity aimed at, or that we should aim at: the unity which
proceeds from a reflective representation of the self and from deliberate initiative.[26]

The construction and perception of the self has been a major
subject of interest and debate in psychology and sociology ever
since William James's seminal chapter 'The Consciousness of
Self' in his *Principles of Psychology* (1890). It has no immediate
relevance to the present study focused on the presence and
permanence of individual characteristics in literary creation.
The typology of personality studies, usually called in France
'caractérologie', has a more direct bearing since it is based on a
selection of traits and on the existence of structures and systems
founded on patterns of correlations, that is co-variation in a
number of behavioural acts.[27] It is assumed that 'the ultimate
objective of psychology is to know and to state the intimate web
of all these interrelationships'. The aim is 'to embrace personality in all its aspects', for partial approaches lead only to partial
understanding, yet, despite the claim of 'functional unity', the
psychologist has first to build 'separate systems' (for perception,
learning, feeling, etc.) before discovering how they interact and
intertwine.[28]

The methods of investigation and the criteria of personality
studies are seldom applicable to literature. Physiological
measures (for activity, excitability, manic-depressive, or paranoid
tendencies) can apply only to living individuals though symptoms may be traced in their writings. Among the behavioural
'traits' selected many are not really 'structures': e.g. relaxation in

---

[26] *Topique*, 38 (1986), 37. My translation.
[27] H. J. Eysenck, *The Structure of Human Personality* (London, 1953), 1–9,
317 ff.; David Krech and George Klein, *Theoretical Models and Personality Theory*
(Durham, NC, 1952), 6–17.
[28] Krech and Klein, *Theoretical Models*, 17, 7; Eysenck, *Human Personality*,
319.

posture, love of physical comfort, of eating, of polite ceremony, etc.[29] Most psychologists have refrained from an extension of their investigations to the revelation of personality in literary works or works of art.

Some elaborate attempts at applying 'characterology' to authors are noticeable in France. The wide-ranging treatise of René Le Senne, using the documents and ratings of G. Heymans and E. Wiersma, distributed writers, artists, and other historical figures among eight fundamental types—nervous, sentimental, choleric, passionate, sanguine, phlegmatic, amorphous, apathetic—resulting from various combinations of six dominant factors: emotive/non-emotive, active/non-active, primary/secondary.[30] My reservations were expressed in 1960; I can only recall some of them here. Though Le Senne admits that the various profiles can shade off into one another, his categories sharply separate authors who seem to belong to the same spiritual family in several respects. Montaigne and Donne, for instance, would be placed at temperamental extremes; yet they have in common an inclination to scepticism, an intense self-awareness, and a desire for a conscious death which I consider important features of their literary 'identity'.[31] Among the 'supplementary' traits of character we find such notions as the 'love of nature' or 'the love of animals', but one may love nature or animals for different reasons and in different ways. As in all personality studies, Le Senne's distinctions are often based on variations in quantity or intensity; but it is the 'form', rather than the degree, of emotiveness that may be discerned in literature and may prove particular to one individual. Even the opposition between primary and secondary proceeds from degrees of perseveration and Eysenck rightly argued that 'the apparently complete lack of inter-relationship between different types of perseveration makes it meaningless to use the general term at

---

[29] In W. H. Sheldon's *The Varieties of Temperament* (New York, 1942).

[30] *Traité de caractérologie* (Paris, 1943). Le Senne's notions, combined with the traditional biographical approach, have been used for monographs, like Pierre Mesnard's *Le Cas Diderot* (Paris, 1952).

[31] Montaigne is said to be phlegmatic (*Caractérologie*, 476). Donne shows several of the characteristics ascribed to the nervous type: see my *Poètes métaphysiques*, I. 257–64.

all'.[32] From a structural point of view Jung's distinction of introversion and extroversion and Le Senne's opposition of 'egocentricity' and 'allocentricity' are more fruitful, but call for qualifications and nuances.[33] The criterion I found most relevant to literary study is the extension of the 'field of consciouness', but it proves only a general frame for the various ways in which space and duration are apprehended in the unveiling of the world to the individual consciousness.

I am aware that the search for individual modes of thought in literary works is open to several objections even if the existence of a personal identity is unchallenged. Proust himself reminds us that 'a book is the product of another self than the self we hold up to view in our habits, in society, in our vices'.[34] This distinction suits me since I am concerned with the deeper self and with structures which are not evident and may not be conscious. Another objection arises from the conviction that the good poet, as Yeats maintained, always speaks from behind a mask, and the particular claim that the speaker in a Renaissance poem is not the author, but a *persona* he creates. Again I could be content to point out that the deep-lying structures I seek to bring out are bound to influence the creation of *personae* and may be unaffected by the choice of attitudes or points of view different from the author's own inclinations and experiences: the same characteristics are traceable in Donne's libertine elegies and lyrics, in poems apparently of passionate love, and in his Divine Poems. I am inclined, however, to challenge the assumption now current, that the 'I' of the speaker in a Renaissance poem is commonly intended to be different from the 'I' of the poet.[35]

The poem, of course, can be the utterance of a particular 'character', usually historical or mythical, in the tradition of Ovid's *Heroïdes*: Drayton's 'Heroicall Epistles' antedate Browning's *Dramatis Personae*. The writer can also assume a fictitious name in a fictive frame, as Spenser did in *Colin Clouts*

---

[32] *Structure of Human Personality*, 283.

[33] See *Poètes métaphysiques*, I. 63–4, 126–35.

[34] Marcel Proust, *Contre Sainte-Beuve*, ed. Pierre Clarac (Paris, 1971), 221–2; cf. p. 224: 'ce qu'on a écrit seul pour soi-même, c'est bien l'œuvre de soi'.

[35] See J. Mazzeo, *Transformation in the Renaissance English Lyric* (Ithaca, NY, 1970), ch. 5.

Come Home Again, or as Thomas Nashe dramatized his own personality in *Pierce Pennilesse*; yet in this case the *persona* was meant to speak for the author.[36] Poetry in general was admittedly the art of 'feigning'. The Elizabethans knew the original meaning of *persona*, a mask, and their notion of the 'person' was closer to 'impersonation' than to a 'self': the term could be used for a role played in society as on the stage, the role of father or husband, of merchant or lawyer, of king or subject, as well as the role of lover or melancholy man, of satirist or malcontent, or any sort of attitudinizing.[37] Erasmus had described the orator as a Proteus[38] and the poet too was endowed with the faculty of 'expressing various affections, representing various persons so accurately . . . that he seemed a very Proteus'.[39] This was obvious in dramatic or epic poetry as in heroical epistles. In lyric poetry, however, there is to my knowledge no evidence that the author intended the speaker to stand for someone else, unless he or she was of a different sex. Inversely, there is plenty of evidence that many readers and collectors of poems assumed that the latter were based on personal experience since they provided biographical titles for them.[40]

Conventions and the eagerness to display wit may seem to turn Renaissance poems into a mere play with signifiers, but this is a different thing. The Elizabethan poets, of course, confessed, as Giles Fletcher did in the dedication of *Licia* (1593), that 'a man may write of love and not be in love'. Yet, from the troubadours to the Renaissance, it was also assumed that the poet

36 Cf. R. B. Gill on 'The Persona of Late Elizabethan Satire', *SP* 72 (1975), 409: 'The satirists themselves would have us think that the voice is their own, and there is evidence that their contemporaries as well as readers for three hundred years have regarded it as such.'

37 See Robert C. Elliott, *The Literary Persona* (Chicago, 1982).

38 Erasmus, *De Copia*, ed. B. I. Knott, in *Opera Omnia* (Amsterdam, 1988), I. 34, 76.

39 Daniel d'Augé, *Deux dialogues de l'invention poétique* (1560), quoted by Jean Lecointe, *L'idéal et la différence: La perception de la personnalité littéraire à la Renaissance* (Paris, 1993), 442.

40 'Dr Donne his wife would have gone as his Page' (for 'By our strange and fatall interview'), 'Dr Dunne on his Departure from his Love' (for 'Sweetest love'), 'Dr Donne. On his Picture which hee left with his mris when he went to travaile' (for 'His Picture'): D. A. Larson, 'Donne's Contemporary Reputation', *JDJ* 12 (1993), 124–6. This was often wrong or naive, but not unexpected in an age when a tale had to be presented as real to be more attractive.

must have had at least an experience of love to write a success-
ful love poem, even if he wrote in different circumstances.[41]
Donne's admission 'I did best when I had least truth for my
subject' is well known, but ambiguous in context.[42] Sir Philip
Sidney implied he spoke his mind in his poetry when he
declared: 'over-mastred by some thoughts, I yeelded an inckie
tribute unto them'.[43] It did not prevent him from taking model
on his predecessors in many sonnets, but he did mean to express
a real experience—or his memory of it—when he said to
himself: 'Come, let me write, and to what end? to ease | A
burthened hart?'[44]

Many modern critics when they use the term *persona* mean
no more than role-playing. One can argue that 'there is no layer
deeper, more authentic than theatrical self-representation'.[45]
There is, however, a major difference between playing a ready-
made part entrusted to you as an actor and playing a part one
has to choose and invent: a full revelation of a man's authentic
personality can only be expected when he himself truly 'creates'
the part he acts. In Donne's elegies, satires, and love poems, as
in contemporary Petrarchan sonnets, there is often a mere
posing for effect. It is in keeping with the Elizabethan tendency
to look upon the world as a stage; in keeping, too, with the
prevailing fantasticality of the age, as well as Donne's own
confessed 'humorous' disposition and temperamental instability
which invited constant changes of mood. When attitudinizing in
this way, however, the author does not intend to be taken for
someone else: it would spoil his pretence. One may feel at times

[41]   Maurice Valency, *In Praise of Love* (London, 1958), 108–16. My conception
of poetic sincerity as 'truth to oneself', irrespective of autobiographical experience,
was set forth in *Poètes métaphysiques*, I. 165–72.

[42]   It was an excuse for writing a mediocre 'Hymn to the Saints, and to
Marquesse Hamylton' (*Epithalamions*, 209). See my article 'Poésie et vérité chez
John Donne', *EA* 40 (1987), 1–14.

[43]   *An Apology for Poetry*, in *Elizabethan Critical Essays*, ed. G. G. Smith
(Oxford, 1904), I. 195.

[44]   *Astrophel and Stella*, xxxiv. Donne may be echoing Sidney in 'The triple
Foole': 'I thought, if I could draw my paines, | Through Rimes vexation, I should
them allay', but he also wrote to Mr T. W.: 'My verse, the strict Map of my misery'
('At once, from hence . . .') and 'Hast thee, harsh verse . . . my pain and pleasure I
have given thee'.

[45]   Stephen Greenblatt, 'Psychoanalysis and Renaissance Culture', in *Learning
to Curse* (London, 1990), 142–3. A theory illustrated in his *Sir Walter Ralegh: The
Renaissance Man and His Roles* (New Haven, 1973).

that Donne might have described himself as Tristan Corbière in his Epitaph: 'Ne fut quelqu'un ni quelque chose: | Son naturel était la pose.'[46] The critics who turn the *Songs and Sonets*, or the poems of Marvell, into a gallery of *personae* substitute a series of *flat* figures for one *round* and rich character. As in Shakespeare's Hamlet the very contradictions between the various moods and attitudes reflect the diversity and depth of a personality. Hugh H. Richmond's view of Donne's complexity comes, in fact, close to mine when he proposes a single *persona*:

Donne chose systematically to create for himself *both in and out of his lyrics* [my italics] a *persona* as complex, subjective, and volatile as any of Shakespeare's most gifted heroes: whether we think of Petrucchio or Berowne, Benedick or Faulconbridge, Hamlet or Antony.[47]

The distinction between the *persona* and the man here becomes tenuous. The personality is not dissolved in a multiplicity of roles. Some of the roles may be held for a short time, others may turn into habits, but we always hear the same voice, as Helen Gardner contended[48] and George T. Wright admitted, though he assumed the presence of many 'speakers':

Donne certainly is in his speakers in the sense that they use his own voice—not only his words and manners, his irony, his wit, the toughness of his language, but his personal force, his style of perceiving, his sense of relations between men and women, his apprehension of the world's structure generally and his way of registering its emblematic patterns.[49]

No more is needed to justify my use of these alleged speakers' words in an attempt to trace the permanent modes of imagination and sensibility of their unique creator. The search can extend to the *Devotions* and the *Sermons* though the sick man and the preacher chose another pose, created another artistic self. The pose can even introduce an element of impersonality since it is 'self-reflecting, man-reflecting, and God-reflecting simultaneously',[50] but I would not say that 'in the realm of

---

[46] *Œuvres complètes*, ed. C. Cros (Paris, 1970).

[47] 'Personal Identity and Literary Personae', *PMLA* 90 (1975), 217.

[48] *In Defence of the Imagination* (Oxford, 1982), 6.

[49] 'The Personae of Donne's Love Poems', *Southern Quarterly*, 14 (1976), 174.

[50] Kate Gardner Frost, *Holy Delight: Typology, Numerology, and Autobiography in Donne's Devotions Upon Emergent Occasions* (Princeton, 1990), 37 (quoting Jonathan Goldberg's Ph.D. diss.).

grace all Christian experience is essentially common', for I hope to prove that the modes of it vary for each believer.

Strangely enough some modern critics have resorted to the assumption of *personae* in order to free Donne from the charge of libertinism in his early poems.[51] He certainly seems at times to over-indulge in cynicism in order to surprise or shock the reader, but he is quite unlikely to have intended to deride his 'speakers' and confute them implicitly by using false arguments. It is true that he said of his own Paradoxes that they 'are rather alarums to truth to arme her then her enemies',[52] but he had to be apologetic about them in a letter to Wotton. In fact, it was the flouting of the moral law or common opinion that made them exciting: the self-exposure of the speaker, a technique practised by Swift and Browning, was not intended. Since Donne himself later deplored his youthful transgressions in his Holy Sonnets, there is no reason to look upon his libertine poems as satires on libertinism. On the other hand, to maintain that the Holy Sonnets reveal 'a Donne behind the scenes—an artist who has set a persona on stage to act out a parable of conversion'[53] is to doubt the reality of his grief for his sins. He seemed to be doing violence to his own nature in his attempt to love God, as Chapter 1 will show, but his fear for the consequences of his sins was all too real.

In a survey of *Donne's Religious Writing*,[54] P. M. Oliver draws subtler distinctions. He assumes we hear 'the authentic voice of John Donne' in his letters to his friends (pp. 214, 239); he discovers only 'fabricated speakers' and 'a range of voices' in the satires and the *Songs and Sonets* (53, 200), finds a 'world of fantasies' in the Holy Sonnets (chapters 4 and 5), yet acknowledges the presence of 'a complex amalgam of the real-life Donne and a literary persona' in his post-ordination poetry and in the *Sermons* (239). He even admits that the 'Hymn to Christ' reflected 'real-life fears' about his safety (218–19) and the 'Hymn to God my God' was 'literally a product of his sickness'

[51] P. G. Pinka in *This Dialogue of One* (Alabama UP, 1982), L. A. Mann in *UTQ* 50 (1980–1), 284–99, L. D. Tjarks in *Southern Quarterly*, 14 (1976), 207–13.
[52] *Paradoxes and Problems*, p. xxvi.
[53] G. A. Springer, 'Donne's Religious *Personae*', *Southern Quarterly*, 14 (1976), 193.
[54] Provocatively subtitled 'A Discourse of Feigned Devotion' (London, 1997).

(231). I have no objection to the 'fantasizing' discerned in Donne's poetry (12), whether profane or sacred. I usually refrain from distinguishing what was 'real' and what was 'fantasized' for the fantasies of a writer are a part of his self as real as the facts of his life since they bear the imprint of his fundamental forms of thought, imagination, and sensibility.[55] I further claim that these forms are unaffected by the 'inconsistencies' Oliver discovers: they were part of Donne's complex personality.

Critics have made a more temperate use of *personae* in the interpretation of George Herbert's *Temple*.[56] When the poet is said to speak as a Christian Everyman in 'Redemption', 'Man's medley', or 'Ungratefulnesse' I can agree;[57] yet he speaks with his own voice in a distinctly personal way. In the poetry of Marvell some have discovered a 'dual self' or 'fragmented selves', or a 'threefold personality' in 'Appleton House';[58] which means little more than various aspects of a single self.[59] Vaughan and Traherne claim to be autobiographical—a claim which, of course, leaves any writer free to live a life of allegory and seek 'to epitomize human history in his own life'.[60]

A more serious objection to the tracing of individual modes of thinking is the lack of originality in some poems. The extreme postmodernist position does not worry me for it may be rejected as contrary to evidence. A text to Barthes is 'a multi-dimensional

---

[55] Oliver agrees that 'all artistic creation is linked in some way to its creator' (53), but doesn't say why. In *Christ Revealed: The History of the Neotypological Lyric in the English Renaissance* (Gainesville, 1982), Ira Clark assumes that Donne 'presents personally dramatic, exemplary self-portrayals' in which 'he becomes a neotype of Christ' (77), which also implies a presence of his personality.

[56] In *Too Rich to Clothe the Sunne: Essays on George Herbert*, ed. Claude J. Summers (Pittsburgh, 1980).

[57] Diana Benet in *Secretary of Praise: The Poetic Vocation of George Herbert* (Missouri UP, 1984), 40–2, 71–4. Harold Toliver sensibly remarks that Herbert 'presents himself to us as a person', but his 'many sided exploration of ego . . . is accompanied by a parabolic lifting of self into type': *George Herbert's Christian Narrative* (Pennsylvania State UP, 1993), 252.

[58] Charles Molesworth, 'Marvell's "Upon Appleton House": The Persona as Historian, Philosopher, and Poet', *SEL 1500–1900*, 13 (1973), 149–62. See Ch. 4.

[59] When Barbara Harman in *Costly Monuments: Representations of the Self in George Herbert's Poetry* (Cambridge, Mass., 1982) speaks of 'the self as a plurality of selves' about George Herbert (152), it also means 'a fluid identity' (159), not a real plurality.

[60] Ira Clark on Traherne in *Neotypological Lyric*, 153.

space in which a variety of writings, *none of them original*, blend and clash' (my italics).[61] A text is a chain of signifiers, but the chain is formed in an individual consciousness, and it is not formed in 'absolute randomness'. Since, according to phenomenology all consciousness is a 'position-taking',[62] when writing consciously the 'place-where-from' the words issue is a mind stored with individual memories of particular texts and particular experiences. In writing, unlike perception, the mind's 'intention' must create its 'object' out of this store: the choice and collocation of the words for the emergence of a 'new' text will be determined at once by the writer's intention (a foreglimpsed theme or idea, however vague), by his individual inclinations, and by the particular mental structures that emerged from my analyses. Originality lies in the individual choice, conscious or unconscious. With the least imaginative writers ready-made remembered phrases and images will be dominant, as in some imitators of Petrarch. Creative writers, particularly in the modern age, may choose to echo earlier texts, yet make an original use of their borrowings, as T. S. Eliot did in *The Waste Land*. Among the poets studied in this book Donne, George Herbert, and Traherne obviously had 'no purpose to come into any mans debt', as the author of 'Metempsychosis' proclaimed ('Epistle'). Both Crashaw and Vaughan at times take model on George Herbert, though in different ways; I shall show how they nevertheless betray their own proclivities. Lord Herbert was influenced by Donne, Jonson, and Carew: that is one of the reasons why distinctive characteristics are harder to trace in his poetry.

In the search for these characteristics my approach was empirical, starting from the individual achievement. The observations that emerged from my analyses of the texts were uninfluenced by philosophical or psychological preconceptions. Yet a coherence was gradually discovered and seemed to be dictated by an inner necessity, by permanent habits of thought. Personality studies, though based on types, allow for some change for they take into consideration impulses and affects that experience and age may modify, and for some psychologists

---

[61] 'The Death of the Author', in *The Rustle of Language*, ed. R. Howard (Oxford, 1986), 52.
[62] Richard Harland, *Beyond Superstructuralism* (London, 1993), 72 ff.

the identity of the individual proceeds from unceasing destructurations and restructurations. No one can deny that the self undergoes evolutions and even dramatic changes which may result in a deep alteration of behaviour. I only claim that such changes did not modify some structures of the individual mind revealed in the works of seven poets.

The definition of the permanent modes of thought and imagination traceable in the writings of each author had to be based on an exhaustive exploration. For the apprehension of temporality Georges Poulet had been an innovator in his penetrating *Etudes sur le temps humain*,[63] but his empathy and intuition recreated the subjectivity of each writer from a limited number of significant examples in fairly short essays. I thought it necessary to give a full survey of all relevant examples and prove that the structures may be discerned even in poems or passages apparently alien in theme or form to the predominant tendencies of each poet's mind. Thus, in the case of Donne, the poet of 'presentness', past and future are apprehended in terms of the present, the past by inclusion or recreation, the future by anticipation (Chapter 6). In other cases, one will discover that the writer passively followed a tradition or a convention, but I show in Chapter 12 that Crashaw's invitation to 'shut our eyes that we may see' in the *Epiphanie Hymn* does not truly make it an isolated poem among his other compositions: even in this sole flight of negative mysticism, he, unlike Vaughan, does not allow his imagination, nor the reader's, to sink into the night of the senses.

The possible conjunction of individual and social factors in the production of the text was not ignored. In fact, my conception of the relationship between the individual and his environment in the process of literary creation was not unlike the type of relationship Michel Foucault described some years later:

The significant sequence by means of which the unique experience of the individual is elaborated is perpendicular to the formal system according to which the significations of a culture are elaborated: at every moment the particular structure of individual experience finds

---

[63] Translated as *Studies in Human Time* (Baltimore, 1956): 'one of the major works of our time' according to Paul de Man: *Blindness and Insight* (2nd edn., 1983), 101.

among the systems of society a certain number of possible choices or solutions, and excludes other possibilities; conversely the social structures, wherever a choice is required, come across a number of suitable individuals and others that are unsuitable, just as the linear structure of language always makes it possible, at a certain moment, to choose between several words or phonemes, but will exclude all others.[64]

In a similar way, though not in linguistic terms, I had argued that each of the poets I studied had been in a position to choose among the various modes of expression available to all authors in his own age, though his individual modes of thinking, imagining, and feeling excluded some choices.[65] Conversely, social structures in a given environment seemed to be responsible for the statistical predominance of certain characteristics in the available modes of literary expression chosen by a certain number of suitable individuals, though not by all the individuals living in this environment. An interplay of individual and social structures articulated in this way imparts intelligibility to the literary creations of the individual mind and to literary history. It introduces a certain amount of necessity in both; yet, in my perspective, it preserves a certain amount of freedom, as will be further argued.

Though a balance seems to be maintained between society and the individual in the text I quoted, Foucault focused his interest on collective forms of culture and apparently deprived the individual of his autonomy. My priority, on the contrary, was given to the structures which determined individual modes of perception and thought, imagination and sensibility for each of the Metaphysical poets. These modes build up what I consider as the 'formal personality' of a writer. This book presents again, though in a different order, three systems of correlated traits:

[64] *Les mots et les choses* (Paris, 1966), 392; my trans.

[65] In a different approach Barbara Harman later seemed to offer a similar balance: noting that Barbara Lewalski in her *Protestant Poetics* assumed 'that culture determines the possibilities for selfhood', whereas William Empson and Helen Vendler insisted on 'the individual's power to refine and discard prescriptions', she concluded that 'writers do indeed rewrite cultural materials' but that cultural ideas 'shape the self's power to write itself up', and she called for 'an analysis of the dialectical relationship between the two' (*Costly Monuments*, 21–30). In her study of Herbert's poems, however, she claimed to discover 'a process of displacement or evacuation' in which the self is lost (48), thus blurring the individual modes of thought.

- the various modes of self-awareness;
- the forms of perception of time and space and the modes of world-awareness;
- the predisposition of the individual mind to apprehend the sensible and the spiritual, the natural and the transnatural, the human and the divine, either jointly or separately, and when jointly, either distinctly or confusedly.

In each system the various structures are shown to have a direct influence on the modes of literary expression and account for stylistic particularities. It would be hazardous to unify the three sets of correlations and we need not assume that the personality is controlled by a single system, or by a single existential 'project' as Sartre would have it.

The permanence of these structures throughout an author's life and, to some extent at least, their presence in all his works was also based on evidence, not on a theoretical assumption. Several of the Metaphysical poets underwent conversions which affected their opinions, their sensibility, and their way of life, and yet their fundamental modes of consciousness remained unchanged. John Donne himself, a shrewd observer, had noted it, perhaps in himself as in others:

A covetous person, who is now truly converted to God, he will exercise a spiritual covetousness still, he will desire to have him all, he will have good security, the seal and assurance of the holy Ghost . . . So will a voluptuous man, who is turned to God, find plenty and deliciousnes in him, to feed his soul, as with marrow and with fatness . . . and so an angry and passionate man,will find zeal enough in the house of God to eat him up.[66]

Since common trends or notions of the period must not be mistaken for personal traits—an error the earlier New Critics were prone to—a knowledge of them is a prerequisite. Yet in this book, as in the previous one, though in a different way, I chose to give priority to the presentation of individual characteristics for both practical and theoretical reasons. Practical, since a preliminary exposition of the habits of thought and literary conventions that influenced the Metaphysical poets would require inordinate space: I have already devoted a whole volume

[66]   *Sermons*, I. 236–7.

to the circumstances that favoured the emergence of Metaphysical poetry in the social environment of the Donne generation.[67] Theoretical, since the individual modes that determine which social or literary influences will be privileged by each writer are unlikely to be all inborn; many are probably developed like the successive schemata that a growing child applies to reality. Piaget 'locates this *a priori* in the mind of the individual subject', but 'the *a priori* of the Piagetian model is an evolving *a priori*, not set down in one go from the start'.[68]

I therefore placed first the chapters in which I analyse the personal modes of thought of the seven poets. In the texts or the notes, however, I call attention, whenever necessary, to the relationships between the distinctive individual trait and the contemporary intellectual, theological, or literary current to which it may be related. There is a constant interplay between active selves and brute historical circumstances. The self can oppose a resistance to the prevailing trends of thought and doctrines. The self alone is responsible for innovation in its own sphere of activity and the larger movements in society are only the consequence of the combined or contradictory exertions of individual selves confronted with changing circumstances. The personal structures brought to light in this study of several poets may therefore allow us to discern a historical evolution in the modes of self-awareness, the perceptions of space and time, and the response to the social environment, as the chapters on 'historical landmarks' will show. This evolution, however, is not to be perceived as a global transformation of a mythical 'collective consciousness', or a Foucauldian episteme,[69] but as the result of changes or discoveries in a multiplicity of minds and the impulsion given by the most imaginative and boldest ones.

If literary creation is controlled by pre-established structures in each individual mind, what is the difference, one may ask, between this kind of inner coherence and psychological or social determinism? My conviction is that this assumption leaves room for freedom: freedom in the interpretation of experience,

---

[67] Volume III of *Poètes métaphysiques*.

[68] Harland, *Beyond Superstructuralism*, 80, 83, citing Piaget's *The Child's Conception of the World*, 23.

[69] Foucault's epistemes abruptly 'isolate the epochs from one another', as Hayden White noted: *Tropics of Discourse* (Baltimore, 1978), 130 ff.

in the creation of values and the orientation of life. When Donne decided he would no longer make love to woman, but make love to God, he made a choice, and choice is freedom, but his new effort did not alter his fundamental modes of imagination and sensibility. When Lacan, pointing to Bernini's *Saint Teresa*, claimed that the saint experienced an orgasm, he gave a wrong or reductive account of experience. Even if it could be proved that Teresa's ecstasy was attended by all the physiological symptoms of orgasm, her own interpretation of the experience and its consequences for her life, her actions, and the life of her mind (her writings) would make it utterly different from the common experience of sensual pleasure.

When we consider the concrete content of the individual consciousness, the self is found to be plural, unstable, changing, as it appeared to Montaigne and to all analysts of the inner mind long before postmodernism. Yet a study of several poets led me to the conclusion that the forms imposed upon their individual experience by the structures of their minds were subject to laws. Whether the conclusion can be generalized is, of course, open to question: the answer cannot be expected from the literary critic alone, but he can take part in the search. There is no science of literature in the older sense, but may not the study of literature make a contribution to science? Deconstructionists have attempted to justify their assumption of indeterminacy in writing by assuming (wrongly) that 'new science'—like 'new philosophy' in Donne's eyes—brought evidence of a total lack of order in the universe. Yet determinism cannot be ruled out on all occasions; even apparent chaos is amenable to laws of probability and physicists agree that chance 'may be given a corset'.[70] Though the stricter forms of scientific inquiry that make prediction possible are beyond its scope and attainment, literary criticism need not renounce the search for law and order which alone can impart intelligibility to our experience.

In my exploration of the structures of various selves I shall use different words for the different ways in which each author has

---

[70] As argued in my article 'Literary History and the Search for Certainty', *NLH* 27 (1996), 529–43. My objections to postmodernist cognitive relativism were not chiefly directed at the misuse of scientific notions (exposed by the physicists Alan Sokal and Jean Bricmont), but at the assumption that certainty is unattainable in all fields of knowledge, including history.

apprehended his own self. 'Self-awareness' is the more comprehensive term, devoid of implications. 'Subjectivity' is also used in
a general way. But there is a particular kind of self-awareness I
called 'self-consciousness' rather than coin a special word. It is
not the philosophic consciousness of our individuality, but the
self-awareness which comes spontaneously into play whenever I
perceive an action, a thought, or an emotion as *mine* in the very
moment of experience, whenever the experience and the experiencing self are apprehended in the same instant. I can then watch
myself act, feel, and think. This kind of self-observation creates
an inner distance and may breed irony directed at oneself. It may
also beget a sense of unreality since the experiencing self, when
so observed, is seen by the detached 'I' as an actor playing a part.
My analysis of Donne's and George Herbert's self-consciousness
will, I hope, justify this special meaning.[71] Joan Webber's later
definition of 'literary self-consciousness' in *The Eloquent I* bore
on 'consciousness of self as style', or 'consciousness of self in the
eyes of the reader',[72] which had not been my perspective though
this posture and the 'primary' self-consciousness I describe are
often closely associated.

For an immediate apprehension of our mental operations,
unattended by any reaction to, or scrutiny of, our emotions, in
other words, for a purely objective awareness of our perceptions
and thinking—including the Cartesian *cogito*—I had used the
French term 'conscience de conscience' in my *Poètes métaphysiques*; 'self-reflexivity' is here substituted for it. The
philosopher Charles Taylor has recently coined the phrase 'radical reflexivity' for an act of consciousness which 'brings to the
fore a kind of presence to oneself which is inseparable from
one's being the agent of experience', but the self-reflexivity I
analyse in the works of Lord Herbert or the poetry of Traherne
may give us a broader view of the self than 'Locke's punctual
self'.[73]

---

[71] The modern use of 'self-conscious' (*OED* 2) may also justify my choice:
when a man is unduly conscious of being an object of 'observation by others', he is,
in fact, uncomfortably aware of his own self and may fear to become the butt of
criticism. In the case of 'self-observation', the criticism will be self-criticism.

[72] J. Webber, *The Eloquent I* (Madison, 1970), 4.

[73] *Sources of the Self: The Making of Modern Identity* (Cambridge, 1994),
130–1 and ch. 9.

PART I

Modes of Self-Awareness

CHAPTER 1

John Donne: Self-Oriented Self-Consciousness

> I am a Man, I have my part in the Humanity . . . God hath
> afforded me my station, in that Church, . . . There is our
> Nos, . . . We, our Nation, we, our Church; There I am at
> home; but I am in my Cabinet at home, when I consider
> what God hath done for me, and my soule; There is the
> Ego, the particular, the individuall, I[1]

This balanced statement, acknowledging each man's link with a community, but ending on a splendid assertion of individuality, couched in terms that seem so modern—'the Ego, the particular, the individuall, I'—invites us to trace in the poetry of Donne, written 'in [his] Cabinet at home', the workings of his self-awareness. An inordinate egotism, an acute self-consciousness of a special kind, and an ever-defeated search for his own identity are characteristics of his inspiration which Chapter 16 will set in a historical perspective for a fuller appreciation of his originality.

Donne's self-centredness, obvious in his lyrics and elegies, pervades all his writings.[2] When he attempted an epic—or mock-epic—his first words were to state: 'Others at the Porches and entries of their Buildings set their Armes, I, my picture' (*Metempsychosis*, Epistle), and he prayed that he might 'understand | So much [him] selfe' as to know at least the length of his

---

[1] *Sermons*, V. 70–1; Whitsunday 1623.

[2] John Carey also stressed Donne's 'self-absorption': *John Donne. Life, Mind and Art* (London, 1981; rev. edn. 1990), 96–101. About his poetry of 'mutual love' Judith Scherer Herz notes: 'She, you, the silent presence in the we—these exist largely to make accessible the solipsism of this speaking I', *JDJ* 13 (1994), 139. Donne's stance, however, is not solipsistic for Donne's speaker 'always conducts his self-examination in relation to another being': cf. Carol Sicherman, 'Donne's Discoveries', *SEL 1500–1900*, 11 (1971), 69.

life (st. iv). In his *Anniversaries* the death of Elizabeth Drury was only a pretext for the expression of a personal anxiety about the human condition. In 'Obsequies to the Lord Harrington' he claimed: 'I discerne by favour of this light, | My selfe, the hardest object of the sight' (29–30). An epistle to the Countess of Bedford 'on New Years day' opens with this proclamation: 'This twilight of two yeares, nor past nor next, | Some embleme is of mee'.

The narcissism of the lover is disclosed when the eyes or tears of the beloved become a mirror in which he can 'Pitty [his] picture' ('Witchcraft by a picture'). Yet in 'The Extasie', 'The Good-Morrow', and 'The Canonization' the contemplation is mutual, and in an age when conceits about eyes and tears were rife, one may hesitate to discern here a trait of Donne's character. But his narcissistic penchant is betrayed in other poems: his own name, not the woman's, is engraved on a window in 'Valediction: Of my Name' and in Elegie XII the reason why he grows enamoured of her mind is: 'my own thoughts I there reflected find'.[3] No love poem of Donne reveals an absorption into the beloved; one poem at least suggests his appropriation of her: 'My body then doth hers involve' ('Dissolution'). In Elegie V, 'His Picture', when rivals tax the woman with foolishness for loving a worn and weather-beaten lover, one would expect her to say why she still loves him; she says instead that there is no reason why 'hee | Should now love lesse, what hee did love to see'. Donne seems to assume that the woman's love will persist so long as his own does. In 'The Token' the mistress is asked not to send him gifts, nor her own picture, but to 'swear thou thinkst I love thee, and no more', as if her belief in his love was an assurance she would love him. When leaving his mistress, the poet makes her dream he will be murdered 'O'r the white Alpes, alone' (Elegie XVI), and in all his Valedictions he calls attention to the dangers that will threaten him, but shows no anxiety for the woman left behind, though Walton assumed that two of the farewell poems ('Sweetest love', 'Valediction: Forbidding Mourning') were inspired by the fears of his wife for herself and

---

[3] 'His parting from her' is among the *Dubia* in Helen Gardner's edition, but internal evidence is in favour of Donne's authorship: see my review in *EA* 20 (1967), 284.

the child she bore.[4] Replying to complaints about Donne's self-hauntedness, Joan Bennett claimed that he wrote not about a woman as an individual, but 'about the oneness of two persons'. This is true of his greatest love poems; but Donne is the poet of 'oneness' because he cannot lend feelings different from his own to the woman loved nor impart to her a recognizable individual existence. This does not mean that he was incapable of genuine love, tenderness, and altruistic feelings. I am only concerned with the psychic structure which determined the usual direction of his attention.

When he turned to divine love, the orientation of Donne's mind did not change. When choosing a liturgical form, 'The Litanie', he made of it one of his most idiosyncratic poems, praying first for himself alone in the first nine stanzas. That the Holy Sonnets should be about his own devotional moods and anxieties is not surprising. More distinctive is the intensely personal character of his hymns and their self-centredness when he invites God to look at him: 'Looke Lord, and finde both Adams met in me' ('Hymne to God my God'), or to love him and be jealous ('Hymne to Christ'). The last word of the hymn he caused to be sung in his own church is not the 'Name Above Every Name', but a pun on the sinner's name, 'done'.[5] His prose treatises, *Biathanatos, Ignatius his Conclave*, even *Pseudo-Martyr* written to please James I, reflect his personal preoccupations: death, suicide, martyrdom, the 'new philosophy'.

In his sermons Donne is nearly always dramatically present.[6] He often speaks in the first person, using such phrases as: 'I hear', 'I see', 'I find', 'I wonder', etc. He often seems engaged in self-examination in presence of the faithful. He does not make

---

[4] P. M. Oliver recently found another example of 'self-absorption': 'Writing to Sir Henry Goodyer to condole with him on the death of his wife, Donne is more attentive to his own plight than Goodyer's': *Donne's Religious Writing* (London and New York, 1997), 197. This attitude may be compared with Ralegh's in his letter informing his wife of their son's death: S. Greenblatt, *Sir Walter Ralegh* (New Haven, 1973), 169.

[5] 'Hymn to God the Father'. He had previously and obviously punned on his own name—'I have, and you have DONNE'—at the end of a letter to Wotton, 'Sir, more then kisses'.

[6] Oliver also emphasizes his 'self-absorption' in his sermons: *Donne's Religious Writing*, 242.

us hear the voice of Everyman, but lends Everyman his own voice, as when he speaks of original sin: '*Adam* sinnd, and *I* suffer . . . I had a *Punishment*, before I had a *being*, And God was displeased with *me* before *I* was *I*' (*Sermons*, VII. 78). Most revealing is the spontaneous, almost unconscious upsurge of personal experience in moments of intense emotion: they are the moments when he considers the human body, disease, or sin, confesses the imperfection of his own devotion, contemplates death or the Last Judgement. They are not the only, nor perhaps the most frequent, themes, but they always call for this intrusion of personality. A significant example is offered by *Deaths Duell*. The beginning is impersonal, the end collective, and the first person plural is dominant throughout; yet the preacher several times chooses to describe the human condition as his individual experience. From 'But for us that die now . . .' he moves to this expostulation: '*Miserable riddle*, when the *same worme* must bee *my mother* and *my sister*, and *my selfe* . . . when my *mouth* shall be *filled* with *dust*, and the *worme* shall *feed*, and *feed sweetely* upon me' (*Sermons*, X. 238). As the initial quotation in this chapter has shown, the preacher still consciously sees the individual self, the Ego, as the centre of his spiritual life.

It is therefore ironical that Hemingway should have borrowed a famous epigraph from a passage in the *Devotions* (xvii) in order to justify a rejection of individualism:

No man is an *Iland*, intire of it selfe; every man is a peece of the *Continent*, a part of the *maine*; if a *Clod* bee washed away by the Sea, *Europe* is the lesse, as well as if a *Promontorie* were; . . . any mans *death* diminishes *me*, because I am involved in *Mankinde*; and therefore never send to know for whom the *bell* tolls; it tolls for *thee*.

This declaration fits the character of Robert Jordan, who never gave much importance to what happened to himself and uttered this comment on his father's suicide: 'You have to be awfully occupied with yourself to do a thing like that'[7]—which was the very reason why Donne was obsessed with the idea of suicide, just as he was obsessed with his own disease and fate throughout the *Devotions*. Is this particular text in contradiction with his usual tendency? It is not, if one looks closely at it. The

---

[7] *For Whom the Bell Tolls* (New York, 1943), 4, 338.

preacher starts from the consideration that 'the *Church* is *Catholike, universall*, and so are all her *Actions*'. His application of this principle does not invite the individual to forget himself and think only of the human community. Donne only rises to universality as a means of heightening his sense of individuality: when the Church '*buries a Man*, that action concerns me', for 'any mans *death* diminishes *me*'. His consciousness retains its structure and viewpoint even when he asserts the integration of the individual in a community. Self-centredness does not imply selfishness or morbidity.[8]

Donne always had a keen sense of the community and of tradition which prevented the kind of dissolution of the self observed in the post-Romantic period.[9] The Lincoln's Inn student, the secretary of Sir Thomas Egerton already had a desire to be involved in that political body which is to the nation what the 'mystic body' is to the Church ('Satyre I', 7–8). Even when he boldy invited an individual quest for the true Church, he presented it as a quest for an authentic tradition: 'aske thy father which is shee, | Let him aske his' ('Satyre III', 71–2). In his 'libertine' poems his individualism was confined to claims for man's natural instincts. His self was obtrusive, but he did not delight in the kind of self-assertion which characterized the Machiavellian or Stoic heroes of Marlowe, Webster, and Chapman.[10]

His constant search for self-knowledge is not a distinguishing trait by itself since it might have been dictated by the current humanistic ideal or the Christian tradition. In his early verse

---

[8] I can accept Joan Webber's assertion that Donne 'makes his individual "I" a symbol representing all men' (*The Eloquent I* (Madison, 1968), 34) provided the priority of self-centredness is acknowledged.

[9] On Donne's insistence on social bonds and the preacher's rejection of singularity (*Sermons*, II. 279, VIII. 153) see *Poètes métaphysiques*, I. 127–9. We constantly find in Donne 'l'exigence de communication' which Starobinski noted in Montaigne; he always confronts an interlocutor—or, as Joan Webber noted, 'imagines himself under observation' (*Eloquent I*, 25). Terry Sherwood thought modern readers did not pay 'equal attention' to the 'two dimensions' of Donne's consciousness 'of the self and the community': *Fulfilling the Circle. A Study of John Donne's Thought* (Toronto, 1984), 101, cf. 186. I think I have, but I wished to stress what was new and singular in Donne's consciousness rather than what was inherited. Why I would not ascribe to him an 'intensely social sense of self'—as Michael C. Schoenfeldt does in 'The Poetry of Supplication', *New Perspectives on the Seventeenth Century English Religious Lyric*, ed. J. R. Roberts (Columbia, 1994), 85—was explained in *Poètes métaphysiques*, I. 129–35.   [10] See Ch. 16.

epistles he mainly echoed the Roman Stoics and satirists. 'Be thou thine owne home and in thy selfe dwell' expands the terse injunction of Persius, *tecum habita,* and 'Seeke wee then our selves in our selves' seems reminiscent of Seneca's *Recede in te ipse.*[11] Among English writers there was then a close connection between the prevailing satirical mood and the theme of self-knowledge, so obtrusive in Marston's *Scourge,* lamenting that Nature had not 'turn'd our eyes | Into our proper selves'.[12] Even a poet so little given to introspective self-analysis as Jonson harped on the same string in his claim to moral autonomy: 'What I am not and what I fain would be | Whilst I inform myself, I would teach thee . . . | For that is first required, a man be his own' (*Underwood,* xlv).

Donne's call to self-knowledge was neither novel, unexpected, nor distinctive at the turn of the century. In his later poems and his sermons the Christian self-searching and self-assessment which superseded the Stoic note equated self-knowledge with an awareness of the sinful condition of man: 'Thinke further on thy selfe, my Soule, and thinke, | How thou at first wast made but in a sinke' (*Second Anniversary,* 157–8). Donne's individuality asserted itself in his imagery of dissection, not uncommon however in his age.[13] His insistence on tracking the impure motive had been anticipated by St Augustine and was characteristic of Jesuit and Protestant devotion alike. As a poet Donne, like George Herbert, and Marvell later,[14] made a particular application of the danger of self-deceit in 'The Litanie' (st. xxi): 'When wee are mov'd to seeme religious | Only to vent wit, Lord deliver us.' Like Augustine[15] he was aware of the subtlest danger, 'pride issued from humility': 'So may a selfe-dispising

---

[11] 'Sir, more then kisses', 47; Persius, *Satires,* I. 5. 'Like one who'in her third widdowhood'; Seneca, *Epist.* viii. 7.

[12] *The Scourge of Villanie* (1599), ed. G. B. Harrison (London, 1925), satire I, p. 14; cf. Persius, *Satires,* IV. 24–8, and Shakespeare, *Coriolanus,* II. i. 41–4.

[13] 'We understand the frame of mans body, better when we see him naked, than apparrelled, howsoever; and better by seeing him cut up, than by seeing him do any exercise alive; one desection, one Anatomy teaches more of that, than the marching, or drilling of a whole army of living men. Let every one of us therefore dissect and cut up himself' (*Sermons,* I. 273). Jonathan Sawday's *The Body Emblazoned* (London, 1995) has emphasized 'the culture of dissection' in Renaissance England.

[14] See Chs. 2 and 4.

[15] Augustine had noted that those who profess to despise vainglory take pride in their scorn of it: *Confessions,* X. 38.

get selfe-love' ('The Crosse', 37–42). The personal relevance of these statements and the distinctive flavour of the style prove that Donne, if he was no initiator in this field, at least fully made his own what tradition may have suggested. Besides, his writings disclose two original traits in his self-examination.

The quest for self-knowledge brings into play his egotism; it is ultimately directed to an achievement of personal identity which apparently becomes an end in itself. When alluding to the universal knowledge attained by a soul in Heaven ('Harrington', 29–32) the poet seems more deeply moved by the prospect of discovering his true self than by the beatific contemplation. The world grows transparent

> And I discerne, by favour of this light,
> My selfe, the hardest object of the sight.
> God is the glasse; as thou when thou dost see
> Him who sees all, seest all concerning thee.

The self in its wholeness can only survive through the resurrection of the flesh, and man will only discover on the Day of Judgement what he could not discover in his life. *Veniet dies, quae me mihi revelabit,* the preacher said in a late sermon, 'that day that shall show me to my selfe; here I never saw my selfe, but in disguises: There, Then, I shall see my selfe, and see God too.'[16] The order of the words, 'see my selfe, and see God too' seems to betray a different intensity or urgency in the wish. Despite the splendour and sincerity of the Dean's longing for a vision in which 'I my selfe shall be all light to see that light by', may not the yearning for an epiphany of the self remain Donne's innermost and deepest desire?

The second original trait is the anguished acknowledgement that the self is elusive and full self-knowledge unattainable in this life. Only Montaigne declared himself so thoroughly baffled in his search for his own identity.[17] Donne's disquisition on this

---

[16] 22 Nov. 1629; *Sermons*, IX. 129.

[17] Other Renaissance writers complain that self-knowledge is not sought for, or not easily attained, but would agree with Jonson that man may 'know [him]self a little' (*Underwood*, xlvii). I have developed the parallel between Montaigne and Donne in 'The Search for Identity: from Montaigne to Donne', in *John Donne and Modernity*, ed. Himy-Llasera (Paris, 1995), and 'L'interrogation sur l'identité de Montaigne à Donne', in *Renaissances européennes et Renaissance française* (Ed. Espaces 34, Montpellier, 1995).

theme—'Poore soule, in this thy flesh what dost thou know? . . . Thou art too narrow, wretch, to comprehend | Even thy selfe' (*Second Anniversary*, 254–63)—might be only a particular expression of Christian pessimism. What is more remarkable is the way in which incidental statements of this impossibility crop up almost irrelevantly in other poems: 'we cannot see | Through passions mist, what we are' ('Lady Marckham', 15–16), 'What we know not, our selves' ('Negative love'). Even more distinctive is the expression of the preacher's perplexity when he turned his gaze inward and described himself as a 'Poore intricated soule! Riddling, perplexed labyrinthicall soule!' (*Sermons*, VIII. 332).

Addressing the Countess of Bedford on New Year's Day, the poet had found his own identity as difficult to define as a meteor:

> This twilight of two yeares, nor past, nor next,
> Some embleme is of mee, or I of this,
> Who Meteor-like, of stuffe and forme perplext,
> Whose *what*, and *where*, in disputation is,
> If I should call mee *any thing*, should misse.

These questionings about his own identity apparently arise from a particular form of self-consciousness. Self-knowledge with Donne meant more than a review of past actions. Just as an emotion or a thought was always apprehended by the poet in the present moment, as Chapter 6 will show, self-awareness would flash upon him in the midst of an action or preaching, as in this surprising interruption (*Sermons*, III. 110):

I am not all here, I am here now preaching upon this text, and I am at home in my Library considering whether *S. Gregory*, or *S. Hierome*, have said best of this text before. I am here speaking to you, and yet I consider by the way, *in the same instant*, [my italics] what it is likely you will say to one another, when I have done.

This is the kind of self-awareness I call *self-consciousness*, as I explained at the end of my Introduction. It has important consequences. In his constant 'awareness of awareness' the 'self-conscious' man will be keenly aware of contradictions and contrarieties which would not be perceived in an unreflecting surrender to impulses. Conversely, inner conflicts will call attention to themselves, and when we grow aware of them, they may thrive and expand, as all the analysts of the inner life have observed. Donne defined himself as 'humorous' and deplored his own changeableness and instability.[18] Humorousness and fantasticality were hardly distinctive in a humorous and fantastical age, but their frequent self-conscious proclamation seems to be closely related to a heightened sense of individuality among Jack Donne's contemporaries.[19] The man who is aware of the mobility of his humours is likely to hesitate on the threshold of action or before making a decision.[20] There was in Donne a Hamlet-like irresolution combined with a Hamlet-like impulsiveness. He seems to have been incapable of making a choice with deliberation. His marriage—a stolen match—betrayed more precipitation than resolution. He afterwards engaged in various studies, formed many plans without coming to a decision. In 1608 he deplored that 'an Hydroptique immoderate desire of humane learning and languages' had diverted him from the study of law. In his worst period of financial distress he was ready to become a lawyer, but he later denied having contemplated it.[21] Apparently he was not always certain of his own desires and observed 'we know not what we would' when writing to the Countess of Bedford ('T'have written, then', 34). Even when sailing on the Azores expedition he had been unable to account for his decision and discover a definite purpose: the very clear-sightedness of his self-conscious mind opened up too many prospects, descried too many motives for one particular choice ('Calme', 39–43). He only took orders after years of procrastination when the king 'descended to an intimation, to a perswasion, almost to a solicitation' that he would embrace this calling and thus forced him out of 'a vertiginous giddines, and irresolution'. Left to himself, what was he doing? His own anwer was: '[I] almost spent all my time consulting how I should spend it.'[22]

---

[18] See Holy Sonnet XIX, 'Litanie', st. xv.

[19] See Ch. 16 and *Poètes métaphysiques*, III. 127–32.

[20] P. M. Oliver also stresses Donne's 'distaste for passionate engagement' and 'his predilection for being in two minds about anything': *Donne's Religious Writing*, 18–19; cf. 78, 180, 243–5.

[21] Hayward, 456; R. C. Bald, *John Donne. A Life* (Oxford, 1970; 1986 edn.), 227.

[22] *Devotions*, Exp. 8, ed. Raspa, 44. There may be a link between this indecision and the 'anxiety' justly noted by Carey, *John Donne*, 109–11, 130. Barbara Everett also observed 'a ceaseless awareness of the mind's and will's alternatives': *Donne: A London Poet* (British Academy Lecture, 1972), 16.

This indecision was not confined to Donne's period of forced inaction from 1602 to 1614. The tendency was enhanced by untoward circumstances, but it was ingrained in his character and persisted after his taking orders. Bredvold read the sonnet 'Show me, deare Christ, thy spouse so bright and clear' as a testimony to a prolonged 'indecision as to which was the true church'; Helen Gardner read it as 'not merely compatible with loyalty to the Church of England', but as a poem which 'could hardly have been written by anyone but an Anglican',[23] yet the note of perplexity and melancholy irony is unmistakable. The pragmatic sincerity of Donne's allegiance to the Church of England did not exclude doubts and misgivings: Anglicanism did suit his mind and temper inasmuch as it left undetermined many things which Roman Catholics or extreme Protestants maintained dogmatically. The admission that there were 'things indifferent' was welcome to the author of the Third Satire.

The origin of Donne's irresolution and changeableness is suggested by a Paradox despite the proverbial origin of the saying: 'Men . . . that have the most reasonn are the most alterable in there designes, and the darkest and most Ignorant, do seldomest change.'[24] This is not true of all minds, but it was certainly true of his own.[25] His rational awareness of multiple issues and multiple answers bred a critical and occasionally sceptical turn of mind which invites a comparison with Montaigne despite obvious differences.

With Montaigne the old theme of inconstancy had taken on a new meaning. His self-consciousness seems to anticipate Gidian 'disponibilité' or Sartrian 'liberté' in statements which imply that our affections and convictions are never so firmly rooted but we may discard them at any time to assume different affections and convictions. 'If I speake diversly of my selfe', the essayist pointed out, 'it is because I looke diversly upon my selfe.' Which means that the contrarieties observed are not

[23] *Divine Poems* (Clarendon Press, 1978), 122.
[24] 'A Defence of Womans Inconstancy'; *Paradoxes and Problems*, 51. Probably by Donne himself, though classed by Peters among the *Dubia*.
[25] Donne's changeableness is stressed in Carey's *John Donne*, ch. 6. Elizabeth Tebeaux has analysed 'his often tortuous position on man's search for certainty' in the sermons: *Renascence*, 43 (1991), 195–213.

merely found in the object considered, the self as distinguished from the ego: they proceed from a mode of consciousness:

The blast of accidents doth not only remove me according to his inclination; for besides, I remove and trouble my selfe by the instability of my posture, and whosoever looketh narrowly about himselfe, shall hardly see himselfe twise in one same state. Sometimes I give my soule one visage, and sometimes another, according unto the posture or side I lay her in.[26]

This goes beyond a perception of inconstancy or a sense of relativity. Montaigne does not describe a succession of moods; he shows how he can throw himself into a mood. He can take in several aspects of his own self at a glance and choose to emphasize one of them. 'All contrarieties are found' in the self, but 'according to some turne or removing' (ibid.). The same ability to give his soul one visage, and sometimes another, according to the posture he laid her in, is suggested in a letter of Donne: 'sometimes when I find myself transported with jollity and love of company, I hang leads at my heels; . . . when sadness dejects me, either I countermine it with another sadness, or I kindle squibs about me again and fly into sportfulness and company'.[27] Donne here does more than show himself sad and gay in turn: he *makes himself* sad or gay. This capability may partly account for his vivid recreation of experience in dramatic monologues.

Montaigne like Donne knew he could not define himself:

Shamefast, bashfull, insolent, chaste, luxurious, peevish, pratling, silent, fond, doting, laborious, nice, delicate, ingenious, slow, dull, froward, humorous, debonaire, wise, ignorant, false in words, true-speaking, both liberall, covetous, and prodigall. All these I perceive in some measure or other to bee in mee, *according as I stirre or turne my selfe*; And whosoever shall heedfully survay and consider himselfe, shall finde this volubility and discordance to be in himselfe, yea and in his very judgement. I have nothing to say entirely, simply, and with soliditie of my selfe, without confusion, disorder, blending, mingling.[28]

This essay was entitled 'De l'inconstance de nos actions', an inconstancy already observed by the Latin moralists, elegists,

---

[26] *Essays*, II. i; Everyman, II. 11–12.
[27] 'To Sir H. G.', Spring 1608; Gosse, I. 184.
[28] *Essays*, II. i; Everyman, II. 11–12; my italics.

and satirists. But in this passage (though not throughout the essay) the contrasts are not merely perceived as a succession of moods and attitudes. The various aspects of the self are here embraced as if a many-faceted personality were discovered by turning the object before one's eyes and much depended on the observing gaze: 'according as I stirre or turne my selfe', 'selon que je me vire'. The instability discovered in the conflicting impulses is traced to an ever-shifting point of view:

It is a counter-roule of divers and variable accidents, and irresolute imaginations, and sometimes contrary: whether it be that my selfe am other, or that I apprehend subjects, by other circumstances and considerations . . . Were my mind setled, I would not essay, but resolve my selfe.[29]

This declaration betrays the deeper meaning of the title chosen:[30] in his *Essays* Montaigne was 'essaying' himself, exploring and trying out his many possible selves. And he never 'resolved' himself, since he never could attain fixity. Yet his aim was to communicate his essential self: 'c'est moi, c'est mon essence',[31] he gave us assurance, speaking of his self-portrait. He could claim that his book was the faithful reflection of what he called his 'forme maistresse' or his 'forme essentielle'.[32] The apparent contradiction is removed if we recognize that the essence here is in 'the passage', that the universal being, 'l'estre universel', of Michel de Montaigne was best revealed through this calling in question of his own self, through this search for an elusive identity.

The first phase in the exploration of the self discovered to Donne not only its changeableness but a kind of vacuity.[33] Montaigne had observed an infinite diversity; Donne expresses at times a sense of *nothingness*. He may be playing with the

[29] *Essays*, III. ii; Everyman, III. 23.
[30] The other meanings were noted by Richard Sayce in *The Essays of Montaigne* (Oxford, 1972), 21–2.   [31] *Essais*, II. vi; Pléiade, 417.
[32] *Essais,* II. vi, III. ii, and III. v; Pléiade, 417, 907, and 920.
[33] My interpretation is reconcilable with R. V. Young's recent assertion that 'Donne manifests a vivid awareness of the inconsistency and insubstantiality, not only of the poetic persona, but also of the role of churchman and Christian': 'Donne, Herbert and the Postmodern Muse', in *New Perspectives on 17th C. Lyric*, ed. Roberts, 172–3. Yet I think that he was aware of his 'inconsistency and insubstantiality' as a 'self' rather than a mere 'persona', and had no misgivings about his 'role of churchman'.

word,[34] as many Renaissance poets had done,[35] for the sake of witty dialectics or eulogy.[36] But his emotions were undoubtedly engaged on several occasions, notably in *A nocturnall* when grief turned him into 'A quintessence even from nothingnesse'. One may object that this was the result of a sense of loss on a special occasion; but he early wrote in 'The Storme': 'Thou which art I, ('tis nothing to be soe)', and repeatedly described himself to other correspondents as a 'nothing' or a 'chimera'. Again this might be a mere trick of polite self-abasement, but humility was no longer expected when he wrote to Gerrard in 1630.[37] It could be one more sign of his self-pity, conspicuous when he spoke of his ailments, but in the *Devotions* (xx) he traced the progress of his disease along 'all waies to exinanition and annihilation' with a fascinated attention. The notion was universalized when he underlined man's nothingness before God called him into being[38] and evoked the nothingness that preceded the Creation;[39] yet a personal obsession seems to dictate the persistence of the theme.[40] When the preacher studied this notion minutely, it obviously procured him an intellectual excitement, for 'absolutely nothing, meerly nothing, is more incomprehensible then any thing, then all things together' (*Sermons*, IV. 101). His obsession with death, which will be considered later, could account for this fascination. One suspects, however, that his intuition of his own fundamental indetermination was at least partly responsible for it. In September 1608 he wrote to Goodere: 'I would fain do something; but that I cannot tell what, is no wonder. For to chuse is to do; but to be no part of any body, is to be nothing.'[41] Of

---

[34] In the poems the word is only used 74 times, but often in a full sense, cosmic or theological.

[35] In their variations on *Nihil* or *Nemo*: see Caspar Dornau, *Amphitheatrum Sapientiae Socraticae Joco-Seriae* (Hanoviae, 1619).

[36] See 'T'have written then', 7; 'Huntington', 15; 'Boulstred', 26.

[37] Gosse, I. 171 ('infinite nothings are but one such'); 216 ('if I writ nothing since I am so'); II. 265 ('To George Gerrard', October 1630: 'because I am nothing').

[38] 'Calme', 52–3; 'Salisbury', 21; *Sermons*, IV. 100–1.

[39] 'Valediction: Of Weeping', 13; 'Huntington', 37; *Essays* (Simpson), 19, 27–32.

[40] Like the constant play on 'all': see *Poètes métaphysiques*, I. 136–7. L. C. Knights later made similar remarks in 'All or Nothing: A Theme in John Donne', in *William Empson: The Man and His Work*, ed. Roma Gill (London, 1979).

[41] Gosse, I. 191; also in Hayward, 456.

course, his solitary inaction in his Mitcham years invited such uncertainties and broodings on himself. It certainly heightened his self-consciousness, but did not create it: it had appeared in his early poems (even in *Metempsychosis* written when he was in active service), and remained conspicuous in his writings throughout his life.

Donne's self-dramatization was probably part of his desire to define himself. To engrave his own name on a window or to pun on his own name when addressing God was a way of 'inscribing' his elusive self, projecting it into a self-perpetuating image. To have several portraits painted was not in itself unusual, but his juvenile motto, *Antes muerto que mudado*, 'Rather dead than changed', at first sight surprising for the apologist of 'change', may express a wish for a constancy of the self that would rid him of his own doubts about his own identity. The portrait of himself in a shroud which he kept under his eyes on his death-bed was more than a *memento mori*: it must have been to him a reminder of himself and a supreme assertion of this mysterious self at the moment of death and beyond death.

Self-consciousness, as I defined it, is bound to affect our emotions and our expression of them. The consequences are traceable in Donne's attitude to love and death and in his religious feelings.

How far Donne's poems, whether libertine or passionate, had an autobiographical basis need not concern us. The best ones are about 'situations' dramatically recreated or conceived and the poet must have had at least an imaginative experience of the emotions he pretended to express or sought to excite. Critics disagree about the poems in which the tone seems to oscillate between emotion and irony; some commentators treat them as mere witticisms, others offer serious interpretations of supposedly sarcastic remarks. But emotion and irony may be allied and the poet may be 'serious' without being 'grave', as T. S. Eliot assumed. The origin of this complexity of tone, however, is not to be found in a mythical 'unified sensibility': it results from a self-awareness characterized by a self-conscious duality.

Knowing that Donne was haunted by the prospect of death and dissolution, one cannot doubt that he was moved by the scene conjured in 'The Relique'; nevertheless irony slips in in the sardonic parenthesis, creating a modulation of tone:

When my grave is broke up againe
Some second ghest to entertaine,
   (For graves have learn'd that woman-head
   To be to more then one a Bed)
     And he that digs it, spies
A bracelet of bright haire about the bone,
     Will he not let'us alone,
And thinke that there a loving couple lies,
Who thought that this device might be some way
To make their soules, at the last busie day,
Meet at this grave and make a little stay?

In 'Aire and Angels' the first lines breathe wonder and love in a mode of Platonic adoration, but the poet moves from wonder at 'some lovely glorious nothing' to admiration of the woman's bright hair before reaching the conclusion that since his soul 'Takes limmes of flesh, and else could nothing doe, | More subtile then the parent is, | Love must not be, but take a body too'. The poem ends, however, on a trait of irony, implying that women are incapable of the ideal or contemplative love felt by the man at first. 'The Extasie' expands the idea that 'Loves mysteries in soules doe grow, | But yet the body is his booke', and also ends on an ironic twist. There will be indeed 'Small change, when we'are to bodies gone' since the spiritual ecstasy of the lovers was already close to physical union: their clasped hands were sweating and their eyebeams intertwined as their limbs will do (5–10). In each poem, as I have argued,[42] the experience described—whether real or imaginary—is true to life, the emotion or longing is modified in tone, but not destroyed by the poet's critical awareness, his distancing of himself in ambiguous self-mockery. In such poems unselfconscious passion would be untrue to Donne's nature.

Yet there are poems in which passion, triumphant and absolute, admits no impediment or abatement. They are the

---

[42] In *Poètes métaphysiques*, I. 174–81 and III. 401–10, I assumed that Donne and Montaigne unwittingly anticipated the Sartrian analysis of an inevitable 'bad faith'. 'We are double in our selves', Montaigne had remarked, 'which is the cause that what we beleeve, we beleeve it not' (II. xvi; Everyman, II. 342), an observation which could proceed from the same insight as Sartre's 'on ne croit jamais à ce qu'on croit'.

poems in which union with the beloved is said to give the lover an assurance of immortality. Irony can be held off when a time-less moment seems to give access to a permanence of being: 'If our two loves be one, or, thou and I | Love so alike, that none doe slacken, none can die.'[43] This hope, however, is preceded by 'if' and in 'The Anniversarie' the lovers are invited to 'refrain' their 'fears'. The intensity claimed for the experience evoked is undeniable, but it may be the intensity of desire rather than fulfilment; the emotion is genuine, but one may be deeply moved by the imaginary realization of a wish. The poems of triumphant love were probably written at a time when Donne's hopes had been ruined by his stolen match. The defiant opening of 'The Canonization' suggests he sought in the enjoyment of the beloved a compensation for a world well lost:

> For Godsake hold your tongue, and let me love,
>   Or chide my palsie, or my gout,
> My five gray haires, or ruin'd fortune flout,
>   With wealth your state, your minde with Arts improve,
>   Take you a course, get you a place,
>   Observe his honour, or his grace,
>   Or the King's reall, or his stamped face
>   Contemplate, what you will, approve,
>   So you will let me love.

Yet Donne's letters in the Mitcham period disclose a growing despondence. The poems seem to record moments of poetic exaltation rather than a stable mood, a reaching for an experi-ence of which reality can offer only a foretaste. He knew that love was first 'An unripe willingnesse which nothing did, | A thirst, an Appetite which had no ease, | That found a want, but knew not what would please' ('Huntington', 44–6). This, of course, applied to the innocent yearnings of adolescence, but

[43] 'The Good-Morrow'. Donne, however, may be playing here on the equation of 'dying' with detumescence in sexual union, but the wit is subservient to the deeper impulse. Like Catherine Belsey ('Worlds of Desire in Donne's Lyric Poetry', in *John Donne and Modernity*, ed. A. Himy and M. Llasera (Confluences XI, Paris, 1995), 99) I think that Donne plays here on the erotic meaning of *slacken* and *die*; but unlike her, I do not think he wants desire to remain 'unfulfilled'. The impression of faintness is felt not at the culmination of the orgasm but at the beginning of its decline or expiration: Donne assumes the absence of detumescence would eternize a pleasure otherwise 'onely for a minute made to be' ('Farewell to Love', 29), thus conferring an imaginary immortality upon the lovers.

Donne felt a 'want' in love even after fruition. His 'Farewell to Love' and 'Loves Alchymie' are unlikely to be mere youthful evaporations like the libertine poems of enjoyment. He had discovered that love 'Being had, enjoying it decayes' and 'leaves behinde | A kinde of sorrowing dulnesse to the minde' ('Farewell'). He despaired of ever finding love's 'centrique happinese' and 'hidden mysterie' ('Loves Alchymie'). Whether this was written before or after the poems celebrating an experience of that mystery — 'Wee dye and rise the same, and prove | Mysterious by this love' ('Canonization') — is not ascertainable. But if human love had truly fulfilled his highest expectations at any time, he might not have spoken of it with such crude contempt in the *First Anniversary* (105–10), many years after his marriage, yet several years before entering holy orders.[44] This pessimistic view, no doubt, was here called for by the poet's theme, but it is consonant with other statements. 'Negative Love', though apparently an ingenious trifle, seems to be the truthful confession that the poet, aware of the limitations of both sensual and ideal love, never knew 'what [he] would have'. The deeper reason for this uncertainty is suggested when he spoke of 'What we know not, our selves'. The ultimate cause of the failure of passion is the split between the conscious I and the feeling self.[45]

An unsatisfied desire to know himself may also account for Donne's brooding over the prospect of his own death. He wrote in the *Devotions*: 'I feare not the hastening of my death, and yet I do fear the increase of the disease.'[46] Though a fear of hell was expressed in the Holy Sonnets, death, indeed, was not fearsome in itself to Donne: he had felt attracted to it from his 'first breeding and conversation with men of suppressed and afflicted Religion [the Jesuit priests in Elizabethan England], accustomed

[44] Christopher Ricks has expressed a fairly similar, though darker view of 'Donne After Love', in *Literature and the Body*, ed. Elaine Scarry (Baltimore, 1988), 33–69.

[45] Donne's recurrent insistence on the distinction between the substance and its accidents may have the same origin: there is a yearning for 'essence' in such oppositions as: 'theirs not them' (the naked body and its ornaments in Elegie XIX), 'from her to hers' (Elegie XVIII), 'having' versus 'being' ('T'have written then', 24; 'Man to Gods image', 25–32; 'Carey', 13–36).

[46] Raspa, p. 30; cf. letter to Mrs Cokain, Jan. 1631, Gosse, II. 272, also in Hayward, 501.

to the despite of death, and hungry of an imagin'd Martyrdom'
(*Biathanatos*, Preface). This longing to die was expressed in
many poems and letters[47] and was wilfully ascribed to Christ in
'The Litanie' (st. x). But Donne's death-wish has a characteristic feature which sharply distinguishes it from Crashaw's: it
never was a desire to lose his self, much less to sink into nothingness.[48] In his *Essays in Divinity* (Simpson, 30) he reminded
us, like Milton later, that even the devils in Hell cannot long for
annihilation. In his self-conscious egotism he sought in death, as
in love, an ultimate experience of identity. He often imagined
himself dead or buried and had his portrait painted in his
shroud because death objectified him, imparted to him a definite self, an unchanging reality which his restless and divided
mind could never grasp in his self-analysis. He expected it to fill
the 'want' he always felt in all his experiences. Just as he looked
for his image in a woman's eye, he sought his own image in
death; in both cases he called for a 'canonization' that would
show him to himself 'Tel qu'en lui-même enfin l'éternité le
change'. To become a 'legend' was a means of self-definition. He
later wished in the same way to forge his own legend as a
converted sinner and to give others and himself the spectacle of
an exemplary death.

In his anticipation of death Donne satisfied the same craving
as in his moments of passion. Yet one has to be alive in order to
imagine oneself dead. Therefore his desire of death was less the
desire of a consummation already accomplished than the yearning expectation of the moment when this miracle would be
achieved in his consciousness: the utmost intensity of being in
the very experience of dying, death as a climax of self-awareness. Once more the parallel with Montaigne is illuminating.
'This is my playes last scene' reminds us that death was for the
author of the *Essays* 'l'acte à un seul personnage'.[49]
Montaigne's attention was focused on this experience of the self
in 'a death united in it selfe, quiet and solitarie, *wholly mine*'.[50]

---

[47] See letters to Goodyer, 1608 (Gosse, I. 191; Hayward, 455), Sir Robert Kerr,
1614 (Gosse, II. 15), Gerrard and Mrs Cokain, 1631 (Gosse, II. 268, 272; Hayward,
498, 501); 'Corona', 1, 11–12; 'Hymne to Christ' (31–2).
[48] John Carey pointed out that Donne endeavoured to 'treat death as a form of
life' (*Donne*, 202).   [49] *Essais*, III. ix; Pléiade, 1096.
[50] *Essays*, III. ix; Everyman, III. 224, my italics.

Donne longed for death to achieve this self-possession in the instant when death—like love in its supreme intensity—would impart stability and substantiality to a self so often perceived as fragmentary or changing. Just as Montaigne thought it best to remain conscious in order to 'taste and savour' this experience, he claimed 'I would not that death should take me asleep. I would not have him meerly seize me, and onely declare me to be dead, but win me, and overcome me.'[51]

An essential continuity in Donne's aspirations, whether profane or sacred, is thus confirmed.[52] In his most devout elevations his self remained the object of his attention. His quest for reality and substance was unending. The man who found all joys in 'Full nakedness' (Elegie XIX) was the man who sought a 'firme substantiall love' in passion or tenderness ('Valediction: Of my Name', 62), and he became the man who aspired to the 'essential joy' only attainable in Heaven (Second Anniversary, 443).[53] The quest for truth in which he had engaged ('Satire III', 79–84) became one with the quest for reality when he discovered that he would never embrace truth in its wholeness before a coincidence of the mind and its objects was achieved in the divine mind 'For it is both the object and the wit' (Second Anniversary, 442).

This coincidence is only possible, if it ever is, in mystic intuition—an intuition foreign to Donne's mind. Passiveness and a surrender of the self are required: they were hardly compatible with his egotism and his flickering attention in prayer or contemplation, openly confessed in a sermon as late as December 1626.[54] A genuine love of God is also indispensable.

---

[51] Essays, II. xii, Everyman, II. 331; 'To Sir H. Goodere', Sept. 1608: Gosse, I. 191, Hayward, 455.

[52] The continuity between Donne's secular love poems and his divine poems has been stressed again by Wilbur Sanders, A. J. Smith, Robert J. Jackson, etc.: see Anthony Low in New Perspectives on 17th C. Lyric, ed. Roberts, 202 n. 5.

[53] A comparison with Keats, mutatis mutandis, is of interest. In both Keats and Donne a pre-eminently tactile sensuality is associated with a yearning for 'a fellowship with essence' conceived as the 'highest intensity'. See my 'Présentation' in Keats: Poésie (Paris, 2000).

[54] Sermons, VII. 264–6: 'I throw my selfe downe in my Chamber, and I call in, and invite God, and his Angels thither, and when they are there, I neglect God, and his Angels, for the noise of a Flie, for the ratling of a Coach, for the whining of a doore.' There are other examples: V. 249–50 and X. 56. Augustine had mentioned his moments of inattention, but not so vividly: Confessions, X. xxxv.

But Donne's human love was a desire for possession of the beloved and the self-assurance arising from a sense of union with her: it never was a forgetting of self.[55] The repentant sinner at first felt only fear—not a sacred awe, but the terror of a man faced with a destiny dependent upon an angry God.[56] Self-interest seems to be still dominant in the expression of love when the preacher says (*Sermons*, III. 308): 'I love my Saviour as He is *The Lord*, He that studies *my* salvation' (thrice repeated, my italics). The Christian poet does occasionally, but not very often, exhort himself to love God, but the language is the language of a man who seeks to *make himself* in love: 'let myne amorous soul court thy mild dove'.[57] He knew that God could only enter his heart by violence: 'Batter my heart, three person'd God . . . for I | Except you'enthrall mee, never shall be free, | Nor ever chast, except you ravish mee'.[58] His sincerity is not to be impugned since a genuine desire is frustrated and the splendid 'Hymne to Christ' is a moving acknowledgement of failure: 'O, if thou car'st not whom I love | Alas, thou lov'st not mee'. He did long to experience the mystical death of St Paul, but his evocation of it shows him again deeply moved by a contemplation of himself and his own fate:

. . . I will finde out another death, . . . a death of rapture, and of extasie, that death which S. *Paul* died more then once, . . . and in this death of rapture, and extasie, in this death of the *Contemplation of my interest* in my Saviour, I shall *finde my self*, and all *my sins* enterred, and entombed in his wounds, and like a Lily in Paradise, out of red earth, I shall *see my soule* rise out of his blade, in a candor,

---

[55] When the preacher later had to define love, he spoke, of course, according to tradition: love 'changes him that loves, into the very nature of that that he loves and he is nothing else' (*Sermons*, I. 185). But he was only concerned here with the love of 'Pureness', by which man becomes pure: this is not love for another *person*, human or divine, but a desire to create a new state of mind in *oneself*. Besides this love of pureness is finally said to enable us to live in the *fear* of God (I. 222, l. 1145).

[56] Holy Sonnets I, IV, V, VI. The insistence on fear as the beginning of wisdom is particularly noticeable in the early sermons: I. 224, 233, 243, 264, etc., though the preacher knew that 'love is the consummation' (I. 43). Even before his 'conversion' Donne advised Goodyer: 'love him [God] as now, but feare him more' ('Who makes the past', 38).   [57] Holy Sonnets XV, XVI, XVIII.

[58] Holy Sonnet XIV. This characteristic has been emphasized in a different way by A. Low in *The Reinvention of Love* (Cambridge, 1993), 73–85, and in *New Perspectives on 17th C. Lyric*, ed. Roberts, 211–17.

and in an innocence, contracted there, acceptable in the sight of his Father.[59]

Donne did aspire to a Pauline regeneration. He knew that the 'new creation' must be accomplished in 'this minute', by the action of grace alone. His nature at once disposed him to feel this desire and denied him its realization. He was bound to seek for a contact with ultimate reality that would heal the rift created in his mind by his self-consciousness; but his inability to forget himself kept him at a distance from God and from himself. His sensibility demanded present experience; knowing the desired good to be beyond earthly reach, he required a *present* assurance of a *future* possession. That is why, though he rejected the Calvinistic doctrine of reprobation, fundamentally at odds with his humanism and the spirit of tolerance which usually accompanies self-consciousness,[60] he came to believe passionately in the predestination of the elect, admitted by St Thomas.[61] His melancholy nourished the obsessive thought of damnation and he craved for a 'modest but infalible assurance of a final perseverance'.[62] But he conceived this perseverance as a gift of God's grace 'renewed to me every minute',[63] with an emphasis on the moment characteristic of his 'presentism'. According to Walton he came to receive 'some assurances' of his

---

[59] *Sermons*, II. 210–11; my italics, save *Paul*. This sermon was preached on 28 March 1619. Donne had been highly sceptical about mystical states in a sermon preached in March 1617 (I. 186). His wife's death in August 1617 may account for the change. Donne later expressed a wish for an exemplary death in the pulpit (To George Gerrard, 7 Jan. 1630/1; Hayward, Letter xxxix, 498), which implies again self-dramatization.

[60] He believed in a *copiosa redemptio* (*Sermons*, VIII. 370) and even admitted that a man who was not a Christian might be saved: *Sermons*, IV. 78, VI. 161–3.

[61] *Summa*, Ia, q. 23, art. 3. Donne never blindly follows either Calvin or the Angelic Doctor: he even goes beyond the latter in his rejection of 'reprobation', which St Thomas, in fact, almost accepts, quibbling on the difference between 'rejection' and 'non-admission'.

[62] A need expressed in his very first sermon, 30 April 1615: *Sermons*, I. 164. The fear is recurrent in the Holy Sonnets: I, II, IV, V, VI, VII, IX, XIII. Donne was in agreement with the Renaissance physicians in his views on religious melancholy: cf. ch. xxxv of Timothy Bright's *Treatise of Melancholy* (1586) and *Sermons*, VII. 68 and VIII. 249. According to Richard Strier his anguish was not that of a convinced Calvinist (I agree), but rather of a person 'who would like to be a convinced Calvinist': 'John Donne Awry and Squint', *MP* 86 (1988–9), 357–84. Why not simply 'one of the elect'?

[63] A clear parallel with the doctrine of continuous creation; *Sermons*, VIII. 368.

election, and publicly proclaimed it in sermons preached in 1628 and 1629.[64] But the preacher's assurance, like his spiritual joy in the 'Hymne to God my God', sprang from his success in his efforts to bring faith and hope to others, not from any mystical experience.

With his usual perspicacity he had noted that conversion does not alter the fundamental tendencies of character: 'A covetous person, who is now truly converted to God, he will exercise a spiritual covetousness still.'[65] If this is true of a conversion which uproots a man from himself, it applies as well to a conversion which slowly ripened out of an effort of will. The profane poet had found his inspiration in present experience; in the religious poetry only the sinner's anguish is present: the Redemption, the Resurrection, and the Last Judgement have to be lived in imaginative anticipation and the preacher's God proves eminently 'a future God' (*Sermons*, VIII. 75). This distinction may explain why the religious poetry of George Herbert, who had an immediate, though fitful experience of divine love, has more in common with Donne's love poetry than it has with his Divine Poems.

---

[64] *Sermons*, VIII. 249 and 371: 'I doubt not of mine own salvation'.
[65] *Sermons*, I. 236–7, cf. Introduction, p.19.

CHAPTER 2

George Herbert: God-Oriented Self-Consciousness Richard Crashaw: The Surrender of the Self

Joseph Summers early observed that 'the primary purpose of [George Herbert's] poem was not what we understand by "self-expression" for "personality" and personal experience were of interest to the poet exactly in so far as they could be profitably used'.[1] This approach accounts for Herbert's inclusion of obviously didactic poems in *The Temple*, and even for his effort at thrusting the lyrics into some sort of liturgical order. It cannot account for the creative impulse. The religious lyric of the Middle Ages often was a self-communing as well as a colloquy between the soul and God. Petrarch's later debates with his own thoughts, in the *Canzoniere* as in the *Secretum*, were permeated with his recollection of the Augustinian soliloquy. If Herbert did describe *The Temple* as 'a picture of the many spiritual conflicts that have passed betwixt God and my soul', there is no reason to doubt his sincerity.[2] Even if Walton's testimony is called in doubt, one may nevertheless trace the structures of the author's mind in *The Temple* as well as in the published or widely circulated poems of Donne.

Herbert's poetry is even at times distinctly autobiographical.[3]

---

[1] *George Herbert* (London, 1954), 84–5.

[2] For Helen Vendler 'the picture of his own conflicts . . . was his main poetic interest': *The Poetry of George Herbert* (Cambridge, Mass., 1975), 201. For Diana Benet 'the sequence gives the reader not fact, but insight into what Ferrar called Herbert's "inward enforcements", what Walton categorized as the "many conflicts" about his vocation': *Secretary of Praise* (Missouri UP, 1984), 196.

[3] Barbara L. Harman has studied this autobiographical impulse in *Costly Monuments* (Cambridge, Mass., 1982), 89–105, and noted 'the collapse of a coherent

In his self-dramatizations Donne only recreated an isolated moment of experience all the more vivid for standing out against a background of obscurity or tantalizing allusions. Not utterly fascinated by the present, Herbert can survey his whole life, enclose it in narrative, as in 'Affliction I', or in drama, as in 'The Collar', gather in one past and present as in 'The Flower' and 'The Glance', or retrace his steps to a distant point: 'And now me thinks, I am where I began | Sev'n yeares ago' ('Bunch of Grapes'). Besides, as a parson, he is too highly conscious of his sacerdotal office to confine his attention like Donne to his 'naked thinking heart'.[4] Yet his attention remains largely self-centred. The priest meditates on the perfection expected from Christ's minister, but he meditates in privacy: the poem comes to a close when the invitation is spoken: 'Come people; Aaron's drest' ('Aaron'). The inner world proves more spacious than the outer world in 'The Agonie' and 'Content'. 'Miserie' defines what Fulke Greville called the wearisome condition of humanity and the hero is Everyman; yet, when the sick-tossed vessel is dashed on 'his own self', the personal meaning is flashed: 'My God, I mean my self'.

His self, however, does not arouse Herbert's curiosity to the same extent as Donne's. He will, of course, invite self-examination in the Christian mode ('Church-porch', 'H. Scripture', 'Even-song') or in Stoic phrase, as in the close of 'Content'. But he hardly ever practises as keen a vivisection as Donne's on his own heart, nerves, and brain. We miss the note of perplexity, for Herbert's genuine desire is not to seek himself, but 'to seek God only', as the Dean of St Paul did urge himself to do in his 'Hymne to Christ', though with doubtful success.

---

view of the self' (103), a vision of the self 'provisional and open to revision' (161); which, in a way, parallels the uncertainty about the self observed in Donne. I agree that Herbert's self-portrait discloses 'a condition of ontological insecurity' as argued by John R. Mulder in 'The Temple as Picture', in Too Rich to Clothe the Sunne, ed. C. J. Summers (Pittsburgh, 1980), 10. For G. E. Veith Herbert's poetry is 'logocentric', but I would not go so far as to say that 'man is ultimately a hearer' since Herbert repeatedly addresses his God (Reformation Spirituality: The Religion of George Herbert (London and Toronto, 1985), 129).

    [4] I have no objection to Deborah Shuger's distinction: 'There is both a hidden selfhood and a public one, and their double motion informs the discontinuity between the first two parts of The Temple' (Habits of Thought in the English Renaissance (Berkeley, 1990), 91–2).

Herbert's poetry is talk, and God, silent or speaking, is the poet's constant interlocutor. Donne only created an illusion of dialogue; one feels he might have told his mistress: 'For Godsake hold your tongue, and let me [talk]' ('Canonization'). There is no give and take in his poems, even when he meets objections: they are raised by his own mind. In his religious poetry the true centre of interest is still the poet's self. Emotions of fear and love, acts of worship, egotistic petitions are directed to God, but no action of a Divine 'subject' is ever felt, with the single exception of the thrilling invocation: 'Heare thy selfe now, for thou in us dost pray' ('Litanie', xxiii): only through his own prayer is Donne able to *realize* the presence of God and the circle runs from self to self.[5] Herbert's God does speak to his 'Child' in 'Dialogue', in 'Artillery', and most movingly, to check his impatience, in 'The Collar': 'Me thoughts I heard one calling, *Child*! | And I reply'd, *My Lord*.' Open dialogue is infrequent, but there is no interruption in the soul's intercourse with the divine lover, constantly addressed as 'my God', 'my Lord', 'my Master'. Donne analysed in a sermon (IV. 310) 'those *ejaculationes animae*, (as S. *Augustine* calls them)', but only to stress their 'occasionall and transitory' nature: they are absent from his religious poems. Herbert's ecstatic apostrophes 'My joy, my life, my crown!' repeated 'all the day' ('A true Hymne') spring from his sense of a personal relation with the divine Thou.[6]

This intercourse with God is the reason why self-consciousness is not so apparent or constant in *The Temple* as in Donne's poems. When Herbert addresses his heart or his thoughts, one might even assume he reverts to the rhetorical figures of the early Renaissance poets who still personified their mental states.[7] The resemblance, however, is superficial. Donne, too, addressed his heart, not to 'objectify' a faculty as in the elementary stages of subjectivity, but with a perfect awareness of an indivisible 'subject', his 'naked thinking heart' ('Blossome'); his aim was self-definition. When he asks 'Busie enquiring heart,

---

[5] Friedman noted that Donne's God is 'largely a silent one', in *Too Rich to Clothe the Sunne*, ed. Summers, 141.

[6] This contrast between Donne and Herbert was later emphasized by Terry Sherwood in *Herbert's Prayerful Art* (Toronto, 1989), 91, 150.

[7] On the allegorization of the inner life see Ch. 16, pp. 303–4.

what wouldst thou know?' in 'The Discharge', Herbert likewise is trying to assess his whole personality; in the next stanza the pronoun which earlier stood for the heart now stands for the speaker himself: the jumbled syntax shows that the heart and the person are interchangeable in the poet's mind.[8] At other times self-examination may be veiled in allegory, or may thicken into emblem or metaphor, but through the close-woven imagery introspection does search the closets of the heart and will disclose an open breast, fit to challenge 'the clearest diamond' ('Confession').

Yet irony directed at oneself may creep in.[9] Humour is not uncommon at the very heart of earnest devotion and Herbert shares a sense of it with an English medieval mystic, Walter Hilton.[10] In 'Gratefulnesse' he displays a rueful, yet playful insight into the ruse of the human heart who makes God's gifts 'occasion more, | And sayes, If he in this be crost, | All that thou hast giv'n him heretofore | Is lost'. Donne put forward a similar argument: 'Thou hast made me, and shall thy worke decay' (Holy Sonnet I), but his intense fear of damnation obscured the irony of the situation. The love relationship between Herbert and his God allows a certain slyness when he makes Time, angered by his useless talk, say to him: 'This man deludes . . . He doth not crave lesse time, but more' ('Time'). When a passionate outburst in 'The Thanksgiving', 'Affliction I', or 'The Collar' ends in the sudden recognition of its futility, one feels the very surge of emotion was controlled from the beginning by the poet's critical self-awareness.

In several poems the sad admission of man's essential foolishness is attended by a touch of humorous acceptance. Human nature appears more ridiculous than hateful. In 'Miserie' the contrast between man's desires and the true good, the paradoxes in his conduct, his 'strange wayes' are so calmly evoked that we may watch this 'human comedy' without anger or indignation,

---

[8] So they were in 17th-c. devotion; cf. Joseph Hall: 'this monosyllable . . . comprises all that intellective and affective world, which concerneth man' (*Works*, 140).

[9] Helen Wilcox has recently emphasized the presence of irony and humour: 'Irony in Herbert's *Temple*', in *George Herbert: Sacred and Profane*, ed. H. Wilcox, R. Todd, and A. Macdonald (Amsterdam, 1995), 127–51.

[10] In *The Scale of Perfection*, ed. Evelyn Underhill (London, 1923).

but with a sense of the infinite disproportion between the perfection of the Creator and the imperfection of the creature, between
the ineffective wilfulness of man and the omipotence of a divine
lover who will not even suffer 'those | Who would, to be [His]
foes'. 'Giddiness' harps on the theme of human inconstancy in the
spirit of Montaigne. A Christian poet can see life at once as a
tragedy and a comedy. He can at once think in jest and feel in
earnest about the human condition. Irreverence about divine
things is the privilege of the saint when he is capable of humour.
With an almost Rabelaisian gaiety Herbert threatens to expel
conscience with cleansing physic or use the bloody cross as a staff
to silence those that trouble him ('Conscience'). He can delight in
grotesque images of the Resurrection of the flesh, when dust will
'stirre, and rubbe the eyes' and 'this member jogs the other'.[11]

His self-consciousness allowed Herbert to exercise control over
his emotions, but unlike Donne, Herbert was less concerned with
himself and self-definition. He was at times tempted to call in
question his commitment to a religious life, but he had a deeper
love of God and knew it would prevail: 'Let me not love thee, if I
love thee not' ('Affliction I'). That is why, despite the structural
homology discerned in the two poets' minds, their religious feelings are so different. There is no fear of hell or the devil in *The
Temple*,[12] though there is often a fear of being estranged from
God, the fear of a true lover. Mortality, too, evokes no fear, with
the possible exception of 'Church-Monuments'.[13] Herbert's

---

[11] 'Dooms-day': cf. and cst. Thomas Hardy's ironical burlesque in 'The Levelled
Churchyard'.

[12] Hence the major difference, *pace* Richard Strier, between Herbert's religious
sensibility and Luther's. R. V. Young, refuting Strier's interpretation of 'The Flower',
notes that 'the possibility of damnation is raised, but this, far from dampening the
joyousness of the poem, heightens it' ('Donne, Herbert and the Modern Muse', in
New Perspectives on the Seventeenth Century English Religious Lyric, ed. J. R.
Roberts (Columbia, 1994), 183). In his view of Herbert's God 'as a torturer'
Schoenfeldt seems to express only a modern and personal reaction to Christianity
(*Prayer and Power: George Herbert and Renaissance Courtship* (Chicago, 1991),
15). The absence of fear could be due to the Calvinistic doctrine of the perseverance
of the saints which Herbert is supposed to have entertained (G. E. Veith,
Reformation Spirituality (Lewisburg, Pa., 1985), 129), but this is open to question
since, like the Country Parson (*Works*, 290), the poet always speaks as if God had
died for *all* men ('Sacrifice') and *all* Christians are invited to the Lord's Supper:
'Invitation', cf. 'Elixir', 13.

[13] I thought this poem 'superficially Donne-like' in 1960, but now agree with

distinctive approach is best exemplified by the serenity of 'Death'. Donne's fascinated anguish before the grave is here absent and yet the same underlying mode of consciousness can be traced, provided we think of 'The Relique' rather than the Holy Sonnets. The poet faces the skeleton in a matter-of-fact way and does not shrink from 'the uncouth hideous thing'. The contemplation is pervaded with a quiet irony—'Thy mouth was open, but thou couldst not sing'—and horror is absent, for the Christian knows that 'all [these] bones with beautie shall be clad'. There is therefore no shudder and no rapture, for the simultaneous awareness of the stark reality of death and the glory of eternity tempers both fear and exultation. The last stanza takes up the well-worn comparison of death with sleep:

> Therefore we can go die as sleep, and trust
>   Half that we have
>   Unto an honest faithfull grave;
> Making our pillows either down, or dust.

The sober assertion of immortality through the stillness of sleep in an 'honest grave' rests on the fearless acceptance of the gruesome image. Dissonance lurks under a deceptive simplicity. The mention of the body as 'half that we have' reminds us with Herbertian restraint that 'gluttonous death will instantly unjoynt' body and soul, as in Donne's sonnet 'This is my playes last scene', but the final balance between the symbols of downy sleep and dreadful dissolution expresses the poet's composure in front of life and death.

This capacity for ironical detachment accounts for Herbert's insistent use of understatement, at first sight so different from Donne's delight in hyperbole. Again the difference obscures a deep-lying similarity. Donne's most characteristic use of hyperbole was not a mere display of Baroque *Schwulst* or *outrance*, even in the *Anniversaries* and *Verse Letters*.[14] His hyberboles

Barbara Harman that it is 'the representation of a self in the process of losing its identity' (*Costly Monuments*, ch. 4); the fear of dissolution (also experienced by Donne) is different from the fear of going to Hell or 'we know not where' (like Shakespeare's Claudio).

[14] Donne's use of hyperbole was discussed at length in *Poètes métaphysiques*, I. 188–96. Donne's rejection of extremes, noted by Healy in the political and religious sphere (*Ignatius His Conclave*, xli), extended to other domains.

are not mere *over* statements, even in praise, but conceits meant
to express a logical or metaphysical truth. Once the Countess of
Huntington has been identified with virtue by transubstantiation, the following statements are truths. The poet who flatters
the lady, yet says to her 'If you can thinke these flatteries, they
are', is at once aware of exaggeration, yet earnest in his speculations on essence and identity. If Donne's distinction between
'ours' and 'wee' in 'The Extasie' (51) betrays a genuine preoccupation, why should we refuse to discern it too in the distinction between 'you' and 'your' when he addresses the Countess
of Bedford?[15] When his religious emotions were most deeply
felt, therefore highly self-conscious, as in the balanced statements of 'The Litanie' and the Hymns, or in some of his sonnets
of fear and trembling, Donne refrained from overstatement. In
his love poems hyperboles are of two sorts. Some are obviously
not meant to be taken seriously, as in 'The Fever'. Others are the
fittest means of expressing intense emotion truthfully. Unlike
the lyrical exaggerations or rhetorical ranting of Elizabethan
poets and heroes, they compel our assent to a conceptual equiv-
alence, as when the notion of absolute possession is expressed
by the assertion 'She'is all States, and all Princes, I, | Nothing
else is' ('Sunne Rising'). This is not Romeo's 'O she doth teach
the torches to burn bright' (I. v. 46), an emotional cry and a
flash of imagination which can provoke a momentary suspen-
sion of disbelief in the reader, for the lover does 'feel' that the
absence of Juliet would put out the light for him. In the more
intellectual conceits of Donne, hyperboles, usually integrated
into a dialectical movement, can convey a subjective truth even
though we remain aware that they have no claim to an objective
reality. Emotion appears to be under the control of a vigilant
mind and the conversational language and tone further temper
all excess, achieving a delicate balance between an apparently
preposterous claim and a quiet restraint in tone and rhythm, as
in the delicately modulated opening of 'The Legacie': 'When I
dyed last, and Deare, I dye | As often as from thee I goe.' With
the same mastery of tone, the same artistic self-control, dictated
by the same self-consciousness, Herbert chooses to convey the
highest religious truths in deliberate understatement rather than

[15] 'Man to God's image', 49; 'T'have written then', 25; cf. Ch. 1, n. 45.

hyperboles. His constant reticence and his preference for homely phrases need hardly be illustrated: one can open the book at random and note them. His easy conjunction of the commonplace and the divine is suggestive of the privilege of Adam: 'He might to heav'n from Paradise go | As from one room t'another' ('The H: Communion'). In its transparency and depth his poetry works like the glass described in 'The Elixir':

> A man that looks on glasse,
> On it may stay his eye;
> Or if he pleaseth, through it passe,
> And then the heav'n espie.

The mere use of prosaic images does not create a kinship between Herbert and Donne: such images occur in Elizabethan poetry and drama. Besides, Donne often combines matter-of-factness and hyperbolic expressions of scorn and disgust, as in 'The Perfume' and 'The Apparition', or irreverence, as in 'The Sunne Rising'. He may announce the poetics of Herbert when he invites us to look on death as 'but the unbinding of a pack | To take one precious thing, thy soule, from hence' (*Second Anniversary*, 94–5). Yet, even here there is no 'understatement' since the poet's aim is to belittle death. Herbert's familiar presentation of Redemption or divine love, on the contrary, does not belittle but elevates.[16] What characterizes his poetry is the conscious reticence of the expression, well studied by William Empson in 'Hope' and 'The Pilgrimage'.[17] What Empson failed to note is its psychological origin: a faculty of critical detachment which Donne and Herbert had in common. Through the delight of the former in hyperbole, as through the preference of the latter for understatement, a deeper-seated affinity is disclosed: the fundamental ambiguity of an acute self-consciousness.

There are, of course, in *The Temple* more poems in which the self does not intrude than could be found in the poetry of

---

[16] I must admit that the holiness of the ordinary was a theme of Protestant divines; Perkins wrote that 'whatsoever is done within the lawes of God though it be wrought by the body, as the wiping of shoes and such like, howsoever gross they appear outwardly, yet are they sanctified' (quoted by C. Taylor in *Sources of the Self* (Cambridge, 1994), 161).

[17] *Seven Types of Ambiguity* (London, 1947), 118–20, 129–31.

Donne: this is not unexpected since self-centredness is not so prevalent.[18] Yet a reader on the alert may discern the workings of a critical self-awareness even in the absence of personal expression. The complaint of Christ crucified in 'The Sacrifice' is an evocation of the Passion modelled on a liturgical tradition which Rosemond Tuve has traced to the Middle Ages.[19] But she failed to notice the difference between the objective paradoxes found in medieval poetry and a handling of paradox and irony which implies a subjective approach in Herbert's poem. Throughout 'The Sacrifice' the emphasis is not laid on the sufferings of Christ, nor even on the mystery of Redemption as in the *Improperia*, but on the blindness of man as it is perceived by a divine omniscience and love. This is in some ways close to Sophoclean irony, but differs from it since we are constantly reminded that man could open his eyes if he wished. As the words of Christ are, in fact, the reflections of a poet who knows that his sins crucify Christ daily, irony here becomes irony directed at oneself though elevated to impersonality. This note is struck from the beginning: men are blind to Him who took eyes that He might find them, and condemn Him with that same breath that He gives them daily. Christ will die betwixt two thieves 'As he that for some robberie suffereth. | Alas! what have I stollen from you? Death.' The subjective implication is more obvious in this quietly terrific allusion to the *Deus absconditus* and the double darkness of man's soul:

> My face they cover, though it be divine.
> As *Moses* face was vailed, so is mine,
> Lest on their double-dark souls either shine.

In the medieval treatment of the theme pathos is foremost and the dramatic irony arising from the blindness of the creature is not perceptible. The clear-sighted balance between emotion and intellect in Herbert's poem is a mark of self-control in a mind given to self-examination. Self-consciousness informs and subtly modifies the objective expression of the Christian mystery.

---

[18] R. B. Rollin, noting that 'Donne's only subject is John Donne', agrees that Herbert 'often takes as his subjects things other than his own subjectivity', but his elaborate classification of the poems in three groups is questionable (*Too Rich to Clothe the Sunne*, ed. Summers, 147–61).

[19] *A Reading of George Herbert* (London, 1951), 49 ff.

Donne and George Herbert have been found to be much closer to one another than one would have expected in their dominant mode of self-awareness, with similar consequences for the expression of their emotions. For a sharp contrast we should now turn to Richard Crashaw.

Richard Crashaw: The Surrender of the Self

Donne's devotion was self-centred. Herbert's attention centred on the intercourse between God and his own soul. Crashaw's ecstatic piety aims at self-annihilation. 'Leave nothing of my SELF in me', he cries out to the Foundress of the Carmelites: 'Let me so read thy life, that I | Unto all life of mine may dy' ('The Flaming Heart').[20] Lyrical, intensely emotional, his poetry nevertheless proves mainly impersonal. He is lost in the contemplation of some outer object: Christ, the Virgin, or a Saint. Whereas the inner presence of God in the soul invited Herbert's self-questionings, Crashaw's faith and imagination are centrifugal: 'Goe, Soul out of thy Self' ('To the Name Above Every Name'). His love of God ignores the self-centred anguish of Donne. It also differs from the devotion of Herbert, which, though focused on Christ, never was a mere contemplation of his life and figure, but an emotional and intellectual experience in which attention was transferred from the feeling to the feeling subject. Crashaw's attention is always directed to a sensible object, the Virgin or Saints as well as Christ.[21] There is no hint of autobiography and the 'I' is almost absent though not deliberately banished.[22] The impersonality of the poetry is spontaneous: it is a blend of sensations and emotions which are not analysed, nor even referred to an experiencing subject.[23]

---

[20] Crashaw's tendency to 'self-sacrifice' has been attributed to 'the Feminine Animus' by Maureen Sabine in *JDJ* 4 (1985), 69–94; cf. her *Feminine Engendered Faith: The Poetry of John Donne and Richard Crashaw* (London, 1992).

[21] Anthony Low stressed his 'wonderful empathy' in *The Reinvention of Love* (Cambridge, 1993), 111.

[22] It is found mainly in paraphrases of liturgical hymns in which it takes on a universal character. In his own hymns, Crashaw commonly uses a collective 'we'. Though written in the first person his early profane poems were objective.

[23] Lorraine M. Roberts thinks that 'Crashaw's intent is to be impersonal' and assumes that impersonality can be traced to Counter-Reformation poets and theorists

From a mind so little given to self-examination the subjective irony and ambiguity of Donne and Herbert cannot be expected, even when he revels in paradoxes. The fundamental feature of Crashaw's inspiration is the ambivalence of pleasure and pain and a wish for death different at once from Herbert's quiet welcome of it and from Donne's search for a 'canonization'. Its most obvious and admirable expression is found in the Teresa hymns:

> O how oft shalt thou complaine
> Of a sweet and subtile paine.
> Of intollerable joyes?
> Of a death, in which who dyes
> Loves his death, and dyes againe,
> And would for ever so be slaine!
> And lives and dyes; and knowes not why
> To live, But that he still may dy.[24]

Besides celebrating the numerous deaths of a saint eager for martyrdom the poet seemed to make the wish his in a short lyric:

> Though still I dy, I live again;
> Still longing so to be so slain,
> So gainfull in such losse of breath,
> I dy even in desire of death.
> Still live in me this loving strife
> Of living DEATH & dying LIFE.
> For while thou sweetly slayest me
> Dead to my selfe, I live in Thee.[25]

That 'dying lives and short-lived dyings' did not become the poet's favourite theme only under the influence of the Spanish

---

('Crashaw's Sacred Voice', in *New Perspectives on the Life and Art of Richard Crashaw*, ed. J. R. Roberts (Columbia, 1990), 66–71). The influence is undeniable, but a creative poet is only influenced when his own imagination and sensibility respond to the suggestions. Crashaw, brought up a Protestant, would not have been attracted to Counter-Reformation poetry and would not have ultimately joined the Roman Church if he had not obeyed a personal impulse.

[24] 'In memory of Madre de Teresa that sought an early Martyrdome', 97–104. In the revised version the last line reads: 'To live, But that he thus may never leave to DY'.

[25] 'A Song'. Parallels have been pointed out in St Teresa's works (see R. V. Young, *Richard Crashaw and the Spanish Golden Age* (New Haven, 1982), 49–50), but in the lyric, unlike the hymn, the speaker expresses his own wish and the unidentified speaker here may be assumed to be the poet rather than a *persona*.

mystics[26] is shown by their profane presence in an early poem
about 'the pretty twilight strife | of dying maide and dawning
wife' ('Epithalamium') and by the paraphrase of an Italian love
poem:

> When my dying
> Life is flying;
> Those sweet Aires that often slew me;
> Shall revive mee,
> Or reprive mee,
> And to many Deaths renew mee.
>
> (*Out of the Italian*. A Song)

The fear of death as annihilation never haunted Crashaw. When
Teresa's physical death is finally evoked at the close of the
Hymn, the uniqueness of the experience is not perceived; all the
previous dying ecstasies are rolled into one:

> When these thy DEATHS so numerous,
> Shall all at last dy into one,
> And melt thy Soul's sweet mansion;
> Like a soft lump of incense, hasted
> By too hot a fire, & wasted
> Into perfuming clouds, so fast
> Shalt thou exhale to Heaven at last
> In a resolving SIGH . . .

Gone is the anguish of the marrow, the spectre of dissolution.
Death to Donne was a wrenching apart of soul and body (Holy
Sonnet VI) but they now 'part like friends . . . A KISSE, a SIGH,
and so away' ('Temperance'). Crashaw belongs to the second
Baroque generation, so intent on the *cupio dissolvi* that they
averted their eyes from the gruesomeness of the grave. He was
undoubtedly influenced by a Christian tradition—'the Holy
Ghost', Donne pointed out, 'is amorous in his Metaphors'
(*Sermons*, VII. 67)—and by the erotic language prevailing in his
spiritual circle. But once again an individual disposition alone
can fully account for the poet's insistent choice of this language
since other believers did not adopt it.

---

[26] As R. V. Young assumed (*Crashaw*, 85–90). He was right, however, in pointing out that in the Teresa poems at least 'Crashaw manages his material in such a
way that the suggestion of erotic sensation is very slight' (87). This is the result of
the gradual 'purification' I had noted.

An unselfconscious sensuality pervaded the early poetry of Crashaw, though no chaster love can be found than 'That not impossible She' addressed in his 'Wishes To his (Supposed) Mistress'.[27] The deflowering of a virgin bride was a common theme in the celebration of a marriage, but it usually did not fill ten stanzas out of twelve as in Crashaw's 'Epithalamium'. This sensuality is not only suggested by his *Hymnus Veneri* and his epigrams on Pygmalion or the nakedness of Venus, but more subtly betrayed by his fascination for the 'crimson streame' of blood 'warme in its violet channel', a recurrent image in several poems.[28] It is no less obvious in the *Epigrammata Sacra* even if psychoanalysts are not justified in gloating over the lines on the Divine babe tabled at the Virgin's teats: 'He'll have his Teat e're long (a bloody one) | The mother then must suck the Son.'[29] The lingering over the Infant martyrs, the Circumcision, and the bleeding Wounds of Christ have erotic connotations and the epigrams Crashaw later chose to turn into English are among the more heavily laden with sensual impressions. In the poems written before 1637 the obsessive imagery of milk issuing from

---

[27] The evolution I trace here and in Ch. 12 is at once psychological and stylistic. R. V. Young reduced it to 'a progressive slackening' of the influence of the neo-Latinists and Marino (*Crashaw*, 10), leaving unexplained the reason for the 'slackening'. The 'erotic undertow of imagery' is acknowledged, but related to a tradition of 'sacred parody' (24–39). This is true, but cannot account for Crashaw's peculiar insistence.

[28] 'Elegy on the death of Lady Parker', 38–9; 'Upon the gunpowder treason', 41–2; 'Elegy upon the death of Mr Stanninow', 22–4.

[29] 'Blessed be the paps which Thou hast sucked'. There were precedents for these metaphors, even in Herbert's Latin verse (*Lucus*, 'In Johannem'), and breast imagery was common in devotional literature: see Marc Bertonasco, *Crashaw and the Baroque* (Montgomery, 1971), 79–82; Maureen Sabine, *JDJ* 4 (1985), 7; and E. R. Cunnar, 'Opening the Religious Lyric. Crashaw's Ritual, Liminal, and Visual Wounds', in *New Perspectives on Crashaw*, ed. Roberts, 237–67. I agree that a stereotyped language meant to convey spiritual emotions is apt to lose its sensual connotations; but one may still suspect an *original* confusion of the erotic and the mystic in the creation of this language. Moreover the frequency of such images in the early poetry of Crashaw and the later chastening of the sensual language remain personal characteristics. The sexual connotations recently pointed out in Herbert's *Temple* are offered in disregard of context and tone. I can give only one instance: the sexual meaning of 'slacken' makes sense and sharpens the wit in Donne's 'The Good-Morrow'. It doesn't, when applied to 'slack' in Herbert's 'Love (III)'; besides, 'slack' was obviously chosen here instead of 'slow' or 'hesitant' in order to rhyme with 'back'. In 'Investigating Herbert Criticism' Stanley Stewart rightly criticized this uncontrolled search for 'sexual meaning' or 'sinister motive': *Renascence*, 45 (1993), 146–7, 152.

a woman's breast,[30] as well as the frequent mingling of milk and blood,[31] is noticeable and the early attraction to martyrdom is not yet invested with a mystic aura.

With the 'Nativity' and 'Assumption' Hymns, as well as the lines 'On a prayer booke', the poet moved away from blood to clearer themes: 'soft exhalations | Of soule; deare, and divine annihilations', but the 'raryfied delights' called up in verse of Shelleyan lightness are not free from a cloying sweetness reminiscent of Salesian devotion. Crashaw had proclaimed himself Herbert's disciple in *Steps to the Temple*, but those steps were mostly laid before 1634 and *The Temple* had been published only in 1633. 'On Mr G. HERBERTS Book sent to a Gentlewoman' was still written in a key of devout gallantry and mystical mawkishness alien to the spirit of Herbert. The actual influence of *The Temple* is not traceable before the second edition of 1648 and is best exemplified by 'Charitas Nimia. Or the Dear Bargain':

> Lord, what is man? why should he cost thee
> So dear? what had his ruin lost thee?
> Lord what is man? that thou hast overbought
>   So much a thing of nought?
> Love is too kind, I see; & can
> Make but a simple merchant man.

The poet's own voice was now more distinctly heard, but this awareness of self is still attended by a desire to lose himself: 'That lost again my LIFE may prove | As then in DEATH, so now in love' (65–6). The reading of the Spanish mystics, shortly after the encounter with Herbert, allowed him to give a more intense expression to this wish, but the wish must have been embedded in his nature. Even in a profane poem, he had seen himself as 'a melting sacrifice' ('To the Morning. Satisfaction for sleepe', 51). In his liturgical hymns the rare intrusion of his self is a means of expressing his innermost tendency to self-loss or absorption of the desired object in an imagery of drinking and sucking, now fortunately freed from the embarrassing concreteness of the

---

[30] '*Et quid si biberet Jesus vel ab ubere vestro*', 'Nativity', st. xi, 'Sancta Maria', st. xi; cf. 'Weeper', st. v–vi; 'On a prayer-book', 111.
[31] 'In lactentes Martyres', 'Upon the Infant Martyrs'.

Epigrammata: 'When this dry soul those eyes shall see, | And drink the unseal'd source of thee' ('Adoro te'),

> O let me suck the wine
> So long of this chaste vine
> Till drunk of the dear wounds, I be
> A lost Thing to the world, as it to me.

('Sancta Maria Dolorum')

A confirmation of this imaginative constancy, despite stylistic changes, will be found in his use of paradox and imagery studied in Chapter 12.

CHAPTER 3

Henry Vaughan: Emotional Subjectivity

The inspiration of Vaughan is intensely subjective: the poet cultivates a 'sweet self-privacy' ('Rules *and* Lessons'). One cannot doubt that he expresses personal feelings even on the rare occasions when he uses the plural or resorts to a traditional dialogue between the soul and the body. There are autobiographical hints even in his profane poetry, as the recurrent allusions to the first meeting with the beloved suggest.[1] In *Silex Scintillans* a spiritual autobiography, implied in *Authoris (de se) Emblema*, is outlined in 'The Garland' and 'Vanity of Spirit'. In 'The Authors Preface' the 'private' character of the poems is emphasized and is an excuse for the obscurity of occasional allusions: 'you will (peradventure) observe some *passages*, whose *history* or *reason* may seem something *remote*; but were they brought *nearer*, and plainly exposed to your view . . . yet would it not conduce much to your greater *advantage*'. The best poems, indeed, are a record of private experience, secretive self-communings. In a series of elegiac meditations which call to mind Tennyson's later *In Memoriam*,[2] Vaughan addresses God as 'Thou that know'st for whom I mourne', not the reader who will only discover incidentally that the loved one lost is now a brother, now a wife (my italics):

> Come, come, what doe I here?
> Since *he* is gone
> Each day is grown a dozen year,
> And each hour, one.

---

[1] See F. E. Hutchinson, *Henry Vaughan* (Oxford, 1947), 52.

[2] Tennyson had read George Herbert shortly before writing *In Memoriam*. He may have read Vaughan as well. Both poets feel the presence of the lost friend in nature: 'There's not a wind can stir, | Or beam passe by, | But strait I think (Though far,) | Thy hand is nigh' ('Come, come, what doe I here?'): cf. *In Memoriam*, lxxxv: 'And every pulse of wind and wave | Recalls, in change of light and gloom, | My old affection of the tomb'.

> Joy of my life! while left me here,
>   And still *my Love*!
> How in thy absence thou doest steere
>   Me from above!

These poems disclose a kind of self-consciousness different from Donne's and George Herbert's. I called it 'sentiment de soi' to stress its emotional nature which brings Vaughan closer to the Romantics. He has also a different way of being present to himself. In the *Songs and Sonets* Donne usually speaks in the presence of the beloved. In the *Satires* and *Elegies* he addresses an interlocutor or a spectator. Even in his self-analysis he commonly has a witness: we seldom see him in solitude. Herbert's devotion is solitary, but he is so vividly alive to the presence—or momentary absence—of God that he never seems to be conscious of his sole existence. Vaughan's feeling of, and for, solitude pervades his poetry. His translations of 'Temperance and Patience', 'Life and Death', 'The World Contemned', and 'The Life of Paulinus'—treatises unconcerned with solitariness—were purposely gathered under the title *Flores Solitudinis*, the solitude of a man said to be writing 'in his Sicknesse and Retirement'. The book was sent abroad '*to bee a companion of those wise* Hermits, *who have withdrawne from the present generation, to confirme them in their solitude*' ('To the Reader'). A volume of prayers, *The Mount of Olives*, was subtitled *Solitary Devotions*. 'Retirement' was a common theme and that two poems should be so entitled (*Works*, II. 462, 642) would not be a significant choice, had not Vaughan so clearly and insistently expressed his predilection for 'solitary years' spent 'in sighs and unseen tears' ('Joy'). A desire for secrecy is linked at once with a spiritual longing for 'the life . . . hid above with Christ | In God' ('Palm-tree') and a more personal aware-ness of the 'secret growth' of plants, as in 'The Seed growing secretly': 'Then bless thy secret growth, nor catch | At noise, but thrive unseen and dumb.' Visions are only granted by God to the 'solitary self': ' 'Tis number makes a Schism' ('Jacob's Pillow, and Pillar'). Perfect solitariness is attained in the night by Jesus and by the dreaming soul in its 'dumb watch' ('Night').[3] Dreaming is also the source of poetic inspiration in 'The World'

---

[3]   Cf. 'Day-spring', 'Cock-crowing', 'Morning-watch'.

and 'The Search'. Now, in a dream our consciousness surrenders to desires, but seems incapable of self-reflexivity.[4] Even when the poet is awake, his state of mind is often initially close to reverie, though the conscious intrusion of articulate reflection on the experience may obscure the fact: hence a vagueness never found in Donne or Herbert.

Vaughan's mode of consciousness is characterized by a tendency to expansion and dispersion, therefore diffuseness. There is no clarity of vision: we enter with this Welsh poet a world of 'mists, and shadows' ('Resurrection and Immortality', 51–4). Chiaroscuro is attractive to his imagination for 'shades set off light' ('Timber'), and 'light is never so beautifull as in the presence of darknes' (*Flores Solitudinis*, 'To the Reader'), unsurprising statements in the age of Rembrandt. What is surprising is the image chosen to illustrate this truth: 'there are bright starrs under the most palpable clouds'. Not a sharp contrast but a veiled splendour and faint beams, as in 'They are all gone into the world of light':

> It glows and glitters in my cloudy brest
> Like stars upon some gloomy grove,
> Or those faint beams in which this hill is drest,
> After the Sun's remove.[5]

Vaughan thus has a vision of a diffuse or refracted light whose distant source is beyond human sight. At other times, addressing his childhood, he only perceives its luminous fringe through the mist of memory; his 'striving eye | Dazzles at it, as at eternity' and he can 'onely see through a long night | Thy edges, and thy bordering light! | O for thy Center and mid-day!' ('Childehood'). Yet, even in heaven, light never seems to have a centre for a poet eager to 'rove in that mighty, and eternall light' ('Resurrection and Immortality', 63), elsewhere called 'a sea of light' ('Water-fall', 18). The 'everlasting Saboth' of Eternity runs 'Without Succession, and without a *Sunne*' ('Resurrection', 70). When Eternity is seen 'Like a great *Ring* of pure and endless

---

4 The dream itself, of course, can be analysed by the awakened mind, which Vaughan never does, unlike Donne in Elegie X.

5 Cf. 'The Pious soul by night | Is like a clouded starre' ('Morning-watch').

light' ('World'), again Vaughan's imagination embraces an
expanse of light. If he had like Traherne always perceived light
as irradiating from a centre toward the circumference, night
might not have had for him the same attraction and spiritual
value: in light and darkness alike he loved a fluid homogeneity
in which his individual consciousness could roam. His aspiration, however, was not to lose himself like Crashaw in a beloved
object. To 'live in God' meant for him to dwell in 'that night!
where I in him | Might live invisible and dim!' ('Night', 53–4).
A diffuse consciousness is not so apt as Donne's or Herbert's to
be self-reflexive. It tends to spill itself abroad rather than apprehend itself inwardly. Having no centre it will easily become a
wandering consciousness.

Vaughan, indeed, was a 'wanderer' like Wordsworth. The
very title of an early poem, 'To Amoret, Walking in a Starry
Evening', is suggestive of his deambulatory inspiration,
confirmed by several other poems such as 'I walkt the other day
(to spend my hour)'.[6] This is significant. Donne practises
(or imagines) self-analysis either at rest (as in 'The Extasie'), or
when he is just about to act ('act the rest' in 'The Dreame')
or move, as in the several 'Valedictions'.[7] Marvell does love to
wander through a garden or a landscape, but he only becomes
introspective when lying under a tree ('Garden', 'Appleton
House', lxxv–lxxviii). One is usually at rest, or will come to a
halt, when the mind turns in upon itself. Motion, walking or
boating, will rather incline to the expansion of reverie. The
Romantics later indulged in such *Rêveries du promeneur soli-
taire*. Vaughan's affinities with them, especially with Wordsworth, were early noticed, but later sharply called in question.
Rightly from a historical point of view; yet, in a search for
psychological correlations, the Silurist does appear at times
closer to Wordsworth than he is to Donne or even Herbert.

Vaughan's attraction to 'flying winds and flowing wells',[8]
rivers, and waterfalls is not only a love of a liquid or fluid
substance, but a love of a 'motion' seen as the very 'form' or

---

[6] See also 'To Amoret gone from him'; 'Upon the Priorie grove', 4, 36;
'Religion'; 'To *Etesia* going beyond Sea', 8.

[7] George Herbert, too, describes himself *about* to perform his office as a priest
in 'Aaron', or *about* to stray from his calling in 'The Collar', but never in movement.
In 'Church Musick' the 'rising and falling' is only a rhythmical experience.

[8] 'Bee', 29; cf. 'Christs Nativity', 8.

essence of water or air: 'Water's refin'd to *Motion*, Aire to
Light' ('Tempest'). The wind is not only the spirit of God[9] but
the symbol of true liberty in 'Misery':

> Lord, bind me up, and let me lye
> A Pris'ner to my libertie,
> If such a state at all can be
> As an Impris'ment serving thee;
> The wind, though gather'd in thy fist,
> Yet doth it blow stil where it list,
> And yet shouldst thou let go thy hold
> Those gusts might quarrel and grow bold.

'Gusts' and 'giddy blast[s]' of passion may indeed turn man into
a different kind of wanderer, 'sadly loose', who 'strays and
roams' ('And do they so', 'Man'). This is traditional Christian
symbolism, but a difference may already be noted in a comparison with Herbert: in *The Temple* man's 'restlessness' ('Pulley')
and 'Giddinesse' are stressed rather than his 'roaming'. Such
assertions as 'I will abroad' ('Collar'), or 'Full rebellion, I would
die, | Or fight, or travell' ('Nature') only disclose an impulse in
a moment of instability. Vaughan alone conveys a sense of
actual wandering through space, which is at times deplored as a
straying from God. Whereas Herbert's common desire is to be
'enclosed' ('Paradise'), to 'roost and nestle' ('Temper I'),
Vaughan's deepest aspiration is to 'rove in that mighty and eter-
nall light' ('Resurrection and Immortality', 63).

A real nostalgia for a different mode of being is only perceptible in *Silex Scintillans*. When Herbert wishes to become a tree
or a flower ('Affliction I', 57; 'Employment I'; 'Employment II',
21), the wish, which arises from his examination of his inner
life, remains symbolic. With Vaughan the starting-point in
'Man' and in 'And do they so?' is a wistful contemplation of the
natural order—*res creatae* expecting the Revelation of the
Son—which reveals his imperfection to man: 'I would I were a
stone, or tree, | Or flowre by pedigree, | Or some poor high-way
herb, or Spring | To flow, or bird to sing!' ('And do they so?').
Here the wish does seem to express a spontaneous and real aspiration, almost a desire for metamorphosis, which can only be
accounted for by a genuine feeling of 'sympathy'.

---

[9] 'Regeneration', st. 9–10; 'Law and Gospel', 9; 'Mount of Olives', 4–8.

Vaughan's notion of sympathy was, of course, related to the natural philosophy of his age and his Hermeticist convictions, which will be examined in Chapter 13. Such bonds between living creatures were 'conceived' by the minds of Donne or Herbert, elaborated by their wits: Vaughan alone seems to have an emotional and almost sensuous experience of the working of sympathy when he claims in these opening lines: 'Sure, there's a tye of Bodyes! . . . Absents within the Line Conspire, and *Sense* | Things distant doth unite.' In 'The Timber' the common notion that the blood of a murdered man will run at the approach of the murderer serves only as an analogue to the 'deep hate and dissent' observed in dead wood at the approach of a storm; both the wasting 'senseless' and the 'strange resentment' seem to be felt by the poet himself in an animistic intuition:

> But thou beneath the sad and heavy *Line*
> Of death, dost waste all senseless, cold and dark;
> Where not so much as dreams of light may shine,
> Nor any thought of greenness, leaf or bark.

Emotional self-awareness in Vaughan may take the form of this awareness of a bond with other creatures. Sympathy does not rule out introspection, as the poetry of Wordsworth shows, but a poet who has no acute curiosity for his own inner life may be content with feeling instead of analysing his feelings. Vaughan is no pantheist, if pantheism implies an absorption of personality in the cosmic whole: being highly conscious of the contrast between the ordered life of other creatures and his own straying, he remains intensely aware of his individuality. Sympathy and subjectivity are reconciled. In such projections into other lives, or in the dispersion of reverie, the Silurist, unlike Herbert, first goes out of himself; but, unlike Crashaw, he returns to himself. In his self-diffusings he remains self-centred, but without a keen interest in his states of mind, without the feverish self-obsession of Donne or the self-probings of Herbert.

The author of *Silex Scintillans* is therefore prone to generalize his experience. In conclusion to his own 'spilt thoughts', he will say: 'Such is mans life, and such is mine', inverting the order of discovery ('Miserie', 89). The universal and the individual are similarly intertwined in 'Man' and in 'Mans fall, and Recovery'. This is almost inevitable in devotional poetry since the sinner in

front of God must be aware of his humanity; Donne and
Herbert, however, prove more acutely conscious of their indi-
viduality even when praying. The very choice of subjects in *Silex
Scintillans* discloses a tendency towards impersonality in reflection though not in feeling. A didactic intention is no less obvious in many poems of Herbert; what is characteristic is
Vaughan's selection of Biblical episodes—'Abels blood', '*Isaacs
Marriage*', 'The Daughter of Herodias', Jesus on the 'Mount of
Olives'—and the profuse scattering of Biblical verses which are
at once epigraphs and themes. Obviously the poet's subject is
often provided by the outer world or by his reading, whereas
Donne and Herbert found an occasion—whether real or
pretended—in an inner experience or an immediate reaction to
some event. The dramatic impact of personality is lost.

Accordingly there will be little psychological complexity in
the poetry of Vaughan. He followed Herbert in his description
of his intermittent spiritual experiences; but poems like
'Unprofitableness' or 'Disorder and frailty' propose images apt
to stir an emotion rather than define it. With Herbert's delicate
analysis of a state of mind in 'The Flower' one may contrast this
profusely descriptive simile which hardly takes us into the poet's
heart:

> 'Twas but Just now my bleak leaves hopeles hung
>   Sullyed with dust and mud;
> Each snarling blast shot through me, and did share
> Their Youth, and beauty, Cold showres nipt, and wrung
>   Their spiciness, and bloud.[10]

'Misery', under the close influence of Herbert, supplies an
insight into the workings of divine grace through what may
seem 'meer tempers'. But Vaughan usually presents the inner life
in a succession of opaque images as in 'The Mutinie':

> My thoughts, like water which some stone doth start
> Did quit their troubled Channel, and retire
> Unto the banks, where, storming at those bounds,
> They murmur'd sore . . .

---

[10] 'Unprofitableness'; the contrast is the more striking since Vaughan here obviously imitates Herbert's way of opening a poem *just* after the moment of experience
recorded: cf. 'Temper II'.

Self-examination, when attempted, may be conducted through allegory and the search is not ultimately directed to self-discovery. In 'Vanity of Spirit', an epitome of his mystic quest and favourite symbolism, the poet, we are told, leaving his 'Cell' (a symbol of solitude) by 'dawn' (the hour of inspiration), lingered by a 'spring' (living waters as a source of life and grace) and 'gron'd to know' the Author of Nature. Like an alchemist he 'summon'd nature' and rifled 'Her wombe, her bosome, and her head'—all the spheres of the cosmic order. 'Having past | Through all the Creatures', the poet tells us, 'I came at last | To search myself'. But not after the manner of Donne, seeking 'the Ego, the individuall, I'. The 'traces' and 'Hyerogliphicks' he discovers in a 'nook' of his own soul, like the 'Ecchoes beaten from th'eternal hills', are intimations of a divine mystery and only build up another fantastic world of 'weake beames' and 'Moone-shine night'. Thus the poet's thought first turns to Nature, then from the contemplation of Nature moves to self-exploration, but with no Augustinian sense of opposition. In his comparison of Vaughan's quest with the questioning of Nature by the author of the *Confessions* (X. 6), Martz slurred over the movement of recoil—*Interrogavi terram et dixit non sum*—because it cannot be found in the poem. Unlike Augustine, or Herbert, Vaughan traces no clear boundary between the world of objects and the subjective experience; unlike Traherne, he does not enclose the outer world in the sphere of soul. His longing for a fuller revelation in death, unlike Donne's, is not a search for his own identity but a yearning for the discovery of the Divine, were it 'but one half glaunce', through the rending of 'these veyls' ('Vanity of Spirit') or 'mists' ('They are all gone'), either in nature or in the soul. This is closer to the Hermetic approach than to Augustine's patient analysis of memory in his journey of the mind towards God as a reality *interior intimo meo* (III. vi).

With Donne, with Herbert, with Marvell too, self-consciousness often led to irony or ambiguity which seem foreign to Vaughan's subjectivity, dominated by an inclination to reverie: irony is unknown to a dreaming consciousness.[11] It is only

---

[11] The 'oneiric irony' of German romanticism lies in the contrast between our deeper life and our 'serious' diurnal occupations that is perceived by the waking consciousness: Albert Béguin, *L'âme romantique et le rêve* (Paris, 1937), vii. 2; 1991 edn., p. 110.

traceable in a traditional acknowledgement of human inconstancy and unconsciousness largely inspired by Herbert in 'Misery': 'The mighty God, th'eternal King | Doth grieve for Dust, and Dust doth sing.' Intense emotion in *Silex Scintillans* tends to be a pure cry: 'O my God, hear my cry; | Or let me dye!——' ('Anguish'). There are no sharp contrasts or changes of mood as in so many of Donne's or Herbert's poems. There is no suggestion either of the kind of ambivalence which characterized the sensibility of Crashaw, no secret equivalence or fusion of contraries: Vaughan is the poet of osmosis rather than metamorphosis or transubstantiation. A unity of tone and feeling prevails. Emotions freely mingle in a nostalgic 'pensiveness' or 'melancholy'.[12] Vaughan's 'debased' use of 'mystical' (the 'mystical, deep streams' of 'The Water-fall') has been criticized by Empson, but it is the only apt word to convey this emotional halo about things, this sense of their spiritual depth, at once intense and vague, though more precise than the later Romantic emotions because of its associations with a definite theology or natural philosophy.

A certain plasticity in Vaughan's imagination, a submission to influence may account for an occasional departure from his proper strain or tone, but will not mask them. A comparative analysis of his feeling for death again will provide an illustration of his originality. He can write about the 'Charnel-house' after the manner of Donne's illegitimate heirs, Cleveland or Benlowes, in a macabre and semi-burlesque mode, descrying in it 'Fragments of man, Rags of Anatomie, | Corruptions ward-robe, the transplantive bed | Of mankind, and th'Exchequer of the dead.' This is alien to the complexity and dissonance noted in Herbert's 'Death'. 'The Check' may remind us of Donne standing before a grave opened for digging up a corpse and the theme of decomposition this time is handled in the language of Herbert:

> Peace, peace! I blush to hear thee; when thou art
>   A dusty story
> A speechlesse heap, and in the midst my heart
>   In the same livery drest
>   Lyes tame as all the rest;
> When six years thence digg'd up, some youthfull Eie
>   Seeks there for Symmetry

---

[12] 'Water-fall', 14; 'Regeneration', 15; 'Resurrection', 67; 'Fair and yong light'.

> But finding none, shal leave thee to the wind,
> Or the next foot to Crush,
>   Scatt'ring thy kind
> And humble dust, tell then dear flesh
>   Where is thy glory?

With Vaughan, however, anguish is impersonalized in an apostrophe to the 'flesh' and irony is diluted in the pathos of humble dust, trodden and scattered. Even in the meditation 'Death. A Dialogue', centring on Christ and the hope of resurrection, a unity of tone prevails and the passage from ignorance ('by none art thou understood') to revelation (21–30) is free from the contrasts and ambiguities analysed in Herbert's 'Death'. The original accent of the Silurist is best heard in 'They are all gone into the world of light!':

> Dear, beauteous death! the Jewel of the Just,
>   Shining no where, but in the dark;
> What mysteries do lie beyond thy dust;
>   Could man outlook that mark!

> He that hath found some fledg'd birds nest, may know
>   At first sight, if the bird be flown;
> But what fair Well, or Grove he sings in now,
>   That is to him unknown.

Death is here associated with beauty (though not in Herbert's manner) and with the poet's favourite themes and images expressing his deeper emotions. The poem achieves a balance between mystery and lucidity, sentiment and reflection, which is characteristic of Vaughan's best moments.

The balance is upset in the opening of 'Death. A Dialogue', which anticipates the pre-Romantic sensibility when the imagination dwells in 'a sad Land', 'Where shadowes thicken, and the Cloud | Sits on the Suns brow all the yeare, | And nothing moves without a shrowd'. But the physician-poet next offers an extraordinary evocation of the first conjunction of body and soul in the throes of childbirth: the babe in the womb struggling in darkness to be born. The obstetrical progress, which might have been evoked crudely in organic terms by the author of *The Progresse of the Soule*,[13] is here, however, veiled in the favourite

---

[13] Cf. stanzas l–li of Donne's *Metempsychosis*.

natural imagery of Vaughan: the 'blushing East' and the rending of 'Clouds' in whose 'Cranies light appear'd'. The comparison is inaccurate when the poet claims 'Just so it is in death', for death disjoins body and soul for a long while before the second birth of resurrection; but defective logic and deep feeling are often associated in the poetry of the Silurist.

These poems on death denote a susceptibility to influence which may occasion a certain inconstancy of temper or manner. One feels in reading Donne or George Herbert that their tone and language reflect a genuine complexity in their modes of imagination and sensibility; Vaughan's originality asserts itself more hesitantly, sometimes only in borrowed robes, and is not marked at any time by the same self-conscious blend of emotion and irony: his self-awareness is definitely attuned to simpler modes of feeling.

CHAPTER 4

Andrew Marvell: Elusiveness and Self-Reflexivity

Marvell's elusiveness is acknowledged.[1] One can imagine what it must have felt like to be John Donne or George Herbert, Richard Crashaw or Henry Vaughan. What is imagined (with sympathy or distaste) need not be the actual truth: I only mean one can make a consistent picture out of the facts of their lives and the ideas and emotions expressed in their writings; even their contradictions and conversions seem to fit in. With Marvell the facts known mainly relate to his public career and allow different interpretations. What the poems disclose or suggest about his opinions and experiences is not only controversial: they leave out some essential aspects of the man's personality and inner life. The very portrait we have of the man is mute. Donne's effigies are speaking pictures of his eloquent self, but Marvell's inquisitive eyes look out of an expressionless face with sensual lips which, like his conversation before strangers,[2] betrays no secret. An attempt to define the nature of his self-awareness seems bound to be defeated.

The first step in this inquiry must be the recognition of his

---

[1] This elusiveness was reasserted in my essay on 'Marvell's Mind and Mystery', in *Approaches to Marvell*, ed. C. A. Patrides (London, 1978); it was stressed with regard to his political views by C. Condren and A. D. Cousens (eds.), who concluded that 'Marvell . . . is a shorthand term for a various family of texts from which we customarily hypothesize there to have been a unified informing mind' (*The Political Identity of Andrew Marvell* (Aldershot, 1990), 4–8). I maintain that some structures of Marvell's mind at least can be ascertained. B. Everett rightly insists that 'the public Marvell . . . seems to be a blank', but I cannot agree that 'he does not appear to have had a personality at all' (*Poets in their Time* (Oxford, 1991), 38); nor would I reduce him to a collection of 'fragmented selves' like D. Benet (*On the Celebrated and Neglected Poems of Andrew Marvell* (Missouri UP, 1992), 194).

[2] 'He was . . . of very few words . . . He had not a general acquaintance': Aubrey, *Brief Lives*.

unique ability to be dispassionate in his views on contemporary events. Within the realm of politics shifting attitudes may not be surprising given the circumstances of his life. We need not dispute whether he should be placed among the Trimmers,[3] or whether he was guided throughout the Commonwealth and the Restoration by a 'devotion to strong and responsible government'.[4] We may agree with William Lamont that 'there is no real evidence that Marvell ever was a republican', or with Annabel Patterson that the *Miscellaneous Poems* were arranged to lead 'through private versions of puritanism to the more unstable model of Fairfaxian politics in retreat, until they arrived at active republicanism'.[5] Change is to be expected in opinions, though not in structures of the mind. But why does Marvell leave us in doubt about his feelings in one and the same poem, the 'Horatian Ode'? The case for the covert expression of royalist sympathies in ironical praise of Cromwell is undoubtedly weak despite the contrast between the Ode and 'Tom May's Death'.[6] The alleged contradiction between reverence for Charles and admiration for Cromwell has been removed by Wallace (*Destiny His Choice*, 104). Yet the host of parallels offered for willing compliance with 'the forced Pow'r' should not blind us to a difference in approach and in tone. When the Engagers argued for 'the right to obey an unlawful government in lawful things' they spoke like casuists and often sounded apologetic (ibid. 47). Marvell is not concerned with justification of any sort. Neither the death of the 'Royal Actor' nor the ruin of 'the great Work of Time' call for a bad conscience. The strange power of the Ode lies in the very fact that it does not engage emotions of pity, love, or fear, but only invites a controlled exultation in the display of power—'angry heavens flame'—or tragic dignity on 'that memorable scene'. The poet is a detached spectator of history

³ Donald Smith, 'The Political Beliefs of Andrew Marvell', *UTQ* 36 (1966–7), 55.

⁴ J. M. Wallace, *Destiny His Choice: The Loyalism of Andrew Marvell* (Cambridge, 1968), 144.

⁵ *Political Identity*, ed. Condren and Cousens, 149 and 208.

⁶ The thesis of Cleanth Brooks, revived by J. M. Newton in *Cambridge Quarterly*, 6 (1973), 125–46.

in the making who makes a dispassionate evaluation of character and destiny.[7]

Since the later 'Poem upon the Death of O.C.' shows 'all the force of Marvell's sentiments for Cromwell after years of loyal service', it must be out of prudence rather than indifference that the Member for Hull refrained from any expression of grief or indignation when relating how the carcasses of Cromwell, Bradshaw, Ireton, and Pride were to be 'hanged up for a while & then buryed under the gallowes'.[8] Yet the callous mention makes a strange contrast to the outraged and anguished allusion in *Samson Agonistes* to God's unfair dismission of His servants, 'their carkasses | To dogs and fowls a prey' (ll. 693–4). It cannot be denied, however, that Milton's friend acted honourably and courageously on many occasions 'under change of times'. Besides, the sincerity of his various political poems—from eulogy to satire—has hardly ever been impugned. When other poets praised Charles I, Cromwell, and Charles II in turn, some of the tributes at least could be dismissed as lip-service; but if all of Marvell's political statements or attitudes reflect genuine, if partly changing, convictions, some form of consistency must be discovered.

Legouis stressed Marvell's religious and patriotic earnestness: he was always 'ready to welcome any régime, whether authority resided in "a single person" or in a "representative" [assembly], provided all protestants were safe and the greatness of England assured'.[9] To Wallace, Marvell was among the few 'who believed that moderation was the very essence of government': hence his 'adherence to the ideal of balance' and the flexibility of policy which would be necessary to achieve it while retaining 'the standard of decency'.[10] But deeper motivations for this flexible consistency may be found in the conjunction of intellectual freedom, active will, and a belief in 'a necessity that was preeternal to all things'.[11] Marvell never opposed 'Fate'

---

[7] Annabel Patterson has also discerned Marvell's ability to create 'a delicate structure of objectivity, if not of non-alignment' in several poems which have 'Roman Catholic texts or genres as models or analogues' (*Political Identity*, 200). This is further evidence of his dispassionateness and tolerance.

[8] Wallace, *Destiny His Choice*, 143; Marvell, *Poems and Letters*, II. 7.

[9] *Andrew Marvell* (Oxford, 1960), 147.

[10] *Destiny His Choice*, 205, 213.

[11] I. G. MacCaffrey, 'Some Notes on Marvell's Poetry', *MP* 61 (1963), 265.

since 'all things . . . happen in their best and proper time'.[12] Yet, while disclaiming 'officiousness', he passed judgement. Ancient rights 'do hold or break | As Men are strong or weak' ('Horatian Ode', 39–40), and men of will are not to be resisted or blamed when they are the instruments of 'Fate'. Like Shakespeare's Octavius he 'let determin'd things to destiny | Hold unbewail'd their way' (*Antony and Cleopatra*, III. vi), but, as his praise of Cromwell's alleged stratagem shows ('Ode', 49–52), he knew that tactics and manoeuvres may be required to open up the way.

'Fate' to a Christian could only mean the Will of God. We have profuse evidence of Marvell's Protestant convictions, his abhorrence of Popery and the Anglican prelacy, but, as Legouis observed, 'we can tell more easily what he attacks than what he approves'.[13] Besides, neither his prose nor his religious lyrics supply the kind of information about his spiritual life that Donne and George Herbert give us in their divine poems. The love poems bring us no nearer to his heart. Most of the situations in Donne's lyrics may be of imagination all compact, but we know at least that he is not speaking of love and sex, ecstasy or disgust, without any experience of such emotions. Marvell did not marry; we have no record of a love affair, and there are only rumours about his sex life—rumours of impotence or homosexuality. His religious poems never evince the intense sin-consciousness paraded by Donne when he remembered his 'profane mistresses', but there is as little evidence for the kind of chastity that must have been Crashaw's. I do not think the daring language used in 'To his Coy Mistress' can suffice 'to settle contemporary doubts cast on the poet's virility, and to prove that he was at least once in love—body and soul—with a real live mistress'.[14] The final lines convey the breathless urgency of physical passion, but it is a passion that seeks no more than the spending of sexual energy. In 'The Match', 'The Definition of Love', and 'The unfortunate Lover' the poet seems to be more interested in the hyperbolical or emblematic expression of love than in the passion itself. Love conventions are handled in an ironical way in 'Mourning', in 'Daphnis and

---

[12] *Complete Works*, ed. A. B. Grosart (London, 1872–5), III. 212–13.
[13] *Marvell*, 221.   [14] Ibid. 34.

Chloe', even in 'The Gallery' and the Mower poems. Sexual love is rejected in the dialogues between 'Clorinda and Damon' or 'Thyrsis and Dorinda'; it is banished from 'The Garden' and does not concern the poet himself in 'Upon Appleton House'. A conscious exclusion of lust and womanhood characterizes 'Young Love' and 'The Picture of little T.C.' The variety Legouis claimed for Marvell as a love poet cannot be found in a wide range of moods comparable to Donne's, but only in the diversity of literary motifs and art forms.

It is tempting, indeed, to consider Marvell as a poet mainly interested in art for art's sake. Whereas Donne sought to be original in form as in matter, he has been described as an 'inveterate imitator'.[15] When Leishman offered a profusion of parallels with Latin, Neo-Latin, Renaissance, and seventeenth-century poetry he only confirmed T. S. Eliot's terse description of Marvell's best verse as 'the product of European, that is to say Latin, culture'.[16] From this angle the puzzling problems of political allegiance might vanish, and the 'Horatian Ode' might be seen only as 'a view of Cromwell appealing to Marvell's thought and imagination as engaged in the making of a *poem*'.[17]

Yet if Marvell was a literary artist mainly concerned with surpasssing what had been written before, why was he so little solicitous about what he himself had achieved? Crashaw and Vaughan had their poems printed in their lifetimes. George Herbert, who left the decision to Nicholas Ferrar, must have known his friend was unlikely to 'burn' his *Temple*. Donne, though he affected the pose of the gentleman who does not condescend to print, projected an edition of his poems in 1614. Lovelace, an aristocrat, prepared his poems for publication while in prison. Marvell apparently took no steps either to let his lyrics come into print or to preserve them for posthumous publication. Though a manuscript copy of 'To his Coy Mistress' has come to light, there is no evidence that he allowed his unpublished poems to circulate as freely as other amateur poets did. Can this attitude be reconciled with the 'professionalism'

---

[15] J. B. Leishman, *The Art of Marvell's Poetry* (London, 1966), 202.

[16] In his essay on 'Andrew Marvell' (1921); cf. Rosalie Colie, *'My Ecchoing Song': Andrew Marvell's Poetry of Criticism* (Princeton, 1970), 20.

[17] A. J. N. Wilson, in *Critical Quarterly*, 11 (1969), 326.

and 'the preoccupation with poetry's problems' emphasized by several critics?[18] If Marvell wrote his non-political poems (including the 'Horatian Ode') only to please himself or a narrow circle of friends, it does suggest a genuine delight in poetry for its own sake, but the kind of delight that will lead an amateur poet to write as he chooses, and therefore to betray his own inclinations, even when seeking to emulate or excel his predecessors. This assumption may justify an attempt to build a coherent pattern for Marvell's world of imagination. A coherence in his perceptions of time and space, as well as his world awareness, will be demonstrated in Chapter 9. Chapter 14 will trace the workings of a fundamental mode of thought in the expression of his religious sensibility. This chapter is only concerned with the nature of his self-awareness.

Marvell's 'Puritan inwardness' has been stressed,[19] but this claim must be qualified. His prose and poetry alike show little evidence for the kind of self-interest and self-analysis which is so characteristic of Donne and George Herbert. His attention is usually centred on a world of objects. When he calls up the temptations that assail 'The Resolved Soul' (not necessarily *his own*), he paints the objects and pleasures offered, asserts the moral resolve, but he does not convey the experience and the strain of a soul in conflict. When he invites his mistress to 'view' his soul, he presents to her a gallery of paintings ('Gallery'). When he pretends to 'define' his love, he only describes the interposition created by Fate to place the lovers at distant Poles ('Definition of Love'). 'The Unfortunate Lover' is an enigmatic projection of emotions into pictures. The Mower poems express their hero's passion through an evocation of incidents in a natural scene, but he mainly plays the part of a spectator or a commentator.

The lines of *Thyestes* that Marvell translated are an invitation to self-knowledge: 'Who expos'd to others Ey's | Into his own Heart ne'r pry's | Death to him's a Strange surprise.' But this Senecan chorus only incited men to shun celebrity in rustic retirement. Marvell interpreted the Socratic advice in the Stoic and Horatian sense, not after the manner of Montaigne. His few

---

[18]   Notably Colie in *My Ecchoing Song*, 105, 137.
[19]   See MacCaffrey, 'Some Notes on Marvell's Poetry', 261.

religious poems are impersonal, and he does not intrude into his satires or epicedes as Donne did.[20] Even when they are 'familiar' rather than official, his letters only give news of events: they never reveal his personality.

Marvell, however, was aware that 'Christianity has obliged men to very hard duties, and ransacks their very thoughts.'[21] As a Protestant of Puritan inclination he was bound to be conscious of the deceitfulness of man's heart stressed by Augustine and Calvin. In 'The Coronet' the poet shows a keen awareness of impure motives. Weaving a garland of verse to crown his Saviour's head, and thinking—'(so I my self deceive)'—to honour 'the king of Glory', he finds that the serpent old 'About the flow'rs disguis'd does fold, | With wreaths of Fame and Interest'. This intuition is akin to Donne's, who knew that we can be 'mov'd to seeme religious | Only to vent wit',[22] as George Herbert, too, surmised and feared. This discovery is not surprising and the poem derives its power from the mastery of form, not from any subtlety of psychological analysis.

Several poems are tinged with irony, and irony requires a capacity for critical detachment.[23] It can take a worldly form when satirizing feminine hypocrisy in 'Daphnis and Chloe' and in 'Mourning'. In each case the speaker's impassiveness underlines the contrast between a hyperbolical expression of grief and the absence of any deep feeling. The poet pretends that all doubts about the sincerity of the young widow's grief are unjustified:

> How wide they dream! The *Indian* Slaves
> That sink for Pearl through Seas profound,
> Would find her Tears yet deeper Waves
> And not of one the bottom sound.
>
> I yet my silent Judgment keep,
> Disputing not what they believe:
> But sure as oft as Women weep,
> It is to be suppos'd they grieve.

---

[20] With the exception of his reminiscence of Cromwell on his deathbed—'I saw him dead' ('Poem upon the Death of O.C.', 247)—but his attention here was focused on what he saw, not on his own feelings.

[21] In *The Rehearsal Transpros'd, Complete Works*, III. 391.

[22] See Ch. 1, p. 30 ff.

[23] In *Marvell's Ironic Vision* (New Haven, 1965), 4–5, H. E. Toliver went further than I had, claiming the poet offered 'irony and vision together, not separately'. To my mind Marvell's 'ironic self-exploration' comes short of Donne's.

Donne's irony could be directed at the expression of his own passion as in the closing lines of 'A Valediction: of my name, in the window'. Marvell is only the spectator of an emotion watched from outside. Irony here is the cool appraisal of the contrast between attitudes and an inner reality, which in 'Mourning' (though not in 'Daphnis and Chloe') evades judgement, for the reserve affected by the poet need not be taken as a pure negation of the woman's grief: the mind to Marvell is indeed an 'Ocean' ('Garden', 43) and its depths cannot be sounded.

Through the hysterical deportment or hyperbolical language of these puppets, Marvell's objective irony seems to dissolve all emotion: the very quietness of his tone suggests some contempt on his part for any kind of 'passion' in the seventeenth-century sense. This is not mere worldly cynicism; it is an instance of a detachment which finds a deeper expression in the poems that propose retirement 'When we have run our Passions heat' ('Garden', st. 4). Marvell himself, we suspect, may never have experienced this 'heat'. He never 'retired' from the world for a long time, but he seems to have always lived as if he stood back to look at life from a distance in a dispassionate way, in the attitude of someone who contemplates a painting, as he so often did, at least in imagination, when composing his poems and satires.

A serious expression of passionate love only occurs in two poems which, on close examination, confirm rather than contradict this impression of dispassionateness. The 'Definition of Love' is an adventure of the mind; the poet's recognition of 'Impossibility' becomes an acquiescence to a 'Magnanimous Despair' which is a refined form of detachment. In 'To his Coy Mistress' sexual desire and the realization of the human condition combine in an effort to triumph over time. The playful opening is not suggestive of any deep feeling for the woman; emotion is stirred when Time's chariot hurries near and the prospect of the grave is opened. Marvell's irony here may seem as powerful as Donne's:

> The Grave's a fine and private place,
> But none I think do there embrace.

Yet in this acknowledgement of a stark reality there is no irony directed at oneself. In 'A Dialogue between the Soul and Body' the irony is again objective and lies in the perception of contrasts and the masterly coining of paradoxes in the Soul's complaint: 'Here blinded with an Eye; and there | Deaf with the Drumming of an Ear. | . . . I feel, that cannot feel, the pain. | And all my Care its self employes, | That to preserve, which me destroys; | . . . And ready oft the Port to gain, | Am Shipwrackt into Health again.' The Mower's love, a love watched, not felt by the poet, is exposed to this kind of objective irony, which may turn into superficial playfulness.[24] In the opening stanzas of 'The Garden' irony is still pitched in a minor key: 'Two Paradises 'twere in one | To live in Paradise alone'. What is admirable here, as in 'To his Coy Mistress', is the Horatian ease with which this poet moves from gay to grave; but this flexibility of tone is different from the simultaneous presence of emotion and ironical comment arising from the self-consciousness of Donne or George Herbert.

There is, however, in Marvell a capacity for self-reflexivity, but his introspectiveness is of a different nature. In the famous lines on 'The Mind, that Ocean where each kind | Does streight its own resemblance find' ('Garden'), he may or may not allude to the 'Platonic doctrine of the correspondence of forms as objects of thought with forms as they exist in their own realm', or to the Cartesian 'theory of representative perception in which thought possesses a symbolic relation to object'.[25] Such philosophic considerations are to my mind unlikely, but the poet undoubtedly expresses a living awareness of the interiority of perception. Thomas Traherne later described the same experience when writing: 'And evry Object in my Soul a Thought | Begot, or was' ('My Spirit', st. 3). Since the world is seated in the mind by the very act of perception, the mind can create

> transcending these,
> Far other Worlds, and other Seas;
> Annihilating all that's made
> To a green Thought in a green Shade.

This may or may not be a Cartesian reduction of the world to 'a *res cogitans* and a *res extensa*', but I take it to be primarily the

---

[24] 'For *Juliana* comes, and she | What I do to the Grass, does to my Thoughts and Me' ('Mower's Song'); 'By his own Sythe the Mower mown' ('Damon *the Mower*').

[25] Daniel Stempel, 'Marvell's Cartesian Ecstasy', *JHI* 28 (1967), 106–7.

concrete experience of the poet's mind looking at the natural scene. The next stanza will show him lying 'at the Fountains sliding foot, | Or at some Fruit-trees mossy root'. His eyes must be filled with greenness. The 'green Thought' may have all the connotations of freshness, innocence, or hope ascribed to the colour in various readings of the poem; yet I think the first and foremost meaning is the actual sensation of greenness which pervades and satisfies the poet's consciousness in the quiet bliss of contemplation. This interpretation may sound oversimple,[26] and I admit Marvell himself intellectualized his experience, but I claim that the experience, not its intellectual elaboration, makes the lines imaginatively convincing. In such a state of quietness, later known to Wordsworth,[27] the contemplating mind will lose all sense of confinement to the body. Traherne will later anticipate Berkeley's and Whitehead's assertion that there is no distance between the mind and the object in the act of perception.[28] There is no conscious expression of a philosophic view in 'The Garden', but the poet's projection of his soul into the green boughs seems to rest on the same experience as Traherne's. Anyone lying under a tree and dreamily gazing on the sunlit foliage will forget his body and have the impression of being among the boughs, 'immanent there' as Whitehead would have phrased it:

> Casting the Bodies Vest aside,
> My Soul into the boughs does glide:
> There like a Bird it sits and sings,
> Then whets, and combs its silver Wings;
> And, till prepar'd for longer flight,
> Waves in its Plumes the various Light.

Marvell did not anticipate the idealism of Traherne but there is in his poetry a consciousness of the perceiving mind which relates him to the Divine Philosopher.[29] His own use of the term

[26] Particularly when compared with R. I. V. Hodge's sophisticated interpretation, *Foreshortened Time: Andrew Marvell & 17th Century Revolutions* (Cambridge, 1978), 67.
[27] 'Lines Written above Tintern Abbey': 'that serene and blessed mood' when 'the motion of our human blood | Almost suspended, we are laid asleep | In body, and become a living soul'. Marvell, of course, never experiences a pantheistic ecstasy.   [28] See 'My Spirit', st. ii, and Ch. 10.
[29] I could have added, as Warren Chernaik did, that 'Marvell shares the epistemological concerns of the Cambridge Platonists' (*The Poet's Time: Politics and Religion in the Work of Andrew Marvell* (Cambridge, 1983), 33).

is characteristic when he grows conscious that what he contemplates is mirrored within his mind:

> How safe, methinks, and strong behind
> These Trees have I incamp'd my Mind.
>
> ('Appleton', st. 76)

> My Mind was once the true survey
> Of all these Medows fresh and gay;
> And in the greenness of the Grass
> Did see its Hopes as in a Glass.
>
> ('Mower's Song', st. 1)

Reflections in water have attracted many Baroque poets.[30] However, when Marvell describes a river as 'a *Chrystal Mirrour* slick; | Where all things gaze themselves, and doubt | If they be in it or without' ('Appleton', 636–8), this doubt again reminds us of Traherne's 'Shadows in the Water' and seems to herald a more philosophical interrogation: are the things reflected in the mind without it or within it? To trace individual modes of apprehension may be more rewarding than to search for borrowed concepts. From this standpoint even the comparison of the soul to a drop of dew may take on a richer significance. The drop that fell from 'the clear Fountain of Eternal Day', 'recollecting its own Light',

> Does, in its pure and circling thoughts, express
> The greater Heaven in an Heaven less.
>   In how coy a Figure wound,
>   Every way it turns away;
>   So the World excluding round,
>   Yet receiving in the Day.
>
> ('On a Drop of Dew', 25–30)

Through his world-awareness Donne reached a higher self-awareness. Marvell shuts out the world of men when 'incamp-

---

[30] In '*Miroirs flottants* . . . with a new look at Marvell's French connexion' (*New Comparison*, 19 (1995), 145–66) Werner von Koppenfels, after Leishman, suggests an influence of French poets on Marvell, adding Etienne Binet to Saint-Amant and Théophile. He offers interesting examples of 'floating mirrors', and points out that Marvell 'has made a literary cliché come literally true' in the flooded meadow of 'Appleton House' (161); but the French poets do not call attention to the mirroring of the outer world in the consciousness of the contemplator.

ing' his mind behind the trees, and at times excludes even the world of nature; but at other times he contemplates the outer world as mirrored in his consciousness. In both cases attention turns to the thinking mind in its act of perception or creation.

This kind of introspection allowed a simultaneous involvement in and detachment from Nature and the world of the senses. Marvell could indulge in a Keatsian life of sensation and yet retire into a thought since sensations could also be apprehended as 'ideas' of the mind in the Lockean sense. Reflection would show him the vanity of men's labours 'To win the Palm, the Oke, or Bayes' ('Garden') and yet allow his involvement in the world of action since, in the service of Cromwell and later in Parliament, he could remain a detached observer of the social and political scene 'in busie Companies of Men' as well as in retirement. Thus the poet's awareness of his thinking mind may prove a key to the mystery of his personality and account for the seeming contradictions and the elusiveness of his poetry.

CHAPTER 5

Edward Herbert of Cherbury and Thomas Traherne: From Self-Reflexivity to Solipsism?

Lord Herbert is definitely a minor poet. As a philosopher he is not of major importance, yet he is an interesting figure in the history of ideas. A combined survey of his prose works and his rather slender corpus of poetry will shed some light on the emergence of his mode of self-reflexivity, with which Traherne's, despite major differences, seems to have some kinship.

Herbert's account of the operations of the mind in the *De Veritate* is based on an analysis of his own subjective states, though the argument takes the impersonal orientation expected in a philosophic treatise. The difference between Donne's or George Herbert's self-consciousness and what may be called his 'awareness of awareness' therefore throws light on a different mode of subjectivity. He believed himself 'to be the first to describe the sphere of all the faculties of man'.[1] He intended to break with the logical or metaphysical systematizations of scholastic philosophy: his method was to be purely introspective and appealed insistently to a scrutiny of the individual experience of one's own perceiving and thinking mind:

I invite the Reader especially to have recourse in this matter to his internal perceptions, and these I require him to employ, not in a casual or sluggish manner but with sensitivity, alertness and vivacity. For the internal perceptions may be closed as the ears may be stopped up or the eyes shut.

Here I refer the Reader to his inner consciousness. I am not attempting to construct a new philosophy based upon pure theory, or upon

---

[1] *De Veritate*, VIII, trans. Meyrick H. Carré (Bristol, 1937), 234.

authority, or upon deception; but at every point I refer the Reader to his own faculties for proof . . . The failure of the Schools in this regard cannot be sufficiently emphasized; for they judge matters which refer to the forms of apprehension by means of discursive thought.[2]

Distinguishing between 'the truth which is in things in themselves' and 'the truth which is in things as they appear', he admitted that 'the Truth of Appearance' is not easily 'brought into conformity with things in themselves', but he maintained that 'false appearance possesses its own truth, for it will appear truly as such' (De Veritate, I. 84). This was a recognition of subjectivity. He therefore found it absurd to assume there are only five modes of apprehension because we have five sense-organs: would one judge a house 'by the number of its doors and windows without troubling about the inside?' (ibid. VII. 209). Because of his exclusive attention to the 'inner sense', Herbert multiplied the modes of apprehension; his discovery of subjectivity made him keenly aware of the particularity of each representation. He reckoned 'the number of the senses according to the number of different sensations which are the sole source of evidence, not according to the sense organs'; thus, regarding touch, different faculties are needed to apprehend hardness and softness, pointedness and bluntness, rarity and density, thickness and thinness, etc. (ibid. VII. 229). This subjective point of view was at variance with not only scholastic philosophy but also the objective 'new philosophy' of Galileo which, through the distinction of primary and secondary qualities, denied reality to the more concrete and particular aspects of our perceptions.

Did Lord Herbert show in his poetry the kind of attention the philosopher had wished to bestow on the 'subjective faculties'? As an aristocrat he mainly wrote verse to show his wit in particular circumstances or in love poetry. When he ingeniously praised 'black beauty' in several poems to his mistress, his query whether blackness is discerned by 'some other sense, | Then that by which it doth py'd colours see' may be a vague allusion to the philosopher's assumption that a specific faculty is needed to perceive each specific difference.[3] His conceits on blackness,

---

[2] De Veritate, VI. 148, 154–5; cf. 121, 151, 153, 159, 163, 172, 203.
[3] 'To her Hair', 25–30. The various poems in praise of blackness addressed to Lady Diana Cecyll were probably written in 1621; Herbert was at the time at work on the De Veritate.

however, mainly derive from heraldry or the mystic tradition. One might have expected the poet to take some interest in the inner life, but, unlike Donne or his brother George, he almost never allows us to enter his consciousness in a particular situation, under the stress of an emotion calling for self-analysis. The immediacy and self-awareness of his bitter and tortuous rumination in '[Loves End]' is exceptional:

> Thus ends my Love, but this doth grieve me most,
>   That so it ends, but that ends too, this yet,
> Besides the Wishes, hopes and time I lost,
>   Troubles my mind awhile, that I am set
> Free, worse then deny'd . . .

Even 'Parted Souls', a poem obviously reminiscent of Donne's Valedictions, will glide from the personal drama of the lovers' separation to general considerations on immortality. The more famous 'Ode upon a Question moved', like the poems on 'Platonick Love', lacks the dramatic urgency of Donne's 'Extasie' and does not explore the feelings of the lovers; it only offers an answer to a general question: 'Whether Love should continue for ever?'

Should we be surprised? Perhaps not. The philosopher himself, after all, was content with vague generalizations about the data offered by his personal observation of the workings of his mind. Though he minutely studies the 'subjective' conditions of truth, he never considers the influence of the passions on judgement. In his analysis of 'the inner forms of apprehension' he is concerned with 'the affective analogies between mind and its objects', but his explanations are 'obscure and confused'.[4] His introspection only yields to him a sense of freedom and infinity (*De Veritate*, VI. 163). His analysis of the 'happy activities which take place in the soul' is based on Neoplatonic metaphysics rather than psychological observation (ibid. VI. 159–61). In his account of man's emotional life, reduced to his 'internal physical apprehensions', he resorts to the traditional physiology of the humours and the 'analogy between the microcosm and the macrocosm' (ibid. VI. 165–71).

To offer an insight into the origin, nature, and effects of the

---

4 Carré, in *De Veritate*, 44.

passions was not, one may say, the purpose of the *De Veritate*. Let us turn to Lord Herbert's autobiography. He is unlikely not to have known Montaigne's *Essays* and even seems to echo his address to the reader when he declares: 'I have thought fit to relate to my posterity those passages of my life, which I conceive may best declare me, and be most usefull to them.'⁵ Yet he only relates the events of his life: his travels, diplomatic missions, or duels, and a few love affairs about which he gives the circumstances, not the feelings experienced. The only traits of his character evoked, but not analysed, are his choleric impulsiveness and his courage.⁶

One is bound to conclude that Lord Herbert, despite an obvious egotistic concern with himself, only entertained an intellectual curiosity about his psychic life. His inquisitiveness concerning the modes of apprehension that all men have in common never extended to the particularities of his individual affective experience. This type of curiosity for the universal operations of the human mind may be styled 'epistemological' to distinguish it from Donne's or George Herbert's interest in the human heart. The author of the *De Veritate* had an ideal of self-knowledge which he also expressed in a Latin poem, '*De Vita Coelesti*'. He took up in it an idea also used in Donne's 'Obsequies to the Lord Harrington': man will only attain full knowledge of himself in the beatific vision, when seeing himself in God as in a mirror.⁷ Characteristically, however, Lord Herbert expects an impersonal revelation of 'our Mind'—*Mens nostra*—whereas Donne wrote 'And I discerne by favour of this light, | My selfe'. This illumination, attended by an aesthetic rapture—'fair' is the 'form' revealed—is closer to the Platonic knowledge of the soul than to Donne's search for the self.

Though the poem has been for a time attributed to Donne, the 'Ode: Of our Sense of Sinne' confirms the difference between these two approaches to self-knowledge. The title is

---

⁵ *The Life of Edward Lord Herbert of Cherbury. Written by Himself*, 3rd edn. (London, 1778), 2; cf. Montaigne, *Essais*, 'Au Lecteur'.

⁶ E. D. Hill claims that 'the object of Herbert's aubiography is not to review the author's life, but to reform the reader into a proponent of natural religion': *Edward, Lord Herbert of Cherbury* (Twayne, 1987), 116. This purpose is far from obvious: only a few pages in the autobiography could support Hill's interpretation.

⁷ Cf. '*De Vita Coelesti*', 50–5, and 'Harrington', 29–35.

misleading; the speaker is not labouring under a sense of sin as the author of the Holy Sonnets was. The 'subject' is 'we', not 'I'; what is deplored is man's usual blindness to his sins. This runs contrary to Donne's affliction for having often in his youth, like St Augustine, sinned deliberately out of 'bravery'.[8] It is the confession of a man who can be unmindful of his own motivations, as Lord Herbert seems to be in his self-flattering autobiography. From the point of view of the moralist his inquiry into our modes of perception may prove as unfavourable to self-knowledge as a preoccupation with 'outward shews':

> But we know our selves least; These outward shews
>   Our mindes so store,
> That our soules, no more then our eyes disclose
> But forme and colour. Onely he who knowes
>   Himselfe, knowes more.

The egotism revealed by Edward Herbert's autobiography is different from Donne's. In his early childhood he wondered 'how I came into this world', which seems to anticipate the kind of self-interest shown later by Thomas Traherne. He is almost silent about his inner life, but he expatiates on his health, his height, his weight, and other outward details (*Life*, 43–5). His 'epistemological' curiosity directs his attention to the universal operations of the mind: in this kind of introspection the thinking and feeling self becomes an object of observation, but the vivid awareness of the self disappears. His love poetry, too, is less subjective than Donne's; he often takes the qualities of his mistress for a theme and gives her a distinct individuality even in the celebration of a perfect union. In an 'Ode upon a Question moved' Celinda has an identity and a voice of her own.

Though tempered in his love poetry, perhaps by an absence of interest in his own emotions, Lord Herbert's egotism is elsewhere displayed with an ingenuousness which is irreconcilable with the kind of ironic self-consciousness discerned in Donne's or George Herbert's presentation of their selves. His autobiography parades his conceit in quixotic situations with an earnestness which

---

[8] See *Essays in Divinity*, 31; *Sermons*, II. 107.

invites ridicule.[9] He composed epitaphs for himself in a Renaissance spirit of self-praise: Donne did take a pose for posterity, but his lucidity and his sense of human imperfection did not allow an expression of overweening pride.[10] Despite his self-reflexive observation of his mind, this philosopher proves incapable of irony directed at himself. Like the Divine Philosopher, Thomas Traherne, he appears singularly humourless.[11]

Thomas Traherne

Alone among the Metaphysicals Traherne expounds a philosophy and delivers a message in his poetry. He was certainly influenced by the Hermetic writings, Plato and the long line of Platonists, from Alexandria to Florence in the Renaissance and Cambridge in his own age. He was well-read, too, in the moralists of Antiquity. His Commonplace Book confirms his debts, but he only borrowed what responded to the needs of his mind and sensibility.[12] He modified and made his own such ideas as entered into his Gospel of Felicity, including the Biblical texts that he turned to his own ends. In 1960 my attempt to define his highly personal modes of consciousness, perception, and sensibility was based on the original works which were thought to be indisputably his: the *Centuries of Meditations*, *Roman Forgeries*, *Christian Ethicks*, the *Thanksgivings*, and the *Poems*.[13] Since 1968 new manuscripts have come to light—*Select Meditations*

---

[9] See *Life*, 80, 127, 144, etc. A new reading of the *Autobiography* has been proposed by E. D. Hill, who claims that it 'tells a comic story with wry self-directed humor' (*Herbert of Cherbury*, 108 ff.). It undoubtedly makes the work more interesting, but it is more attractive than convincing: no reader had earlier detected this 'self-directed humor'. Hill may be right in discerning a parody of 'unnatural prodigies' (111, 115), but this is an *objective* form of irony.

[10] Cf. 'Epitaph for himself' and '*Epitaph in se Romae factum, 1615*' with Donne's 'Epitaph on Himselfe'.

[11] The touches of satiric irony in 'The State Progress of Ill' and 'Of Travellers' and the macabre humour of 'To his Mistress for her true Picture' are purely objective.

[12] See my study of Traherne's sources in *Poètes métaphysiques*, II. 263–70. In 'Thomas Traherne and Hermes Trismegistus' (*Renaissance News*, 19 (1966), 118–31, n. 29) Carol Marks came to the same conclusion.

[13] *The Poems of Felicity* edited by his brother Philip are used when the original is missing in the Dobell MS; the purely prosodic or stylistic corrections made by Philip are poetically disastrous but do not alter the modes of thought.

and *Commentaries of Heaven*—and works of doubtful authorship—*Daily Devotions* and the *Meditations on the Six Days of
Creation*—are now generally ascribed to him. I therefore depart
from the mode of exposition used for the other poets and
reshape my earlier analysis to include in it the consideration of
new texts and recent criticism instead of confining the discussion
to the notes. The conclusions, however, are not substantially
altered. Critics have usually stressed the differences between the
early and the later works, yet, as my references will show,[14] a
vast majority of Traherne's characteristic modes of thought,
imagination, and sensibility were already clearly apparent in the
Select Meditations: egocentricity coupled with communicative-
ness, an insatiable desire for self-aggrandizement dating from
early childhood, the assurance that God gives all things to each
man alone, a spiritual possession of the world through the
unlimited powers of the soul, a passion for infinity, a spatial
conception of eternity, a constant play on the sphere and centre
image, Neoplatonic rather than Christian paradoxes, an intuition of the divine in nature, the opposition between natural
treasures and false riches, the assumption that Eden may be
recovered here and now, etc.

With Traherne we move from egocentricity to a kind of solipsistic illusion, at least in his record of the alleged intuitions of
his infancy. His claims might be thought purely symbolic in the
poems since in 'The Improvment' he stops short after a philosophical disquisition and confesses he could not have had an
intellectual apprehension of such mysteries as in infant:

> But Oh! the vigor of mine Infant Sence
> Drives me too far: I had not yet the Eye
> The Apprehension, or Intelligence
> Of Things so very Great Divine and High.
> But all things were *Eternal* unto me,
> And *mine*, and *Pleasing* which mine Ey did see.

The impressions recollected in the *Centuries* (III. 1–25),
however, required no intellectual speculation and Traherne
seems to have had genuine faith in their reality. When compared

---

[14] References to *Select Meditations* and *Commentaries of Heaven* are mainly
given in the notes since the *Centuries* and the *Poems* are at once more interesting
and more easily available.

with the simpler account of his childish impressions given in the earlier *Select Meditations*, they may appear to be a 'late construct',[15] yet the allusion to the child's delighted discovery of the outside world in both texts is a guarantee of authenticity. I only quote from the earlier work (III. 29) since the version of the *Centuries* (III. 2–3) is well known and more accessible, but I print in italics expressions and ideas found in both texts:

I remember the time when its [the City wherein he lived] *Gates* were Amiable, its *Streets Beautifull*, its *Inhabitants Immortall*, its Temples glorious, . . . Soe they appeared to the *little Stranger*, when I first *came into the world*. . . . For I saw them all in the light of Heaven. And *they were all mine* . . . The people were my *Living joyes* and *moveing Jewells*, sweet Amazments, walking Miracles.

Section 30, which relates his disappointment with the subjects discussed at the University, is a more critical version of the account given in the *Centuries* (III. 36–7) but it confirms its autobiographical foundation. A section in verse (III. 99) probably combines memories of 'The Gates and streets mine Infancy did view' (cf. *Centuries*, III. 3: 'The Gates were at first the End of the World'), of the child's impression that 'the Citie seemed to stand in Eden' (*Centuries*, III. 3; cf. 'make the Eden mine'), and of the flights of imagination by which the boy's soul would be carried away to 'New Kingdoms Distant' (cf. 'New Kingdom beyond the Seas' in *Centuries*, III. 24), with the sense of seeing all things 'as in a Sphere of Light'.

These poems and meditations were composed after a spiritual crisis leading to an illumination, and in a sudden illumination one may discover a brave new world. Furthermore, we know that in a certain state of mind we may have a sense of something seen or lived through before, though there is no justification for this strange feeling of revived experience. Such an illusion may have been responsible for Traherne's faith in his recollections of childhood. When speaking as a 'Christian philosopher', he undoubtedly did not abstain from interpreting his reminis-

---

[15] Sharon C. Seelig, 'The Origins of Ecstasy: Traherne's *Select Meditations*', *ELR* 9 (1979), 419–31. The impersonal account of the Babe's progress in *Commentaries of Heaven* is an even later construct, yet reminiscent of the impressions earlier recorded: see A. Pritchard's selections from the manuscript in *UTQ* 53 (1983), 19–21.

cences; yet he maintained the reality of the babe's silent enjoyment of the world, of an original sense of pleasure and possession which he claimed to be at the same time an experience of
eternity through the sheer ignorance of death. He may have
found support for his views in the writings of the Hermetist
Thomas Vaughan, who had made a similar claim for his childish experiences:

certainly Nature, whose pupil I was, had even then awakened many
notions in me which I met with afterwards in the Platonic philosophy
. . . This consideration of myself when I was a child hath made me
since examine children, namely, what thoughts they had of those
elements we see about us; and I found thus much of them: that Nature
in her simplicity is much more wise than men are . . . A child, I
suppose, *in puris naturalibus,* before education alters and ferments
him, is a subject [that] hath not been much considered . . .
Notwithstanding, I should think, by what I have read, that the natural
disposition of children, before it is corrupted with customs and
manners, is one of those things about which the ancient philosophers
have busied themselves even to some curiosity.[16]

Once the poet's description of the child's consciousness is
divested of Platonic assumptions, it also offers surprising similarities with some of the conclusions reached by Jean Piaget
through the close scientific observation of children.[17] One may
note, besides, that Traherne, though well read in philosophy
and theology, expounds his Gospel of Felicity with a kind of
naive candour not found among the contemporary Cambridge
Platonists: he seems to have been one of those happy souls who,
despite their intellectual development, hardly achieve the kind
of maturity apt to make us sadder, if not wiser, men. I am aware
that my analysis of his modes of thought will make him appear
more ingenuous than he is supposed to be by many critics and
may impair his stature as a philosopher or a mystic, but it will
in no wise diminish his originality.

No poet has so subtly and sympathetically observed the awakening of the senses in early infancy. In 'The Salutation', provided
we overlook the shaping of the impressions by the grown-up

---

[16] Thomas Vaughan, *Euphrates or the Waters of the East* (1653), in *Works*, ed.
A. E. Waite (London, 1919), 396.

[17] The parallels I gave in 1960 and in *Revue de la Méditerranée,* 64 (1954),
648–56, anticipated the brief allusions of later critics.

mind, we may trace a truthful expression of what the infant feels when he discovers the several parts of his body with evident interest and wonder, tasting the pure pleasure of existence in the exercise of his senses: 'such Joys as Ears or Tongue, . . . Such Sounds to hear, such Hands to feel, such Feet, | Beneath the Skies, on such a Ground to meet'. This discovery of the world is to the child himself an inexhaustible source of surprise. Like Shakespeare's Miranda, he sees a world that is new to him. Psychologists have noted that very young children have aesthetic emotions.[18] Traherne's recorded experience sounds like a genuine epiphany: 'The Green Trees when I saw them first through one of the Gates Transported and Ravished me; their Sweetnes and unusual Beauty made my Heart to leap, and almost mad with Extasie, they were such strange and Wonderfull Things!'[19]

From an awareness of strangeness to the awakening of an intellectual curiosity there is but one step. One may hesitate to believe in so rapid a progress (despite the definiteness of the setting) when Traherne claims that he was only four years old when, prompted by 'a real Whispering Instinct of Nature', he started to reason with himself 'in a little Obscure Room in [his] Fathers poor House' and asked himself: if there is a God 'infinit in Goodness . . . how comes it to pass therfore that I am so poor?' In such moments of solitariness the child's thoughts 'would be deeply Engaged with Enquiries, How the earth did End? Whether Walls did Bound it, or Suddain Precipices, or Whether the Heavens by Degrees did com to touch it . . .' (*Centuries*, III. 16–17). Such speculations at the age of four seem incredible; yet both Piaget and Bovet observed the emergence of this kind of curiosity in children from the age of six: speculations about the origin of all things, the coming into being of the earth, and the appearance of man.[20] Traherne may be slightly mistaken about his age but not about his recollections.

[18] Pierre Bovet, *Le sentiment religieux et la psychologie de l'enfant* (Neuchâtel, 1926), 14.

[19] *Centuries*, III. 3; cf. *Select Meditations*, III. 29.

[20] Jean Piaget, *La représentation du monde chez l'enfant* (Paris, 1938), trans. *The Child's Conception of the World* (London, 1973), ch. 7; Bovet, *Le sentiment religieux*, chs. 6 and 7. In his *Principles of Psychology* (London, 1890, I. 267) William James recorded the reminiscences of a deaf and dumb child who, by the age of eight or nine, before he had received any education, wondered how the world had come into being and was obsessed by his own questionings.

We are the more easily persuaded of the essential truthfulness of this testimony when we turn to poems inspired by early experiences which bear the hallmark of childish imagination. According to Piaget one of the most general manifestations of the child's animism is his spontaneous assumption of being followed by the sun or the moon when he moves from one place to another.[21] This happens to be the very theme of a short poem in which Traherne records the feeling of wonder experienced by his younger brother when, after a journey, he beheld the moon he had watched the day before shining upon another place ('To the same purpos'). The stamp of authenticity is also impressed on another experience of the same child recorded by his elder brother. By night he leapt over a stream in which he saw a reflection of the orb of the moon; coming home, he 'with Joy related soon | How *happy he* o'r-leapt the Moon' ('On Leaping over the Moon'). Equally genuine may be another 'sweet Mistake' ascribed by the poet to 'unexperienc'd Infancy' when he did 'by the Water's brink | Another World beneath me think' and 'fancy'd other Feet | Came mine to touch and meet'. To the poet this sweet mistake reveals 'many Secrets ... | Which afterwards we com to know' ('Shadows in the Water'). Was the scene imagined for the sake of instruction? If it was, it was at least with a surprising intuition of what a child's reaction would be.[22]

The infant is all eye, all ear, all smell, all touch and taste. But he rapidly becomes all imagination. Traherne's evocation of his dreams in childhood is again in accordance with the conclusions reached by Piaget. To the young child the dream is an image which comes from outside and which he thinks he sees with his eyes, though with closed lids.[23] The dream image is first located in the imagined surroundings, but the child soon realizes that the image is in his head; yet, while recognizing its illusory nature, he still assumes it has a real existence. To him the dream

---

[21] Piaget, ch. 7, §2 (the division into short sections is the same in the French and the English editions). Another apparent motion of the moon when observed by a running man was, however, a philosophic instance of our errors of perception: Malebranche, *De la recherche de la vérité*, I. vii. 4–5.

[22] For a Lacanian interpretation of the mirror effect see Alvin Snider's essay in *UTQ* 55 (1986), 313–27.

[23] Piaget, ch. 3, §1; *Représentation*, 113 ff.

is not characterized by a false perception, but by the fact that we truly perceive something different from waking reality. Distinctions are not so finely traced in Traherne's poem 'Dreams', but it records a similar experience:

> 'Tis strange! I saw the Skies;
> I saw the Hills before mine Eys;
> The Sparrow fly;
> The Lands that did about me ly;
> The reall Sun, *that* hev'nly Ey!
> Can closed Eys ev'n in the darkest Night
> See through their Lids, and be inform'd with Sight?

This contemplation of the world and the first workings of the imagination are the source of a pure feeling of wonder. The infant's soul is declared insatiable, but Traherne assumes that desire is exempt from the frustration of unfulfilment as long as the child follows the instinct of nature, as long as his judgement is not corrupted by society (*Select Meditations*, III. 13, 85; *Centuries*, III. 7–13). This is wishful thinking; yet the recorded experience is reconcilable with the observations of Piaget for the child spontaneously sees himself as the centre of the world.[24] Despite the accretion of Hermetic notions[25] Traherne's rapturous 'thanksgivings' for having been made 'A living Inhabitant | Of the great World, | And the Centre of it!' ('Thanksgivings for the Body', 86–8), his conviction that all things 'by their Service End in *me*' ('The Improvment', 22), seem to retain the freshness and naivety of the child's egocentricity. Hence a perfect communion between the self and the world. In his initial narcissism and his undifferentiated apprehension of his active self and the world acted upon, the baby, when moving his limbs, thinks himself in command of the only world he knows. The universe is supposed to obey the self. When babies obviously delight in moving their toes, Piaget claims, they seem to feel the joy of a god directing the motions of the stars at distance.[26] Such are the impressions conveyed by the poems in which Traherne celebrates the unlimited powers of the infant mind and its sense of harmony with the whole creation.

---

[24] Piaget, ch. 4, §5, 'Logical and ontological egocentricity'.
[25] See *Poètes métaphysiques*, II. 271–3.
[26] Piaget, ch. 4, §3; *Représentation*, 140.

The interpretation of this alleged inner experience given in 'The Preparative' and in 'My Spirit' is, of course, expressed in terms of a Neoplatonic philosophy. What is new is the recreation of a state of mind in its immediacy: it confers an individual and affective value on metaphysical tenets. It may proceed from a dim rememoration of some primal experience. Even the joy which suffused the adult consciousness of Wordsworth in a surge of pantheistic emotion seemed due to the revival of a long-buried state of mind, a return to the original indistinction between the self and the world.

Not society alone, as Traherne assumed, but a natural evolution will ruin this original sense of bliss. The child will grow conscious of the duality of the world and the self when his desires meet with a resistance. Unhappiness or disquiet will follow the birth of self-consciousness. When the child becomes aware of his own being-in-the-world, in this first confrontation of the self and the universe lies the awakening of *angst*, or existential anguish; this moment for most of us is overlaid by the successive amnesias of our psychic life. With Traherne the precocious awakening of an acute self-consciousness, heightening the infant's egotism, may have been due to the deep disquiet provoked by a separation from his mother.[27] Then came the moment when the young child had his first experience of awe, closely linked to an anxious sense of his individual condition. It was convincingly recorded both in the poem *Solitude* and in the *Centuries* (III. 23). I quote from the prose for its autobiographical quality is more obvious:

Another time, in a Lowering and sad Evening, being alone in the field, when all things were dead and quiet, a certain Want and Horror fell upon me, beyond imagination. The unprofitableness and Silence of the Place dissatisfied me, its Wideness terrified me, from the utmost Ends of the Earth fears surrounded me. How did I know but Dangers might suddainly arise from the East, and invade me from the unknown Regions beyond the Seas? I was a Weak and little child, and had forgotten there was a man alive in the Earth.

Though his 'first impressions' were often transposed in the language of the Divine Philosopher, I therefore incline to think

---

[27] A suggestion of Gladys Wade in *Thomas Traherne* (Princeton, 1944).

that Traherne's doctrine was genuinely based on the common structures of the child's consciousness. It may not be an isolated instance. Piaget himself noted a close correspondence between the Platonic doctrine of reminiscence and a natural phenomenon of amnesia in the young child who forgets the origin of newly acquired knowledge and therefore believes all knowledge originates in the mind.[28] A similar coincidence between the workings of the child's imagination and ancient philosophy may also be observed in a minor instance. Traherne's description of the infant's way of seeing by 'visiv Rays' acting like 'Beams of Light' ('An Infant-Ey') is, no doubt, reminiscent of the Platonic theory of extramission, but it may reflect a genuine impression. The child originally confuses vision and light and believes 'seeing comes from the eye, it gives light'.[29]

More important is the link between the spontaneous solipsism of the infant, acknowledged by modern psychology, and the poet's moments of solipsistic meditation. There is, however, an important difference. The baby according to Piaget is solipsist as long as he identifies himself with the images perceived and therefore with the very world unveiled to his consciousness; he therefore has no sense of his individuality. Traherne, when reviving the experience, ascribes to the infant a vivid consciousness of his own self which belongs to a maturer mind. Yet the analogy remains perceptible when he writes about his infant thoughts: 'There I saw all the World Enjoyd by one; | There I was in the World my Self alone' ('Dumnesse', 35–6). This privilege of the infant's mind implies no denial of the existence of others, but an original transmutation of the solipsistic viewpoint is apparent from the beginning in the *Select Meditations* when he 'sees Himselfe Advanced there a Lone' (III. 58) and assumes that God's wisdom 'could make every one Sole' (IV. 50).

Structural affinities may also be discerned between the

[28] Piaget, ch. 1, §3; *Représentation*, 27.
[29] Piaget, ch. 1, §2. Traherne does not evoke the long conflict between the theories of extramission and reception: see Carl Havelange, *De l'œil et du monde* (Paris, 1998), 142–63. It was not brought to a close by the optics of Kepler and Descartes which 'interposed the image on the retina between the eye and the world' (ibid. 347), though by 1646 Sir Thomas Browne pointed out that the theory of extramission was 'now sufficiently convicted [disproved] from observations of the dark chamber' (*Pseudodoxia Epidemica*, III. vii).

philosophic idealism or immaterialism of Traherne and child-hood impressions. This is a paradoxical claim since the child's mind is pre-eminently realistic, lending a perceptible external reality to all his representations. But a closer inspection is needed. Traherne seems to anticipate Berkeley when he writes:

> And evry Object in my Soul a Thought
> Begot, or was; I could not tell,
> Whether the Things did there
> Themselvs appear,
> Which in my Spirit *truly* seemd to dwell;
> Or whether my conforming Mind
> Were not alone even all that shind.

('My Spirit', st. 3)

The poet, however, ascribes this doubt to the child as a living intuition which is not reached by reasoning. The Divine Philosopher himself never denies the existence of an external world; yet, just as he tends to assimilate dream images to reality, or imaginative presence in a place to real presence, he is inclined to blur the distinction between thoughts and things. As several poems entitled 'Thoughts' reveal, thoughts to him are not pure abstractions, but rather insubstantial images of things: the 'world' becomes 'Effectuall' when 'received by our Thoughts and Exprest within' (*Select Meditations*, IV. 12). Now, in the child's mind the distinction between his thoughts and the outer world develops slowly: all his representations, according to Piaget, are laid out before him, as it were on a single screen.[30] The child thus takes his own thoughts for things, but Traherne wonders whether the things seen are not his own thoughts. In each case, despite a different orientation, there is a spontaneous tendency to confuse rather than dissociate the mind's representations and external reality.[31] This tendency may have generated the philosophic systems of Platonic inspiration.

---

[30]   Piaget, ch. 4, §5; *Représentation*, 155.
[31]   On the representation of space in the child's mind see J. Piaget and B. Inhelder, *La représentation de l'espace chez l'enfant* (Paris, 1948), 536–9. One may note, too, in Traherne's account of the development of the child's mind that the discovery of the world and the discovery of the self precede the discovery of God: both Bovet and Piaget have shown that the conception of God is a fairly late acquisition.

Whatever its origin may have been, there was in Traherne's mind an intense awareness of his individual existence and a demanding egocentricity. 'Hydropick Nature thirsteth after all, | And still retains its Primitive Desire.'[32] He early proclaimed that 'the Possession of all Treasure' was necessary to his happiness (*Select Meditations*, IV. 2). The insatiableness of his desire, traced to his early childhood in the *Centuries* (III. 16) and in 'Poverty', was proclaimed and universalized:

> There's not a Man but covets and desires
> A Kingdom, yea a World; nay, he aspires
> To all the Regions he can see
> Beyond the Hev'ns Infinity.
>
> ('Misapprehension')

Traherne's discovery that this desire is satisfied, though men may be unconscious of it, was made in two stages. His wish for 'a Book from heaven' (*Centuries*, III. 27) was met when he read in the Bible that he was 'Heir of the Whole World alone' (III. 30). Yet this illumination apparently waned during his stay at the University (III. 36 ff.) and was only recaptured when he 'came into the Country' at Credenhill and devoted his time 'wholy to the study of Felicitie' (III. 52-3). In his early *Select Meditations* his assurance of being 'Lord and Heir of world', possessor of all things (II. 81, III. 48, 69; IV. 31) was apparently only based on the Biblical promise and on the conviction that the soul, being a 'Temple of the Deitie' (II. 95), was 'an Interior Temple of all Eternity' (III. 72), that it could 'Enjoy infinity' and be 'infinitly Rich in working as in Essence' (IV. 3) The Neoplatonic and Hermetic origin of these ideas is obvious and they constantly recur in his later writings. Yet the *Poems* alone bear full testimony to Traherne's own discovery of what was for him at once an experience and a philosophic proof that the intuition he ascribed to the infant in the 'Salutation' (23-42) could be recaptured:

> An Object, if it were before
> My Ey, was by Dame Natures Law,
> Within my Soul. Her store
> Was all at once within me . . .[33]

---

[32] *Commentaries of Heaven*, No. 87, 'Avarice I'.

[33] 'My Spirit', 37-40. In *Commentaries of Heaven* this spiritual possession of all things was expressed impersonally: Nos. 18, st. iii; 35, ll. 15-28; 63, ll. 25-7.

Like Donne, therefore, but in a very different way, he could claim to possess the wealth of 'both the Indies'.[34] Since the world is seated in the mind through the very act of perception ('Misapprehension', 49), the Biblical promise is already realized: 'all things are yours' (1 Cor. 3: 21). The Gospel of Felicity is summed up in the precept: 'behold the World as thine' ('Vision', 17).[35] Seneca had experienced this feeling, uttered this injunction, but the power he conferred on the human mind was not related to an apprehension of the world as representation.[36] Plotinus spoke of the individual soul as having 'all things in itself' like the Universal Soul[37] through the possession of the forms of sensible things 'stripped of their mass',[38] yet, like all Neoplatonists he seems to have in mind a purely intellectual intuition different from the miracle of sensible perception which *usually* excites Traherne's wonder.

There is no trace of this wonder in the other metaphysical poets. When Donne claims that the universe is enclosed within the eyes of the lovers ('Good-morrow'), this particular, momentary and metaphorical miracle has nothing in common with Traherne's exaltation of the universal phenomenon of perception. Marvell's inclination to see the world mirrored in his mind has some kinship with Traherne's, but the brief suggestion is not expanded and a major difference appears when he seeks to 'exclude' the world rather than absorb it ('Drop of Dew'), or annihilates all that's made to a green thought ('Garden'). In some poems Traherne seems at times to isolate the soul of the infant in an inner contemplation, but it soon appears that this 'Naked Simple Pure *Intelligence*' ('Preparative', 20) is only ascribed to the newborn babe in the early days when, his 'Body

---

34 *Commentaries*, No. 7, 'Abundance'; cf. and cst. Donne's 'The Sunne Rising', 17.

35 The assurance that 'all Things in the World are mine' persists in the late *Commentaries of Heaven* (Nos. 65, l. 40; 67, l. 51; 78, end; 86, l. 31 etc.), but is more often based on the Biblical promise than on the act of perception.

36 *De Beneficiis*, VII. iii. 3, viii. 1, x. 6. On the similarities and differences see *Poètes métaphysiques*, II. 276–7.

37 *Enneads*, IV. 3. 6; *Plotinus*, trans. A. H. Armstrong (Cambridge, Mass., and London, 1966–88), vol. IV, p. 49.

38 *Enneads*, III. 6. 18; Armstrong, p. 283. Plotinus speaks here of 'the [Universal] Soul', as the translation by G. S. Mackenna and R. S. Page (*The Six Enneads* (Chicago, 1952), 118) implies, but also of its operations in the individual souls since he started by discussing various views on the passions.

being dead, [his] Lims unknown', his soul 'Did seem no Outward thing to note, but flie | All Objects that do feed the Eye' ('Innocence', 13–16). When the author of the *Centuries* speaks of the child he only ascribes to him a *sensible* intuition of the splendour of God's works, an aesthetic ecstasy and an advantageous 'Ignorance' of death, of sin, of custom, of property and divisions (III. 2–3, 5–9). 'The Salutation' speaks of the revelation to the newborn child of 'These Brighter Regions which *salute mine Eys*, | . . . The Earth, the Seas, the Light, the Day, the Skies, | The Sun and Stars' (my italics). But since the Divine Philosopher was convinced that he had recovered 'those Pure and Virgin Apprehensions' (*Centuries*, III. 4) through the exercise of the 'higher reason', the poet felt free to ascribe to the newborn soul the direct intuition of truths he could only express in Platonic language. Yet, after stating that the soul 'Did *seem* no Outward thing to note, but flie | All Objects that do feed the Eye', he asserts: 'I *on the Earth* did reign, | Within, *without me*, all was pure' ('Innocence', 14–15, 58–9; my italics), which implies a perception of outward things. In reality Traherne lends to the infant soul the later adult awareness of the inner presence of all things in the mind. His use of the terms 'Simple Sence' or 'Naked Sence', rather than Intellect, shows he had not in mind a transcendental intuition of Platonic Ideas, but the revelation of its own contents to his consciousness:

> My Naked Simple Life was I.
>   That Act so strongly Shind
> Upon the Earth, the Sea, the Skie,
>   That was the Substance of My Mind.
>   The Sence it self was I.
>
> ('My Spirit')

This intuition is expressed as if there was no conscious distinction between the thought and the self: this is no Cartesian *cogito*. The Cartesian subject, wholly self-enfolded, constituted itself in utter solitariness through an effacement of the world. Traherne's next lines stress the 'capacity' of the soul to apprehend 'all things', which means, as we later discover, to embrace a multitude of concrete objects (ibid. 35–46).

This kind of reflexivity has nothing in common with the self-consciousness of Donne and George Herbert. It rather reminds us of the attention bestowed on the operations of our 'inner sense' by the author of the *De Veritate*, but Lord Herbert was objectively concerned with the working of the mind, not with the thinking subject and his enjoyment of his representations as Traherne constantly is. The poet's egocentricity is reinforced by this discovery of a 'spiritual possession' of the world, but his self-reflexivity is of a general nature and therefore its character-istics and privileges are universal: they can be extended to all other men, since each man is a conscious 'subject'. He shows no interest in the particularities of individual experience. He is interested in the mechanism of perception, but he never seeks to analyse an emotion or discern the hidden motives of human actions. He cannot be expected therefore to show the kind of irony directed at oneself displayed by 'self-conscious' authors. Like Lord Herbert, he is singularly humourless.

Had Traherne been capable of self-criticism he might not have indulged in an exaltation of self-love. He was not unaware of his shortcomings and sins: he confessed them in general terms, frequently in his early *Meditations*, occasionally in the *Centuries*, and again insistently in the *Commentaries of Heaven*.[39] What he seems incapable of is the kind of critical self-exploration practised by Donne and George Herbert. In his conviction that God did for us 'the Best of all possible Things', he even comes to regard sin as 'an infinit Treasure Forbidden and Permitted at the Same time' (*Select Meditations*, III. 41, 81).

Just as the solipsistic illusion of the infant is only a first stage, self-love in his eyes is assumed to lead to the 'lov of all others' (*Centuries*, IV. 55). Traherne bids his disciple see himself first as the centre of the world and the possessor of it, borrowing the words of Seneca: 'God gave me alone to all the World, and all the World to me alone' (*Centuries*, I. 15). Man is alone in the world, though the world is peopled with millions of creatures, since he is 'alone to Enjoy and rejoyce in all' (II. 15). To be enjoyed, the world therefore must be filled with riches and with inhabitants. Solitude only brought fear and dismay to the child ('Solitude'; cf. *Centuries*, III. 23). Traherne even realized, in

---

[39] *Select Meditations*, II. 100, III. 68, 74, 97, 98, 100. *Commentaries of Heaven*, Nos. 74, 87 (ll. 113, 158), 90, 93.

nearly Hobbesian terms, that man unsocialized would be 'Naked and hungry, | Blind and brutish' ('Thanksgivings for the Body', 302–3). In his rhapsodies (Whitmanesque according to Dobell) he declared himself 'a sociable Creature', 'a lover of company' ('Thanksgiving for the Nation', 215–17). His doctrine of felicity allowed him to find happiness at once 'in Solitud alone, in communion with all, by Action and Contemplation' (*Centuries*, II. 99). How was this miraculous conjunction effected? As a Christian he was bound to give moral pre-eminence to the altruistic forms of enjoyment; but enjoyment still takes precedence in the acquisition of this wisdom:

All these relate to Enjoyment, but those Principles that relate to Communication are more Excellent. These are Principles of Retirement and Solitude; but the Principles that aid us in Conversation are far better: and help us, tho not so immediatly to Enjoyment in a far more Blessed and Diviner maner. For it is more blessed to giv then to receiv: and we are more happy in Communication then Enjoyment, but only that Communication is Enjoyment; as indeed what we giv we best receiv, for the Joy of Communicating and the Joy of receiving maketh perfect Happiness.   (*Centuries*, IV. 18)

The underlying structure remains egocentric. There is no real contradiction between the rejection of solitude and the earlier solipsistic inclination. The moralist compares the world to a theatre pleasurable only if the actors are on stage (*Christian Ethics*, VIII. 59). Fellow beings are first in his eyes 'objects' to be viewed, a 'spectacle' in which he can take delight. This is again an attitude close to the interest taken by the child in the discovery of the world and other creatures apt to divert him like toys or coloured pictures. What he calls 'communication' means conversation and commerce, but his consciousness seems hardly eager to engage in communication with another consciousness. Other men contribute to the felicity of the individual and since his consciousness absorbs what it contemplates, everything remains within the sphere of the self. Even in the late *Commentaries of Heaven* a solipsistic impulse may spontaneously emerge: 'I Know that for my sake the World doth stand. | I am the Sole spectator of this All' (No. 87, 'Avarice', 134–5).

At times, however, Traherne will consider the other as a 'subject' and show himself aware of an apparent contradiction between 'two Inclinations, that are both in our Natures, yet seem Contradictory', the 'Avaricious Humor' and the 'Communicativ Humor'. He gives thanks to God for 'satisfying two such Insatiable Humors that are contrary to each other' (*Centuries*, II. 79). Their reconciliation, however, is less miraculous than he thinks. He expects another man to be happy in order to give him 'Himself and all his Happiness': he wants to be 'Magnified in his Affections, represented in his Understanding Tenderly Beloved Caressed and Honored' (IV. 19). Other men are still mirrors in which he contemplates his own image 'Enlarged by the Multitud of Spectators' (II. 61). This is the unexpected turn he gives to the Neoplatonic idea that the lover lives in the beloved:

We need Spectators; and other Diversities of Friends and Lovers, in whose Souls we might likewise Dwell, and in whose Beauties we might be Crowned and entertained. In all whom we can dwell exactly; and be present with them fully . . . And as in many Mirrors we are so many other selvs, so are we Spiritualy Multiplied when we meet our selvs more Sweetly, and liv again in other Persons.   (*Centuries*, II. 70)

He could not have more distinctly revealed that he was incapable of conceiving a gift of self that would be a surrender of his own self.[40] I do not question the sincerity of his love for others and for God; *amans amare* like Augustine, he felt, however, 'we cannot Delight in God . . . till we Lov to be Beloved' (*Select Meditations*, II. 87), and he was ecstatic when persuaded of God's love for him.[41]

This self-centredness is characteristic of his conception of love as originating in self-love both in man and in God. In the *Centuries* (II. 56), appropriating a Platonic notion, he argues that the lover, since his spirit resides in the beloved Object, 'can Enjoy a Sweet Communion with it self: in contemplating what it is in it self, and to its Object'. Self-love, he admits, is 'Dishonourable . . . when it is alone', but it is the starting-point: he 'would have first his Self Lov satisfied, and then his Love of

---

40 In two instances only did Traherne speak of 'Annihilateing [him] selfe' before the glory of God (*Select Meditations*, III. 71, IV. 38), a traditional expression which is not distinctive.

41 *Select Meditations*, IV. 39; in this work he repeatedly addresses God as the Bridegroom and sees himself as the Bride of the Song of Songs, but this type of 'erotic' relationship is hardly perceptible in later works.

all others . . . That Pool must first be filled, that shall be made
to overflow' (IV. 55). That God's love for His creatures proceeds
from His self-love is theologically correct,[42] but Traherne again
takes an original stand: to do all things for one's own glory
would be 'vain Glory', therefore the 'True Glory' of God is 'that
he seeks the Happiness of Angels and Men as his Last End', 'He
loves himself because he is infinit and Eternal Lov to others',
'His Lov unto them is Lov unto Him self' (IV. 63–5). Two interpretations are possible. Like some mystics, like Eckhart,[43]
Traherne may genuinely feel that God needs man: 'for He |
Doth place his Whole Felicitie | In that, who is despised and
defied | Undeified almost if once denied' ('Recovery', 17–20).
But one may see in these lines a transfer of the poet's own desire
to be glorified by God, to be 'the sole Object of His Ey, and the
End of all His Endeavors' (*Centuries*, I. 70; cf. *Select
Meditations*, IV. 38–48). The conviction that in the creation of
the world God 'intends thy single Self' ('Dialogue', 39) is
another testimony of Traherne's inordinate egocentricity.

It would be unjust not to acknowledge the moving beauty of
a passage in *Christian Ethicks* (ch. 32, p. 265) which conse-
crates the metamorphosis of self-love into the love of God:

when I see my self infinitely beloved . . . I live for the sake of my infinite Blessedness. Now that is GOD. And for his sake it is that I love my
self . . . Thus is God infinitely preferred by Nature above my self, and
my Love to my self, being thoroughly satisfied, turns into the Love of
GOD, and dies like a grain of Corn in the Earth to spring up in a new
and better form.

Yet I wonder whether the root of this better love is not still in
the 'Heavenly Avarice' of the self ('Desire', 6) for the same treatise offers a cool appreciation of the benefit we may derive even
from egotistic inclinations:

I do not look upon Ambition and Avarice . . . as things that are evil in
their root and fountain. If they be, temperance has a strange vertue in

---

[42] See Augustine, *De Trinitate*, IX. Hooker asserted that God loves His Son and
us as reflections of Himself (*Works* (ed. Gauden, 1662), II. 246–7). Eckhart
proclaimed that 'God loves Himself' and in His self-love, loves all creatures (*Traités
et sermons*, trans. M. de Gandillac (Paris, 1942), 245).

[43] Notably in 'Predigten', 12–13; *Meister Eckharts Predigten*, ed. J. Quint
(Stuttgart, 1958).

its Nature, for as Chymists make Antidotes of Poysons, so doth this vertue turn the matter of all these into a Quintessential perfection. Nay Selfishness and Pride it self escape not its influence. A little touch of something like Pride, is seated in the true sence of a mans own Greatness . . . A little Selfishness puts our Companions in mind of our own Interest, and make them perceive that we understand it: which adds a lustre to our Self-denial, and renders our Liberality more safe and precious.   (Ch. 22, pp. 173–4)

This is worldly rather than 'holy sagacity'. It is definitely oppposed to Donne's view of self-love as 'the greatest treason we can commit against God' (*Sermons*, I. 242), or Shakespeare's 'Sin of self-love' (Sonnet 62). It shows Traherne parting company with Theophilus Gale and Plotinus, whom he followed in other respects,[44] and moving closer to Hobbes, though he severely condemned 'that arrogant *Leviathan*' for making our love to our selves 'inconsistent with Charity towards others'.[45] It looks forward to Locke's defence of the innocence of natural self-love[46] and the ethics of a new age which will proclaim 'That true self-love and social are the same'.[47]

[44] Self-love was condemned in Gale's *Anatomie of Infidelitie* (London, 1672), 228–9; Plotinus ascribed all destructions in the universe to the self-love of the World-Soul (*Enneads*, IV. iv. 32).

[45] *Christian Ethicks*, XXXII. 261. Traherne's views were adumbrated by William Pemble (1592–1623) in *A Summe of Morall Philosophy* (Oxford, 1632); this Puritan divine pointed out the benefits of 'true self-love' (as distinguished from self-love 'fancyed according to sense'), wishing and working the best to our selves, 'Joying at our own good, and grieving at the contrary' (pp. 23–4). The link between the rehabilitation of self-love and certain trends in Puritanism may be of interest.

[46] See C. Taylor, *Sources of the Self* (Cambridge, 1994), 242–4.

[47] Pope, *An Essay on Man*, Ep. iv, 396.

PART II

Time, Space, and World

CHAPTER 6

John Donne

Donne's attention is usually focused on the here and now. This is a habit of his mind, not a mere characteristic of his art. The celebrated immediacy and dramatic quality of his *Songs and Sonets* had precedents in Roman elegies and satires and even in some sonnets of Petrarch and Sidney.[1] But Donne's arresting of the present tenuous instant in a close-up is peculiar: 'So, so, breake off this last lamenting kisse' ('The Expiration'). The poet pinpoints the moment in his numerous 'Valedictions', in 'The Anniversarie', in 'A Nocturnal': 'Tis the yeares midnight, and it is the dayes . . . let mee call | This houre her Vigill'. The past may be evoked, but only to be abolished, as in the first stanza of 'The Good-Morrow', or to lead up to the present as in 'Aire and Angels' ('and now | That it assume thy body, I allow'), in 'Loves Diet' ('Now negligent of sport I lye'), and 'Woman's Constancy' ('Now thou hast lov'd me one whole day . . . what wilt thou say?'). When indulging in retrospect, the poet revives what had been a present moment of experience: 'I heard mee say, Tell her anon' ('The Legacie').

This turn of mind may be traced as well in Donne's *Satires*, *Elegies*, and *Verse Letters*[2] and even some of the *Epicedes*, as in 'Obsequies to the Lord Harrington': 'Thou seest mee here at midnight . . .'. It is illustrated by the Holy Sonnets,[3] by the Hymns and other religious poems, notably 'Good Friday, 1613.

---

[1] See *Poètes métaphysiques* on the dramatic vividness of Roman satire and elegy (III. 300–10) and Petrarch's sonnets (III. 208–10). Sidney's brusque openings anticipate Donne's: 'Alas, have I not pain enough, my friend' (*Astrophel and Stella*, 14, 20, etc.).

[2] One might argue that the influence of Latin models here prevailed, but I have shown that it can account only for the prevailing trends among poets of Donne's generation, not for each author's individual inclination and achievement: *Poètes métaphysiques*, III, ch. vi.

[3] With the exception of 'La Corona', built on a conventional scheme.

Riding Westward'. Even the traditional 'Litanie' was not written in the timeless present of impersonal prayer: 'come | And re-create mee, now growne ruinous'. The *First Anniversary* laments the loss of Elizabeth Drury for its abiding effects on the world; in the *Second Anniversary* (85 ff.) the future death of the poet and the liberation of his soul are envisaged as a present experience: 'Thinke then, my soule, that death is but a Groome . . .' (85).

With Donne, indeed, the future is never a far-off event: all sense of distance is suppressed. In 'The Apparition', 'The Funeral', 'The Relique', duration comes to a stay in the contemplation of a unique, hallucinatory detail: the flickering candle-light, the wreath or bracelet of bright hair. The poet does not merely foresee the future but calls it from the void and contemplates the image he creates with a fascinated attention. In the Holy Sonnets as well, when anticipating his own death ('This is my playes last scene . . ., my minutes latest point'), the world's end ('What if this present were the worlds last night?'), or the Resurrection ('At the round earths imagin'd corners, blow | Your trumpets . . .'), he seems to hurl himself into a future already 'realized',[4] just as a man walking dizzily at the edge of an abyss sees himself falling down to the bottom.

Donne is only capable of present emotion: even his 'Extasie', narrated in the past tense, is lived over again rather than recollected. His energy is often strained in an effort to carry and then maintain emotion—love or anguish, fear or hatred—at an acme of intensity, for 'his first minute, after noone, is night' ('A Lecture upon the Shadow'). This may be felt in the sonnets of 'fear and trembling' as well as in 'The Good-Morrow', 'The Sunne Rising', or 'The Apparition'. Quieter moments seem to crystallize into a state of permanence, though not of stillness: the very pulse of life is caught in a throbbing instant. 'The Canonization' emblematizes a solstice of love; its enduring power is celebrated in 'The Anniversarie' through the return of a definite day, of the very moment 'When thou and I first one another saw'; its culmination is the triumphant assertion of 'The Sunne Rising':

---

4 For Donne 'death doth touch the resurrection' ('Hymn to God my God'); see John Carey, *John Donne* (London, rev. edn. 1990), 290.

Love, all alike, no season knowes, nor clyme,
Nor houres, dayes, moneths, which are the rags of time.

This intuition of eternity within the space of a moment seems
to be a privilege of human love in the poetry of Donne. In his
divine poems eternity is conceived rather than felt, so true it is
that the love of God was for him less an affair of the heart than
of the imagination: religious ecstasy was not part of his experience. Yet the notion of eternity as the *nunc stans*, an eternal
present moment, fascinated him. Just as he described the entire
duration of the Creation as the coincidence of two points in
time, for God made Creation 'With the last judgement, but one
period',[5] he conceived of divine eternity as a circle 'Whose first
and last concurre' ('Annuntiation and Passion', 5). Not the
luminous symbol of endlessness, dear to Henry Vaughan, nor
the infinity of duration extolled by Traherne, but the instantaneous coincidence of two extreme points was for Donne the
most exact image of absolute perfection, 'For a point and one |
Are much entirer than a million'.[6]

Donne's prose statements confirm the characteristics
observed in his poetry.[7] He emphasized in a letter the strange
virtue of the instant which, 'though it be nothing, joynes times
together'.[8] In the *Essays in Divinity* he marvelled at the idea of
'a beginning [of Creation] so near Eternity that there was no
Then, nor a minute of Time between them'.[9] The preacher
reminds us that 'there is not a more comprehensive, a more

---

5 'The Annuntiation and Passion', 37–8; cf. *Sermons*, VI. 331: 'The First Fiat
in the Creation of Adam, and the last note of the blowing of the Trumpets to
Judgement (though there be between these . . . 2000 yeares of Nature . . . and 2000
yeares of the Law . . .) . . . yet this Creation and this Judgement are not a minute
asunder in aspect of eternity, which hath no minutes.'

6 'Lord Harrington', 67–8; cf. 'As a circle is printed all at once, so his beginning and ending is all one': *Sermons*, IV, 95. Carey (*John Donne* (London, 1981),
127) rightly speaks of Donne's 'urge to outsoar the *mind*'s boundaries' (my italics):
when he mentions 'a thousand millions of millions of generations', 'an infinite,
a superinfinite, an unimaginable space', he is, indeed, trying to *conceive* the *unimaginable*.

7 K. G. Frost recently noted that 'the *Devotions* both begins and ends on the
needle's point of a present moment' (*Holy Delight* (Princeton, 1990), 138).

8 A V[uestra] Merced (*c*.1609); Hayward, 459; Gosse, I. 215.

9 Ed. Simpson, p. 19. Just as 'the stars were created at once', 'so the *Christian
doctrine necessary* to salvation, was delivered at once' (*Sermons*, III. 369): cited by
Achsah Guiborry in *The Map of Time* (Urbana, Ill., 1986), ch. iii.

embracing word in Religion, then . . . *Now*' (*Sermons*, II. 250). The grace of God 'doth everything suddenly':[10] his mercies 'worke *momentarily* in minutes' (*Sermons*, X. 240). The future 'is reduced to an infallible present': 'it is not, *Ecce veniam*, but *Ecce venio*' (*Sermons*, I. 304). 'If all this earth were made in that minute, may not all come to the generall dissolution in this minute?' (*Sermons*, IX. 48); 'In an instant, we shall have a *dissolution*, and *in the same instant* a *redintegration*' (*Sermons*, X. 238). God gave the Church 'an instant fullnesse; in this exanination, instant glory; in this grave, an instant Resurrection' (*Sermons*, VI. 67). Eternal bliss is characterized by the intensity of each moment, the exaltation of 'every minute', 'infinitely multiplied, by every minutes addition' (*Sermons*, VIII. 82). As in the poems, eternity therefore is identified with the instant, with the point: 'such a point as admits, and requires a subtle, and a serious consideration . . . this point, *this timeless time*, time that is all *time*, time that is no *time* . . .' (*Sermons*, II. 139).

These statements proceed from a philosophical, Biblical, and theological tradition, acknowledged in Chapter 17, and one might argue that they need not disclose any personal inclination. The special emphasis, however, cannot be denied and the close correspondence with poems mainly written earlier shows that experience preceded speculation: the value of the instant was felt by the lover before it received 'the serious consideration' of the preacher.

The contraction of space by Donne's imagination is no less remarkable than his contraction of time. The flux of time could be brought to a standstill in a privileged moment. Space cannot be reduced to a point, but the poet will focus his attention on a definite object, whether at rest or in motion within a circumscribed setting. This is again more than a dramatic device. There is no horizon, no perspective in the poetry of Donne, which does not mean it lacks the dimension of the infinite. Just as the womb of the Virgin 'shuts[t] in little roome, Immensity cloystered' ('Annunciation'), cosmic space may be enclosed in the exiguity of a room for love 'makes one little roome an every where' ('The Good-Morrow'), the sun can make 'This bed [his]

---

[10]   To Sir H. Goodere [Sept. 1608]; Hayward, 457.

center, these walls, [his] sphere' ('The Sunne Rising'), eyes can mirror the world's hemispheres ('The Good-Morrow') and a tear become a 'globe, yea world', by the impression of a face ('Valediction: Of Weeping'). 'The Canonization' achieves the impassioned convergence of the universe and of all experience, past and present, towards a point in time and space, a unique centre, the lovers' eyes:

> Who did the whole worlds soule contract, and drove
> > Into the glasses of your eyes
> > So made such mirrors, and such spies,
> That they did all to you epitomize,
> > Countries, Townes, Courts . . .

When he cannot 'contract' space the poet captures it in the mesh of thought and science: 'For of Meridians, and Parallels, | Man hath weav'd out a net, and this net throwne | Upon the Heavens, and now they are his owne' (*First Anniversary*, 278–80).

When space is traversed by a dynamic motion, some sort of duration is expressed without losing a sense of instantaneity: one of Donne's favourite images is the trajectory of a discharged bullet.[11] Duration itself may take on a certain density: time does not flow, the present moment stretches out 'Like gold to ayerie thinnesse beate' or follows the motion of the mobile leg of the compass turning around the stationary one ('Valediction: Forbidding Mourning'). In 'The Extasie' the lovers' eye-beams, threading their eyes upon one double string, seem to fill up both space and time for a whole day.

The close-up is dominant: the speaker calls attention to a flea ('The Flea'), a wreath of hair ('Relique', 'Funerall'), a moving shadow ('Lecture upon the Shadow'), a winking taper ('Apparition'), a pair of compasses, a name engraved upon a window or a book (in the various 'Valedictions'), an undisturbed heap of feathers and dust ('Calme'). The lovers, as we have seen, often peer into each other's eyes and 'Witchcraft by a Picture' offers another instance: 'I fix mine eye on thine, and there | Pity my picture burning in thine eye'. The eye seems to touch the foregrounded object. What the poet sees is felt to be

---

[11] 'Dissolution', 23–4; *Second Anniversary*, 81.

at hand or at his fingertips;[12] the willing body of the mistress whom he caresses ('To his Mistress Going to Bed'), the inter-grafted hands of the lovers ('Extasie'), the roundness of a map of the world ('Valediction: Of Weeping'), the dry asperity of vertebrae (*Second Anniversary*, 212), or of a wrist-bone in a tomb ('Funerall').

In this circumscribed space attention is most often called to solid objects:[13] rooms, beds, window panes, glass, tapers, pictures, coins, gold, medals, books, maps, compasses, limbecks, crosses, graves, sun-dials, minerals, stones, bullets, chains, rings, bracelets, nails, lovers' hearts, hands, hair, and eyes. Blood and sweat are more prominent fluids than water; tears 'fall', are 'coined' ('Valediction: Of Weeping') or taken into vials ('Twicknam Garden'), but never 'flow' as in Crashaw's poems. Nor does water really stream:[14] it eddies in 'curled whirlepooles' (Elegie VI), or is stirred to produce concentric circles ('Loves Growth'). The sea is mentioned not for its waves or swell, but for its shores and straits, its distancing, swallow-ing, and drowning power ('Hymne to God my God', 'Valediction: Of Weeping', 'Hymne to Christ').

Donne's absorption in the here and now may have had consequences for his emotional life. When the present imposes itself so forcefully upon the imagination, consciousness does not integrate it into the continuity of life but rather detaches it, in all its brilliance, from the pale, fluid backgound of the past in 'The Good-Morrow':

> I Wonder by my troth, what thou and I
> Did, till we lov'd? were we not wean'd till then?
> But suck'd on countrey pleasures, childishly?
> Or snorted we in the seaven sleepers den?
> 'Twas so; But this, all pleasures fancies bee.

---

[12] In 'But yet the body is his book' Elaine Scarry has brilliantly developed the remark that 'for Donne touch is the model for all the senses' (*Literature and the Body* (Baltimore, 1988), 88).

[13] John Carey has rightly emphasized Donne's fascination with the structures and functions of the body, hence with blood and all 'secretions' (*Donne*, ch. 5). My perspective here was different, but I should have added the 'spongy' to the 'solid'; this sponginess, comparable to the 'viscous' in the phenomenology of Sartre, is a kind of nauseating perversion of fluidity.

[14] Except as an emblem of mutability in the *Second Anniversary* (395–6) and of 'tyrannous rage' in Satyre III.

If ever any beauty I did see
Which I desir'd, and got, 'twas but a dreame of thee.

Every man has probably known one of these moments when the intensity of an emotion makes the past appear as a shadow or a dream. But the extreme vivacity of Donne's immediate impressions and his way of looking at them point-blank isolate them as a microscope isolates an object. The way in which the enlarged image completely invades the poet's field of consciousness, as well as his field of vision, is a constant feature of his attention. Emerging instantaneously, the impression is apt to disappear in the same way, without transition; when love attains its culmination, 'his first minute, after noone, is night' ('Lecture upon the Shadow').

Now, there are two ways of warding off the inner darkness that follows the fading of the present impression in the consciousness of a man for whom the past and memory have neither charm, nor substance, nor reality. The first is to renew the impression constantly; the second is to fix and eternalize it. The contradiction between Donne's libertine poems, in which he takes the role of an apologist for inconstancy,[15] and the poems in which the unique moment of pleasure, love, or adoration tends towards perpetuity[16] only concerns the nature of the feeling and attitude, not the mode of imagination. The younger man may have inclined towards change and variety; a more fervent, more exclusive sentiment probably inspired the desire for permanence asserted in his most passionate poems. Yet, however deeply a new experience or 'conversion' may have affected his emotional life and behaviour, it did not require an alteration of the fundamental psychic structure which determined his exaltation of the instant. An *immediate* impression was felt and proclaimed to be precarious in the search for variety; it was desired and proclaimed to be permanent and imperishable in more passionate moments. In the second case, duration was expected; but duration in 'The Anniversarie' is experienced as the recurrence of an identical moment. 'Loves

[15] 'Change', 'Variety', 'Womans Constancy', 'The Indifferent', 'Communitie', 'Loves Diet'.
[16] 'The Good-Morrow', 'The Sunne Rising', 'The Canonization', 'The Anniversarie', 'The Extasie'.

Growth' describes a passion that perpetually grows in intensity, but this apparent progression is first perceived by the poet through the contrast between the intensity of the present moment and an erroneous judgement in the past: 'Me thinkes I lyed all winter, when I swore | My love was infinite, if spring make'it more.' Furthermore he discovers that 'no greater, but more eminent, | Love by the spring is growne'. The present moment perpetually displaces the past in a movement which is a way of transcending pure continuity, of straining toward an ever more intense experience, an absolute beyond all change: this is the lesson taught by 'A Lecture upon the Shadow'. Yet, at the same time, the poet discerns the profound identity of human love in the diversity of its manifestations: he wants this love to be always 'all alike' ('Sunne Rising'). What he seeks is not the simple continuity of existence, but the permanence of being, which can only be attained in the instant. We never find Donne feeding his passion with memories, and when he projects his feelings into the future, it is with the purpose of perpetuating an experience he has already enjoyed, not to forge a mere imaginative anticipation.[17]

The consequences of Donne's apprehension of time and space for the composition of the poems must be evaluated with due diffidence since more factors than the poet's own cast of mind may come into play. I have argued that his reading of the Roman elegies and satires could not have *determined* his insistence on the here and now, but his practice of the pseudo-dialogue in his own poems certainly owed much to his predecessors.[18] However, the reason why Donne's satires are more dramatic than Joseph Hall's academic imitations of Juvenal is to be sought for in their conversational vivacity. Though they fall far short of Donne's in liveliness, the satires written by other members of the Inns of Court, Lodge, Marston, Henry Fitzgeffrey, occasionally prove colloquial in the same way: this was the hallmark of the new urban inspiration in the

---

[17] 'To his Mistress Going to Bed' only apparently contradicts this assertion; the lover finds a *present* pleasure in his exploration of the woman's body before he will 'act the rest' (as in 'The Dreame').

[18] See *Poètes métaphysiques*, III, ch. vi, 4.

closing years of the sixteenth century.[19] But the transfer of the satiric or epistolary mode of composition and style to the lyric was Donne's achievement, dictated, I assume, by a bent of mind observable in all his writings.

The influence of the London theatres must be taken into account. Donne had been 'a great frequenter of plays' in his youth and, despite an affectation of contempt for dramatists and 'ideott actors', he could 'tell of new playes' (*Satires*, II. 11–16, IV. 95). His poetry is studded with allusions to the theatre;[20] a few can even be spotted in his sermons.[21] But was the influence decisive for the adoption of a 'dramatic' style in his poems? At the time when he wrote his satires and elegies, as well as some of the *Songs and Sonets*, the language heard on the stage was still highly rhetorical and would hardly have suggested the colloquial tone of Donne's poems. Only with the monologues of Brutus and Hamlet do we approach the spontaneity of conversation and the genuine soliloquy.[22] Yet Shakespeare, though he came to practise this conversational style in his plays, gives scant evidence of it in his early Sonnets,[23] and Ben Jonson, a professional dramatist, did not adopt a 'dramatic' mode of composition for his lyrics and epistles. With due allowance for his debt to the Roman poets, to the London theatres, and to the Inns of Court environment, Donne's individual bent of mind still appears to be the predominant cause of these unchanging characteristics in his handling of time and space and his dramatic manipulation of the lyric in the *Songs and Sonets*.

Because of his acute, exclusive perception of the present Donne was disinclined to cultivate the literary genres that call for a sense of continuity. He did not write the kind of narrative

[19] See Ch. 18 and *Poètes métaphysiques*, III. 37–9, 272–5, 300–3.

[20] 'Expostulation', 61; 'Calme', 14–15; 'To Mr. E. G.', 8–10; 'Here's no more newes', 19–21; *Second Anniversary*, 67; Holy Sonnet VI.

[21] See *Poètes métaphysiques*, III. 188–92; cf. M. Mahood, *Poetry and Humanism* (London, 1950), 89–90, and P. Crutwell, *The Shakespearian Moment* (London, 1954), 84–5.

[22] Cf. my 'Self-consciousness in Montaigne and Shakespeare', *Shakespeare Survey*, 28 (1975), 45–50.

[23] The later sonnets prove more dramatic or colloquial than the earlier ones: see 'Shakespeare the non-dramatic poet', in *The Cambridge Companion to Shakespeare Studies*, ed. Stanley Wells (Cambridge, 1986), 43–4.

poetry practised by the Elizabethans. He attempted one long poem, *Metempsychosis* [*The Progresse of the Soul*], and left it unfinished. Besides, when announcing 'I launch at paradise, and I saile towards home' (57), he characteristically takes his stand 'here' (58) and 'now' (41, 61), and the present tense often crops up in the narrative;[24] the poet's aim is always to 'arrest [the reader's] thought' (513) on an image or an idea. The prose *Devotions*, a journal of his sickness wholly written in the present tense, is made up of a series of momentary meditations on distinct episodes. Descriptive poetry, when it might call for narration, had also little appeal for Donne. In 'The Calme' and 'The Storme' he made of it a fabric of conceits; juxtaposed and mutually reinforcing impressions depict an unchanging condition of the sea, as well as a single mood, without any development in time.[25] Even in his way of reasoning Donne does not display the continuity of a dialectical movement. His logic is best described in Dr Johnson's word as 'analytical'. The poet is not progressing towards the discovery of a truth: he usually starts from a truth of experience and only aims at defining, refining, justifying what is felt to be a compelling evidence.

One suspects a close link between the poet's 'presentism' and his usual avoidance of repetition, symmetry, or regularity in structure and verse forms. He would, of course, favour the revival of a previous impression when it could be experienced as an identical and ever present moment as in 'The Anniversarie'. The construction of 'Lovers Infinitenesse' can be symmetrical because the logical articulation radiates from a unique point, the present instant: 'If *yet*, I have not all thy love . . ., Yet I would not have all *yet*.' But Donne's poetry offers few instances of parallelism or periodicity. He was not attracted to the regular, ordered succession of similar impressions. He never uses a

[24] Notably in stanzas xvi, xix–xxii, xxvi–xxviii, xxxii, xxxiii–xxxvi, xliii, xlvi. Spenser also resorts at times to the historic present in the *Faerie Queene* but not so frequently nor so vividly.

[25] According to Terry Sherwood, Donne had 'a strong sense of sequential movement in time' (*Fulfilling the Circle* (Toronto, 1984), 26). I still think he only has a sense of 'concatenation', with no sense of duration. When Sherwood writes about the *Devotions* that 'Donne's conception of typology invests time with a crucial importance that incarnates all value, past, present, and future, in the *immediate moment* within the believer' (178, my italics), he acknowledges the primacy of the instant.

refrain; if he repeats a verse, as in 'Lovers Infinitenesse' or the 'Hymne to God the Father', it is only to play with an idea, as one would inspect the facets of a diamond by turning it over and over again. The harmonious swell of rhythm which, like the rising and ebbing waves of the sea, calls upon the memory of what is past, did not charm the imagination of a poet whose main preoccupation was to fix the present impression. The eruptive quality of the emotion expressed in each poem does not allow for change or progression in time: the surprise endings brought about by an ironic self-consciousness merely reverse or transpose the initial emotion. The brusque changes of rhythm and tone reveal different aspects of a single state of mind. The poem develops through the discovery of relations or alternatives which give a sense of intellectual order, an impression of spatiality. A single dramatic moment is broken up into logical moments, the distinct propositions of a demonstration or syllogism used to express a single truth.

Donne himself suggested a link between instantaneous apprehension and quickness of wit in 'Obsequies to the Lord Harrington' (81–98):

> As when an Angell down from heav'n doth flye,
> Our quick thought cannot keepe him company,
> Wee cannot thinke, now he is at the Sunne,
> Now through the Moon, now he through th'aire doth run,
> Yet when he's come, we know he did repaire
> To all twixt Heav'n and Earth, Sunne, Moon, and Aire,
> And as this Angell in an instant knowes,
> And yet wee know, this sodaine knowledge growes
> By quick amassing severall formes of things,
> Which he successively to order brings;
> When they, whose slow-pac'd lame thoughts cannot goe
> So fast as hee, thinke that he doth not so;
> Just as a perfect reader doth not dwell,
> On every syllable, nor stay to spell,
> Yet without doubt, hee doth distinctly see
> And lay together every A and B;
> So, in short liv'd good men, is'not understood
> Each severall vertue, but the compound good.

Though based on traditional angelology this passage seems to disclose a distinctive feature of the poet's own mind besides the usual fascination of the instant. The 'quick amassing' of several forms of things brought successively to order implies a singular 'presence of mind' and suggests the brilliant emergence of the conceit. Conceited poetry, of course, was common in the Renaissance, but Donne's 'quickness' of wit can only be challenged by Shakespeare's.[26]

A mind so riveted upon the present impression is likely to be incapable of the vaster syntheses of philosophical speculation. He will grasp analogies without co-ordinating them. Donne has been said to 'unify experience' because he constantly brings into relation the physical and the spiritual, the temporal and the eternal; but to 'relate' is not necessarily to 'unify'. In the historical context his originality did not lie in the perceiving of analogies, always present to the Elizabethan mind, but in the fact that he grasped and multiplied correspondences one by one without seeking to illuminate the panorama of universal harmony. Donne's poetic world, when compared with that of Spenser or Milton, is an uncertain world, illuminated by brief flashes of light when traversed by a sudden conceit which momentarily opens up a startling perspective and links heaven and earth, but only for a while.

This is one of the reasons why Donne's 'metaphysical poetry' is not 'philosophical poetry': it never is the exposition of a system. It is founded upon the principle of universal analogy, but Donne cannot be distinguished from his contemporaries by his perception of multiple correlations though he often surpassed them in intellectual agility. His originality is denoted rather by his scepticism about astrology, alchemy, and many vulgar errors,[27] and his readiness to envisage the ruin of the entire edifice of correspondences in the *Anniversaries*.

The analysis, however, must be carried further to define the structures of a mind. To base the metaphysical character of Donne's poetry on the presence of metaphysical concepts borrowed from Scholastic or Neoplatonic philosophy would be

---

[26] In a survey of the contemporary vogue of the epigram and the paradox, the spontaneity and superiority of Donne's wit were demonstrated in *Poètes métaphysiques*, III, ch. vii.

[27] See my articles 'Le fabuleux et l'imagination poétique dans l'œuvre de John Donne', *De Shakespeare à T. S. Eliot: Mélanges Fluchère* (Paris, 1976); 'Divination et esprit métaphysique', *Du Verbe au Geste: Mélanges Danchin* (Nancy, 1986); 'Poésie et vérité chez John Donne', *EA* 40 (1987).

erroneous. We must disregard this obsolete debris of traditional systems, thrown out in the individual creative operation of a thinking mind, to take up again Gabriel Marcel's existentialist distinction between 'pensée pensée' and 'pensée pensante'. The fresh analogies the poet's mind offers are uniquely destined to illuminate a particular situation, as his use of paradox will show in Chapter 11. Yet his tendency to conceive and express his own experience in connection with universal problems and the ultimate destiny of man can justify the epithet 'metaphysical'.[28] The 'metaphysical' mind is characterized by an aptitude for transcending the immediate facts of human experience. We have already seen how natural it was for Donne's mind to enclose eternity within the moment and realize through love his aspiration to immortality. His passion for substance and essence has been noted.[29] His eagerness to go beyond the particular experience in search of a totality is exemplified by his awareness of the world and his own 'being-in-the-world'.

The statistical frequency of the word 'world' in Donne's writings is not meaningful by itself, but his use of it is distinctive. The traditional Christian meaning—'For thus I leave the world, the flesh, the devill' (Holy Sonnet VI)—is rare. The poet's allusions to the cosmos are not original: the obliteration of the world by the death of the mistress or the person eulogized was a common conceit. Though William Empson described him as a 'space man',[30] he never creates a sense of cosmic expansion: his narrow field of consciousness precludes panoramic visions. When he describes the soul threading her way among the planets in the *Second Anniversary* (ll. 206–13) the voyager

> At once is at, and through the Firmament.
> And as these stars were but so many beads
> Strung on one string, speed undistinguish'd leads
> Her through those Spheares, as through the beads, a string,

[28] This was discussed at length in *Poètes métaphysiques*, II, 'Conclusion'.
[29] In Ch. 1, n. 45.
[30] In his 1957 essay, reprinted in *William Empson: Essays on Renaissance Literature* (Cambridge, 1993), 78–128. I agree with John Carey that 'Donne has a colossus mentality and a cosmic apprehension of space' (*Donne*, 118–22); yet this apprehension is predominantly intellectual, not visual, with the exception of the shipwrecked moon over Tenerife; I mentioned it as an instance of his sensitiveness to contrasts of light and darkness (*Poètes métaphysiques*, I. 246–7); yet, even here, attention is focused on a single image with no sense of the surrounding space.

> Whose quick succession makes it still one thing:
> As doth the pith, which, lest our bodies slacke,
> Strings fast the little bones of necke, and backe;
> So by the Soule doth death string Heaven and Earth.

This is a cosmos 'conceived' rather than 'surveyed': the poet does not seek to embrace it in his gaze. Donne is here, as in all his other poems, apprehending the world through his consciousness of 'being-in-the-world'. The movement supposed to take him through the spheres proves instantaneous and does not take him out of this 'world-surrounding-the-self'. When outside the material world, he will not turn back to contemplate it from afar, nor will he describe the divine world: the progress of the soul is not a movement towards Vaughan's 'country beyond the stars', but a yearning after 'essentiall joy', inseparable for Donne from a sense of his own being. In the elegy on Lord Harrington (27–30), the revelation of the world to the poet is attended by a revelation of the self to the self.

The same mode of consciousness leads the poet to constitute his surroundings as a world at once particular, since it is an aspect of the objective world, and universal, because this aspect, or moment, is apt to become the only existing world in his consciousness, as when on a ship assailed by a storm 'Darknesse . . . his birth-right | Claims o'er this world' ('Storme', 67–8; cf. 37–40). In 'A Nocturnall' a universe of death surrounds a concrete, closely localized centre: at first the deathbed, then the lover himself, who can be imagined kneeling by the bedside. The dramatic situations created by Donne are enclosed within a world focalized on the poet, an eternity focalized on the moment.

In many love poems the beloved is no longer seen by the lover 'on the ground of the world as a *this* among other *thises*, but the world must be revealed in terms of him [or her]'. The beloved must be 'the very condition of the upsurge of the world', 'the one whose function is to make trees and water exist, to make cities and other men exist, in order to give them later to the Other who arranges them into a world', for the beloved is 'the object through whose procuration the world will exist for the Other', and, in another sense, the beloved is the world. Rather than being a '*this* detaching itself on the ground of the world', the beloved is 'the ground-as-object on which the world detaches itself'. Thus the lover is reassured: the Other's look no longer paralyses him or her with finitude, for each lover is 'secure within the Other's consciousness'. These assertions are taken from Sartre's analysis of love in *Being and Nothingness*.[31] Donne's intuition and the philosopher's are analogous in so far as they both express a similar human experience. 'The Good-Morrow' can be closely re-read in the light of these quotations which provide the most exact philosophical paraphrase of the poem, including the role of the gaze and the lovers' feeling of security. This is not an isolated example: the same experience inspired 'The Sunne Rising', the last stanza of 'The Canonization', and is traceable in some of the 'Valedictions'.

This world-awareness is perhaps universal in structure, but Donne exhibits it with a peculiar acuity, a lucidity exceptional for his age. It can hardly be ascribed to his undeniable and often anxious interest in the world as an astronomical entity. His first certain allusion to the new astronomy is found in *Biathanatos*, composed when he had already written the majority of his poems. Nor could his concrete intuition emerge from the abstract speculations of medieval scholasticism or Renaissance Neoplatonism. A psychological explanation is required, however hazardous it may seem.

Donne's concentration of attention in time and space, as illustrated, leads him to constitute an intense moment of his individual experience as a 'world-for-the-self'. A man with an extended field of consciousness would have had more difficulty in conceiving a diffuse world in its unicity, though his imagination, like Vaughan's or Traherne's, could embrace its expansion. A consciousness which ceaselessly slipped from the present to the past or the future, like Vaughan's, would be less likely to centre its attention on the momentary emergence of the self into the world. Donne's immediate intuition of a world-for-the-self and a totality of experience was, of course, expressed in the language of his age, and was bound to nourish an interest in current views concerning the universe. But the poet proves to be less concerned with the objective signification and fate of the universe than with the immediate world brought into being in a moment of individual experience, and this may also apply to the

[31] Trans. Hazel Barnes (London, 1943), 368–70.

world *destroyed* in the *Anniversaries*. He will elevate this particular meaning to the level of the universal, sometimes by fram-
ing a general law as in 'A Lecture upon the Shadow', but more
often by absorbing the objective world into the immediate
world of his own subjectivity, just as the universe is drawn into
the lovers' eyes in 'The Canonization' or 'The Good-Morrow'.

Donne's world therefore appears to be a universe where the
poet is the centre of reference and where he becomes at times his
own world. Presence in the world then implies at once an
awareness of the world revealed and a reflexive consciousness
of this revelation of the world to the self.[32] This may not be a
necessary consequence of the narrowness of the field of
consciousness, nor of a privileged intuition of the present. It
seems likely, however, that the narrower the field of consciousness, the easier and the more spontaneous is this turning back
upon the self. A diffuse consciousness is willing to be absorbed
in the exterior object of its contemplation; conversely, an intense
self-centredness is likely to restrict the field of consciousness and
favour an exclusive attention to the moment. My concern is not
with cause-and-effect relationships but with the discovery of
permanent correlations. One may at any rate assert that presence to the world meant for Donne presence to the self in accordance with his fundamental mode of consciousness.

[32] Merleau-Ponty assumed that our consciousness of the world and our self-
consciousness are simultaneous ('rigoureusement contemporaines'), *Phénoménologie de la perception* (Paris, 1945), 345). Yet this is only revealed to us when we
are self-conscious!

CHAPTER 7

George Herbert and Henry Vaughan

With Herbert as with Donne 'Onelie the present is thy part and fee' ('Discharge'). In their intuition and use of the present, however, one may discern subtle differences and a close comparison is a means of tracing the influence of the predominant mental structures in the very texture of the poems.

In complaint or prayer, self-communings or apostrophe[1] Herbert records moments of experience with the same immediacy as Donne and the same brusque openings:

> Kill me not ev'ry day   ('Affliction II')
> Full of rebellion, I would die . . .   ('Nature')
> Busie enquiring heart, what wouldst thou know?
>
>   ('The Discharge')

He composes, or pretends to compose, when spurred on by a present emotion or incident: 'My God, I heard this day' ('Man'), 'My God, I read this day' ('Affliction V'), 'Foolish soul who sinn'd to-day' ('Businesse'). In the very process of 'The Holy Communion' he addresses Christ who 'dost now thy self convey'. Music is not merely evoked or invoked as in Milton's 'At a Solemn Musick'; the hearing of the melody and the attendant impressions are described as a present experience:

> Now I in you without a bodie move,
> Rising and falling with your wings.
>
>   ('Church-musick')

The poem may be about the sudden loss of a state of mind, which however remains, as it were, present in absence as a

---

[1] As in (1) 'Affliction IV', 'Submission', 'Complaining'; (2) 'Longing', 'Discipline', 'Home', 'Dulnesse'; (3) 'The Forerunners', 'An Offering', 'The Odour'; (4) 'Content', 'The Familie', 'The Size'.

dream still haunts our consciousness on awaking: 'It cannot be. Where is that mighty joy, | Which just now took up all my heart?' ('Temper II'). Here lies a first difference. With Donne the present leaps into being and may even rob the past of all reality as in the first stanza of 'The Good-Morrow'. But Herbert maintains the remembrance of the past at the very heart of the present. The very intermittence of his gleams of spiritual joy invited a brooding over the vanishing moment: 'Thou cam'st but now; wilt thou so soon depart . . .?' ('Glimpse'). He can be the poet of return and rebirth, though in a different way from Vaughan's, not into a previous state but into the present: 'How fresh, O Lord, how sweet and clean | Are thy returns, ev'n as the flowers in spring':

> And now in age I bud again,
> After so many deaths I live and write;
> I once more smell the dew and rain,
> And relish versing: O my onely light,
> It cannot be
> That I am he
> On whom thy tempests fell all night.
>
> ('The Flower')

By his inclusion of the past in the present Herbert tempers the vehemence of emotion. When noting his first white hairs, before calling attention to them and questioning anxiously, he calmly states a fact, in designedly enigmatic terms to hold us in suspense, and uses a tense—'are come'—in which the present denotes something already accomplished:

> The harbingers are come. See, see their mark;
> White is their colour, and behold my head.
> But must they have my brain?
>
> ('The Forerunners')

Whereas Donne's attention was instantaneous, spasmodic, and easily dispersed,[2] the country parson is capable of prolonged recollection and a more spacious attention may embrace the day 'For if thou stay | I and this day | As we did rise, we die together' ('Repentance'). The role of ejaculatory prayer is noteworthy:

---

[2]   See Ch. I, n. 54.

the ever-welling call of a loving heart fills the day in 'A true Hymn'. Herbert can meditate on a large span of his life: 'And now, me thinks, I am where I began | Sev'n yeares ago' ('Bunch of Grapes'). His true bent, however, is not retrospection but recapitulation.[3] A poem which opens as narrative will lead up to the present moment: 'I made a posie, while the day ran by ... Farewell deare flowers, sweetly your time ye spent ... I follow straight' ('Life'). The self-enclosed narrative can also blur the distinction between the present and the future, which is apprehended as completion rather than grasped in anticipation, as it often was by Donne. At the end of 'The Pilgrimage' the poet places himself, and places us, in present death—his own death: 'After so foul a journey death is fair, | And but a chair.' His imagination can roll up past and future into a ball—one of his favourite images. Distance, whether historical or eschatological, disappears: Christ is 'dying daily' ('Affliction III'). The drama of 'Redemption' is related in the preterite as an apologue, but the words spoken on the cross are intensely present: 'there I him espied | Who straight, *Your suit is granted*, said, & died.'

Herbert's intuition of time and his sense of form in the composition of his poems are interrelated. The building up of the poem may be thought out in order to lead to an unexpected close. Donne's agile mind could bring such surprises on us, but he tacked about from one argument to another through his piled-up statements or questionings. Herbert moves more steadily towards a conclusion which at once unifies and reverses the meaning:

> Then for thy passion—I will do for that—
> Alas, my God, I know not what.
> > ('The Thanksgiving')

> Well, I will change the service, and go seek
> Some other master out.
> Ah my deare God! though I am clean forgot,
> Let me not love thee, if I love thee not.
> > ('Affliction I')

---

[3] After Ricœur, Taylor observed that the basic condition of making sense of ourselves is 'to grasp our lives as a narrative' (*Sources of the Self* (Cambridge, 1994), 47). Harman offered a full analysis of 'Herbert's impulse to have a story' (*Costly Monuments* (Cambridge, Mass., 1982), 98 and *passim*).

> But as I rav'd and grew more fierce and wilde
> 　　　At every word,
> Methoughts I heard one calling, *Child*!
> 　And I reply'd, *My Lord*.

('The Collar')

The premeditated composition turns the dramatic monologue into a single conceit instead of a witty succession of flashes. It is the triumph of form within the recorded moment of experience, within the self-enclosed lyric.

The ideograph has a similar function in the poetry of Herbert. Julien Benda rightly described an 'hantise du simultané', an obsession with simultaneity, and a 'fureur du total', an eagerness for totality, in the typography of Mallarmé and the *Calligrammes* of Apollinaire.[4] When delighting in this identification of words and things on the page, Herbert achieved an apprehension of truth based on a 'presentness' different in nature and form from the dramatic immediacy of other poems, yet capable of answering the peculiar needs of his imagination.

The contraction of space is even more obvious than the contraction of time in *The Temple*. Just as he calls to God to 'contract [his] hour' ('Complaining'), Herbert will ask him: 'Stretch or contract me thy poor debter: | This is but tuning of my breast | To make the musick better' ('Temper I'). Images of extension are images of torture: 'O rack me not to such a vast extent' is the call of a soul attracted by both heaven and earth.[5] Violent tension is suggested by the 'stretched sinews' of Christ on the Cross ('Easter'). 'No scrue, no piercer' can penetrate more searchingly than afflictions ('Confession'). Thoughts wounding the heart are 'a case of knives' ('Affliction IV') and 'Sinne is that presse and vice, which forceth pain | To hunt his cruell food through ev'ry vein' ('Agonie'). The poet, of course, was influenced by the emblematic technique, but he is original when he transposes a visual impression into an organic one: bushy groves 'pricking the lookers eie',[6] the rose's 'hue angrie

---

[4] *La France Byzantine* (Paris, 1948), 47–8.

[5] 'Temper I'. Even the blissful expansion of the soul in Heaven is described as a limited extension: 'If as a flowre doth spread and die, | Thou wouldst extend me to some good, | . . . The sweetnesse and the praise were thine; | But the extension and the room, | Which in thy garland I should fill, were mine' ('Employment I').

[6] 'Faith'; cf. 'Frailtie' ('prick mine eyes'), 'Ungratefulnesse' ('The dust into our eyes').

and brave' which 'bids the rash gazer wipe his eye' ('Vertue').
Donne's imagery was kinetic; Herbert's is often kinaesthetic.[7]
He was contemporary with great Baroque artists who painted
ecstatic ascensions in which Christ, the Virgin, or a Saint rose
vertically among spiralling angels in a fluid movement which
suggested a continuous élan, but he rather chose to leap to
Heaven with the suddenness and discontinuity of a bound or a
projection:

> O let me take thee at the bound,
>   Leaping with thee from sev'n to sev'n,
>   Till that we both, being toss'd from earth,
>   Flie hand in hand to heav'n!
>
>   ('Sunday')

In 'The Pulley' God gives blessings to man, yet refuses rest, so
'that at least, | If goodnesse leade him not, yet wearinesse | May
tosse him to my breast'. The brusqueness of 'tossing' qualifies
the yearning for repose: Herbert does not simply dream of
quiescence, but projects himself into relaxation with the sudden
recoil of a spring, as if violence alone could conquer the
passions or regrets that the country parson, as a former courtier,
had to overcome.

The 'caller' who, in his 'choler', could strike the board in
'The Collar' had, however, a yearning for security which
enhanced his preference for nearness and enclosed spaces: 'O let
me, when thy roof hath hid, | O let me roost and nestle there'
('Temper I').[8] Since space and distance gave him pain and terror,
the only world the poet gladly inhabits will be solid and full,
like the boxes and chests, the cabinets 'packt' with sweets, on

---

7 Some 'metaphors of fluidity' have been traced in Herbert's *Passio Discerpta*
and *Lucus* by Edmund Miller in *Drudgerie Divine* (Salzburg, 1979), ch. ix, and by
Elizabeth Clarke in 'Sacred Singer/Profane Poet: Herbert's Split Poetic Persona', in
George Herbert: Sacred and Profane, ed. H. Wilcox, R. Todd, and A. MacDonald
(Amsterdam, 1995), 26. They are not characteristic, for Herbert is more imitative
in Latin verse than in vernacular; besides these metaphors are comparatively rare,
and the epigram 'In Johannem' (*Lucus*, xxxiv), instead of pursuing the image of
flowing blood, as Crashaw will, ends with a kinetic movement: 'Dipping my shoul-
der thus, surely | I may shake the Throne of God.'

8 E. Pearlman suggested that the preference for enclosed spaces expressed a
longing for infantile security and the wish to recover his mother ('George Herbert's
God', *English Literary Renaissance*, 13 (1983), 108–9).

which he liked to dwell.⁹ Wood was Herbert's privileged
substance, loved for its combination of hardness and definite
form with a natural warmth not found in steel or marble;¹⁰
loved also for its association with the house and the hearth, the
roof and the furniture, the security of home, by a poet who had
the 'complexe de l'habitation' analysed by Gaston Bachelard.¹¹
Wood, of course, had its religious associations: the mystical
carvings of Solomon's temple ('Sion', 5) and Christ's Cross,
which 'taught all wood to resound his name' ('Easter'). In the
Eucharist God is presented 'broken' for 'Pomanders and wood
. . . being bruis'd are better sented' ('Banquet'). The last stanza
of 'Vertue' illustrates the interpenetration of the religious
symbolism and the poet's attraction to the substance:

> Onely a sweet and vertuous soul,
> Like season'd timber, never gives;
> But though the whole world turn to coal,
>   Then chiefly lives.

This apocalyptic prospect of a carbonized world offers a sharp
contrast to the sweetness of a day hailed as 'the bridall of the
earth and skie', yet this image of absolute desolation was
prepared for by the tragic acknowledgement that the rose's 'root
is ever in its grave'. In its starkness the final image of 'season'd
timber', the emblem of a faithful soul, becomes a rustic symbol
of immortality and resurrection as potent as the legend of the
Phoenix: burnt wood turns to coal, and out of coal springs a
clearer flame.

Through the Christian myth Herbert's homely images may
acquire a cosmic background. Yet his didactic poems, such as
'Man' or 'Providence', only mirror the traditional world picture
of his age. Even in a lyric poem like 'Employment I' the allusion
to the 'great chain' of being does not suggest the kind of
personal 'world awareness' discovered in the poetry of Donne.
In lyrics like 'The Good-Morrow', and occasionally in the

---

⁹ See 'Vertue', 10; 'Ungratefulnesse', 7–24; 'Confession', 3–6; cf. 'Even Song',
21; 'Miserie', 68; 'Good-Friday', 24; 'Confession', 1–16. Herbert's 'Images of
Enclosure' and 'Violent Containment' were later studied by T. R. Higbie (*TSLL* 5,
1974, 627–38) and F. L. Huntley (*GHJ* 8, 1984, 17–27).

¹⁰ Wood is associated with Herbert's native North, marble with the South in
'Providence', 96.

¹¹ *La terre et les rêveries du repos* (Paris, 1948), chs. 4 and 5.

Anniversaries, an individual human consciousness could show at times a global apprehension of the world irrespective of the existence of God. Herbert never has the world in mind without thinking of God. To him Christ the Redeemer is the greater world enclosing the created world and the human world of sin:

> Lo, here I hang, charg'd with a world of sinne,
> The greater world o'th' two; for that came in
> By words, but this by sorrow I must win.
>
> ('Sacrifice', 205–7)

More miraculous than the creation of the world, which fascinated Donne, is the fragile, yet perpetual creation of a world of grace:

> The grosser world stands to thy word and art;
>   But thy diviner world of grace
>   Thou suddenly dost raise and race,
> And ev'ry day a new Creatour art.
>
> ('Temper II')

Donne could enclose infinity in the point, eternity in the moment. Herbert, in a quieter, religious way, wants 'one grief' for Christ's sacrifice to devour his 'whole life' ('Good Friday'). By prayer, 'Angels age', man can be raised to an atemporal existence ('Prayer I'). Life must be lived both in the present and for eternity: 'Thy life is Gods, thy time to come is gone, | And is his right. | He is thy night at noon: he is at night | Thy noon alone' ('Discharge'). Here again Donne's concentration on the instant is enlarged to past, present, and future: a whole life, embraced in a single thought *sub specie aeternitatis*.

This is an eternity *sensible au cœur*, emotionally apprehended, not intellectually like Donne's, nor imaginatively like Vaughan's. It implies a desire for constancy: 'O that I once past changing were, | Fast in thy Paradise, where no flower can wither!' ('Flower'). But access to this Paradise is gained through a 'trinitie of light, | Motion, and heat' ('Starre'), not in a passive nightly contemplation of a cold ring of light as in Vaughan's 'World'. The blessed souls enjoy at once the fixity and the 'winding' of stars, which is 'their fashion | Of adoration', like the gyrations in Dante's *Paradiso*.[12]

---

[12]   Cf. 'The Starre', 25–8, and *Paradiso*, XIV. 19; XVIII. 41.

With Herbert, however, no delight in expansiveness can be expected, even in Heaven. He knows 'the soul doth span the world', but his own soul will only 'hang content | From either pole unto the centre' when Heaven shrinks to a local habitation, 'Where in each room of the well-furnisht tent | He lies warm, and without adventure' ('Content'). At times, the substitution of spiritual homeliness for cosmic amplitude or metaphysical profundity implies a limitation in imaginative range, a loss in poetic intensity. At other times it imparts poignancy to the anguish of a soul which, in a different way from Pascal's, experiences its solitude in the immensity of the universe:

> O rack me not to such a vast extent;
>   Those distances belong to thee:
> The world's too little for thy tent,
>   A grave too big for me.
>
> ('Temper I')

The dialectics of the finite and the infinite, immanence and transcendence, is ever present in *The Temple* as in Donne's poetry, though far less obtrusive:

> Thy will such a strange distance is,
>   As that to it
> East and West touch, the poles do kisse,
>   And parallels meet.
>
> ('The Search')

No poet had a finer sense of the Divine presence and 'neareness', 'Making two one' ('Search'). The God who immured himself in his heart ('Decay', 11–12) brought with Him infinite riches in a little room. Allowing for differences in intellectual and imaginative range, Herbert and Donne still have in common a vivid apprehension of the eternal and the infinite in a single point of space and time. 'Shine here to us and thou art every where' the lover said to the 'Sunne Rising'. Herbert shows the same 'metaphysical' confidence when addressing the Sun and Son:

> Thy power and love, my love and trust
>   Make one place ev'ry where.
>
> ('Temper I')

Henry Vaughan

Vaughan is best considered in this chapter for two reasons. His *Silex Scintillans* was written in close imitation of *The Temple*; yet his intuition of time and space offers a clear contrast to both Herbert's and Donne's. His predecessors had been poets of the here and now, he is the poet of distance and retrospection.

The present is not absent from the poetry of Vaughan, particularly when he echoes Herbert's language, but it is always filled with the memory of the past or the expectation of the future:

> How rich, O Lord! how fresh thy visits are!
> 'Twas but just now my bleak leaves hopeles hung . . .
> But since thou didst in one sweet glance survey
> Their sad decays, I flourish, and once more
> Breath all perfumes, and spice.
>
> ('Unprofitableness')

The beautiful description of a waterfall dwells on the lingering flow of water and makes it one with the continuous flow of 'times silent stealth' ('Water-fall'). Vaughan, unlike Donne, never focuses his attention on a unique instant. The present, or present perfect, may be used to describe a repeated action, 'Oft have I seen' ('Resurrection and Immortality'), 'oft have I prest | Heaven ('Showre'), or a permanent psychological state, 'I grieve, my God, that thou hast made me such' ('Distraction'), 'Such is man's life, and such is mine' ('Misery'). A particular moment of emotion will immediately trigger a universal meditation ('Lampe', 'Palm-Tree', etc.). The more authentic present is reminiscent of the past, as in this characteristic union of 'now' and 'since' which forces upon us a sense of distance:

> Silence, and stealth of dayes! 'tis now
> Since thou art gone,
> Twelve hundred houres . . .
>
> ('Silence, and stealth')

Many poems open with the evocation of the past: ' 'Twas so, I saw thy birth' ('Showre'), 'Sure, It was so' ('Corruption'), 'I wrote it down' ('Agreement'). With Herbert this was a means of bringing past and present together in the enclosure of a tale or a life, but Vaughan seeks to move back into the past though an act of reminiscence or reviviscence. Poetry truly becomes emotion recollected in tranquillity in many openings: 'I walkt the other day (to spend my hour,)', or 'As time one day by me did pass', or the famous 'I saw Eternity the other night' ('World') which can be contrasted with Donne's 'What if this present were the worlds last night?'

There is no instant projection with Vaughan; his imagination seems to move up a continuous stream in constant awareness of duration: 'So o'r fled minutes I retreat | Unto that hour | Which shew'd thee last' ('Silence, and stealth'). Retrospection itself becomes the theme of 'The Retreat' and 'Looking-back'. These poems are intimations of a fundamental mode of consciousness which unifies Vaughan's essential longings for childhood, Eden, and the Biblical ages.

Was the poet's imagination haunted by the past mainly because of a love for the purity of childhood, or out of envy of the patriarchs who could converse with God? I doubt it, for the same notions occur in *The Temple*, and *Silex Scintillans* only offers an amplified echo of them:

> The growth of flesh is but a blister;
> Childhood is health.
>
> ('H. Baptisme II')

> Sweet were the dayes, when thou didst lodge with Lot
>
> ('Decay')

Herbert's gaze, however, is not retrospective: 'But *now* thou dost thyself immure and close | In some one corner of a feeble heart' ('Decay'; my italics). Vaughan's reminiscent turn of mind did not create the traditional notions about the glory surrounding childhood or the early ages of humanity, but it disposed him to emphasize them rather than stress the inherited sinfulness of the child or merely complain about the decay of the world. Yet reminiscence with him is not a Proustian delight in the imaginative recovery of time past when he seeks to retrace his steps:

> O how I long to travell back
> And tread again that ancient track!

> That I might once more reach that plaine,
> Where first I left my glorious traine,
> From whence th'Inlightned spirit sees
> That shady City of Palme trees.

('The Retreate')

Past and future meet, since the City is at once the lost Eden and the Paradise to come, the New Jerusalem. Vaughan's poetry is at once retrospection and anticipation. Not with the feverish precipitation of Donne, which did not allow us to feel the *distance* between the present moment and world's end, or the Resurrection, but as an experience of slow progress:

> But the delay is all; Tyme now
> Is old and slow,
> His wings are dull, and sickly.

('Buriall')

This sense of delay imparts to the future the substantial reality of a duration which has to be lived through and gives poignancy to the repeated call: 'Lord haste, Lord come . . .' ('Buriall'; cf. Revelation 22: 20).

In this eschatological perspective Vaughan's intuition of Eternity is different from Donne's or Herbert's present apprehension of it as the *nunc stans*.[13] He most often conceives of it as an eternity *after* time—'while time runs, and after it | Eternity' ('Agreement')—or *before* time, the eternity left behind us at our birth ('Retreate'). Man will enter it again at 'the last gasp of time . . ., man's *eternall Prime*' ('Evening-watch'). The Platonic myth of *Timaeus* (37d), the fashioning of time as a degraded image of eternity, was congenial to his imagination and inspired his vision of the motionless Ring of light and the whirling spheres:

> I saw Eternity the other night
> Like a great Ring of pure and endless light,
>   All calm, as it was bright,
> And round beneath it, Time in hours, days, years
>   Driv'n by the spheres,
> Like a vast shadow mov'd, in which the world
>   And all her train were hurl'd.

('The World')

---

[13] The notion of 'Eternity in time' only appears in one poem, 'Son-dayes', written in close imitation of Herbert.

Eternity is a superior world of light into which one may soar from the Platonic 'grots, and caves' ('World', 46–51) of the material universe. However, it is not a metaphysical eternity opposing the One and the Many, the changing and the unchanging: it is 'a Countrie | Far beyond the stars' ('Peace') in which the sensuous impressions dear to the poet—calm, silence, and light—are gathered and sublimated.

The circumscription of space noticed in the poems of Donne and Herbert is as foreign to the imagination of Vaughan as their concentration of time. He has no sense of limited confines. His gaze, like his mind, will roam to the distant horizon to 'see a Rose | Bud in the bright East' ('Search'). He can climb the sacred hill whence 'this spacious ball | Is but [God's] narrow footstool' ('Mount of Olives'). But there is no clarity of vision: we enter with this Welsh poet a world of 'mists, and shadows' ('Resurrection and Immortality', 51–4), 'faint beams' ('They are all gone', 5–8), and 'clouded starre[s]' ('Morning-Watch'). In his chiaroscuro the *union* of light and darkness even more than their contrast is attractive to his imagination: *there are bright starrs under the most palpable clouds, and light is never so beautifull as in the presence of darknes* (*Flores Solitudinis*, To the Reader).

Vaughan's world is the natural world, as apprehended by the senses and the cosmic imagination, not the world 'conceived' by the minds of Donne and Herbert. It is characterized by an intense awareness of life and its circulation in the universe; it is therefore a world of vegetation and growth, and furthermore a world of sympathy and animism.

Donne's imagination was only moved by the tree of knowledge (*Metempsychosis*, xiii, Holy Sonnet IX) or 'Christs cross and Adams tree' standing in one place ('Hymn to God my God'), and the reason 'why grasse is greene' only puzzled his intellect (*Second Anniversary*, 288). In bucolic Bemerton George Herbert took delight in plants and flowers, but only for their sweet fragrance or medicinal virtue ('Life', 'Flower'). Vegetation only yields images of contempt when he reminds us that '*Man is but grasse*' ('Miserie') or '*deare earth, fine grasse or hay*' ('Frailtie'). He usually thinks of a tree as an emblem of the cross ('Sacrifice', 202–3; 'Unkindnesse', 32; 'Longing', 32), and only wishes to be a tree or a flower because he would then 'grow | To fruit or shade' ('Affliction I', 56–60; 'Employment II', 21) and be 'extended to some good' ('Employment I'). His predilection for wood is directed to wooden objects, man-made, like the boxes, chests, and cabinets he so lovingly mentions. Vaughan alone had an emotional approach to vegetation,[14] an animistic experience that allowed him to 'feel | That God is true as herbs unseen | Put on their youth and green' ('Starre'). He alone durst assert that 'th' herb he treads knows much, much more' than man ('Constellation', 28). He alone was moved by the 'strange resentment after death' of wood wasting

> all senseless, cold and dark;
> Where not so much as dreams of light may shine,
> Nor any thought of greenness, leaf or bark.
>
> ('The Timber')

The analogical imagination only was at work in the Biblical parable which suggested 'The Seed growing secretly', but the poem achieves the perfect fusion of the sensible and the spiritual through the emotion awakened in the poet's soul by the actual life of the seed underground: 'Dear, secret *Greenness*! nurst below | Tempests and windes, and winter-nights'. The notion of 'sympathy', still regarded as scientific truth, was commonly used by seventeenth-century poets, but it was not with Vaughan a mere source of conceits or intellectual perplexity. As Elizabeth Holmes rightly pointed out, 'he not only believed with the Hermetists in the "tye of bodies", but he felt the tie; and the expression of his sense of kinship with the creatures of Nature leaves a curious impression in the reader's mind of a tie as strong as the physical or even the uterine link forged before consciousness in the "wombe of things".'[15]

The pervasive water-symbolism is related to the feeling for life and growth expressed in the symbols of vegetation. Vaughan had a Virgilian love of running waters and springs, evidenced by

---

[14] Natural images, of course, were charged with symbolism; to 'convey the brightness of the glory of God' and celebrate Christ as the 'Root' of spiritual life, the Cambridge Platonist Peter Sterry resorted to the same images as Vaughan: tree, plant, branch, sap, flower (pp. 64, 169, 179, 183, etc., in *Peter Sterry, Platonist and Puritan*, ed. Vivian de Sola Pinto, Cambridge, 1934).

[15] *Henry Vaughan and the Hermetic Philosophy* (1932; New York, 1967), 25.

both his profane and religious poems.[16] That a Christian poet should wish to drink from 'living springs', or 'living wells' as 'sources' of spiritual life is not surprising, but he insistently italicizes these recurrent words, and italics with Vaughan, as Blunden observed, can be meaningful. A deeper link may be suspected: the oneiric imagination associates water with the past and the author of 'The Retreate' may have longed for an immersion in the past.

Dew was not merely attractive to his imagination as a symbol of divine grace. Herbert sharply distinguished between the liquid dew that 'doth ev'ry morning fall' and the spiritual dew 'for which grasse cannot call' ('Grace'). When Vaughan cries 'My dew, my dew! my early love, | My souls bright food',[17] the metaphor for grace becomes suggestive of a substantial affinity, especially when one remembers the emotion aroused by the image of Jesus wandering by night: 'When my Lords head is fill'd with dew, and all | His locks are wet with the clear drops of night' ('Night'). Dew certainly stirred the poet's material imagination. He loved in it the union of liquidity and coolness. He did not congeal it as Marvell, nor did he see it, like Crashaw, as a collection of distinct pearls. Coolness and purity were allied in 'the chast kiss [of] the cool dew' ('Bee'). Among liquids, only watery substances had an attraction for him, unlike milk and blood so profusely flowing in the poetry of Crashaw.[18] Christ's blood shed for man could not be absent from his religious poetry, but his imagination spontaneously turned it into dew and water, refreshing his 'yielding leaves' as if he were a plant: 'Thy bloud | Too, is my Dew, and springing wel' ('Disorder *and* frailty').

Beauty, like purity, is an essential characteristic of Vaughan's

---

[16] The epigraph of *Olor Iscanus*, 'Flumina Amo . . .', was borrowed from the *Georgics*. See 'To the River Isca'; 'Search', 70; 'Dawning', 33; 'Shepheards', etc.

[17] 'Seed growing secretly'; cf. 'Mount of Olives', 24–5; 'Retirement', 25–6; 'Love and Discipline', 7–10.

[18] On Crashaw, see Ch. 8. 'Blood' with Vaughan is positive when life-giving: 'O how it *Blouds*, | And *Spirits* all my Earth' ('Morning-Watch'); cf. Thomas Vaughan, *Lumen de Lumine*: the Star-Soul is 'compounded of the aether and a bloody, fiery, spirited earth'; *Works*, ed. Waite (London, 1919), 293. Vaughan condemns bloodspilling: 'Ad Posteros', *The Mount of Olives* (*Works*, I. 167), 'Righteousness', 'Abels blood'. Unlike most Baroque poets, he never revels in evocations of Christ's bloody sacrifice.

world. Donne very rarely called attention to beauty and George Herbert only offered some images of prettiness. With Vaughan all natural objects—groves and fields, springs and rivers, mounts and hills, rainbows and stars—are radiant with beauty and 'beauteous shapes, we know not why, | Command and guide the eye' ('Starre'): Donne's maps and Herbert's pulleys only commanded the attention of the mind. This feeling for sensuous beauty is in harmony with Vaughan's allegiance to Christian Platonism and his preference for natural theology analysed in Chapter 13. Aesthetic emotion in spiritual natures becomes an intuition of transcendence: the light of Creation is but the shadow of God, *umbra Dei*. The contemplation of the created world feeds the poet's dream of Eden, his nostalgia for a diviner world, meditating 'what transcendent beauty shall be given to all things in that eternall World, seeing this transitory one is so full of Majesty and freshnesse'.[19] The 'gazing soul' is therefore invited to dwell on 'the living works' of God 'And in those weaker glories spy | Some shadow of eternity' ('Retreate').[20]

[19] *The World Contemned, Works*, I. 326.
[20] Vaughan, like Milton, inclines to delineate what surmounts the reach of human sense 'By lik'ning spiritual to corporal forms', as when the ray of God illumines his mind: 'So have I known some beauteous *Paisage* rise | In suddain flowers and arbours to my Eies' ('Mount of Olives').

CHAPTER 8

Richard Crashaw

Everything is or tends to be solid in Donne's, George Herbert's, even Marvell's worlds of imagination; nothing is in Crashaw's world, where everything is either liquid or hovering on the brink of dissolution or metamorphosis. Water and air, light and fire are its elements. But the fluids privileged by his sensibility are organic: milk and blood. Symbolic (since he addresses Hope), yet revealing is the poet's unquenchable thirst for the milk coming from a woman's breast: 'Pande sinus: sitiens laboro' ('Spes Diva, salve'). There seems to be a correspondence between this craving and his desire to lose himself. In his self-centredness Donne sought to make his own what he touched, grasped, or caressed; but one becomes what one absorbs,[1] and in sacred, as in natural, ebriety, one ceases to belong to oneself. To drink milk from the breast is to fill oneself with a desired substance and the otherness of the person loved. 'Two sister-Seas of virgins Milke' are more than Caesar's birthright ('Nativity Hymne', st. 11). Hence Crashaw's recurring dream of 'milky fonts' ('Infant Martyrs') and 'milky rivers' along the 'milky way' ('Weeper', st. 4; 'Assumption', 6).

In Christian symbolism Jesus is 'the well of living Waters' ('On the bleeding wounds'); but on the holy cross, coming from his breast like milk, 'streames of life' 'Flow in an amorous floud | Of WATER wedding BLOOD'.[2] The poet harps upon the bloody theme on all occasions, the Circumcision as well as the Crucifixion. Blood may be dropped from a wound like a tear ('On the wounds of our crucified Lord'), or turn into rivers and

---

[1] Catholic theology even makes it a principle of holy communion: 'Cette nourriture spirituelle ne se transforme pas en celui qu'elle nourrit, mais elle a au contraire la propriété d'assimiler à elle-même celui qui la mange' (*Dictionnaire de Théologie Catholique*, t. III, c. 509).

[2] 'Vexilla Regis', st. ii; this image is not in the Latin hymn.

become a 'Red Sea' or a 'generall flood' ('Bleeding wounds',
25–8). This blood is always to be 'drunk',[3] or sucked like milk,
and this spiritual thirst has all the urgency of a physical need:

> O let me suck the wine
> So long of this chast vine
> Till drunk of the dear wounds, I be
> A lost Thing to the world, as it to me.

> ('Sancta Maria Dolorum')

Crashaw is not attracted to clear water like Vaughan: his
channels, streams, and seas are hyperboles meant to describe the
flow of human milk, blood, or tears. Eyes sweat out tears as
wounds exude blood and paps secrete milk. The water of
baptism, like the water which refuses to wash Pilate's hands,
turns to tears.[4] Tears, of course, had inspired many conceits, but
no poet had spoken of their 'watry Eloquence' ('Upon the Death
of a Gentleman') with this kind of sensuous relish of their liquid
substance though 'their cadence is Rhetoricall' in this poem as
well as in 'The Weeper' and 'The Teare'.

The miracle of water turning to wine was three times celebrated by Crashaw.[5] Equally miraculous seem the manifold
metamorphoses of Mary Magdalene's tears into milk, into wine
or dew, drops of amber, or sap of 'the Balsame-sweating bough'
('Weeper'). They can be changed also into apparently hard
substances—crystal, pearls, gold, silver—but they only borrow
their brilliance, not their hardness, when we hear of 'Thawing
Christall', 'Warm silver showres' (st. i, xxi). They may be
'gems',[6] but of the first 'water':

> A watry Diamond; from whence
> The very Terme, I think, was found
> The water of a *Diamond*.

> ('The Teare')

---

[3] 'Our Lord in his Circumcision', 7; '*Heus conviva! bibin'?*' The metaphorical
use of 'thirst' was present in the liturgical '*Adoro Te*' (st. vi: 'tam sitio'), but
Crashaw's elaboration of it turns 'signs' into 'sensations'.

[4] 'In aquam baptismi', 'On the water of our Lords Baptism', 'To Pontius wash-
ing'.

[5] 'Aquae in vinum versa', 'Ad Christum, de aqua in vinum versa', 'Thou water
turn'st to Wine'.

[6] 'Each blest drop', 'Rich Lazarus', 'O these wakefull wounds'.

This tear will further change into a star, but a trembling star about to fall, a drop of dew or sweat in a rose, a juicy grape, the 'watry Blossome' of the vine, before becoming 'an eye of Heaven', a metamorphosis also suffered by the soap bubble— *ocellulus* (136)—in the Latin poem 'Bulla', an epitome of the poet's universe. For this bubble, born like Venus 'in the midst of the foam' (11), is liquid as well as airy: it flows (29) and swims as if drunk (34), it contains wandering streams (43), water, waves, and milky rivers (68–75).

Fire, like air in the myth of 'Arion', is always wedded to water. Not torrid or consuming heat, for Crashaw dreams of the gentle warmth of the maternal breast and milk, of a 'rarely-temper'd kisse' that 'Warmes in the one, cooles in the other' ('Nativity Hymne', st. 11). The Pentecostal fire falls from a cloud with the softness of rain ('Quae vehit auratos nubes dulcissima nimbos?') and paradoxically a flame has 'brighter beames' when 'quench't' ('Her eyes flood lickes his feet'). In the eye of Mary Magdalene the poet sees only 'a moist spark' ('Teare'). St Teresa, however, revealed the intensity of light and fire to her devotee, but her influence did not change his mode of sensibility, which had always called for 'liquid love' ('Joh: 13: 34.', 'Sic magis in numeros'). The fire of mystic desire or ecstasy is still expressed by 'thirsts of love' for 'draughts of intellectual day', or a 'draught of liquid fire', drunk in 'brim-fill'd Bowles' ('Flaming heart', 97–100) and the saint herself is a 'Fair floud of holy fires' ('Apologie').

Each thing in this world seems to have a precarious existence and all things tend to interfuse, like the ever-changing reflections in the 'rainbow' and the 'lovely chaos' of the bubble, which now 'grows red with green' and now 'grows green with red', so that, 'all colours being seen, no colour is seen' in these 'wandering visions'.[7] All things are a-tremble: drops of dew or water, tears, colours, day and light, even panellings.[8] In this universe the very substance of things seems uncertain. The bubble, which is the image of this poetic world, includes all fluid elements—waves, fire, and air—and yet is 'nothing': 'O

---

[7] 'Bulla', 21, 42, 88–9, 64–5. The rainbow is 'Iris lubrica', at once slippery, moving, and deceiving.

[8] 'Weeper', st. 7; 'A drop, one drop'; 'Teare', st. 6; 'Bulla', 108; 'Votiva Domus Petrensis', 20, 28.

sum (scilicet) O nihil' ('Bulla', 149–51). Yet this world does not evaporate into thin air like Prospero's pageant: [9] it always melts or thaws into liquid substances. That is why shapes and colours, though changing, have the strange distinctness of an aquatic landscape: nothing is blurred or hazy.

As there is no air in this world,[10] there is no emptiness, hence no distance. This focus on the foreground and lack of perspective may remind us of Donne and Herbert. But the latter project solid objects through a dense space. There is no sense of space in Crashaw's imagination of movement. A fluid, flowing, or gliding motion is, of course, different from a dynamic, brusque, or instantaneous impulse. But an even more important difference is the absence of a definite orientation in a physical or geometric space. Crashaw's favourite Latin epithet is *vagus*;[11] it describes a movement which has no direction, no goal, no guide mark: 'wandering' is its essence. It may be the 'trembling' already observed. We never notice a 'progress', only a 'flowing', we know not whither, of streams and rivers, drops, tears, or stars; often a flowing into one another or a final gathering into a 'general flood' ('On the bleeding wounds'). There is no one-way current and no law of gravity. 'Upwards thou doest weepe' ('Weeper'), of course, is a conceit, but it is hardly sensed as a miracle by a reader immersed in this world. This poetry is too intellectual to invite an oneiric interpretation, yet it conveys an intuition of 'pure' movement when Crashaw evokes, in terms at once concrete and abstract, a melting of the year 'into a weeping motion' ('Weeper', st. 16). This fusion of movement, liquidity, and continuity is also an abolition of temporality.

Temporality requires a distinction between past, present, and future. Even the perception of the instant implies a consciousness of being poised between past and future in ordinary experience, though it may seem to give access to eternity in moments of highest intensity. Unlike Donne and Herbert, Crashaw,

---

[9] Prospero's term, 'melted' (*Tempest*, IV. i. 150), indicates dissolution, not liquefaction.

[10] The bubble is described as air and there is air *inside* it, but the poet is not interested in the air on which it floats: 'Bulla', 122, 149.

[11] It recurs in 'Bulla', 22, 48, 59, 67, 100, 125, 145, but also in 'Veris descriptio', 35, 51, though the theme did not call for it.

despite his raptures, shows no intuition of such 'instants'. Nor
is he given to retrospection like Vaughan. In relating past events
he commonly relies on the narrative present, for he is concerned
with the immediate impact of the emotion excited, as in
'Musicks Duell' and the 'Teresa' poems. In the 'Hymne' the
episodes of her life are retraced in the future tense, but this
rhetorical future does not create a sense of expectation as in the
poetry of Vaughan: Crashaw's imagination is usually looking
forward, but only to an immediate future, the swelling of an
emotion which keeps enlarging or intensifying. The poet places
no interval between a hope and its realization. The distance
between the present and the future is blurred in his celebration
of a '(supposed) Mistress': 'Her whose just Bayes, | My future
hopes can raise, | A trophie to her present praise'. Hope itself
becomes an imaginary present:

> Sweet *Hope*! kind cheat! faire falacy! by thee
> We are not where, or what wee bee,
> But what, and where wee would bee: thus art thou
> Our absent presence, and our future now.

('On Hope')

Living in a present world of love and adoration this Christian
poet was not inspired by the theme of the end of time, of
Doomsday, so prominent, though differently, in the poems of
Donne, Herbert, and Vaughan.[12] Change, too, can be independent of time for beings and things change in this world without
'becoming'. They are not transformed by the incessant renewal
of nature, so deeply felt by Spenser and other Renaissance poets.
They undergo instant metamorphoses of the same nature as the
transubstantiation in which Crashaw, alone among the
Metaphysicals, came to believe. We have no sense of duration in
his universe.

Since this poetry discloses no intuition of the instant, nor of
duration, nor of the distance between the present and the past
or the future, what then is its relation to time? In poems like
'The Weeper' or 'The Teare' we find a chain of discontinuous
impressions without any logical or temporal progress. This was

---

[12] It only appears in the paraphrase of the *Dies Irae* and at the close of the
hymn 'To the Name of Jesus'.

common in compositions of this type, but longer poems which retrace the life of Teresa or the events of the Nativity were hardly composed differently. These impressions are like musical notes, now in accord, now in dissonance, played on a single theme. But a piece of music creates an ordered 'time'. Pure 'duration' is best experienced not as a flow, but as the stationary rocking of a sea-swell: it has no orientation, no beginning and no end. 'Time', as here understood, comes into being with the first act, the first movement forward, the first words—*fiat lux*—the first chord struck in music. 'Time' introduces death into the timeless stagnancy of duration; but a death which is the end of time, whether the 'time' of our world or the space of time allotted to a piece of music. Music seems to give access to eternity—or at least allows us to escape from the Sartrian nausea[13]—because it triumphs over the formlessness of duration by a rhythmic succession of notes ending on a final chord. The last chord tends to become the moment of greatest intensity since it is the moment when, as we were about to enter eternity, 'time' is abolished and we lapse back into duration with the sweet regret of a failed approach like the mystic coming out of his ecstasy.

Before turning to 'Musicks Duell', which might be a mere mimetic exercise, the profound identity between the genius of Crashaw and the musical aspiration may be again best perceived in the variations he played on the theme of mystical death:

> Of a DEATH, in which who dyes
> Loves his death and dyes again.
> And would for ever so be slain.
> And lives, & dyes; and knowes not why
> To live, But that he thus may never leave to DY.

> ('Teresa Hymn', *Carmen Deo Nostro* version)

Here is no mere counterpoint of various impressions as in 'The Weeper'. In a unique heart-throb emotion rises to a paroxysm, subsides, and rises again. The climax reached in an élan

---

[13] J.-P. Sartre, *La Nausée* (Paris, 1938), 36–7. Sartre opposed 'la durée de la musique' and our 'temps misérable', but I choose to invert the terms, for 'la durée' best expresses the common experience of formless duration.

heightened by repetition is death, for all intense delight 'existe pour mourir'. The poetic rhythm here is both erotic and musical, for music has its fulfilment in reaching out toward the silence out of which it springs and to which it returns. And since music only exists through this impulse and expectation, one may say that music is heard in a 'future NOW' (Crashaw's definition of hope); not a distant future divorced from the present, but a future which is at once the horizon and the depth of a present sensation, the very essence of its being.

This may be the reason why Crashaw so often chooses the mode of anticipation in narrative. Narration in the past tense allows musical divisions, but they only make dead music. Action in the narrative present is only an unforeseeable accident. Placing himself initially in Teresa's childhood or at the 'advent' of the Magi, the poet can announce the saint's mystic deaths or the sun's eclipse in the future tense, thus fashioning a 'musical time' which is at once a creation and the announcement of its abolition. The construction of 'The Weeper', 'The Teare', 'On the bleeding wounds' is not essentially different: an image succeeds an image, a sensation succeeds a sensation as in a sequence of chords, until the poet exclaims: 'I counted wrong; there is but one, | But ô that one is all o're' (*Poems*, p. 102). This gathering of the preceding chords in a finale which is the consummation of repeated efforts is paralleled by the moment when Teresa's 'DEATHS, so numerous, | Shall all at last dy into one'.

'Musicks Duell' is not a mere exercise in imitative harmony like Dryden's 'Ode to Saint Cecilia'. There is a correspondence between its lyrical beauty and Crashaw's modes of imagination and sensibility. Music here is not aerial as in *The Tempest*: it comes from and reaches a soul 'Bathing in streames of liquid Melodie' (68). The 'sleeke' and 'lubricke' throat of the nightingale (37, 64) is an 'ever-bubling spring' (66) which gives out a 'slippery song' in 'wav'd notes' (60–1). The 'torrent of a voyce' (45) becomes a 'forward streame' (86); the singing bird 'opes the floodgate, and lets loose a Tide | Of streaming sweetnesse' (93–4). The musician's fingers 'struggle with the vocall threads, | Following those little rills, hee sinkes into | A Sea of *Helicon*', and 'The Lutes light *Genius* now does proudly rise, | Heav'd on the surges of swolne Rapsodyes' (122–36). The poem is composed of variations widening like concentric circles on the surface of water: the lute player's and the nightingale's melodies are at first alternately described in batches of 5, then 7 and 10 lines (17–21, 21–5; 27–33, 34–43); 13 lines are devoted to a more vigorous effort of the man, who seeks to close 'the sweet quarrell, rowsing all | Hoarce, shrill at once' (54–5). A second movement of greater amplitude (56–104) is taken up by the bird's song; the third and last is the triumphant reply of the musician (105–56). In each case the conclusion of the movement expresses the poet's own aspirations. The bird's soul is 'ravisht' and 'so pour'd | Into loose extasies'; the 'blest soule' of the lute player is 'snatcht out at his Eares | By a strong Extasy'. Besides, one may note the same rise and fall as in the description of St Teresa's rapture, the same acceleration in the rush of the music toward a finale and a silent close, of the sensations toward their climax and expiration, of the rapture toward its culmination and death:

> In many a sweet rise, many as sweet a fall
> A full-mouth *Diapason* swallowes all.

'Musicks Duell' was written ten years at least before the hymn 'To the Name of Jesus' and its splendid 'Fitt-tun'd Harmony' in which Nature and Art conspire (50, 69–71). In the different imagery and the Platonic allusion to the 'Architects of Intellectuall Noise' (77) one perceives again a 'purification' of the pleasure expected from sense impressions. Yet muted erotic suggestions survive in the evocation of the Day-break of Christ's Dawn: 'Thou | Womb of Day! | Unfold thy fair Conceptions' (161–3). The lands and the poet are still 'thirsty' for 'Golden Showres' (130) or 'balmy showrs' (169). The poet makes clear his wish to gather all the strains of his music and all his delights in 'An universal SYNOD of All sweets' (176).

Crashaw's sensibility aspired to a fusion of sounds and sensations and mystic deaths. This 'All-imbracing SONG' aims at mixing 'All your many WORLDS, Above, | And loose them into ONE of Love' (86–7). This is different from Donne's aspiration to transcend a particular experience and reach an intuition of eternity or infinity; different too from Herbert's perception of a moment, a day, or a life *sub specie aeternitatis*: in each case there was a mental leap from one plane of reality to another for their notion of the eternal or the infinite was not attained by the mere 'embracing' of multiple instants or worlds. What we find in Crashaw is not an intuition of a present eternity, but a musical preconception of an eternity always about to be, an ever-swelling tide of ever more high-pitched sensations until the Multiple seems to become One. Time to him is, indeed, a liquid element which 'shall be pour'd out | Into Eternity' ('Upon the Death of Mr. Herrys'). The prospect of this final effusion appealed most intensely to his imagination. Hope was to him an 'earlier Heaven' for, by hope, 'Young *Time* is taster to Eternity' ('On Hope', 52). The end of time is the realization of Hope (56–60):

> Till in the lap of Loves full noone
> It falls, and dyes: oh no, it melts away
> As doth the dawne into the day:
> As lumpes of Sugar lose themselves, and twine
> Their subtile essence with the soule of Wine.

Time, too, suffers a mystic death into eternity; it 'melts', loses itself in it, but its 'subtile essence' survives in a kind of mixture. There is no ontic discontinuity between time and eternity, for the rapturous experience is an extension of the moment when time is dissolved: a moment at once musical, erotic, and mystic. The most intense joy will not arise from the intuition or contemplation of the Eternal and the Unchangeable, but from the ultimate élan of a love dying like a spent wave on the shore. With a series of sounds music creates its own time; with a series of distinct sensations or renewed deaths Crashaw creates his substitute for eternity: 'the long | And everlasting series of a deathlesse SONG' ('To the Name of Jesus', 85).

In the 'Epiphanie Hymn' (26–31) the poet seeks to give a philosophical definition of the deity by first restating a ready-made commonplace of the Neoplatonic tradition: 'All-circling point. All centring sphear, | The world's one round, Aeternall year'. The metaphysical significance, however, is muddled in the next lines, which conjure up an image void of meaning and yet disturbingly precise:

> Whose full & all unwrinkled face
> Nor sinks nor swells with time or place;
> But every where & every while
> Is One Consistent solid smile.

This disharmony between abstract thought and its concrete expression is not unexpected in a poet whose pre-eminently musical sensibility seeks to convey the emotions aroused in him rather than define them. Crashaw will at once project inner feelings into images and weave these images into a tissue soliciting our visual imagination. His failure to achieve an interpenetration of the abstract and the concrete in the same way as Donne or Herbert will be studied in Chapter 12.

CHAPTER 9

Andrew Marvell and Edward Herbert

Marvell's imagination, unlike Vaughan's, is disinclined to rememoration.[1] Like Donne and Herbert, he lives his experiences in the present, but in a mobile rather than static instant. Behind him there is no expanse inviting retrospection, only the threatening approach of death chasing him. Hence this striking image of a man dispossessed of his past, hemmed in by his own future:

> But at my back I alwaies hear
> Times winged Charriot hurrying near;
> And yonder all before us lye
> Desarts of vast Eternity.
> Thy Beauty shall no more be found;
> Nor, in thy marble Vault, shall sound
> My ecchoing Song . . .
>
> ('To his Coy Mistress')

Our ultimate future is a tomb in a desert; the only reality for us is this moving present. Within our life, the future is not something we should expect or long for at a distance, as Vaughan does; it must be 'antedated':

> So we win of doubtful Fate;
>   And, if good she to us meant,
> We that Good shall antedate,
>   Or, if ill, that Ill prevent.
>
> ('Young Love')

> Oh sweet! oh sweet! How I my future state
> By silent thinking, Antidate.
>
> ('Thyrsis and Dorinda')

---

[1] The present tense appears even in narrative: cf. 'Bermudas', 'Appleton House', st. xiii ff.

More quietly than Donne's, Marvell's 'presentness' can invite the creation of a definite 'situation' in a precise setting. 'The Garden' opens with general considerations, but they are immediately followed by a clear indication of the 'here and now': 'Fair quiet, have I found thee *here*', 'What wond'rous Life in *this* I lead!' (my italics). 'Upon Appleton House' moves more amply from description and narrative to present pictures and emotions as the contemplator progresses through the estate and the day: 'And now to the Abbyss I pass' (xlvii), 'And now the careless Victors play' (liv), 'But I, retiring from the Flood' (lxi), etc.[2] 'To his Coy Mistress' is not a mere illustration of a hedonistic theme; from the opening apostrophe about '*this* coyness' it is the creation of a climactic moment with the three times repeated 'now', when the lovers face each other in the culmination of their desire.

Yet Marvell's poetry, though mostly written in the present tense, is less dramatic than Donne's.[3] His pastoral or religious dialogues are opportunities for wit rather than the creation of a situation. Being less self-centred, he is willing to give us 'pictures' in which the descriptive present in the poet's absence no longer conveys a unique moment of experience and takes on a universal value as in 'On a Drop of Dew'.[4] Even when the 'instant' is recorded, it is not attended by an intuition of being or permanence as in some lyrics of Donne and Herbert. Time, to Marvell, is always 'flowing Time', not 'pour'd out | Into eternity' as a river into the sea,[5] but a 'Watry Maze' which closes upon the sinking man in the 'First Anniversary' (1–6):

> Like the vain Curlings of the Watry maze,
> Which in smooth streams a sinking Weight does raise;
> So Man, declining alwayes, disappears
> In the weak Circles of increasing Years;
> And his short Tumults of themselves Compose,
> While flowing Time above his Head does close.

Marvell's imagination was attuned to the Heraclitean view of reality. As he never experienced the fullness of being in the

---

[2] See also stanzas lxvii, lxxi, lxxv, lxxix, lxxxii, lxxxxvii.

[3] Anne Ferry pointed out that Marvell is often closer to Jonson in this respect (*All in War with Time* (Cambridge, Mass., 1975), 199–201).

[4] In 'Eyes and Tears' and 'The Gallery' the speaker's voice, heard at the beginning or the close, hardly changes the objective and atemporal nature of the poem.

[5] As in Crashaw's 'Upon the Death of Mr Herrys'.

instant, he sought to conquer time by controlling its pace. A comparison between Donne's poems of triumphant love and 'To his Coy Mistress' will bring out the difference. For the earlier poet time can be suspended and abolished by love-making. Marvell assumes the slow, indifferent pace of clock time can be hurried by the lovers' passion if they choose:[6]

> Rather at once our Time devour,
> Than languish in his slow-chapt pow'r.
> Let us roll all our Strength, and all
> Our sweetness, up into one Ball:
> And tear our Pleasures with rough strife,
> Thorough the Iron gates of Life.
> Thus, though we cannot make our Sun
> Stand still, yet we will make him run.

Cromwell will be praised for ' 'Tis he the force of scatter'd Time contracts' ('First Anniversary', 13–15).[7]

Yet this acceleration or crowding of time did not meet the poet's deeper longing. In the slow growth of plants he found an image of time freed from the fever and the fret. In 'The Garden', where 'all Flow'rs and all Trees do close | To weave the Garlands of repose', even desire has no other end than fixity, as when 'Apollo hunted Daphne so, | Only that she might Laurel grow'. Time is certainly suspended when the Mind annihilates 'all that's made | To a green Thought in a green Shade', for the single impression invading the poet's consciousness will not allow him to be conscious of any change. The very sense of duration becomes a sense of permanence for the world as a green thought is not a flux: it is felt to exist and subsist. This is Edenic time,[8] and unsurprisingly the scene becomes an earthly paradise (st. viii): the threat of death or corruption is removed. In this vegetable world the hours reckoned by the plants and

---

[6] Poulet argued that this was 'an act of fixation and determination' of the 'moment' rolled 'into one Ball' (*Les métamorphoses du cercle* (Paris, 1961), 37–8); but the Ball here is the united bodies of the lovers, not the moment.

[7] Ann Berthoff later wrote that the theme of the Cromwell poems is 'the conquest of time' (*The Resolved Soul: A Study of Marvell's Major Poems* (Princeton, 1970), 55).

[8] L. S. Marcus later argued that the poet tries to regain the timelessness of Eden in loving children, for whom time has no meaning (*Childhood and Cultural Despair* (Pittsburgh, 1978), 219); on the significance of childhood see Ch. 14, p. 252.

flowers no longer measure the fluid elapsing of existence but a compact permanence of being in the natural world. The last stanza on the sundial would be a weak conclusion if the reader failed to discern this metamorphosis of time:

> How well the skilful Gardner drew
> Of flow'rs and herbes this Dial new;
> Where from above the milder Sun
> Does through a fragrant Zodiack run;
> And, as it works, th'industrious Bee
> Computes its time as well as we.
> How could such sweet and wholsome Hours
> Be reckon'd but with herbs and flow'rs!

When time has become consubstantial with all living things, it is no longer a disease diminishing their vitality: it is, indeed, 'whole' as well as 'wholesome'. Yet, within this untainted time the poet has no sense of eternity. When the question is raised in 'Thyrsis and Dorinda'—'But in Elizium how do they | Pass Eternity away?' (my italics)—he seems unconscious of any difference between the 'passage' of time and an eternity described as *vitae tota simul et perfecta possessio*.[9]

In his apprehension of space as in his perception of time Marvell shows some initial resemblance with Donne and George Herbert before parting company with them. He often brings the object close to the observer: 'He makes the Figs our mouth to meet; | And throws the Melon at our feet' ('Bermudas'; cf. 'Garden', st. v). Attention is focused on foreground objects clearly detached against a flat background: 'He hangs in shades the Orange bright, | Like golden Lamps in a green Night' ('Bermudas'). The meadow described as an unfathomable 'Abyss' is not seen as a wide expanse of tall grass waving in the sun: Marvell's imagination chooses to dive into it, giving us an experience of close environment and proximity with the 'Grashoppers' and 'Flow'rs' ('Appleton', 369–84). The forest, too, 'stretches still so closely wedg'd | As if the Night within were hedg'd' ('Appleton', 503–4). When the poet has to evoke a wide 'levell'd space', he circumscribes and narrows it by a comparison with the canvas of a painting or the '*Toril*', circular figures

---

[9] The definition of Boethius given by St Thomas, *Summa*, Ia, q. 10, art. 1.

embraced at a glance. A taste for clear images and a predilection for the close-up are allied. In Marvell's world the macroscopic and the microscopic vision may be superimposed:

> Such Fleas, as they approach the Eye,
> In Multiplying Glasses lye.
> They feed so wide, so slowly move,
> As *Constellations* do above.
>
> ('Appleton', st. lviii)

From this world of definite objects fluidity is banished, as from the worlds of Donne and George Herbert, but the privileged objects and substances are not the same. A distinction here must be drawn between the imagination of form and the imagination of matter. Bachelard's 'law of the four elements' is not a safe ground for a comparison beween different poets. To give an example, the predominance of 'air' is illustrated at once by Shelley and by Nietzsche, but one fails to discover a real kinship between the poet of *Epipsychidion* and the author of *Zarathustra*. Bachelard, of course, was aware of the differences and he distinguished the combination of 'cold, silence, and height' in Nietzsche from the association of 'softness, music, and light' in the Shelleyan imagination,[10] but these associations can hardly be considered as necessarily related to 'air': they only disclose the subjective disposition of an individual sensibility. Besides, Shelley's 'aerial' imagination was also attracted to water;[11] it responded to a 'quality', fluidity, which also characterized his style and prosody. A 'quality' may be found in different substances and sensations: otherwise would we feel that, besides fresh air and fresh water, there are fresh voices of children, fresh colours, fresh fragrances?

Marvell is at one with Donne and George Herbert in privileging hardness or density in substances and images. Music to him is 'the Mosaïque of the Air' ('Musicks Empire'). The sky is a solid 'Vault' whence 'rebounding' the Pilgrims' song 'may | Eccho' ('Bermudas'). Tears are 'Amber' or 'crystal' ('Nymph complaining', 100–2); they fall like 'Plummets', are weighed in 'Scales of either Eye'; their liquidity is, in a way, given 'form' when they 'melt in these Pendants' or fetter Christ's feet like 'liquid Chaines' ('Eyes and Tears'). A fountain is imprisoned

---

[10]   *L'Air et les Songes* (Paris, 1948), 161–2.   [11]   Ibid. 49.

'within the concave Shell' ('Clorinda and Damon'). Even when 'Cataracts' turn a meadow into a sea, attention is called not to the expanse of water but to the creatures swimming in it, or, when the waves are fallen, to the grass which 'Seems as green Silks but newly washt' ('Appleton House', 465–80, 625–8). We discover in Donne, Herbert, and Marvell a 'formal' analogy between their absence of interest in fluidity and their search for precision and firm delineation in both imagery and analysis; but differences appear in their choice of material substances.

Donne deals in maps and compasses, books and pictures, glass and tapers, rings and bracelets, beds and graves; all dry objects and substances. He seems to be fascinated by hair and bones, by the structure and excretions of the human body.[12] Herbert, as we have seen, is attracted to the dryness, scent, and warmth of wood. Marvell has his own distinctive preferences. He mostly chooses to evoke cold substances, metals, alabaster, crystal,[13] and he comes closest to Donne's famous compasses when he materializes a spiritual extension and the interposition of fate as the stretching of his soul and the driving of 'Iron wedges'.[14] But he alone seems to delight in a peculiar phenomenon: the conversion from a fluid to a solid state.[15] The culminating scene in 'Appleton House' (673–8) is the coming of the Halcyon, 'Flying betwixt the Day and Night':

> The viscous Air, wheres'ere She fly,
> Follows and sucks her Azure dy;
> The gellying Stream compacts below,
> If it might fix her shadow so;
> The stupid Fishes hang, as plain
> As *Flies* in *Chrystal* overt'ane.

The 'Drop of Dew' is 'congeal'd and chill'. The fountain in 'Damon the Mower' is 'gelid', like the strawberries in 'Appleton

---

[12] John Carey has called attention to this interest (*John Donne* (London, 1981), ch. 5). See n. 13 in Ch. 6.

[13] 'Nymph complaining', 28, 64, 120; 'Coy Mistress', 44; 'Definition of Love', 11, 17; 'Appleton House', 192, 636, 694.

[14] See also 'Dialogue between the Soul and Body', 1–8.

[15] In *Andrew Marvell, poète protestant* (Paris, 1997), 59, Claudine Raynaud called attention to the crystal imagery in the Book of Revelation, 21: 11, 22: 1. Marvell must have been aware of the religious connotations, yet crystal in his poetry is part of a distinctly personal image cluster.

House' (530). But the poet also enjoyed the moment when a
solid substance begins to melt, when fruits boil in 'The Sugars
uncorrupting Oyl' ('Appleton', 174) or 'crush their Wine' upon
his mouth ('Garden', 36). He liked 'Grass, with moister colour
dasht' ('Appleton', 627). Sensations had to be cool and wet, but
his mind cared for definiteness. As a poet he relied on liquid
consonants and clear vowels (e, i, u) to impart a lustrous moist-
ness to his verse, but a consonantal sharpness and a forcible
rhythm ensure a firmness of outline, never allowing the 'liquid'
sounds to flow or melt into indistinction. A single line—'And
therefore her Decrees of Steel' ('Definition of Love')—may
suggest this quality of the material imagination which becomes
a quality of style. Marvell's poetry, to use words applied by
Charles Du Bos to the prose of Gide, 'participates of two reigns,
the mineral and the liquid, but the latter is only collected in
ewers of crystal'.[16]

Edward Herbert of Cherbury

Any attempt to discover the deep-lying structures of Edward
Herbert's mind in his poetry is hazardous; not only because the
corpus is slender, but because of a lack of originality. Even in his
translations and paraphrases Crashaw showed a distinctive
style and created his own world of imagination. So did Marvell,
even while conforming to the decorum of several poetic genres.
Lord Herbert at times closely imitated some superficial characteristics of Donne's style—harshness, obscurity, scholastic or
erudite imagery—yet he was influenced by the Neoplatonic
philosophy of love. He seems to have had even more affinities
with the Court poet he called 'my witty Carew'; they both wrote
in the Petrarchan vein as well as in the new 'metaphysical' style.
How can we determine his individual perception of time?

His failure or disinclination to create a truly dramatic situation
may be a first indication. We have seen that he does not isolate a
moment of experience in order to introduce us into his consciousness. A particular circumstance is only a starting-point for a
discussion of a general subject or philosophic problem. The apos-

---

[16]   *Dialogue avec André Gide* (Paris, 1929), 3.

trophe 'To his Watch, when he could not sleep' and the
'Meditation upon his Wax-Candle burning out' invited the 'localization' and immediacy displayed by Donne and George Herbert
in many poems; but he did not avail himself of the opportunity
and handled the theme only as an emblem illustrating a general
truth. In the late poem entitled 'October 14. 1644' only the question 'What, is't not done?' seems to reflect a spontaneous utterance in the moment of experience. Though modelled on Donne's
Valedictions, 'Parted souls' soon strays from the problem of
immediate separation to the larger issue of the immortality of
love. Lord Herbert's best achievement, 'An Ode upon a Question
moved' is reminiscent of Donne's 'Extasie',[17] but the lover's argument here is not meant to bring about an immediate action like
the invitation 'To'our bodies turne we then', which implied a definite place and time. The philosophic demonstration seeks to allay
an anguish which is individual, but does not require a location in
a particular setting at a precise moment: it answers the general
question 'Whether Love should continue for ever?' Both the 'Ode'
and 'The Extasie' find the solution of a personal problem in
universal principles; yet to abstract the argument from its
dramatic context would work a deep change in Donne's poem,
whereas it would hardly alter the meaning and import of Lord
Herbert's Platonizing dialogue.

Furthermore, half a dozen poems only invite a comparison
with Donne's dramatic monologues. Lord Herbert usually does
not take a situation, nor even a state of mind, for a theme: he
offers what he himself calls 'A Description' or 'A Vision' of his
mistress, apostrophizes 'her Face', 'her Body', or 'her Mind',
'her Eyes' or 'her hair', shows her 'Combing her Hair', paints a
'Black Beauty' or a 'Brown Beauty', a 'Green-Sickness Beauty'
or 'The Sun-burn'd Exotique Beauty'. Such poems as 'Platonic
Love', 'The IDEA', 'An appeal to his hopes not to fail him' are
straightforward disquisitions. The predominance of descriptive
or philosophic themes cannot have been dictated by a particular perception of time or place, but it does betray the poet's lack
of interest in any kind of 'localization', spatial, temporal, or
even psychological, and proves in harmony with his usual mode
of thinking and imagining.

[17] See E. D. Hill, *Edward Lord Herbert of Cherbury* (Twayne, 1987), ch. 7.

To check this assumption we must again turn to his treatise *De Veritate*, which, indeed, reveals no concrete intuition of duration. The perception of time is assigned to distinct 'faculties': 'some are concerned with the present, others with the past, others with the future' (*De Veritate*, VIII. 272–5). The 'faculties' to Lord Herbert are, 'as it were, mental beams which thrust through the apertures of the senses and pick out the appropriate specific essences' of the different objects considered (IV. 109). This doctrine seems, in fact, to deny any continuity in the perception of time by our consciousness. Besides, the philosopher reduces the faculty concerned with the past to 'a kind of silent faith . . . in the authors, from which no one would withhold assent', a 'natural instinct' out of which our 'Common Notions arise'. He deliberately excludes from it 'memory and recollection'. Memory 'serves all the faculties', but is 'passive' and dominated by 'recollection' which 'draws out what the former has stored away'; it will 'vanish at death' for its objects are mortal (VIII. 237–8). He has obviously no experience of a spontaneous reliving of the bygone, and therefore, unlike Vaughan, no nostalgia of the past. The active faculty of 'recollection' in a way operates outside time, for it recalls 'the constant features of things', 'ideas imprinted by the mind or spirit' that 'exist for ever'. As to 'the faculty which relates to the future', Lord Herbert again divorces it from any experience of duration, or even distance, since he conceives of it as lifting the soul to a level of perception which opens the future as well as the past to our understanding (VIII. 238). Accordingly there is little difference between 'the faculties which refer to the past and the future' and the faculty 'corresponding to eternity', which 'gathers together the past, present, and future by means of the Common Notions'—again a purely intellectual approach rather than a living intuition (VIII. 274).

One may wonder what the perception of the present becomes in this system. Since the three dimensions of time are supposed to be related to distinct faculties, the present can only be apprehended as an 'instant of time', isolated and static. Time therefore cannot be imagined as a flux; the philosopher even rejects its traditional assimilation to movement.[18] An intuition of the

---

[18]   *De Veritate*, VIII. 273; cst. *Timaeus*, 37d and Vaughan's 'The World'.

instant is said to accompany the 'first modification from which external perception emerges' as 'a vague premonition, which anticipates the actual realisation of perception', an interesting observation suggested by 'a process of careful introspection' (VII. 208).

Though he may seem at one with Donne in reducing time to the dimension of the instant, Herbert confers no privilege on the present moment. The perception of it belongs 'to the animal part of our nature' and is unrelated to the 'faculty corresponding to eternity' (VIII; Carré, 274). In its ideal thinness the instant of the philosopher is very different from the dramatic moment which seems to roll up duration into one ball in some 'metaphysical' poems. As a static description of an object, or a meditation on an idea, Herbert's present tense is timeless and flat. His evocation of 'The first Meeting' with the beloved is made up of a series of discontinuous perceptions; none of them is invested with the unforgettable value of the moment 'When thou and I first one another saw'.[19] The only poem that takes time itself as its theme, 'To his Watch, when he could not sleep', describes the passage of the 'Uncessant Minutes' as a succession of disconnected 'short steps' which 'both divide and summ' our life, thus fragmented into moments. This impression is not contradicted by the uninterrupted syntactic progression which suggests the relentless pressure of time from the initial instant, 'Past a beginning', to the foreordained execution of the Decree. In the closing lines time does not merge in eternity: death occurs in the separate moment represented by a 'minute', and the 'Time' that dies 'in Eternity' is here a time made up of instants dying successively as so many distinct drops. For Lord Herbert time was essentially *number*, defined here and in the Latin poem 'For a Dyal' in words borrowed from mathematical operations: 'tell', 'divide', 'sum', 'numerous', 'addens', 'subtrahit', 'ratio', 'calculus'.

Eternity itself is not apprehended in a Donne-like intuition of the depth of the present moment or in the acts of imaginative contemplation which characterize Vaughan and Traherne. For the philosopher it is even hardly a concept since 'we can only faintly imagine the infinite and eternal after the analogy of the

---

[19] Donne's 'Anniversarie', 5; cf. Elegie XVI: 'By our first and fatall interview'.

finite and temporal'.[20] Lord Herbert's main concern is the permanence of being. The poet and the lover endeavour to prove the immortality of the soul in conjunction with the immortality of love ('Ode upon a Question moved', 65–132). But this assurance of immortality is gained through intellectual speculation, not attained in a privileged moment of experience as in some of the *Songs and Sonets*. Donne could rationalize this experience, resorting even to sophistry as in the close of 'The Good-Morrow', but the immediate intuition remained uppermost. Lord Herbert's arguing in comparison seems impersonal—an impersonality already noted in his objective analysis of the operations of the mind and the senses.

On the perception of space the philosopher is silent, though he is interested in the conditions of visual perception.[21] He only mentions the infinity of space in connection with the Infinity of God, linked with Omnipotence and Liberty (*De Veritate*, IX; Carré, 292). The poetic corpus is too slim to reveal a characteristic mode of apprehension; yet the gallery of static figures contemplated on a flat background without perspective suggests an indifference to distance in space as in time. The absence of any allusion to the new astronomy is surprising since the author of the *De Veritate* claimed to break new ground. Yet in his poems of aristocratic courtship his star-gazing into women's eyes inspired a beautiful image in the 'Ode upon a Question moved':

> This said, in her up-lifted face,
>   Her eyes, which did that beauty crown,
>   Were like two starrs, that having faln down,
> Look up again to find their place.

---

[20] *De Veritate*, III. 91, 104.

[21] *De Veritate*, VII. 213–14. His brief observations only relate to position and 'the differences of local movement'.

CHAPTER 10

Thomas Traherne

Traherne lived in space rather than in time for his mind took possession of space. He has celebrated all the senses; yet, as his brother Philip observed,[1] his deepest wish was to become 'All Ey'. His mode of vision was neither the near vision of Donne, nor the far vision of Vaughan: near and far were united in his self-reflexive mode of perception and instead of feeling 'rack[ed] to such a vast extent' like George Herbert, he could enjoy the presence of the most distant objects in his mind, a privilege already mentioned in *Select Meditations* where it was ascribed jointly to Love and to Sight (IV. 9).

Between the rival theories explaining sight by extramission or intromission Donne had hesitated (*Sermons*, IX. 247). Traherne apparently avails himself of both. In 'An Infant-Ey' the 'visiv Rays' are sent out, quicker than 'the sprightly Winds', and meet their object instantly. In 'My Spirit' (st. 2) the poet first asserts that the mind is present wherever it perceives its objects:

> It Acts not from a Centre to
> Its Object as remote,
> But present is, when it doth view,
> Being with the Being it doth note.

Plotinus had maintained that the form of the object is not imprinted on the soul, as Aristotle had assumed in the *De Anima* (II. 12). He claimed that the impression takes place where the object is; but, unlike Traherne, he argued that this was a means for the soul to perceive the 'distance' between itself and its object (*Enneads*, IV. vi. 1). Our Divine Philosopher is closer to Bergson and Whitehead, for whom the perceiving

---

[1] 'Dedication', 27. In *Select Meditations* Traherne asserted that 'the very substance of the soul is sight' (II. 92).

mind itself is 'immanent there'.[2] In fact, he expressed an experience anyone may share when looking unreflectingly at an
object: a very young child, as yet unaware of distance, will reach
out his hand to grasp what he desires, even though it might be
the far-off moon.

In 'My Spirit' (st. iii–iv) the sense of distance between the
mind and what it contemplates is even more decisively abol-
ished by the realization that 'An Object, if it were before | My
Ey, was by Dame Natures Law, | Within my Soul', so

> That all my Mind was wholy Evry where
> What ere it saw, twas ever wholy there;
> The Sun ten thousand Legions off, was nigh:
>   The utmost Star,
>   Tho seen from far,
> Was present in the Apple of my Eye.

The poet first declares the mind present everywhere, then
assumes that all things are present in the mind. This is not philosophically consistent, but it has a psychological coherence.
Traherne first expresses the sense of expansion felt in the
contemplation of distant objects, but his self-reflexivity reminds
him that he only perceives images formed in his eye, only thinks
ideas formed in his mind. Hence the final paradoxes combining
inwardness and expansion in the description of his mind (st. vi):

> A Strange Extended Orb of Joy,
>   Proceeding from within,
> Which did on evry side convey
> It self, and being nigh of Kin
>   To God did evry Way
> Dilate it self even in an Instant, and
> Like an Indivisible Centre Stand
> At once surrounding all Eternitie.

This is not a purely intellectual illumination revealing the
Platonic world of ideas to the infant soul as in 'The Preparative'
(st. ii–iii) where the powers of the soul 'Themselvs soon in their
Objects Image cloath' (st. vi). In 'My Spirit' the allusion to the

---

[2] As noted by the philosopher Jean Wahl: 'Mon esprit est à l'endroit qu'il
contemple, comme le dira Bergson. Il est "immanent là-bas" comme le dira
Whitehead' (*Poèmes de la Félicité* (Paris, 1951), 128).

presence of the star 'in the Apple of my Eye' (62) implies that the poet's culminating feeling of spiritual omnipresence originates in the perception of the material world.

This perception is conceived as 'immanent' in the scholastic sense, that is wholly inside the subject, and yet present with the object; the object is seen as remote, yet within the mind (st. iv): 'The Act was Immanent, yet there. | The Thing remote, yet felt even here.' If the distance is real, the thing is outside the mind, which only holds its representation. But should the sense of distance prove subjective, things might have no existence outside the mind. This was the dilemma solved by Berkeley's idealism:

Thirdly, it will be objected that we see things actually without or at a distance from us, and which consequently do not exist in the mind, it being absurd that those things which are seen at the distance of several miles, should be near to us as our own thoughts. In answer to this, I desire it may be considered, that in a dream we do oft perceive things as existing at a great distance off, and yet for all that, those things are acknowledged to have their existence only in the mind.[3]

Traherne did not give a clear philosophical answer, but his reflection, we know, was also guided by the remembrance of oneiric impressions. The child takes dream images for things and the adult mind in its self-reflexivity can impart to the world a double reality, outside and inside the self:

> Of it I am th'inclusive Sphere,
> It doth entire in me appear
> As well as I in it: It givs me Room,
> Yet lies within my Womb.
>
> ('Misapprehension', 62–5)

This inner presence of the world was fascinating for an egocentric consciousness and the poet exultantly exclaimed: 'The World was more in me, then I in it' ('Silence', 81).

Traherne's 'idealism' may have been suggested by the *Pimander* (V. i),[4] but his anticipation of Berkeley's idealism

---

[3] *Principles of Human Knowledge*, *Works*, ed. Luce and Jessop (London, 1949), II. 58; cf. *New Theory of Vision*, *Works*, I. 171.

[4] In his edition of the *Hermetica* (Oxford, 1924), II. 158, W. Scott observed: 'As here stated the doctrine resembles Berkeley's idealism. In the world of sense, *esse*

should be qualified. Gladys Wade pointed out that he was more interested in the inverted formula, *percipi est esse* (*Thomas Traherne*, Princeton and London, 1944, 173). This again is only partly true. Traherne extols the human mind's power of creation in the poems entitled 'Thoughts', but this is no more than a flight of the imagination in the expanding universe revealed by the new astronomy: 'new Rooms, and Spaces more, | Beyond all these' ('Nature', 71–2). Besides, this activity of our imagination is bound to cease when the whole of reality will be displayed in the beatific vision at the end of time: 'Nor shall we then invent | Nor alter Things; but with content | All in their places see' ('Consummation', 49–51).

Traherne's insistent message should rather be phrased *non percipi est non esse*. He seems to start from the common experience that 'Things are indifferent; nor giv | Joy of themselves, nor griev'. Since a thing 'can't affect but as it doth appear' ('The Inference I', 9–20), '*Things tru* affect not, while they are unknown'. Our representations, called 'Thoughts' (images as well as concepts), alone affect us, and the poet therefore claims that 'these are Reall things when shewn' (ibid. 23). 'To perceive is to be' only as far as our subjectivity is concerned. Traherne does not elaborate a theory of knowledge nor an ontology. He only wants to show that man's neglect or blindness can bring to naught God's work, the Creation. In *Christian Ethics* (V. 36–7) the principle is clearly stated:

If we would be *perfect, as our Father which is in Heaven is perfect*, our Power of Knowing must be transformed (into *Act,*) and all Objects appear in the interior Light of *our own* understanding. For tho all Eternity were full of Treasures, and the Whole World, and all the Creatures in it transformed into Joys and our Interest to all never so perfect; yet if we are Ignorant of them, we shall continue as Poor and Empty, as if there were nothing but Vacuity and Space. For not to *be*, and not to *appear*, are the same thing to the understanding.

is *percipi*. There are no really existent "external objects"; there's nothing but perceptions, and God who causes the perceptions.' In Everard's translation of *The Divine Pymander* (1650), however, the fact that God's imagination generates the world does not imply that the world is mere appearance: 'Himself [God] is not made, yet in fantasie he fantasieth all things, or in appearance he maketh them appear, for appearance is onely of those things that are generated or made, for appearance is nothing but generation' (V. 1; p. 63). In other words the world is God's dream, but the dream comes true.

The philosopher does not call in question the reality or materiality of the 'objects'; he only states that what we do not perceive does not exist for our consciousness. And so does the poet in 'The Improvment' (23–4):

> Had he not made an *Ey* to be the Sphere
> Of all Things, none of these would e're appear.

Out of this ingenuous recognition of a self-evident truth Traherne's egotism educes a principle: each human consciousness is expected to reflect the Creation. The revelation of the world to the infant is a new Creation for each individual consciousness ('Salutation', 'Wonder'). For the grown-up man the outer world exists only when his mind is active, for the mind 'containeth all Things. *Being a Power that Permitteth all Objects to be*' (*Centuries*, II. 24; my italics). The world will thus come into being to be 'enjoyed' by man; but also to be enjoyed by the angels and by God himself through the consciousness of His creatures. For wholly spiritual natures, Traherne boldly assumes, cannot directly apprehend the qualities perceived by the human senses. The angels see 'by our Eyes': 'They smell thy [God's] Perfumes, | And taste thy Honey, Milk, and Butter, | By our Senses'.[5] God's gifts come down to us but return to Him with 'more value' for 'The GODHEAD cannot prize | The Sun at all, nor yet the Skies, | Or Air, or Earth, or Trees, or Seas, | Or Stars, unless the Soul of Man they pleas' ('Demonstration', st. v). No clearer proof of the sensuous character of Traherne's 'message' is needed. His wonder at the discovery of the inner presence of the objects in the perceiving mind seems at times to suggest a solipsistic idealism. Yet, even when he presents his consciousness as enclosed in a spiritual world, he still reminds us that it is 'A Spiritual World Standing within, | An Univers enclosd in Skin' ('Fullnesse', 7–8). The Gospel of Felicity will not be based on a Neoplatonic idealism, nor a Cartesian *cogito*, but on a spiritual exercise of the senses.

Hence the peculiar nature of Traherne's 'world', material in itself and immaterial in the mind. From Plato or Plotinus to St Thomas, philosophers agreed that only the immaterial 'forms'

---

[5] 'Thanksgivings for the Body', 399–404; cf. *Select Meditations*, III. 9.

of things could enter the mind, 'stripped of their mass'.[6] What is peculiar in Traherne's description of this operation is not only his enthusiasm but his emphasis on the sensuous aspect of perception. In 'My Spirit' (st. vii) he seems to be addressing at once his 'Self', his mind, and his eye in this apostrophe:

> O Wondrous Self! O Sphere of Light . . .
> O Living Orb of Sight!
> Thou which within me art, yet Me! Thou Ey,
> And Temple of his Whole Infinitie!
> O what a world art Thou! a World within!
> All Things appear,
> All Objects are,
> Alive in thee! Supersubstancial, Rare,
> Abov them selvs, and nigh of Kin
> To those pure Things we find
> In his Great Mind
> Who made the World! . . .

That the 'eye' here is not only the inner eye of the intellect is strongly suggested by other Neoplatonic Renaissance celebrations of the eye which can at once receive 'the pictures of all bodies' and the 'ideas of Plato':

> N'est-ce un songe de voir dans sa petite boule
> Qui autour de l'essieu en son vuide se roule,
> De tous corps les pourtraicts tour a tour penetrer?
>   . . . dedans l'œil sont gardées
> Universellement de Platon les idées.
> Sans l'œil tout l'univers, ciel & chaque Element,
> Ne serait qu'un Caos comme au commencement . . .
> Adoncq par le moyen de ce rayon de feu
> Qui a-t-il en ce tout qui ne soit veu & sceu?
> Et l'esternelle essence infinie, accomplie,
> Se laisse à l'œil comprendre, et en l'œil se replie.[7]

---

[6] *Enneads*, III. vi. 18, *Plotinus*, trans. Armstrong (London, 1966–88), III. 283; *Summa*, Ia, q. 12, art. 2, resp.

[7] René Bretonnayau, *La génération de l'homme et le temple de l'âme* (Paris, 1583), fos. 89ᵛ–92ʳ. Sight was acknowledged to be the noblest of the senses from Aristotle to Leonardo da Vinci and Descartes (see Carl Havelange, *De l'œil et du monde* (Paris, 1998), 94, 263, 330), but the presence of the ideas in the eye was a fanciful Neoplatonic assumption. Malebranche pointed out that it was difficult to see a truth distinctly with the eye of the soul when we use the eyes of the body to apprehend it (*De la recherche de la vérité* (1674; Paris, 1979), 10).

Sight had been acknowledged to be 'a spiritual faculty, the most perfect and universal of the senses', by Thomas Aquinas as by Augustine[8] and comparisons between the eye of the soul and the eye of the body abounded.[9] Traherne was not innovating when he stated in *Select Meditations* (II. 44) that 'the very substance of the Soul is sight', or described his own soul as 'A Living Endless Ey' in 'The Preparative' (12) and *Commentaries of Heaven*;[10] yet he often keeps us uncertain whether he has in mind an intellectual or a sensuous apprehension. The opening poems in the Dobell MS lay stress on the 'Meditation' which 'did employ | My Soul within' in infancy ('Innocence'). They could be Platonically interpreted[11] as a contemplation of 'the Idea of Heaven and Earth in the Soul of Man' (*Centuries*, II. 90) and a passage in *Select Meditations* (I. 81) seems to invite this interpretation:

When I retire first I seem to com in my selfe to a centre, in that centre I find Eternity, and all its Riches. By leav[ing] things as they Stand without, I find them within in a richer Manner. They are all in Thee, and Thou art there: O my God I flie unto Thee.

Yet the opening poems are followed by 'The Instruction', which does not invite man to avert his gaze from the outer world, but only from the man-made evil unknown to the child: 'All that is Great and Stable stood | Before thy Purer Eys at first; | All that in Visibles is Good | Or pure, or fair, or unaccurst.' The next poem, 'The Vision', clearly urges us to contemplate the visible universe, 'all that Ey can see'. 'Flight', indeed 'is but the Preparative'—an echo of the earlier poem—to a contemplation of the Creation as it came out of God's hands, before being spoiled by man. Yet 'The Sight | Is Deep and Infinit'. What is the precise meaning of this assertion of infinity? As the undoubtedly concrete 'Vision' of the world culminates in an obviously spiritual invitation 'to see the Fountain', that is God, at least in its 'Effects' (st. 5–6), it must be more than a hint at the infinity of the universe.

---

[8] *Summa*, Ia, q. 78, art. 3, resp.; Augustine, *De genesi ad litt.* I. xii, c. 16, n. 32. Cf. Lord Herbert, *De Veritate*, VII. 213.

[9] See Etienne Gilson, *Le Thomisme* (Paris, 1945), 287.

[10] No. 32, l. 58; cf. No. 90, l. 52, and No. 57: 'All the Faculties | Are in the Ey'.

[11] As R. D. Jordan proposed in 'Thomas Traherne and the Art of Meditation', *JHI* 46 (1985), 29–65.

A passion for infinity is a major trait of Traherne's imagination. The idea recurs throughout his writings, though even more insistently and at times naively in the early *Select Meditations* as if the repetition of the word itself was inebriating to him.[12] In an act of self-reflexivity he had discovered 'A vast and Infinit Capacitie' in his soul.[13] More radically and rapturously than Marvell in 'The Garden' he asserted that the human mind, being present with all objects (*Centuries*, II. 84), can contain every thing and is not merely receptive: it has a power of expansion and can project itself through space and time even towards objects unknown. Traherne was directly influenced by the Pseudo-Hermes, who called upon the soul to be conscious of its possibility of omnipresence in the farthest places and even beyond the sphere of the cosmos.[14] But his point of view is more subjective: he did not start like the Egyptian sage from a speculation on the knowledge of God, but from the wonder he personally experienced when he discovered that his desire to possess all things could be satisfied by their presence in his mind. The 'thought' that the Pseudo-Hermes allowed to roam through all objects in a depersonalized expansion was thus clearly enclosed within an individual consciousness. Besides, the

[12] Nearly all sections could be quoted; as a sample see III. 80 and 90.

[13] 'Silence', 75; cf. 'My Essence was Capacitie' ('My Spirit', 8). The phrasing may echo Thomas Vaughan's description of the soul's 'vast and infinite capacity, which is satisfied with nothing but God' (*Anthroposophia Theomagica*, 1650; in *The Works of Thomas Vaughan*, ed. A. E. Waite (London, 1919), 46), but the *Hermetica* may be a common source. The capacity of the soul was commonly celebrated by nonconformist ministers as R. D. Jordan pointed out in *JHI* 46 (1985), 389 ff. The recurrence of the theme and the intensity of the emotion in Traherne's writings are, however, unequalled.

[14] *Pimander*, XI. 18–20 (*Hermetica*, I. 221); cf. the passages copied under the heading 'Capacitie' in Traherne's Commonplace Book, fo. 24ᵛ. The concept of infinity appealed to the Cambridge Platonists, and Carol Marks quoted from More and Sterry in 'Thomas Traherne and Cambridge Platonism', *PMLA* 81 (1966), 528–9. She assumed, however, as I had, that 'it was Hermes who fired Traherne's imagination'; see *Poètes métaphysiques*, II. 272–3. Other parallels can be offered. In his *Discourse of the Light of Nature* (London, 1652) Culverwell stressed the 'worth' and 'desires' of the soul (it can 'open its mouth so wide that the whole world can't fill it', 201) and insisted like Traherne on the notion of 'Act' (118–21) and on the soul's 'reflex acts' (102–3). But Culverwell emphasized the difference between God's mind and the human mind (118) and had a poor opinion of the faculties of the infant and the child (92), which shows once more that Traherne's use of borrowed ideas is always selective in accordance with the original dictates of his mind and experience.

cosmos remained a sphere and was not infinite in the *Pimander*;[15] God alone was said to be 'uncircumscribed'.[16] The Hermetic books offer no equivalent of the immediate and passionate intuition of the infinite which Traherne presents as a self-evident datum of consciousness, the perfect exercise of our intellectual faculty when it takes model on God's 'One infinit Act of KNOWLEDG' (*Centuries*, II. 84). He alone makes it a condition of felicity.

The author of the *Centuries* had been early convinced that '*All things* in Time and Eternity' were necessary to his 'Felicity' (II. 100). This was not Donne's yearning for an 'All' which could be the world of the lovers absorbing the larger world, all kings, all states, all princes,[17] or the entire possession of the beloved, as in 'Lovers Infiniteness'. Donne's tendency was not to expansion, but to oneness: the oneness of the lovers, of the truly 'catholic' church and of mankind itself, for 'All mankinde is of one *Author*, and is one volume' (*Devotions*, xvii). The Incarnation had cloistered divine 'Immensity' in the Virgin's womb ('Nativitie'). Elizabeth Drury could symbolically become 'all this All' (*Second Anniversary*, 376) and Lady Marckham could be praised as 'th' Elixar of this All' (28). The spaciousness of the world was best apprehended 'on a round ball' when a workman quickly made 'that, which was nothing, *All*' ('Valediction: Of Weeping'). The *concept* of infinity allowed *conceits* and proved attractive as such, for this concept can be 'clear and distinct' as Descartes argued.[18] Donne used it to express an infinite intensity of feeling in 'Loves growth' or contrition in the Holy Sonnet 'Oh, to vex me . . .', or to evoke qualities carried to an infinite extreme, like those of light and Lady Huntington ('That unripe side of earth', 102), or Lady Bedford ('This twilight of two yeares', 30). He could conceive infinity in number, whether of stars in the galaxy or resurrected

[15] X. 11; *Hermetica*, I. 195.

[16] XI. 18: 'All things are in God, but things are not in God as a place: the incorporeal cannot be enclosed by anything but it can itself enclose all things', *Hermetica*, I. 219.   [17] 'The Sunne Rising', 'The Canonization'.

[18] Descartes, *Réponses aux premières objections*, §10: 'l'infini en tant qu'infini n'est point à la vérité compris, mais . . . néanmoins il est entendu, car entendre clairement et distinctement qu'une chose soit telle qu'on ne puisse y rencontrer de limites, c'est clairement entendre qu'elle est infinie' (*Méditations métaphysiques*, ed. Beyssade (Paris, 1979), 217).

souls ('Primrose', 5; Holy Sonnet VII, 3). But the infinitude of
space invites an imaginative apprehension which is bound to
remain indefinite: it may be the reason why it did not appeal to
a poet always so anxious to define, a man who sought a fullness
of being contracted in a point.[19] Traherne's insatiable desire, on
the contrary, sought this fullness in expansion: he aimed at
taking possession of all things at once through the reflection in
the mind of all perceptible objects and the projection of his
thoughts throughout the universe, hence through the boundless
space opened to the imagination by the new astronomy.

Yet the Divine Philosopher maintained that the idea of infinity is inborn in man's soul, for 'The true exemplar of GODS
infinity is that of your Understanding, which is a lively Patern
and Idea of it'.[20] His intuition of infinity, however, is not the
Cartesian notion of infinite being.[21] In the *Select Meditations* it
was still essentially based on the Neoplatonic conviction that
'Infinit space' is a thing 'intimately known to the soul' (IV. 3; cf.
III. 27), yet he argued like the Greek Atomists about physical
space[22] when he added (IV. 3): 'Nor is it Possible there should
be any End of space, beyond which there will not still and ever-
more be space, so that I can Plainly *see* infinit Space' (my italics). The *Poems* celebrate a revelation of 'endless Space' at once
within and without the soul:

> I know not well
> What did me tell
> Of endles Space: but I
> Did in my Mind
> Some such thing find
> To be beyond the Sky
> That had no Bound . . .

('Sight', 37–43)

> Dame Nature told me there was endless Space
> Within my Soul; I spy'd its very face.

('Felicity', 4–5)

---

[19] See Ch. 6, p. 113.   [20] *Centuries*, II. 24; cf. II. 92, IV. 98–100.
[21] 'I say that the notion I have of the infinite is in me before that of the finite
because, by the mere fact that I conceive being, or that which is, what I conceive is
infinite being; but in order to conceive a finite being, I have to take away something
from the general notion of being, which must accordingly be first' (*Philosophical
Letters*, trans. A. Kenny (Oxford, 1970), 255).   [22] See Ch. 17.

Thus in the Mind an endless Space
Doth nat'rally display its face.

('Consummation', 17–18)

This infinity is not 'conceived', but 'seen' or imagined by 'a
mind | Exerted for it saw Infinitie' ('My Spirit', 99–100). It is
emotionally apprehended, for 'We first by Nature all things
boundless see; | Feel all illimited; and know | No Terms or
Periods' ('City', 61–3). In the *Centuries* intellectual and physical
arguments are associated as if Traherne made no distinction
between the idea and the perception of infinity:

Few will believ the Soul to be infinit: yet Infinit is the first Thing
which is naturaly known. Bounds and Limits are Discerned only in
a Secondary maner. Suppose a Man were born Deaf and Blind. By
the very feeling of His Soul He apprehends infinit about Him, infinit
Space, infinit Darkness. He thinks not of Wall and Limits till He
feels them and is stopt by them. That things are finit therfore we
learn by our Sences, but Infinity we know and feel by our Souls: and
feel it so Naturaly, as if it were the very Essence and Being of the
Soul. The truth of it is, It is individually in the Soul: for GOD is
there, and more near to us then we are to our selvs. So that we
cannot feel our Souls, but we must feel Him, in that first of
Properties infinit Space.[23]

The Augustinian echo about a God *interior intimo meo* is noteworthy, yet the *conceptual* intuition of infinity is transmuted
into an apprehension of infinite space imagined as being 'felt'.
In *Commentaries of Heaven* Traherne moved even further from
the metaphysical notion of infinity when he insisted on 'infinite
Variety', though still enclosing it 'In infinit and Endless
Unitie'.[24]

A craving for the infinite is supposed to be a natural instinct
in all men since, 'were there no such Infinitie, there would be no

[23] II. 81. This is comparable with, yet obviously different from, Descartes's way
of arguing in his *Meditations*: 'I must not imagine that I do not perceive the infinite
through a distinct idea, but only through the negation of the finite, just as I perceive
stillness and darkness through the negation of movement and light, since, on the
contrary, I obviously understand there is more reality in the infinite substance than
in the finite, and therefore find my perception of the infinite, that is of God, precedes
my perception of the finite and of myself' ('Meditatio tertia'; ed. Beyssade, p. 117,
my trans.).

[24] Nos. 32, ll. 25–6; 67, ll. 35–6; 80, l. 164; cf. *Select Meditations*, III. 37, 46.

Room for their Imaginations; their Desires and Affections would be coopd up, and their Souls imprisoned' (*Centuries*, V. 3; cf. III. 24). The universality of the craving is questionable; it is belied by George Herbert's preference for 'nestling' in enclosed places. Traherne's own obsession with the theme, apparently stronger even than Henry More's, is peculiar and related to the almost physiological satisfaction he felt at feeling, as he said, strangely 'extended', 'enlarged', or 'expanded'.[25] In his *Commentaries of Heaven* his sense of containing all space and all ages was even conveyed in grotesque physical images.[26]

There is a correlation between this yearning for expansion and the naive questionings of the child who 'Wondered why Men were made no Bigger' and would have had 'a Castle as big as the Heavens'. But he came to consider that 'for him to be made infinite ... would be to no purpose' and even prove inconvenient: 'One Star made infinite would all Exclude' (*Centuries*, III. 18–21). Infinite perfection may be found in a finite being. Nicolas Cusanus had come to the same conclusion in his speculations on infinite being,[27] yet to Henry More it remained 'a marvell of marvells ... That the Goodness of God being Infinite, the effects thereof should be so narrow and finite as commonly men conceit'.[28] Traherne's intuition enabled him, long before Blake and Whitman 'to see a World in a Grain of Sand' and hold it 'perfect':[29] 'there not being a Sand nor Mote in the Air that is not more Excellent then if it were infinit' (*Centuries*, III. 20). This evaluation of the 'excellencies' of all creatures is moral or spiritual rather than metaphysical. What proves most attractive to the apostle of Felicity is the perspective

[25] 'My Spirit', 86; *Centuries*, III. 84; I. 73.

[26] No. 35: 'His very Cranium is it self a Skie, | The Earth a Centre, Ages fill his Ey | And in the Caverns of his Heavenly Brain | He doth the Sea and all the World contain.' The change from personal experience to universal assertion in the *Commentaries* is responsible for their poetic inferiority: see Nos. 32, 44.

[27] Every creature being 'God-created' or 'finite-infinity', 'no creature's existence could be better than it is': *Of Learned Ignorance* (London, 1954), II. 2, 75; cf. II. 5, 85.

[28] *Divine Dialogues*, III. xxxii (London, 1668), vol. 1, 514–16. Whether Traherne had read the *Dialogues* before writing the *Centuries* is uncertain, but he is likely to have read them before composing *Christian Ethicks* (1675) where the theme is taken up again and elaborated in ch. xxiii.

[29] Blake, 'Auguries of Innocence'; Whitman, 'Song of Myself', 31. The image recurs in Traherne's *Commentaries*, Nos. 22 and 73, l. 35.

of unlimited possession and enjoyment, infinite riches and pleasures (*Christian Ethicks*, IX. 67). This subjective approach leads him to ascribe infinity to human desires and joys: 'Infinite Wants Satisfied Produce infinit Joys' (*Centuries*, I. 43).

The association of expansiveness and egocentricity is reflected in Traherne's recurrent use of the combined metaphor of the centre and the circumference.[30] It could express 'infinit unitie', a phrase occasionallly used by Traherne (*Centuries*, I. 74); but 'infinit unitie' was a metaphysical notion based on the concept of pure being, *ipsum esse*, by Aquinas as by Descartes, or on the *Maximum Absolutum* by Cusanus.[31] Traherne most often resorts to the metaphor in order to emphasize the capacity of the human mind:

The spiritual Room of the Mind is transcendent to Time and Place, because all Time and Place are contained therein . . . It is the Greatest Miracle perhaps in nature. For it is an infinite Sphere in a Point, an Immensity in a Centre, an Eternity in a Moment.[32]

The infinity of man's mind seems to become the guarantee of Divine infinity. We are brought back to the initial revelation: the unlimited capacity of the soul. But this capacity extends to all times and even to eternity. The sense of distance is abolished in space by the omnipresence of thought; in the same way a consciousness filled with the vision of eternity is bound to have no sense of duration.

Just as the intuition of infinity was supposed to precede the conception of the finite, the intuition or the feeling of eternity is prior to the notion of time. In *Select Meditations* the soul already was 'an Interior Temple of all Eternity' (III. 73). When the soul of the infant is assumed to enjoy a knowledge of eternal realities in 'The Preparative' and 'Dumnesse' Traherne may be merely following the Platonic tradition. But his record of his early impressions as a child is the expression of a genuine

---

[30] *Select Meditations*, II. 66, 92, III. 82: God is 'an Infinit Sphere, yet an infinit Centre'; cf. *Commentaries*, No. 35.

[31] Thomas, *Summa*, Ia, q. 7, art. 1, resp.; Descartes, see n. 21; Nicolas, *Learned Ignorance*, I. v, 'Oneness of the Maximum'.

[32] *Christian Ethicks*, X. 73. Cf. *Centuries*, V. 4 ('Every man is alone the centre and circumference of it [infinity]. It is all his own') and *Commentaries*, Nos. 39, l. 9; 65, l. 66; 67, l. 44, etc.

experience. Even if it were the experience of a mystic in the stage known as Illumination rather than an accurate rendering of a child's thoughts, it would still reveal an individual mode of apprehension (*Centuries*, III. 3):

The Corn was Orient and Immortal Wheat, which never should be reaped, nor was ever sown. I thought it had stood from everlasting to everlasting . . . I knew not that [men] were Born or should Die. But all things abided Eternaly as they were in their Proper Places. Eternity was Manifest in the Light of the Day, and som thing infinit Behind evry thing appeared . . .

Several poems bear testimony to the reality of this experience: 'When first among his Works I did appear . . . | The World resembled his *Eternitie*' ('Wonder'); 'They seem'd to me | Environ'd with Eternity' ('City', 19–20). This sense of everlastingness, at whatever age it was really felt, is close to the spontaneous impressions of the child who has no knowledge of death and is not immediately aware of the flow of time since the distinction between past, present, and future is acquired progressively. The child's 'perpetual present', however, is different from the *nunc stans* of the mystics and the philosophers. Eckhart, among others, had insisted on the fact that there is only an eternal present for the soul's highest faculty as for God and he may seem to anticipate the impressions of Traherne concerning time and space: 'for this faculty there is no yesterday, nor any day before yesterday . . . but only a perpetual present. What was a thousand years ago and what will be in a thousand years hence is present, as well as every thing beyond the seas.' But Eckhart's assertions were based on the soul's power to 'apprehend God in his unity and his solitude, his desert and his own abyss'.[33] The soul—at least the infant soul—may seem to have a similar power in 'Dumnesse' and in 'My Spirit'; yet, if we look more closely, we discover that attention is not focused on God, but on the oneness of the self and the world enclosed within the self: 'There I saw all the World Enjoyd by one; | There I was in the World my Self alone' ('Dumnesse', 35–6; cf. 'My Spirit', st. vi–vii). When divested of its Neoplatonic trappings, Traherne's intuition of eternity is found to be essentially a *totum simul* made

---

[33] *Meister Eckharts Predigten*, ed. J. Quint (Stuttgart, 1958), Predigt 10, I. 172. My own translation is indebted to an earlier French edition by M. de Gandillac, *Maître Eckhart. Traités et Sermons* (Paris, 1942), 167.

up of a multiplicity of objects supposed to be simultaneously present in the mind, but inevitably evoked distinctly as the poet's long catalogues evidence. His interest in 'variety' may partly account for this trait (*Select Meditations*, III. 37, 47). His insistence on the soul's 'enjoying in it self all Ages, kingdoms, Souls, and Treasures' (ibid. II. 95) betrays a dispersion in multiplicity. Reversing Traherne's statement 'All Time was Eternity' (*Centuries*, III. 2), one could say that this Eternity is nothing more than 'all time' contemplated by the mind, even when all ages seem to be viewed in a single moment of egocentric exaltation:

> With Secret Rooms in Times and Ages more
> Past and to com enlarging my great Store,
> These all in Order present unto Me
> My Happy Eys did in a Moment see . . .[34]

Eckhart described a 'moment' when '*all creatures are a mere nothing*', when 'there is neither here nor there, but an obliviousness of all creatures: there is the fulness of Being'.[35] The Poet of Felicity wants to be 'A constant Mirror of Eternitie' only so 'That while Gods Omnipresence in us lies, | His Treasures might be all before our Eys' ('Thoughts IV', 96, 89–90). Obviously his intuition of spatial infinitude, already manifest in *Select Meditations* (III. 72), commanded his conception of an eternity turned into a receptacle of all periods of time, a 'Space'

. . . wherein all Moments are infinitly Exhibited, and the Everlasting Duration of infinit Space is another Region and Room of Joys. Wherein all Ages appear together, all Occurences stand up at once, and the innumerable and Endless Myriads of yeers that were before the Creation, and will be after the World is ended are Objected as a Clear and Stable Object, whose several Parts extended out at length, giv an inward infinity to this Moment, and compose an Eternitie that is seen by all Comprehensors and Enjoyers. (*Centuries*, V. 6)

Eternity as 'The Object of [man's] View' ('Misapprehension',

---

[34] 'Nature', 63–6. In *The Temple of Eternity* (Port Washington, NY, 1972) Richard Jordan argued that Traherne made time only 'a part of eternity'; but in this case either time and eternity are substantially identical and eternity is only infinite time, or eternity must be conceived spatially as a receptacle for time.

[35] *Eckharts Predigten*, Predigt 11 (ed. Quint, I. 185); *Traités et sermons*, trans. Gandillac, 174. That is why I reject the pretended similarity between the message of Traherne and the mysticism of Eckhart or other followers of the *via negativa*.

21) is not Vaughan's symbolic great ring of light seen in a dream, but an occasion for the soul to 'see before and after its Existence into Endless Spaces' (*Centuries*, I. 55). This notion of eternity grows out of an initial confusion of infinity and boundlessness. Human thought in its expansion finds no end and no beginning. Traherne therefore assumes that all things and all times can come together in his consciousness thanks to the unlimited capacity of the soul. When they are supposed to do so in a moment, we seem to approach the definition of eternity given by Boethius and Aquinas; yet the point of view is different. The convergence of all things in man's mind as in God's is proclaimed and extolled less as a token of the ontological reality of the eternal than as an evidence of the powers of the individual psyche. In this triumph of an egocentric consciousness the intuition of a spatial and temporal infinity only seeks to glut and gratify the insatiable self.

An emphasis on a perpetual present precludes any nostalgia for the past: 'all Ages are Things, neer and present, Solid and Real'.[36] Traherne has no reason to feel like Vaughan estranged and distant from the 'early days when [he] | Shin'd in his Angell-infancy' ('Retreate'). But even had Vaughan recovered, as Traherne felt he had, the 'white, Celestiall thought' of childhood, one feels he would not have lost his sense of distance, so prominent in his wish to 'travel back' and 'return'.[37] When Traherne says 'I must becom a Child again', he does not think of travelling back: he has already recovered a 'Bliss, which most I Boast | And ever shall Enjoy' ('Innocence'). His childhood is not a distant glory but 'a Sphere' in which the visions of the child and the thoughts of the man are enclosed. There is no progress along a 'track': the poet's life is 'a Circle of Delights' ('Review II') for he 'a World of true Delight | Did then and to this Day do see' ('Innocence', 47–8). This is not a reminiscence, but a reviviscence of the past: '*The first Impressions are Immortal all.*'[38]

The notion of a pre-existence also emerges in a different

---

[36] Quoted in Allan Pritchard's article 'Traherne's *Commentaries of Heaven* (With Selections from the Manuscript)', *UTQ* 53 (1983), 12.

[37] The poem of Traherne entitled 'The Return' opens with the line 'To Infancy, O Lord, again I com': he is *immediately* back in infancy.

[38] 'Dumnesse', 85. The spatial conception of eternity is also obvious in the *Commentaries*, Nos. 34 and 35 on 'Ages'.

perspective with Vaughan and Traherne. They both may have read Henry More's philosophical poem *The Praeexistency of the Soul* published in 1647.[39] But the Silurist only drops a mysterious hint and the Divine Philosopher, though inclined to theory, is hardly more explicit. Vaughan may be unwilling to contradict the doctrine of the Church of England, but Traherne took bolder initiatives. In fact, they were both uninterested in the Neoplatonic 'material metaphysics', already used by Spenser in 'An Hymne in Honour of Beautie' (106–19) to describe the descent of the soul from Heaven in a fiery, then airy vehicle, borrowing influences from the planets before fashioning the body. They offer no objective discussion of the doctrine; they express a subjective intuition, an individual aspiration; but they do so in different ways. Vaughan longed to travel back to 'a Countrie | Far beyond the stars' ('Peace') from which he was exiled. His soul yearned to 'return' to its Creator ('Retreate', 32). All believers agree that the soul 'comes' from God, but in pure logic it only means that God created it. The imagination, however, consciously or unconsciously, sets a *distance* between the Creator and his creatures; hence the theories of 'emanation' describing a 'descent' in various stages which some minds conceive as a progress in space and time. Vaughan's gaze, we know, is on the distant horizon and the soul must have a place of origin in the distance, in 'That shady City of Palme trees' whence it came ('Retreate'). When this poet speaks of his 'second race' in this world, he may be thinking of his 'early days', his 'Angell-infancy', as the first phase of his life; but the phrase can imply an earlier existence of the soul, either in Heaven or at least in its first 'race' or descent from Heaven to earth. What is 'the glorious traine' he 'left' behind, if not the glory of the yet unbodied soul? In any case, the sense of distance in time and space is paramount. This was clearly a different conception from Donne's. The poet of instantaneity and simultaneity 'as S. *Augustin* cannot conceive any interim, any

---

[39] The soul is described 'Like to a light fast-lock'd in lanthorn dark' both in More's poem (st. ci) and in Traherne's 'Nature', but Plotinus (*Enneads*, I. 4. 8) may be the common source. Yet the soul and its radiance are described by More and Traherne in strikingly similar images: 'One shining sphear', 'one Orb of Sense, all eye, all airy ear' (st. ci–cii). Cf. '*Sphere of Light*', '*Orb of Sight*', 'all Sight, or Eye' in 'The Preparative'.

distance, between the creating of the soule, and the infusing of
the soule into the body' (*Sermons*, V. 349). This divergence is
one more consequence of the fundamental difference in their
modes of imagination.

Traherne, like Donne, ignores distance and therefore will
not approach the idea of pre-existence in the same way as
Vaughan. In *Select Meditations* he asserts: 'From all Eternity
my being was with God.' Since 'from all Eternity God wanted
us' and 'included us', being all 'in Gods Essence', we were in
God 'from all Eternity' (III. 78, 79; IV. 28). This could imply
no more than a pre-existence among God's ideas. In his opening poem, 'The Salutation', the reality of his own present existence is highlighted by the realization of his own previous
non-existence:[40]

> I that so long
> Was *Nothing* from Eternitie,
> Did little think such Joys as Ear and Tongue,
> To celebrat or see:
> Such Sounds to hear, such hands to feel, such Feet,
> Such Eys and Objects, on the Ground to meet.
>
> .   .   .   .
>
> From Dust I rise,
> And out of Nothing now awake.

This wonder sounds naive; yet this is indeed my first perception
of my self in any act of instantaneous reflexive consciousness.
My existence then is not revealed to me as the existence of a
being with a history, a memory, or a future, but as an inexplicable happening on a background of nothingness. Why do I
exist? Why does this body belong to me? For Traherne this
ekstasis of his consciousness, which makes him aware of his
awareness, is attended by a feeling of joy, a truly ecstatic delight.
From this point of view the doctrine of pre-existence is irrele-
vant. There is already an elaboration of the immediate intuition,
a reference to a prior state, when he exclaims: 'How like an
Angel came I down!' But he does not turn his attention to the

---

[40] In a slightly different way Joan Webber later observed that 'unable to
conceive of a state of non-being, Traherne assumes that essence precedes existence'
(*The Eloquent I* (Madison, 1968), 238).

place of origin, nor to the descent of the soul, but to the journey's end and the place reached, the world he discovers with a Miranda-like feeling of wonder: 'How Bright are all Things here!'[41]

At the very moment when it seems to emerge out of nothing the self-reflexive consciousness paradoxically must assert its existence by projecting the 'I' backward beyond the moment of its emergence. 'I was not' is but an abstraction. The only intuition I can have of my anterior nothingness must be spelt: 'I was non-being.' The poet phrased it so:

> When silent I,
> So many thousand thousand yeers,
> Beneath the Dust did in a Chaos lie
>
> ('The Salutation')

From this point of view there is no pre-existence, but essence precedes existence, as in the strange interrogation: 'Did you not from all Eternity Want som one to giv you a Being?' A want related to Traherne's desire of infinite possession and presence to all times:

Did you not from all Eternity Want som one to giv you a Being? . . . Did you not from all Eternity Want som one to give you infinit Treasures? . . . What you wanted from all Eternity, be sensible of to all Eternity. Let your Wants be present from Everlasting. Is not this a Strange Life to which I call you? Wherein you are to be present with Things that were before the World was made?   (*Centuries*, I. 45)

'Where wast thou when I laid the foundations of the earth?' (Job 38: 4). To the question of the Eternal Henry More boldly replied: 'souls do bear the same date with the creation of the

---

[41] There is a surprising similarity between Traherne's description of this experience and an 18th-c. imaginary account of the awakening of the first man discovering the world through his senses like the statue of Condillac: 'Je me souviens de cet instant plein de joie & de trouble, où je sentis pour la première fois ma singulière existence; je ne savois pas ce que j'étois, où j'étois, d'où je venois. J'ouvris les yeux, quel surcroît de sensation! La lumière, la voûte céleste, la verdure de la terre, le crystal des eaux, tout m'occupoit, m'animoit, & me donnoit un sentiment inexprimable de plaisir; je crus d'abord que tous ces objets étoient en moi & faisoient partie de moi' (Georges-Louis Buffon, *Histoire naturelle de l'homme*, in *Histoire naturelle générale et particulière*, III (Paris, 1759), 364). It confirms my conviction that Traherne fundamentally records genuine sense impressions and anticipates the sensualism of the Enlightenment through the conceptual cloak of Platonism.

World'.[42] Traherne will not say where he was *then*.[43] Probably not out of a cautious avoidance of heresy like Sir Thomas Browne who left the answer to him 'who understands entities of preordination, and beings yet unbeing' (*Christian Morals*, III. 25). The only thing of interest to him was the assurance that he could still be *present now* at the creation of the world: not a pre-existence, but a simultaneous existence was his wish and claim, which he extended to God. The pre-existence of all creatures as ideas in the Divine Mind was a commonplace, but he wanted God to love His creatures before their existence, for '[His] love is infinite: impatient of delay. It could never endure to be distant from them, not a moment could stand between [Him] and them' ('Thanksgivings for God's Attributes', 202–4). The idea that God has loved mankind from all eternity is found among the mystics.[44] Traherne, however, speaks as if the yet uncreated creatures already had in God's mind an existence distinct from God's own. If questioned about it, he might have replied like Sir Thomas Browne that 'it may be somewhat more than a non-entity, to be in that mind, unto which all things are present' (*Christian Morals*, III. 25); but he apparently never asked himself the question, for a mind supposed to contemplate all things in an eternal present can easily conceive 'beings yet unbeing'.

Traherne's mode of composition and his style are in harmony with his imagination of space and time. His expansiveness often defeats all attempts at restraint, particularly in his longer poems, such as the 'Thanksgivings'. He wrote a beautiful line on order—'Order the Beauty even of Beauty is' ('Vision', 9)—and his shorter lyrics show some sense of form, but he avoids the intricacies and subtleties of Donne and George Herbert.

[42] *The Immortality of the Soul*, ch. xii, in *A Collection of Several Philosophical Writings*, 4th edn. (1712), 114.

[43] He remained non-committal in his *Commentaries of Heaven* under 'Babe': 'Before he was conceived he was not, and yet all the Matter of his Body was in the Universe before: Some think his Soul was so too: but he received both by the Gift of His Creator' (Pritchard's 'Selections from the Manuscript', *UTQ* 53, p. 19).

[44] Julian of Norwich wrote: 'For I saw that God began never to love mankind: for right the same that mankind shall be in endless bliss, fulfilling the joy of God as anent His works, right so the same mankind hath been in the foresight of God: known and loved from without beginning' (*Revelations of Divine Love*, ed. Grace Warrack (London, 1912), 128). Cf. *Select Meditations*, III. 79.

Everything seems to be projected on to the same level plane, an impression enhanced by the constant enumerations, the litanies of nouns and epithets. A mind that seeks to grasp a multiplicity of objects at a time is tempted to resort to mere accumulation, often disregarding dialectical and even temporal co-ordination. When a 'Demonstration' is attempted, the same tendency is observed in the profusion of often unrelated arguments or examples; a profusion again noticeable in the meditation on a theme (e.g. 'The Circulation') and in descriptive poems (e.g. 'The World').

The poetic 'world' of Traherne is built out of these enumerations of objects, whether natural or man-made (a distinction studied in Chapter 15). It is a world of contiguity without perspective. A bright-lit world, with no alternation of day and night, or seasons. A world of nature unlike Vaughan's, for it is a world without change, growth, or withering in its eternal present. Nor is it a world of hard materiality like Donne's, or George Herbert's, or a world of fluidity like Crashaw's. It is a world of things, elements, phenomena, conceptualized as objects of perception: 'All things | Visible | Material | Sensible | Animals, | Vegetables, | Minerals, | Bodies celestial, | Bodies terrestrial, | The four Elements, | Volatile Spirits, | Trees, Herbs, and Flowers, | The Influences of Heaven, | Clouds, Vapors, Wind, | Dew, Rain, Hail and Snow, | Light and Darkness, Night and Day, | The Seasons of the Year, | Springs, Rivers, Fountains, Oceans,

> Gold, Silver, and precious Stones.
> Corn, Wine, and Oyl,
> The Sun, Moon, and Stars,
> Cities, Nations, Kingdoms.
> And the Bodies of Men, the greatest Treasures of all.

> ('Thanksgivings for the Body', 243–64)

The senses of the body are, indeed, celebrated, but attention is called to their general operations, despoiled of the 'furry' concreteness of sensation[45] in the mere mention of their general qualities, sometimes reduced to abstractions in a process of generalization: 'a Body ... | Can see | Only visible things, |

---

[45] Gaston Bachelard used to speak of 'la bonne fourrure de la sensation'.

Taste | The Qualities in Meat and Drink, | Feel | Gross or tangible Bodies, | Hear | The harshness or melody of Sounds, | Smell | The things that have Odours in them' ('Thanksgivings for the Soul', 189–99). Colours are lavishly mentioned, but seem unsubstantial in their primary brilliance: 'Rare Splendors, Yellow, Blew, Red, White and Green' ('Wonder', 43). The predominance of the visual imagination is such that even 'Wine and Oyl' are said to be *seen* 'By our Eyes' ('Thanksgivings for the Body', 401). A vague sensuousness only emerges in a process of reflection on man's powers of perception:

> For *Sight* inherits Beauty, *Hearing* Sounds,
>   The *Nostril* Sweet Perfumes,
>   All *Tastes* have hidden Rooms
> Within the *Tongue*; and *Feeling Feeling* Wounds
>   With Pleasure and Delight . . .
>
>   ('The Preparative', st. iv)

The following assertion, 'But I | Forgot the rest, and was all Sight, or Ey', is largely true of the poet though it concerns the infant. He presents to us a world 'aestheticized' in so general a manner that no particular 'thing of beauty' will stand out distinctly in its particular shape. Throughout his writings Traherne kept expressing the breath-taking emotion he claimed he had first felt as a child and recorded in a passage of the *Centuries* (III. 3) throbbing with the intensity of his feeling for beauty:

The Green Trees when I saw them first through one of the Gates Transported and Ravished me; their Sweetnes and unusual Beauty made my Heart to leap, and almost mad with Extasie, they were such strange and Wonderfull Things.

PART III

Modes of Religious Sensibility and Modes of Thought

CHAPTER 11

John Donne and Bifold Natures

> We are . . . that amphibious piece, between a corporeal and
> a spiritual essence; that middle form, that links those two
> together, and makes good the method of God and nature,
> that jumps not from extremes, but unites the incompatible
> distances by some middle and participating nature.
>
> (*Religio Medici*, I. xxxiv)

Among Donne's and George Herbert's contemporaries, very few
minds would have questioned this statement of Sir Thomas
Browne. Furthermore, Christians firmly believed in the dogma
of the Incarnation, the union of two natures, divine and human,
in Christ. The existence of 'bifold natures' was a source of paradoxes and poets were expected to take advantage of them in an
age addicted to conceits. Donne, however, is singular in his
recurrent insistence on the relations between body and soul and
the paradox of the Incarnation: tradition furnished the material,
but it was not responsible for the poet's 'choice' of themes and
his individual inventiveness.[1]

It is important to note that Donne's fascinated attention to
the union of the soul and the body was first manifested in his
profane poetry. 'The Extasie' defines 'that subtile knot which
makes us man' in terms of the current psycho-physiology. 'Aire
and Angels' is based upon the same conception of human nature
and 'Loves growth' implies it when asserting that 'Love sometimes would contemplate, sometimes do'. In 'A Valediction: Of
my Name, in the Window' the contrast between physical separation and spiritual presence is traditional, but Donne's conceits
suggest that the body itself resides in some way wherever the
soul dwells (25–6). In 'Valediction: Forbidding Mourning' the

---

[1] Ramon Selden also emphasized 'John Donne's Incarnational Conviction' in
Critical Quarterly, 17 (1975), 55–73.

union of the lovers' souls (depicted in terms of solid substances, beaten gold or compasses), besides perpetuating their spiritual love, finally brings them together again, restoring their bodily union. Other poems evoke the untying of 'the subtile knot', the work of death 'When bodies to their graves, soules from their graves remove' ('Anniversarie': cf. 'Dissolution', 'Funerall')—a paradox which is another expression of the dual nature of man. The idea of the resurrection of the flesh, before haunting the author of the Holy Sonnets, imparted a strange reality to the conceit of 'The Relique': at the Last Day, will not the 'bracelet of bright hair about the bone' compel the lovers' souls to stop for a moment at the edge of the grave where the body is laid to rest?

The soul or the spirit, the body or the flesh, are indeed the two poles of Donne's speculation: his mind, alert and tense, moves along an axis which at once opposes and unites them. His prose works, even his letters dashed off along his stream of thought, confirm the constancy of this preoccupation. His 'Paradoxes' emphasized the dependence of the mind on the body.[2] He stressed it in earnest in a letter: 'Our nature is meteoric, we respect (because we partake so) both earth and heaven; for as our bodies glorified shall be capable of spiritual joy, so our souls demerged into these bodies are allowed to partake earthly pleasure.'[3] The following text gives a curious personal twist to the notion:

We consist of three parts, a soul, and body, and mind: which I call those thoughts and affections, and passions, which neither soul nor body hath alone, but have been begotten by their communication, as music results out of our breath and a cornet.[4]

---

[2] Paradox iv: 'our Complexions and whole bodyes, we inherit from parents, our inclinations and minds follow that. For our mind is heavy in our bodyes afflictions, and rejoyceth in the bodyes pleasures.' Paradox vi: 'I SAY agayne that the body makes the mind. Not that it created it a mind, but formes it a good or a bad mind ... our Soule (me seemes) is enabled by our body, not this by that' (Peters, 7, 11). Though Donne apologized for the 'lightnes' of his Paradoxes, they certainly reflect his 'inquiring attitude' (Peters, p. xxiv).

[3] 'To all my friends: Sir H. Goodyer'; Gosse, II. 9 (c.1612?).

[4] 'To Sir H. G.', Gosse, I. 184 (Spring 1608). From a different perspective R. Wiltenberg has recently called attention to Donne's play with 'two concepts of the inner life, the self and the soul', in Reconsidering the Renaissance, ed. M. Di Cesare (Binghamton, NY, 1992), 413–27.

That the 'mind' originates in the union of the soul and the body is an idea which occurred to the mind of a poet whose conceits often spring from a conjunction of material and spiritual realities. Donne in a way defines his own wit and the nature of his poetry; at once abstract and concrete, when he claims that neither the soul nor the body can entertain in isolation experiences which are, in fact, engendered by their communication. He further suggests that neither of them has a separate, distinct identity, that neither is capable of individual action, heaven attracting the soul as gravity pulls the body back to earth. Only the 'mind', which comes into being through their union, gives each man a possibility of choice and determines his unique destiny. By a detour apparently unrelated to orthodox theology, Donne seeks to link the bifold nature of man with his own experience of individuality.

The natural inclination of Donne's mind inevitably espoused the Christian conception of human nature while setting the seal of his personality upon it. No religious faith was required to perceive the duality of the mind and the body and their necessary conjunction, but the poet inserted his intuition in the theological tradition which could give it a foundation, as in the 'Elegy on M^{ris} Boulstred' (43–5):

> Death gets 'twixt soules and bodies such a place
> As sinne insinuates 'twixt just men and grace,
> Both worke a separation, no divorce.

Most religious paradoxes originated in the Christian mysteries: the Redemption accomplished by virtue of the Incarnation, the Passion and the Resurrection of the Mediator. The Calvinists, however, stressed the imputation of Christ's merits and the working of grace in each individual soul; from this point of view the mystery was completely interiorized and attention was focused on a single plane, the spiritual one. Their dualistic emphasis on the conflict between the spirit and the flesh did not invite a paradoxical expression. The post-Tridentine Roman Catholics paid more attention to the historical episodes of Christ's life on earth, the Nativity, the Crucifixion, and the Resurrection as sources of emotion and wonder; but their contemplation of the Incarnate God too often dispersed the wonder in a descriptive celebration of particular 'miracles'.

Donne keeps the twofold nature of Christ always immediately present in the reader's mind; he always unites the *concept* of the Redemption with the *event* of the Incarnation, but he shows no interest in the minor miracles of the life of Christ celebrated in Crashaw's epigrams.

What fascinated Donne in the mystery of the Incarnation was not the mere idea of God made man, rather dully expressed in Holy Sonnet XV (13–14). He was only moved and inspired when he evoked the immersion of the divine in the flesh of Mary: 'Thou'hast light in darke, and shutst in little roome, | *Immensity cloystered in thy deare wombe*' ('Corona 2'). He thought of God's descent into the womb of the Virgin as a descent into 'a place | Of middle kind' ('Litanie', 155–6), just as he felt man to be also a mysterious place of union for two natures, carnal and spiritual. His emotion could then flower into a splendid apostrophe to the blessed Mother-maid:

> Whose flesh redeem'd us; that she-Cherubin,
> Which unlock'd Paradise, and made
> One claime for innocence, and disseiz'd sinne,
> Whose wombe was a strange heav'n for there
> God cloath'd himselfe, and grew.
>
> ('Litanie', 38–42)

Donne often played on the traditional paradoxes of the Redemption: the sinless Christ taking upon himself all the sins of the world ('Corona 2'), life and death henceforth exchanging their meaning.[5] He could speak in Calvinistic language of the imputation of merit to fallen man through Christ's sacrifice (To Wooward, 'Like one who'in her third widdowhood', 13–15), but this clear assertion of a judicial relation only satisfied his logical sense though he tried to give it the edge of paradox: 'Thy Blood bought that, the which before was thine' (Holy Sonnet II). Once again his poetic response was more original when man's redemption was felt to be ensured by Christ's Resurrection through a metamorphosis of his entire being, flesh and spirit:

---

[5] 'Marckham', 17; 'Boulstred', 30; 'Elegie on the L.C.', 17–18; 'Corona 6', 5–6.

Hee was all gold when he lay downe, but rose
All tincture, and doth not alone dispose
Leaden and iron wills to good, but is
Of power to make even sinfull flesh like his.

('Resurrection, imperfect')

Redemption, in its individual aspect, was always more passionately desired by Donne in conjunction with the death and resurrection of the human body, often imagined in close conjunction since in his eyes 'death doth touch the Resurrection' ('Hymne to God, my God'). This was a theme on which he spent his eloquence as passionately in his sermons as in his poems.[6] In accordance with his intuition of temporality, he stressed the union of the body and the soul in the *instant* when death severs them, or the *instant* when the soul rejoins the entombed body (Holy Sonnets VI, VII). In the religious poems the frequency and forcefulness of the images is striking. More surprising is the presence of the theme in an early verse epistle, 'The Storme' (47–8), a paradoxical elegy, 'The Autumnall' (41–2), an ironically Platonic love poem, 'The Relique' (10–11). In a letter about the death of a child in 1629 the same urgent need of his sensibility emerged: 'The Grave shall restore me my child . . . and pay me my Earth, when that Earth shall be Amber, a sweet Perfume, in the nostrills of his and my Saviour.'[7] Donne, like Sir Thomas Browne (*Religio Medici*, I. vii), was even tempted by the mortalist heresy. In Holy Sonnet VI he had at first written:

And gluttonous death will instantly unjoynt
My body, and soule, and I shall sleepe a space.
Or presently, I know not, see that Face
Whose feare already shakes my every joynt.

'I know not' implies doubt and suggests anxiety.[8] In the definitive version this was corrected to 'But my'ever waking part shall

---

[6] See 'Harrington', 53–6; 'Marckham', 41–8; *Second Anniversary*, 491–4; 'Corona 6'; Holy Sonnet VII. Among innumerable instances in the *Sermons* attention may be called to his contrast between the immortality of the soul—grasped by 'a naturall mans reason'—and the mysterious raising of the scattered and dissolved body: *Sermons*, VIII. 97–8.

[7] [To Mrs Cokain]: Hayward, p. 495; Gosse, II. 260.

[8] The conscious expression of doubt does not justify Helen Gardner's assumption that Donne, when he wrote this sonnet, 'had given no serious thought to the matter' (*Divine Poems*, p. xlv).

see that face'. Other uncorrected poems, however, suggest the complete immersion of man in the sleep of death (Holy Sonnet X), or the awakening of the soul itself on the day of Resurrection ('Relique', 10; Holy Sonnet VII). Donne later dismissed the idea, but the very ardour with which he debated the question in his sermons, going beyond the cautious views of Calvin and the Anglican Church on the matter, betrays a personal and passionate interest.[9] To have to wait for the enjoyment of heavenly felicity must have been repugnant to him since his imagination always projected itself into an instant future. Yet he remained loath to separate the soul from the body. A paradoxical reconciliation of his contradictory exigencies was achieved in a metaphysical intuition: between the *instant* when the body is abandoned by the soul and the *instant* of its resurrection, there is, in reality, no interval *sub specie aeternitatis*:

Nunc est, Now is the Resurrection come to him, not onely because the last Judgement is involved in the first . . . but because after the death of the Body, there is no more to be done with the Body, till the Resurrection; for as we say of an Arrow, that it is overshot, it is gone, it is beyond the mark, though it be not come to the mark yet, because there is no more to be done to it till it be; so we may say, that he that is come to death, is come to the Resurrection, because he hath not another step to make, another foot to goe, another minute to count, till he be at the Resurrection.   (*Sermons*, VI. 272)

Furthermore, even when he defends the orthodox doctrine, Donne is irresistibly led to ascribe to the soul a resurrection analogous to the resurrection of the flesh. The soul, when leaving the body, forgoes its natural condition:

when in the generall Resurrection, the soule returnes to that state, for which it was created, and to which it hath had an affection, and a desire, even in the fulnesse of the Joyes of Heaven, then, when the soule returnes to her office, to make up the man, because the whole man hath, therefore the soule hath a Resurrection; not from death, but from a deprivation of her former state; that state, which she was made for, and is ever enclined to.   (*Sermons*, VI. 75)

These sermons preached in 1624 and 1625 were contemporary with the elegy in which Donne argued that, since the soul is the

<hr>

[9]   See the numerous texts collected by Gardner, *Divine Poems*, 114–17.

form of the body, the body, in letting it ascend to the 'spheare of formes', anticipated its own resurrection, because, if the form of the body is in heaven, the body, too, in a certain way, must be there ('Hamylton', 25–30). In *Deaths Duell* the dying preacher still insisted that 'the union of the body and soule makes the man, hee whose soule and body are separated by death as long as that state lasts is properly no man' (*Sermons*, X. 236). His theological reflection only confirmed the spontaneous intuition which guided the poet when he spoke of the resurrection of the flesh as an awakening of the whole man from sleep: 'One short sleepe past, wee wake eternally' (Holy Sonnet X). Even in the revised sonnet VI a revealing ambiguity persisted. The sleep of death overcomes the entire *person*, represented by 'I': 'I shall sleep a space'. What remains awake is not a person but only a part of man: 'my'ever waking part'.

Donne's emotions, in verse and prose, were more often and more intensely aroused by the entombed or the glorified body than they were by the liberation of the soul.[10] Definitely unplatonic was his passionate expectation of the moment 'When earthly bodies more celestiall | Shall be, then Angels were, for they could fall' (*Second Anniversary*, 493–4): the hyperbole makes a common dogma singular. Equally remarkable is the poet's insistence on ascribing to the body the attributes of the soul—purity, transparence, and even thought:

> You, for whose body God made better clay
> Or tooke Soules stuffe such as shall late decay . . .[11]

> . . . her pure, and eloquent blood
> Spoke in her cheekes, and so distinctly wrought
> That one might almost say, her body thought.
>
> (*Second Anniversary*, 244–6)

> He would have justly thought this body a soule.
>
> ('Resurrection, imperfect', 21)

Donne never spiritualizes the human body in the Platonic way as Lord Herbert will.[12] The glorified body, as he conceives

---

[10] The way in which Donne's personal interest in bodily resurrection influenced his theology was explored in Carey's *John Donne* (London, 1981), 219–29.

[11] Bedford: 'Honour is so sublime perfection', 22–3. Cf. 'Boulstred', 46–8.

[12] See Ch. 14, pp. 61–2.

it, is not immaterial: it is not different in substance from the living body, it is not a new body.[13] There would be no full restoration of the person if the soul was not reunited with the body fashioned for it even before its creation.[14] He showed a profound sense of the eminent dignity of the human body even in its life on earth. In his early paradox 'That The Gifts of The Body Are Better Than Those of the Mind', his witty arguments were not always frivolous. In a truly religious perspective the Dean of St Paul compared the Christian exaltation of the human body with the Copernican revolution (*Sermons*, VI. 265). It is this respect for the body, even more than the Protestant viewpoint, that inspired his aversion to asceticism, mortification, and flagellation, led him to condemn the use of torture in judicial investigations, and in the century of rising capitalism, to denounce those who impose overtaxing labour upon men (*Sermons*, VI. 271, 266–8).

Yet the author of the *Second Anniversary* had evoked the misery of the soul 'made but in a sinke', contaminated with original sin by this 'lumpe of fleshe', this 'curded milke', the human embryo. With the bitterness of medieval Christian pessimism he had claimed that the Anchorite 'fixt to a pillar', 'bath'd in all his ordures', does not dwell 'So fowly as our Soules in their first-built Cels' (164–72). Was this morbid loathing called for by the theme? The same bitter disgust emerges at times in the *Divine Poems* and in the *Sermons*.[15] Besides, one can trace in Donne's profane poetry a similar duality between his apology for the senses, the 'joys' ('Elegie XIX',

---

[13] This persistent identity, everywhere implicit, is explicit in 'Obsequies to the Lord Harrington', 53–6, and in *Death's Duell*: '*recompacting* this *dust* into the *same body*, and *reanimating* the *same body* with the *same soule*' (*Sermons*, X. 239).

[14] Donne follows St Augustine in his demonstration that the soul of each man is created by God at the very moment when it animates the body: 'As S. *Augustin* cannot conceive any interim, any distance, between the creating of the soule, and the infusing of the soule into the body, but eases himselfe upon that, *Creando infundit, and infundendo creat*' (*Sermons*, V. 349). Donne's rejection of the pre-existence of the soul is not surprising but one may wonder why he rejected traducianism, accepted by Luther and many Reformed theologians, and apparently more consonant with his own 'naturalistic' bent and his sin-consciousness. It may not be merely out of sympathy with the doctrine that had prevailed in the Catholic Church. We have seen he was fascinated by the idea of 'creation' and a simultaneous birth of the soul and the body would be attractive to a mind accustomed to thinking on two levels simultaneously.

[15] 'Litanie', 19–20; *Sermons*, X. 231–2.

33) of the flesh, and his inclination elsewhere to depict its repulsive aspects,[16] an inclination which, though called for by a satiric intent, seems to disclose a genuine repugnance. Even in the *Songs and Sonets* he was always conscious of the wretchedness of the body; with the eye of the anatomist he discerned the skeleton, the nerves, and the viscera beneath the surface seduction. But he felt such a pressing need for a tangible satisfaction, he had such an acute sense of the role played by the body in all our affections that he was compelled as a lover to reconcile body and soul in the 'Extasie' and, as a Christian, to stress equally the corruption and the essential goodness of the body, a balance maintained even by Platonizing theologians when they do not stray from the essential spirit of Christianity. Like Montaigne he would have agreed with this statement of Augustine: 'He that praiseth the nature of the soule, as his principall good, and accuseth nature of the flesh as evill, assuredly he both carnally affecteth the soule, and carnally escheweth the flesh since he is of this mind not by divine verity, but humane vanity.'[17]

The Christian conception of human nature calls for a psychological theory that recognizes the duality of the spirit and the flesh and at the same time surmounts it. The union of the divine nature and human nature is accomplished supernaturally in the God-Man. Since the will of the Creator joined the human soul with an earthly body by a transcendent act, a natural harmony between their operations must also be established. This role was entrusted to the animal spirits, as Donne explained in 'The Extasie' (61–4):

> As our blood labours to beget
>   Spirit, as like souls as it can,
> Because such fingers need to knit
>   That subtile knot, which makes us man.

These spirits are of a 'middle nature' and man could not exist without their mediation:

In the constitution and making of a natural man, the body is not the man, nor the soul is not the man, but the union of these two makes up

---

[16] See Elegies I, II, IV, VIII.
[17] *Essays*, III. 13; Florio, Everyman, III. 384.

the man; the spirits in a man which are the thin and active part of the blood, and so are of a kind of middle nature, between soul and body, those spirits are able to doe the office, to unite and apply the faculties of the soul to the organs of the body, and so there is a man. (*Sermons,* II. 261)

The natural mediation accomplished by the spirits is not structurally analogous to the conjunction of the divine nature and the human nature in the person of Christ and Donne's adoption of the theory is not a distinctive trait of his poetry. It was, however, the psychological theory that would best satisfy a mind accustomed to thinking in terms of dual nature and mediation. Moreover, nuances appear in the very use made of these concepts by Renaissance thinkers and poets. When their mode of thinking is predominantly Neoplatonic, they either stress the essential duality of mind and body, or, like Vaughan and the Hermetists, the unbroken continuity of life throughout the forms of existence.[18] With Donne there are neither multiple emanations, nor imperceptible gradations and indeterminate boundaries: the role of the animal spirits is always to link together two distinct natures and compose out of them a unique person.

This conjunction of body and soul provides a pattern for other conjunctions. It was used by the preacher as a justification of the sacraments (*Sermons,* II. 262). There is even an ironical resemblance between the lover's plea for carnal enjoyment in 'The Extasie' and the preacher's argument borrowed from Tertullian: 'All that the soule does, it does in, and with, and by the body' (*Sermons,* IV. 358). Yet Donne does not display a sacramental sensibility as keen as George Herbert's or Crashaw's. He makes no allusion to the Holy Communion in his religious poetry; in the *Devotions* (Expostulation 7) the fervour of his prayer is less noticeable than his concern with associating the sign and the thing signified. Donne's attitude to the Eucharist was not dictated by the love of Christ but by his need to possess a specific and sensible assurance of God's mercies and his own salvation (*Sermons,* II. 254). The Real Presence answered this need and he had no reason to hanker after the Roman doctrine of transubstantiation since it substituted a kind

[18] See Ch. 13, pp. 230–4.

of metamorphosis for the inexplicable conjunction of the sensible and the spiritual.[19]

The fascination that dual natures held for Donne's mind was reflected in conceits which are quite diverse, yet identical in structure. The way in which they flowed imaginatively, if not logically, from the fundamental paradox of the Incarnation is clearly revealed in this passage from a sermon:

Saint *Bernard* spent his consideration upon three remarkable conjunctions, this Day. First, a Conjunction of God, and Man in one person, Christ Jesus; Then a conjunction of the incompatible Titles, Maid and Mother, in . . . the blessed Virgin *Mary*: And thirdly a conjunction of Faith, and the Reason of man, that so beleeves, and comprehends those two conjunctions. Let us accompany those three with another strange conjunction, in the first words of this Text, *Propterea*, *Therefore*; for that joins the anger of God, and his mercy together.[20]

The Christian liturgy offered the poet an opportunity for multiplying the paradoxes upon the coincidence of extremes in 'The Annuntiation and Passion falling upon one day':

> . . . this day hath showne
> Th'Abridgement of Christs story, which makes one
> (As in plaine Maps, the furthest West is East)
> Of the'Angels *Ave*, and *Consummatum est*.

Hands, in their 'double office', become the symbol of man's dual vocation (Bedford: 'T'have written then', 41–5):

> As dead low earth ecclipses and controules
>   The quick high Moone: so doth the body, Soules.
> In none but us, are such mixt engines found,
>   As hands of double office: For, the ground
> We till with them; and them to heav'n wee raise.

Donne seems to give us the secret of his favourite conceits when, speaking of the Old Testament and the Gospel, he evokes 'that harmony, which made of two | One law, and did unite, but not confound' ('Litanie', 66–7). To unite without confounding, to include one within the other while leaving them distinct—two beings, two things, two concepts, two sentiments—this was the

---

[19] See *Devotions*, Expost. 14 (Raspa, p. 75) and *Sermons*, II. 258.
[20] *Sermons*, VI. 168. Cf. the various 'marriages' accomplished by God in the spiritual and the natural order: ibid. VIII. 94.

natural inclination of a mind passionately concerned at once with synthesis and distinction; a mind able to control the diverse impulses of a complex sensibility and assemble a multiplicity of ideas or impressions within the unity of the consciousness which conceived or experienced them *simultaneously*.

Obviously an individual disposition would not have been enough to produce so many conceits celebrating paradoxical unions if Christian dogma and its Patristic and scholastic elaboration, on the one hand, and, on the other hand, the psychophysiology and metaphysics of the Renaissance had not offered the poet some ready-made models and furnished his imagination with elements for his more original discoveries. Yet it would be an error to consider the age, the environment, or the prevailing episteme as the *origin* of Donne's predilection for paradoxes based upon dual natures. Many minds among Donne's contemporaries accepted the same dogmas, embraced the same concepts, yet did not spontaneously pour into their writings the same profusion of conceits based on twofold natures. Even admitting that a few of them perhaps did, it will be clear that others, such as Edward Herbert, Vaughan, and Traherne, followed other trends of thought. Within each age, more or less diverse spiritual and intellectual 'families' have always coexisted. Historical circumstances certainly contribute to the appearance or the predominance of each 'family'. But the reason why any writer came to belong to one of these families must be sought within the individual. This personal inclination, no doubt, is partly determined by external influences; childhood impressions, the parents and the social group, the profession, etc., but this web of circumstances is particular for each individual.

The homology between various structural traits in Donne's way of thinking and imagining is further proof of their individual character. His insistence on the conjunction of body and soul is in harmony with his conceits on 'form', and more generally with his constant association of the abstract and the concrete.

Donne's fascination with the very idea of form is not surprising, since he had a passion for definition. Form gives being,[21] and to give form is not only to confer existence but to define:

---

[21]   See *Second Anniversarie*, 72; 'Nocturnall', 20; 'Elegie XI', 76.

'Her name defin'd thee, gave thee forme and frame' (*First Anniversary*, 37). In characteristic conceits the poet insists that 'form' itself is capable of a higher 'form': the soul is 'form', but virtue—or grace—may be 'our formes forme and our soules soule'.[22] Noticeable is the tendency to give form an individualizing function: it defines or directs one's being or soul. Although he usually follows St Thomas, Donne often suggests the Scotist and Nominalist theory of individualization through form rather than through matter. In the *Anniversaries* the form of the universe is incarnated in Elizabeth Drury, who is herself a symbol of the particular grace of a personal God. Thus even an abstract notion conveys an individual and concrete meaning.

Critics have underscored the pre-eminence of abstraction in the poetry of Donne;[23] yet, as George Rylands early noted, abstract words in Donne 'nearly always define states of mind or of being'.[24] These abstract realities are conceived as 'things'—occasionally 'things which are not' ('Nocturnall')—and are never personified after the manner of Chaucer, or Spenser, or even Shakespeare in 'She sat like patience on a monument, | Smiling at grief' (*Twelfth Night*, II. iv. 117–18). The abstract word in Spenser is either a bare concept, like the divine attributes in the *Hymn of Heavenly Beauty* (110–11), or a 'subject' which is 'described', as in the processions of allegorical figures in the *Faerie Queene*. With Donne the abstract word, defining a state, becomes a 'substantial' concept. In 'A Nocturnall' even nothingness has weight, becomes palpable:

> For his art did expresse
> A quintessence even from nothingnesse,
> From dull privations, and leane emptinesse.

The epithets at first suggest a condensed personification which is to the personifications of Spenser what metaphor is to allegory. The following lines (my italics)

> He ruin'd mee, and I am re-begot
> Of absence, darknesse, death, *things* which are not.

---

[22] To Mr R.W., 'If, as mine is . . .', 32; cf. 'Goodfriday', 6–10.
[23] From Courthope's *History of English Poetry* (III. 160) to J. Bennett's *Four Metaphysical Poets* (Cambridge, 1934), 41.
[24] *Essays and Studies*, 41 (1931), 53–84.

take away from these abstractions any human character. Yet a tremor of existence is imparted to them, as to the forces that psychoanalysts conceive as impersonal, unconscious, and nevertheless endowed with a capacity for desire and activity. Donne, unlike his contemporaries, never personifies Love, except when he addresses the ancient 'God of Love' satirically.[25] 'Aire and Angels' rests upon the idea of incarnation, not of personification. In 'Twicknam Garden' love has a spider's and a serpent's power of secreting poison: the animal metaphors express psychological and physiological characteristics. Because such metaphors 'define' but do not 'represent' love, the poet elsewhere can 'give it a diet', feed it on sighs and tears without logical incongruity and without producing an allegorical or emblematic effect ('Loves Diet'). He can also present it as a force at times spiritual, at other times physiological in 'The Extasie' (33–44) and in 'Loves Growth':

> But if this medecine, love, which cures all sorrow
> With more, not onelie bee no quintessence,
> But mixt of all stuffes, paining soule, or sense,
> And of the Sunne his working vigour borrow,
> Love's not so pure, and abstract . . .

Donne's interest in scientific thought may partly account for the fact that his abstractions are 'not so pure' and the very words 'quintessence', 'nothingness', 'time', 'space', and 'form' take on a quasi-material value. But the particular resonance of the abstract word in his poetry is largely due to his appetite for substance, his need for the tangible, his constant desire to incarnate spiritual realities. In this 'metaphysical' poetry form is always entrapped in matter and the poet's philosophy has more affinities with Aristotelianism than Platonism.

Just as the opacity of the concrete penetrates the abstraction, the light of the abstract plays upon the surface of the concrete in the poetry of Donne. This trait is not singular; examples may be found in the dramas of Shakespeare, Chapman, and Webster: they correspond to a state of the language which must be studied historically. What is peculiar with Donne is the tension and the balance between a vivid subjectivity and the objectivity of

---

[25] In 'Loves Usury', 'Loves Deitie', 'Farewell to love'.

the concepts used to define an inner state. The author of 'Loves Growth', 'A Nocturnall', 'The Dissolution', 'The Extasie' considers actions and events only as they impinge upon his consciousness; yet he gives his states of mind an objective nature by expressing them in terms of psychic or physiological phenomena or metaphysical truths. A singular aspect of his mind is certainly the constant transposition of the sensible into the abstract.

This tendency cannot be ascribed to dull senses. Donne's sensitiveness to touch is acknowledged. He vividly reproduces the noise heard 'when winds in our ruin'd Abbeyes rore' ('Satyre II', 60). He can conjure a floating moon shipwrecked on Tenerife (*First Anniversary*, 286–8) and create pictorial contrasts of light and shadow (*Second Anniversary*, 85–8; 'Dreame', 11). He is attentive enough to nuances to discern that 'shadows upon clay will be dirty, and in a garden green and flowery'.[26] But these touches are relatively rare. Donne is a man for whom the exterior world exists, but the world perceived mainly interests him in so far as it is conceived. Usually he will not evoke it for its own sake, but through images which have the same function as scholastic or scientific propositions meant to illustrate, prove, or define. When he contemplates the sensible world in and for itself, he renders it through a network of abstractions. One could turn against him his own assertion in the *First Anniversary* (278–80): 'For of Meridians, and Parallels, | Man hath weav'd out a net, and this net thrown | Upon the Heavens, and now they are his owne.'

The erotic poet will not depict nakedness sensuously as the other Elizabethans, but only name it: 'Full nakedness! All joyes are due to thee' ('Elegie XIX'). He will not show the power of a face by depicting its radiance but by proclaiming its effects: 'This face, by which he [Love] could command | And change the Idolatrie of any land' ('Loves Exchange'). His intense desire for a woman is suggested through such abstract notions as 'wealth' or 'honor', or 'all States', and 'both the Indias of spice and Myne' is a concept, not a vision ('Sunne Rising', 17–24).

Donne's only descriptive poems, 'The Storme' and 'The Calme', were early poems, but they already displayed his

---

[26] Letter to Goodyer; Gosse, I. 219.

intellectuality[27] and his tendency to interiorize and humanize the outer world:

> Mildly it [the wind] kist our sailes, and fresh and sweet
> As, to a stomack sterv'd, whose insides meete,
> Meate comes, it came; and swole our sailes, when wee
> So joy'd as *Sara'* her swelling joy'd to see.

('Storme', 19–22)

In the same way he translates cosmic confusion into terms of human experience, avoiding sensory data and placing himself within his own faculty of perception:

> But when I wakt, I saw, that I saw not;
> I, and the Sunne, which should teach mee'had forgot
> East, West, Day, Night, and I could onely say,
> If the world had lasted, now it had beene day.

('Storme', 37–40)

Here again Donne achieves his usual balance between objectivity and subjectivity. The world just projected upon the blueprint of his consciousness according to intellectual co-ordinates is in no way distorted. Donne ignored the pathetic fallacy[28] and the later Romantic subjectivism. In 'Twicknam Garden' the transubstantiation achieved by love takes place within the poet's consciousness but does not affect his perceptions: his sadness does not prevent him from realizing that the garden is a pleasant place untouched by his own melancholy.

A study of colour in the poetry of Donne would show that he was never content with pure sensation. *Blue* and *green* appear only four times and turn into concepts.[29] *Gold* and *golden* refer to the precious metal but do not evoke a colour. A purely concrete use of colour only occurs in a few Elegies, in the Epithalamions, and in *Metempsychosis*. Colour becomes a

---

[27] In the lines praised by Jonson—'And in one place lay | Feathers and dust, to day and yesterday'—a concrete detail *signifies* the perfect immobility of the ship.

[28] Donne in 'Twicknam Garden' wants to be made a mandrake or a fountain so he may *groan* here or *weep out* his year. Yet, in apparent contradiction, he adds 'let mee | Some *senselesse* peece of this place bee' (my italics). One must understand: let me become an unfeeling object which nevertheless displays the outer signs of love, tears and groaning. Donne does not ascribe a feeling to the mandragora or the fountain.   [29] In 'Communitie', 14, and *Second Anniversary*, 287.

'quality' apprehended by the intellect in 'Elegie II' (11) as well as in the *First Anniversary* (361–3). The mournful admission 'Why grasse is greene, or why our blood is red | Are mysteries' (*Second Anniversary*, 288–9) suggests that the 'metaphysical' mind, unsatisfied by the raw data of the senses, acknowledges the unintelligibility of existence.

White and red do not occur in the *Songs and Sonets*, even as abstractions: their value is moral or religious in the poetry of Donne. In the Satires, the Epicedes, and in some epistles, *white* is used as a symbol of purity or integrity.[30] In the Divine Poems the ethical contrast of black and white, however, is rare and only found in alliance with the pre-eminent oppositon of white and red.[31] The light and shadow contrast, so dear to Vaughan and the mystics, appears only once.[32] Donne saw the religious life as a conflict between the *red* appetency of the flesh and the *white* aspiration to chastity and salvation, for God can purge our 'red earth', Christ's blood 'dyes red soules to white', and man will only have access to heaven 'in his purple wrapp'd'.[33] It is the meaning of the colour that is imposed upon the imagination when the poet speaks of his 'mindes white truth' (Holy Sonnet VIII) and his 'muses white sincerity' ('Corona 1'). For a long time critics have opposed Spenser the imagist and Donne the intellectual. Contemporary literary history has had a tendency to ignore or play down the dissimilarities. It is true that sensations and concepts were closely linked in all Renaissance minds; but Spenser, like the emblematists, shows white clothing to denote purity; he does not like Donne associate the epithet 'white' with an abstract term, combining the two in a concrete concept.

The interpenetration of the abstract and the concrete in the

---

[30] 'Satyre V', 68–9; Wotton, 'Sir, more then kisses', 41–2; Woodward, 'Like one . . .', 13; 'Funerall Elegie', 75; 'Marckham', 41; *Metempsychosis*, 404.

[31] 'Hamylton', 33–6. In Holy Sonnet IV Donne can depict his soul as both black and red because he has only the meaning of the terms in mind.

[32] In 'Hymne to Christ', 29–32, but night here is a mere symbol of death or renunciation of the world. Light as a symbol of the divine hardly appears, even when the soul at the end of the *Second Anniversary* reaches a Heaven very different from Dante's.

[33] 'Litanie', st. i; Holy Sonnet IV; 'Hymne to God my God', 26. The opposition is found in *Pseudo-Martyr*, sig. E.1, and in the *Sermons*, II. 210–11. These symbols have a Biblical, liturgical, or Patristic origin; but Donne's insistence is nevertheless significant and related to his obsession with sin and salvation: *Sermons*, VI. 166.

poetry of Donne has a complex origin, at once in the historical evolution of the language and in the poet's individuality, his intellectuality and subjectivity allied to a keen awareness of particular objects in their materiality. One cannot claim it proceeded from the fascination 'bifold natures' exerted over his mind, but it proves at least consonant with it: in each case his mind and poetry achieve a conjunction of two different orders of reality.

CHAPTER 12

George Herbert and Richard Crashaw: Two Versions of the Christian Paradox

With George Herbert as with Donne the awareness of the two natures of Christ—'In Christ, two natures met' ('Offering')— and of man's amphibious nature commanded his vision of the world and his poetic inspiration as if it were a structure of his mind.[1] It favoured the simultaneous perception of distinct, yet indissolubly linked realities or truths.

In 'Affliction IV' the poet describes himself as 'A wonder tortur'd in the space | Betwixt this world and that of grace', but he always seeks to bring both worlds together, knowing that God's power and love 'Make one place ev'ry where' ('Temper I', 28). The Lord's day to him is 'the fruit of this, the next worlds bud' ('Sunday'). He delights in 'The bridall of the earth and skie' ('Vertue') and can find an image of it in a sundial— *Conjugium Caeli Terraeque*—removing the fear that would be inspired 'By the earth without light, by the flesh, without mind' (*Lucus*, xxxi).

That the spirit and the flesh cannot be separated was indeed Herbert's conviction as well as Donne's. Man's middle nature between angel and beast was a Renaissance commonplace, but the author of *The Temple*, unlike the Platonists or the satirists, was never tempted to privilege one of them, nor merely to oppose them as Hamlet did (II. ii. 315–21). In his intuition of the complexities of mire and blood, he will sing to his God:

> Whether I flie with angels, fall with dust,
> Thy hands made both, and I am there.
>
> ('Temper I')

[1] Mario Di Cesare also called attention to the central place of the Incarnation in Herbert's poetry: 'Herbert's Prayer (I) and the Gospel of John', in *Too Rich to Clothe the Sunne*, ed. C. Summers (Pittsburgh, 1980), 107.

'Mans Medley' insists on man's doubleness:

> To this life things of sense
> Make their pretence:
> In th'other Angels have a right by birth:
> Man ties them both alone,
> And makes them one,
> With th'one hand touching heav'n, with th'other earth.

Another poem, 'Man' (34–6), extends this conception of the human condition:

> All things unto our flesh are kinde
> In their descent and being; to our minde
> In their ascent and cause.

Herbert's conception of the Eucharist will shed light on his essential mode of religious sensibility.[2] An examination of his views on the sacrament will be more enlightening from my point of view than the general controversy over his 'Protestantism'.[3]

Lutherans and Calvinists alike, while denying any form of transubstantiation, acknowledged the Real Presence of Christ; what is of interest to me is the way in which they conceived of it. When they were Calvinists, as they mostly were before the Laudian reaction, Anglicans maintained that the Body and Blood of Christ are *verily* and *indeed* taken by the faithful in the Lord's Supper, but usually insisted that they were only 'taken spiritually and with the mouth of our faith'. Calvin himself had shown some distrust of 'humanly devised symbols, being images of things absent rather than marks of things present (which they

---

[2] For a fuller discussion, see *Poètes métaphysiques*, I. 323–41.

[3] As Ilona Bell remarked, 'Scholars have placed Herbert at every point along the spectrum of English Protestantism, from ceremonial Anglo-Catholicism to radical Puritanism' (quoted by M. C. Schoenfeldt in *Prayer and Power: George Herbert and Renaissance Courtship* (Chicago, 1991), 12). The best-balanced view to my mind was presented by Achsah Guiborry: *The Temple* 'expresses not a harmonious, peaceful middle way, but rather the deeply conflicted *via media* of the seventeenth-century English church' (*Ceremony and Community from Herbert to Milton* (Cambridge, 1998), 45). My purpose is to determine mental structures irrespective of ecclesiastical or political allegiances, though a statistical predominance of different views may be expected in the different groups: Milton could be at once a Puritan and an Arminian, but there were few Arminians among the Puritans. A. D. Nuttall's subtle analysis of Herbert's theological Calvinism leads to the admission that his poetry is a 'largely unconscious critique of Calvinism' (*Overheard by God. Fiction and Prayer in Herbert, Milton, Dante and St John* (London, 1980), 75).

very often falsely represent)',[4] a suspicion which seems to anticipate the later distrust of metaphorical language among seventeenth-century scientists. The signs given by God could be trusted because 'so great . . . is their similarity and closeness, that transition from one [the sign] to the other [the thing signified] is easy'.[5] But Calvin's mode of reasoning through analogy proves vastly different from the symbolic mode when he argues that 'when bread is given as a symbol of Christ's body, we must at once grasp this comparison: as bread nourishes, sustains, and keeps the life of our body, so Christ's body is the only food to invigorate and enliven our soul'.[6] Calvin could be content with this kind of 'similitude' because he thought, as Sir John Stradling later put it, that faith was foremost, that 'by believing truly, we do eate, | There is no feeding else the soul to fill'.[7] But the relation thus established between the outward sign and the spiritual substance seems more rhetorical than ontological. Calvin's followers, though repeating that the sacrament is 'no figure bare', either presented the Eucharist as the purely spiritual communication of supernatural life or multiplied mere similitudes, as Richard Bolton did, comparing the treatment endured by corn to be turned into bread with the sufferings of the body of Christ, who feeds the soul as bread feeds the body.[8]

In a version of 'The H. Communion' (Hutchinson, p. 200) excluded from the Bodleian MS of *The Temple*, presumably because of its author's dissatisfaction with it, Herbert, rejecting both transubstantiation and the doctrine of 'impanation',[9] had emphasized the duality of the sensible and the spiritual, and failed to suggest their close union:

> Into my soule this cannot pass;
> fflesh (though exalted) keepes his grass
> And cannot turn to soule.

---

[4] *Institutes of the Christian Religion*, ed. John T. McNeill, XVII. 21 (London, 1961), p. 1385.   [5] Ibid. XVII. 21, p. 1386.
   [6] Ibid. XVII. 3, p. 1363. About the words of institution—'Take, eat, this is my body'—he says: 'this expression is a metonymy, a figure of speech commonly used in Scripture', and gives as an instance: 'the rock from which water flowed in the desert [Exod. 17: 6] was Christ [1 Cor. 10: 4]'.
   [7] *Divine Poems* (1625), V. 248–50 (p. 216).
   [8] *The Saints Selfe-Enriching Examination* (1634), 39–40; there are further similitudes with the pressing of grapes and the shedding of Christ's blood.
   [9] A medieval doctrine (Hutchinson, in *Works*, 548), but Luther revived it.

> Bodyes & Minds are different Spheres,
>   Nor can they change their bounds & meres,
>   But keep a constant Pole.

Though the doctrine is not really different, the perspective has changed in the later version (Hutchinson, p. 52):

> Not in a rich furniture, or fine array,
>   Nor in a wedge of gold,
>   Thou, who for me wast sold,
> To me dost now thy self convey;
> For so thou should'st without me still have been,
>   Leaving within me sinne;
>
> But by the way of nourishment and strength
>   Thou creep'st into my breast:
>   Making thy way my rest,
> And thy small quantities my length;
> Which spread their forces into every part,
>   Meeting sinnes force and art.
>
> Yet can these not get over to my soul,
>   Leaping the wall that parts
>   Our souls and fleshly hearts;
> But as th' outworks, they may controll
> My rebel-flesh, and carrying thy name,
>   Affright both sinne and shame.
>
> Onely thy grace, which with these elements comes,
>   Knoweth the ready way,
>   And hath the privie key,
> Op'ning the souls most subtile rooms;
> While those to spirits refin'd, at doore attend
>   Dispatches from their friend.

On the one hand the poet maintains a clear separation between the sensible and the spiritual, the fleshy heart and the soul to whom the divine grace alone has access. On the other hand, he ascribes to the bread and wine, absorbed 'by the way of nourishment', the capacity to act upon the 'outworks' of the soul and control his 'rebel-flesh'. He even assumes that these material 'elements' have this efficacy because they are 'to spirits refin'd' in his own body. This may not be sound theology, but it is curiously in harmony with Donne's argument in 'The Extasie'. In both poems the frontier between body and soul cannot be crossed by the 'spirits' (though Donne describes them 'as like souls' as the blood can make them), and yet these spirits ensure a close connection. Neither poet apparently would be satisfied by a purely spiritual ecstasy. With his thoughts lifted to heaven by the divine banquet, Herbert cries: 'Give me my captive soul, or take | My bodie also thither' (25–6). Donne assumed that in human love 'soule into the soule may flow, | Though it to body first repaire'. This was not applicable to divine grace and Herbert substituted two distinct actions: that of grace on the soul, that of the elements on the body. But the main point is the same: body and soul have parallel, though not identical, activities and enjoyments, closely linked, yet never confused.[10]

This parallelism is different from the psycho-physiology of the age. Herbert knew that 'an herb destilled, and drunk, may dwell next door, | On the same floore, | To a brave soul' ('Praise I'), but this influence and proximity did not imply the ontological continuity between organic life and the life of the soul assumed by the Hermetists and the Paracelsians.[11] The starting-point in his reflection is the sense of his relationship to God: the Eucharist 'concerneth mee & Thee' (Hutchinson, p. 200). Since man is made up of body and soul, Christ will communicate not only his grace, but his own flesh and blood. How can it be? Calvin agreed that Christ is incorporated in us as we are in him. He rejected the purely commemorative interpretation of the sacrament and maintained that Christ communicates his body to the believer. But, since the bread and wine were only signs, he assumed that the conjunction between our body and the body of Christ was effected by the Holy Ghost, 'the channel by which Christ, and all He is and possesses, is conveyed to us'.[12] He was thus led once more to a similitude: since the Sun through its beams sends its very substance to breed and nourish the fruits

---

[10] I have no 'theological' objection to the later analysis of the two Holy Communion poems by G. E. Veith in *Reformation Spirituality: The Religion of George Herbert* (Bucknell UP, 1985). He concludes that 'the doctrine of the Real Presence seems to have been closest to Herbert's experience' and assumes that he could 'use the various interpretations [of Reformed theology] with unusual flexibility' (218–19). But I do not think that 'his inconsistencies are simply those of the Church of England'; I believe he is perfectly consistent and original in the requirements of his individual sensibility. On the difference between Calvin's and Herbert's views see also R. V. Young, 'Herbert and the Real Presence', *Renascence*, 45 (1993), 179–95.   [11] See Ch. 13, pp. 230–4.

[12] *Institutes*, XII. iv. 11–24.

of the earth, the irradiation of Christ's Spirit may well communicate his body and blood.[13] Hooker retained the simile though
he insisted on the transcendent nature of the communication:
'his body and blood are in that very subject whereunto they
minister life not only by effect or operation, even as the influence of the heavens is in plants, beasts, men, and in every thing
which they quicken, but also by a more divine and mystical kind
of union, which maketh us one with him even as he and the
Father are one'.[14] Before Andrewes, Montague, and Laud,
Hooker, however, assumed 'we need not greatly to care or
inquire' in what way the body and blood of Christ are conveyed
to us in the sacrament.[15]

George Herbert was more precise when he suggested a
parallel action of divine grace on the soul and of the material
elements on the body. I have found no clear theological precedent for this claim,[16] though in the fifteenth-century *Imitatio
Christi* the Eucharist was said to restore the body as well as
the soul.[17] Herbert's sacramental approach in *The Temple*
reveals his mode of thought and sensibility. Constantly aware
of the twofold nature of man as priest and poet, he stresses the
concomitance of two simultaneous actions in divided or
distinguished worlds; in a single flash he grasps two realities,
sensible and spiritual, at once distinct and conjoined. In
Calvinistic doctrine the conjunction seemed gratuitous since
the spiritual alone had efficacy and meaning. Catholic
doctrine, which the sensuous imagination of Crashaw will
espouse of its own accord, blurred the distinction and relied

---

[13] *Institutes*, XII. iv. 24.

[14] *Laws*, V. lvii. 5; cf. lvi. 9–10 on 'divers similitudes' and the notion of participation.   [15] *Laws*, V. lxvii. 6.

[16] D. R. Dickson has recently offered a 'Galenic' interpretation: when the heart
(the seat of the soul) fails to produce enough purified 'spirits', the health of both
body and soul is impaired (*GHJ* 11 (1987), 10–11), but this is hardly a theological
justification.

[17] 'Tanta est aliquando haec gratia, ut ex plenitudine collatae devotionis, non
tantum mens, sed et debile corpus vires sibi praestitas sentiat ampliores': *Imitatio*,
IV. i. 11. Herbert, who often writes about the Eucharist in the spirit of the *Imitatio*,
may have noted this assertion. In his paraphrase Corneille, too, emphasized and
sought to explain the influence on the body: 'Tu descends quelquefois avec telle
abondance | Qu'après l'âme remplie, un doux regorgement | En répand sur le corps
le rejaillissement, | Et l'anime à son tour par sa vive influence' (*L'Imitation de Jésus-
Christ. Traduite en vers par Pierre Corneille*, ed. Bernard de Give (Paris, 1941),
440).

on a kind of metamorphosis. Herbert's mode of apprehension was truly original.

This mode governed his poetic inspiration as well as his religious emotions. His most deeply felt paradoxes bring together but never confuse contrary notions, indissolubly connected in human experience: the finite and the infinite, time and eternity, life and death.[18] The writers influenced by Calvinism, when they expressed spiritual truths, either kept the contrasting notions well apart or abolished the contrast in Neoplatonic idealism. With Crashaw, who joined the Roman Church, transubstantiation seems to become a model for an imaginative interfusion of the sensible and the spiritual which melt into one another.

Herbert's handling of the abstract and the concrete will again illustrate his tendency to bring contraries together without blending them. He even refrains from the kind of interpenetration observed in the poetry of Donne; he seldom offers palpable abstractions and avoids scholastic quiddities. His mind seems to move in a purely material universe, clotted with objects; but the reader's mind is constantly alerted to the meaning of these objects. Not after the manner of allegory, for the image and the meaning are grasped metaphorically in a single mental act: 'Feed no man in his sinnes', 'Dresse and undresse thy soul' ('Church-Porch', 257, 453). This is not by itself a distinctive stylistic trait in Herbert's age though its persistence is peculiar. What is remarkable, too, is the degree of compression achieved. Donne at times offered 'concrete concepts', Herbert produces 'conceptual images' as in 'The fleet Astronomer can bore, | And thred the spheres with his quick piercing minde' ('Vanitie I'), a line perhaps reminiscent of Donne's evocation of the interstellar progress of the soul threading the stars (Second Anniversary, 205–13). Donne mostly relied on explicit comparisons; here between the voyage of the soul and the pith stringing fast the bones of neck and back. In such similes an abstract relation of analogy can be apprehended. Herbert's metaphors do not allow

---

[18] Ted-Larry Pebworth insists on Herbert's 'double vision, an ability to focus simultaneously on two perspectives', in George Herbert: Sacred and Profane, ed. H. Wilcox, R. Todd, and A. MacDonald (Amsterdam, 1995), 146.

us to perceive the image and the meaning separately: abstraction lurks in the image. When bees in 'Praise I' are invited to 'sting my delay', rather than 'sting me delaying', the image does not arrest the attention of the senses, it sets off a conceptual operation of the mind, as in such phrases as:

> He breaks up house, turns out of doores his minde.
>
> Thus clothes being fast, but thy soule loose about thee.
>
> This is but tuning of my breast,
>   To make the musick better.[19]

This intellectuality is recognizable even in a poem like 'The Odour', apparently expressive of a mystic sensuality akin to Crashaw's.[20] The 'orientall fragrancie' of the words *My Master* becomes food for the 'mind':

> With these all day I do perfume my minde,
>   My minde e'en thrust into them both:
>   That I might finde
>   What cordials make this curious broth,
> This broth of smells, that feeds and fats my minde.

Herbert will always 'thrust his mind' into his sensations and emotional experiences. In 'Prayer', a long chain of metaphors (again a usual pattern in Renaissance poetry), the simpler images — 'the Churches banquet', 'Christ-side-piercing spear', the 'milkie way', the 'land of spices' — might have been found under the pen of Southwell or Quarles; some of the conceits — 'Engine against th' Almighty', 'Reversed thunder' — look forward to Crashaw's 'Upwards thou doest weep', and 'Church-bels beyond the starres heard' mainly appeals to the imagination. But 'Heaven in ordinarie' and 'man well drest' give food for thought. 'Gods breath in man returning to his birth' is the compression of two ideas: God gave man the breath of life which returns to God at once in prayer and in death. 'Angels age' implies that prayer gives access to the intemporal existence of the angels since time is suspended in the ecstasy of devotion. As 'the souls blood', prayer inspirits the soul as blood vivifies the body. The final words, 'something understood', seem to be

---

[19] 'Church-Porch', 150, 414; 'Temper I', 23–4.
[20] That is why the discernible Salesian influence had different effects in Herbert's poems and in Crashaw's.

mysteriously loaded with several meanings: prayer as a communication with God is 'secret'[21] and its meaning is 'understood',
implied or only hinted at, for words cannot fully express the
heart's desire; yet prayer is always fully 'understood' by God
who can read in our hearts.

This unified apprehension of the image and the idea is at
times imperilled by the opacity of the concrete, as when the
poet, addressing Holy Scripture, declares 'heav'n lies flat in thee
| Subject to ev'ry mounters bended knee', meaning that it should
be read with humility ('Holy Scriptures I'). But our mind and
imagination are both deeply stirred when human dust and
bones are described as 'The shells of fledged souls left behinde'
('Death'). Unlike the winged hearts of the emblematists, this line
does not call up a precise *visual* image of broken eggs and feath-
ered souls. Its full significance is grasped through the lingering
image of the actual human bones, a faint and almost abstract
impression of white brittleness and dereliction, followed by the
elation of a breaking out, a sense of flight and freedom.

Through this fusion of the image and the idea, Herbert can
bring allegory close to metaphor. He cannot totally change its
nature when he personifies moral notions, Pleasure, Sin, or
Justice ('The World', 'Justice II'). But he often presents a
'person' rather than an attribute, gives us an Overburian
'portrait' in a nutshell: 'Then came brave Glorie puffing by | In
silks that whistled' ('Quip'). Love is no longer a mere allegorical figure when he is the Lover, Christ, and awakes a dramatic
emotion in 'Love III'. The poet's debt to the emblematists is well
known, but the emblem suffers a sea-change in his poetry,[22]
though not on all occasions. When he stays within the convention, as in 'Love Unknown', the heart's progress from fount to
cauldron leaves us unmoved for it is an unreal apologue, a mere

---

[21] The probable meaning of 'understood' in *Paradise Lost*, I. 662.

[22] When I first made this assertion critics had emphasized the debt of 'the most
emblematic of poets'; they recognized his original handling of the form more
recently. Helen Vendler showed how it undergoes 'a constant critique of its own
possibilities, comparable with, but not identical to, the continuing critique of his
own feelings' (*The Poetry of George Herbert* (Cambridge, Mass. 1975), 99). Charles
A. Hutton emphasized 'the freedom which the poet exercised in adapting emblematic material' ('Herbert and the Emblematic Tradition', in *Life's Season'd Timber:
New Essays on George Herbert*, ed. E. Miller and R. Di Yanni (New York, 1987),
69).

fabrication. But a poem like 'The Church-floore' can evoke a poetic thrill:

> Mark you the floore? that square & speckled stone,
>   Which looks so firm and strong,
>   Is *Patience*:
> And th'other black and grave, wherewith each one
>   Is checker'd all along,
>   *Humilitie*:
> The gentle rising, which on either hand,
>   Leads to the Quire above,
>   Is *Confidence*:
> But the sweet cement, which in one sure band
>   Ties the whole frame, is *Love*
>   And *Charitie*.

The 'square speckled stone' *is* an actual slab and *means* intensely. This is not symbolism since the sign and the thing signified are not truly one. Yet 'is' and 'means' become interchangeable when we hear that the stone 'Is *Patience*'. This identification of the sign with the virtue it represents makes our perception of the stone simultaneous with our conception of its meaning; an interweaving of the sensible and the spiritual is achieved in a single apprehension. This is the hallmark of the sacramental imagination, which starts spontaneously from a *given* object to grasp a spiritual reality, whereas the allegorical or emblematic imagination chooses or constructs an image to illustrate some preconceived idea. The significance of the poem so far remains objective: the qualities discerned in the stone fabric of this particular church are the fundamental virtues which can preserve the Christian Church. But the subjective meaning emerges in the closing lines:

> Hither sometimes Sinne steals, and stains
>   The marbles neat and curious veins:
> But all is cleansed when the marble weeps.
>   Sometimes Death, puffing at the doore,
>   Blows all the dust about the floore;
> But while he thinks to spoil the room, he sweeps.
>   Blest be the *Architect*, whose art
>   Could build so strong in a weak heart.

For a moment one could still have in mind the Universal Church weathering the assaults of sin and death; but the final line brings the full revelation of the meaning: God has built His temple in the human heart. Through the chain of images the poet's art and the reader's thought move from the outward object to the inner life.

The 'example' is a form of allegory Herbert cultivated in an original way. Whereas a 'figure' was usually followed by its interpretation, the image of the posy and the abstract idea are closely associated from the very opening of 'Life': 'I made a posie while the day ran by: | Here will I smell my remnant out, and tie | My life within this band'. The apologue, the parable, and the fable did not invite abstraction, yet the distinctive features of Herbert's mind also emerge in his best poems. Comparisons reveal his true genius. The inferiority of 'Christmas' is not merely due to the absence of the dramatic impact created in 'Redemption' by the final encounter and the unexpected revelation; a gratuitously contrived narrative precedes the expression of a meaning merely stated. But each episode of 'Redemption' is at once a fact in the reported action and the figure of an underlying truth: the repeal of the Mosaic law (4), the Incarnation of the Son of God (6–8), the Redemption of mankind effected through his Crucifixion. The coincidence between the sign and the thing signified is so close that in the final image the fictional narrative becomes literal truth:

> At length I heard a ragged noise and mirth
>   Of theeves and murderers: there I him espied,
>   Who straight, *Your suit is granted*, said, & died.

'Peace' and 'The Pilgrimage' are both beautiful poems, but in different ways. The former owes its charm to the calm intensity of an aspiration to repose also found in 'The Pulley', and to the artful modulations of a slow rhythm, particularly at its close. But there is no necessary link between the essential meaning intended and the evocation of the cave, the rainbow, and the Crown Imperial (stanzas i–iii). In the Biblical story of the Prince of Salem the tropological meaning rests on a historical basis, but there is only an artificial or 'mythical' link between the dispersion of the twelve stalks of wheat and the idea that true peace is only given by Christ through the 'bread of life', the Eucharist. Besides, the 'myth' is inserted in the story of an imaginary encounter with the old man: hence an impression of unreality and an inevitable separation of the story and its meaning in the reader's mind. In 'The Pilgrimage' the narrative has from the beginning a dramatic urgency which makes the past experience present: 'I Travell'd on . . . But I was quicken'd by my houre . . . My hill was further: so I flung away.' The allegorical episodes—the cave of Desperation, the rock of Pride, Care's copse—are conventional, but the comparison of human life to a pilgrimage is so natural and the landcape imagery so unobtrusive that the meaning is 'conceived' almost without 'perceiving' the visible sign. This would be a weakness in a narrative by Spenser or Bunyan, but the imagery here is only a language used to convey a spiritual odyssey. It proves most effective when the concrete term, with characteristic ambiguity, takes on an abstract meaning:

> That led me to the wilde of Passion, which
> Some call the wold;

These lines identify Passion—a term including for the poet the desires of the flesh, all his other longings, and even his outbursts of anger—with a *wild* place, a desert and a forest (*wold*). They further suggest that the source of evil is the corruption or obstinacy of the human *will* reduced to a perverse and ineffective velleity (*would*), so that all passion is bound to be unsatisfied. The subtle punning is the oblique and ironical expression of a psychological and Christian truth. Our perception of the meaning does not require a visualization of the images and the last lines again convey the spiritual significance through what might be called a concrete abstraction, the unvisualized 'chair' calling up immediately the idea and the impression of rest: 'After so foul a journey death is fair, | And but a chair.'

Typological images are handled in the same way. The Biblical and iconographical sources of this stanza in 'Sunday' have been fully explored:[23]

> The rest of our Creation
> Our great Redeemer did remove
> With the same shake, which at his passion
> Did th'earth and all things with it move.

23   See R. Tuve, *A Reading of George Herbert* (London, 1951), 159–61.

> As Sampson bore the doores away,
> Christs hand, though nail'd, wrought our salvation,
> And did unhinge that day.

But the essential meaning is not based on the typological correspondences, though Samson's action was a prefiguration of the
removing of Christ's tombstone. The preceding stanza declares
that Christ made·this day, 'this piece of ground', a garden for
those 'who want herbs for their wound', original sin. The parallel with Samson must not distract our attention from the essential correspondence between the Creation and Redemption. The
seventh day had been a day of rest for the Creator of Eden, but
the Passion of the Son of God—the earthquake that 'did
th'earth and all things with it move'—and His Resurrection
were necessary to achieve 'our salvation'.

When he followed the liturgical or typological tradition, as
when he chose the form of the emblem or the apologue, Herbert
had to write within a convention. The persistence of his own
individual modes of thought, imagination, and sensibility is all
the more remarkable. Besides the fusion of the abstract and the
concrete, the other constant features of his individuality I have
already pointed out can be traced in these poems: his self-
consciousness and psychological penetration, his irony and
humour, his reticence and his taste for understatement.[24] The
influence and unchanging characteristics of his personality are
all-pervasive.

Richard Crashaw

Crashaw's poetry again will offer a contrast to George Herbert's
though they seem to be at one in their love of Christ and their
interest in the liturgical tradition.[25]

Different modes of imagination commanded each poet's
apprehension of the Christian mysteries. Herbert's wonder,
like Donne's, was largely intellectual, nearer perplexity than

---

[24] Notably in 'Humilitie' and in the familiar and prosaic handling of the cosmic
in 'Artillerie'.
[25] The contrast was emphasized from a different point of view by R. V. Young
in *Richard Crashaw and the Spanish Golden Age* (New Haven, 1982), 5–9.

admiration. Not only because his Church distrusted miracles but mainly because of his concentration on spiritual experience, he was never attracted to the miraculous. Crashaw was still in the fold of the Anglican Church when he celebrated the miracles of Christ in his *Epigrammata Sacra*; his secular poems on the phoenix, *monstrum dulce*, and on the legends of Pygmalion or Arion show the same taste for the marvellous.[26] Even in the maturer 'Hymn in the Glorious Epiphanie' the description of the 'elaborate love-eclipse' of the sun (152) and the 'new prodigious night' (172) is so elaborate, indeed, that the miracle almost obscures the symbolic significance.

For Crashaw's religious sensibility, therefore, the *spectacle* of the Nativity or the Crucifixion will take precedence over the paradoxes of the Incarnation and the Redemption which fascinated Donne and Herbert.[27] No Christian poet, of course, could fail to mention the union of two natures in Christ in a 'Hymn in the Holy Nativity' (79–82):

> Wellcome, all WONDERS in one sight!
> Aeternity shutt in a span,
> Summer in Winter, Day in Night,
> Heaven in earth, & GOD in MAN.

Yet the poet makes apparently no difference between the metaphysical mystery and the occasional contrasts, the birth of the divine Babe in winter and at night, the strange fact that 'in spite of Darkness, it was DAY' (20). His aim is to call attention to a multiplicity of 'wonders'.[28] He can even lose sight of the essential when he heaps detail upon detail in his attention to the mere circumstances of the Incarnation. When Donne praised the Virgin Mary 'Whose womb was a strange heav'n, for there | God cloath'd himselfe, and grew' ('Litanie', 41–2), the appre-

---

[26] 'Thou Water turn'st to Wine', 'Two Devills at one blow', 'See here an easie Feast', 'Christ bids the dumbe tongue speake', 'Paenitet Artis', 'Squammea vivae', 'Phaenix alumna'.

[27] Many of the 'paradoxes' Anthony Raspa discovered in Crashaw's poetry are only contrasts (e.g. meeting 'love's Noon in Nature's night'), or metaphors (Mary resembling a text in 'Sancta Maria Dolorum'); paradoxes and antitheses are jumbled (*The Emotive Image: Jesuit Poetics in the English Renaissance* (Fort Worth, Tex., 1983), 155, 158, 161).

[28] On the different use of the term 'wonder' by Donne, Marlowe, and Milton, see n. 34 in *Poètes métaphysiques*, I. 424–5.

hension of the mystery was food for thought. Crashaw shows us the Virgin casting an eye on the sphere of her belly where a star is now fixed. Exclaiming ' 'Tis Heav'n, 'tis Heaven she sees', he devotes four lines to the stupendous inversion: ' 'Twas once *looke up*, 'tis now *looke downe* to Heaven' ('That on her Lap she casts'). This is a bad conceit, not for want of taste (a subjective criterion), or want of emotion (Crashaw did worship Mary), but for want of a serious meaning.

We have seen that this poet lived in a world of metamorphosis in which tears turned into milk and dew, pearl and crystal, gold and silver; the Christian was bound to incline of his own accord to the doctrine of transubstantiation even before he became a convert to Rome. Herbert's interpretation of the Real Presence required a mysterious harmony between the world of nature and the world of grace, though it kept them distinct. The mystery is explained away by theological ingenuity in the assumption of a 'transubstantiation', but this process, doing violence to nature, is of a miraculous character: the bread is no longer bread, though it retains the 'accidents', that is the appearance, of bread. In the paraphrase of the *Lauda Sion Salvatorem* attention is dispersed on miraculous side effects. That the believer, when the host is broken, may still find 'whole CHRIST in every crumme' (st. x) is a mere corollary of the essential mystery. In 'The Sacrifice' Herbert had made each episode of the Passion an opportunity for pointing out a relation between the Creator and his creature. In the 'Office of the Holy Cross' Crashaw again dwells on the outward circumstances and only plays rhetorical variations on the common paradox, stressing the 'strange mysterious strife | Of open DEATH & hidden LIFE!'

The poet's paradoxes and wildest conceits are, like the miracles his imagination revels in, mainly a source of wonder and holy inebriation. He often brings contradictory terms together in an oxymoron. But when pain *is* pleasure, transmutation seems to prevail over paradox. Even the death of ecstasy is nothing but a succession of 'intollerable joyes' ('Teresa Hymne', 99), pain in the mode of pleasure. Donne's or Herbert's imagination moved among fixities; their paradoxes and ambiguities opposed or linked definite notions and emotions. In the sensibility of Crashaw 'kind contrarieties' melt into each other and the result is confusion rather than complexity:

No where but here did ever meet
Sweetnesse so sad, sadnesse so sweet.

('The Weeper')

His characteristic inclination to ambivalence emerges when he cries 'Welcome my Griefe, my Joy' (*Divine Epigrams*, Joh. 16), when he calls to the 'soft ministers of sweet sad mirth' ('To the Name Above Every Name', 62), or yearns for 'all those stings | Of love, sweet bitter things ('Sancta Maria Dolorum', st. x). Though its literary or liturgical descent is obvious, this rhetoric of contraries has a personal significance. Joy and grief, day and night, fire and water were apprehended in static opposition by the Petrarchans; they become here suggestive of change or exchange: 'A commerce of contrary powres' ('Epiphanie Hymn', 214).

The relation between the spiritual and the sensible we noted in the poetry of Donne and George Herbert appears to be of a different nature in the poetry of Crashaw, and a similar difference obtains in the interrelation between the abstract and the concrete.

The characteristic feature of Crashaw's imagination is the transposition of a psychical state or a moral quality into a stream of sensations. In Donne's mind 'white integritie' remained a concept.[29] When Crashaw speaks of 'the mild | And milky soul of a soft child' ('Teresa Hymne', 13–14), the white-ness and softness of milk seems to be infused into the child's soul as a substance. When he compares an emotion with a sensation, the analogy is not analytical; the impression created is an indivisible whole: hope melts away 'As lumpes of Sugar lose themselves, and twine | Their subtile essence with the soule of Wine' ('On Hope', 59–60). It has been claimed that 'the basic emotion which Crashaw seeks to create in us is to spring not from the image, but directly from the idea'.[30] It is true that the image, even in the early poems, is not used for the sake of its sensuous value alone, but in order to awaken an emotion. The emotion, however, is not aroused by an 'idea' or 'concept'—the Incarnation, the Redemption, etc.—but by the loving evocation

[29] To Wotton, 'Sir, more then kisses', 42; 'Funerall Elegie', 75.
[30] 'this complex of suggestions, he uses as a sign, or metaphor, of his concept' (R. Wallerstein, *Richard Crashaw* (Wisconsin University Press, 1925), 85.

of a *person*, from the 'supposed Mistress' to Mary Magdalene, the Virgin or the Divine Child, St Teresa or the Divine Lover. As in the Ignatian meditation the aim is to excite the affections through an 'application of the senses', arresting our attention on persons and on sensible details.[31] The consequence is that the sensation tends to fill the whole field of consciousness, which precludes any kind of critical detachment and evaluation.

Crashaw's world of sensations is therefore less permeable to thought than the no less concrete world of *The Temple*. A poem of Herbert does not originate in a concept, but it does not aim only at satisfying an emotional need. It starts from a fact—like Christ's Passion—or from an inner experience, and the poet seeks to analyse and define the initial data, to probe their significance. Rather than scrutinize a pre-existent state of mind and affection, Crashaw strains to arouse the desired emotion by focusing his attention on images apt to stir it more fervidly. Donne proceeded in a similar way in some of his Holy Sonnets when he tried to warm up his affections, intensify his own fear or awake divine love in himself. Crashaw's emotions are different and he seeks to intensify them out of an excess of feeling, not out of a lack of true love.

Intellectuality nevertheless is not absent from the poetry of Crashaw, but its function is usually limited to relating or coordinating the sensations selected to convey an emotion: he does not 'thrust [his] mind' into them as Herbert did. His method of composition is distinctly musical (see Chapter 8). He can impart a logical order to a series of variations on a theme as a composer does in a symphony. In the longer poems the lyrical impulse overrides the epigrammatic tendency noticeable in 'The Weeper', 'The Teare', and other poems; yet their architecture remains largely antithetical: witness the structure of the 'Nativity Hymn' and even the more elaborate argument of the 'Epiphanie Hymn' where the meaning is carried along rhythmic waves in wide undulations of thought. Crashaw does 'construct' his poems, but the form is imposed from outward whereas it seems to come into being spontaneously and dramatically in the most characteristic poems of Donne and George Herbert.

---

[31] As in the contemplation of the Nativity in the Second Week (*Exercitia Spiritualia S.P. Ignatii Loyolae* (Antwerpiae, 1635), 57).

In some of his later poems Crashaw thirsted for 'draughts of intellectual day'; he vowed 'to make brave way | Upwards, & press on for the pure intelligentiall Prey', but the term is used in a Neoplatonic sense to denote a spiritual intuition which transcends our rational faculties.[32] The Teresian 'dowr of LIGHTS & FIRES' ('The Flaming Heart', 94) burned away the sensual dross of the early poems. The stylistic evolution, unsurprisingly, was parallel to the purification earlier noted (Chapter 2) in the poet's sensibility. In his paraphrases of the medieval liturgy his sensuous images tend to become abstract signs of the emotion they seek to express or awake. In the early poems, a sensation was often a mere transposition of another sensation: behind the roses or rubies, there was only blood, and behind the stars or pearls, only eyes and tears. In the paraphrase of the *Stabat Mater* the poet is not concerned with the physical agony of the Crucifixion, but with the moral suffering felt by both Mary and Christ in their reciprocal love; nails, swords, and spears therefore do not merely depict the mangling of the flesh; they evoke the harrowing of the soul.

Following closely St Thomas in his paraphrase of the *Adoro te*, Crashaw concentrated on the essential divorce between the senses and faith and expressed it superbly:

> Down, down, proud sense! Discourses dy.
> Keep close, my soul's inquiring ey!
> Nor touch, nor taste must look for more
> But each sit still in his own Dore.
>
> Your ports are all superfluous here,
> Save That which lets in faith, the eare.
> Faith is my skill; Faith can beleive
> As fast as love new lawes can give.

Yet, despite his aspiration to a contemplation of the divine beyond the evidence of the senses, the poet never dismissed their support.[33] His splendid evocation of the 'mystic night' of the

---

[32] 'Teresa Hymn', 97; 'Epiphanie Hymn', 223. Wallerstein (*Crashaw*, 55) and A. Warren (*Crashaw* (Baton Rouge, 1939), 158) had noted a growing abstraction, but had not linked it with a spiritual development.

[33] Apart from the paraphrase of the *Adoro Te* I find no evidence in any poem of the voiding of the senses from their natural response to the physical world which should precede their application to the image for meditation drawn in the imagination according to the Ignatian technique: Raspa, *The Emotive Image*, 38, 98.

Areopagite reveals the persistence and power of his visionary imagination, still felt even in the semi-abstract splendour of the 'Epiphanie Hymn' celebrating the 'frugall negative light' (210) only perceived when we (232–3)

> Now by abased liddes shall learn to be
> Eagles; and shutt our eyes that we may see.

This Hymn is not an 'isolated' poem in Crashaw's work as Austin Warren claimed (*Richard Crashaw*, London, 1939, p. 151): it shows the utmost boundary his imagination could reach in one direction. The true bent of his mind reasserts itself in the closing lines with the sensuous and emblematic image of the visible sun,[34] so different from Vaughan's call 'for that night! where I in him | Might live invisible and dim':

> Something a brighter SHADOW (sweet) of thee.
> Or on heav'ns azure forhead high to stand
> Thy golden index, with a duteous Hand
> Pointing us Home to our own sun,
> The world's & his HYPERION.

Comparisons are invidious. Crashaw's poetry has other merits: a delight in musical language, a lyrical afflatus of Shelleyan impetuosity. One feels he might have been a greater poet if his imaginative associations had been dictated only by his deeper feelings and his major symbols. He often succumbed to an irritability of fancy which, in the literary atmosphere of his age, bubbled up in superfluous conceits. He only reached the highest intensity when he relied on straightforward assertion and plain symbolism. In such moments his images are not called up by the figurative fancy he had displayed in 'The Weeper'. The metaphors spring from the poet's emotion and bring us the same flush and glow. In the close of 'The Flaming Heart' lights and fires, the eagle and the dove, the thirsts and deaths of love, and

---

[34] R. V. Young observed that San Juan de la Cruz, like Crashaw, employed 'the sensuous symbolism of the mystical marriage' on the subject of the *via negativa* (*Crashaw and the Spanish Golden Age*, 108). This is true, but Juan's sensuous images in *Una noche oscura* are not visual images like Crashaw's. Stella Revard rightly notes that 'like the Vatican Apollo, the Crashavian sun-god can coexist with the other sun as his symbol' ('Christ and Apollo in the Seventeenth-Century Religious Lyric', in *New Perspectives on Crashaw*, ed. J. R. Roberts (Columbia, 1990), 158). The 'coexistence', indeed, is characteristic.

the soul's final kiss appeal to the imagination and no conceit intrudes when he calls to Teresa:

> O thou undanted daughter of desires!
> By all thy dowr of LIGHTS & FIRES;
> By all the eagle in thee, all the dove;
> By all thy lives & deaths of love;
> By thy larg draughts of intellectuall day,
> And by thy thirsts of love more large then they;
> By all thy brim-fill'd Bowles of feirce desire
> By thy last Morning's draught of liquid fire;
> By the full kingdom of that finall kisse
> That seiz'd thy parting Soul, & seal'd thee his.

CHAPTER 13

Henry Vaughan:
Supernatural Naturalism

As a staunch Anglican and as an admirer of *The Temple*, Vaughan was bound to express views close to George Herbert's when writing on Christian themes. The individual and distinctive features of his poetry will be more clearly discerned by starting from the more obvious differences in approach and temper.

The Silurist's religious sensibility has far closer links than Herbert's or Donne's with the aesthetic sense.[1] In his profane poetry he had acknowledged his susceptibility to female beauty ('The Importunate Fortune', 62–3) and only turned away from it, as he claims,

> When first I saw true beauty, and thy Joys
> Active as light, and calm without all noise
> Shin'd on my soul.[2]

The poet's favourite association of beauty, light, calm, and silence with religious emotion is immediately noticeable, and his personal touch is even more evident in the following comparison of the divine 'Ray' with 'some beauteous Paisage' rising 'In suddain flowres and arbours to my Eies' and bringing in the dead of winter 'a lively sense of spring' (16–20). All the beings or objects which awake Vaughan's love or admiration are invested with beauty: springs, groves and fields, stars and angels, and the 'very memory' of the dead, shining 'fair and

---

[1] The parson of Bemerton was keenly alive to the 'beauty of holiness', in Laudian phrase, a beauty also celebrated by Vaughan: 'Give to thy spouse her perfect, and pure dress, | *Beauty* and *holiness*' ('Constellation'); cf. 'this beauty of holinesse' in *Primitive Holiness* (Martin, I. 339). But Herbert's love for God was a love for a 'person' in expectation of 'grace', not a love of the supreme Beauty.

[2] 'Mount of Olives'; cf. 'The hidden Treasure', 19–24.

bright' ('They are all gone into the world of light!'). When dreaming of 'a calm, bright day! | A Land of flowers and spices', the poet adds: '*If these be fair, O what is Heaven!*' ('Proffer', 46–8; cf. 'Fair and yong light!', 23–5). An aesthetic emotion will even pervade the evocation of a dear one in the grave where lies

> A beauty far more bright
> Then the noons cloudless light
> For whose dry dust green branches bud
> And robes are bleach'd in the *Lambs* blood.

('As time one day')

The paradox of the robe bleached in Christ's blood reminds us of Donne's invitation: 'wash thee in Christs blood, which hath this might | That being red, it dyes red soules to white' (Holy Sonnet IV), but what was a theological conceit becomes a pastoral vision suffused with loveliness. Mary Magdalene is traditionally a 'beauteous saint', but Vaughan alone wonders why she weeps though her beauty 'doth still keep | Bloomy and fresh' ('St Mary Magdalen'). To describe Mary, 'Gods Virgin Spouse', as the 'true Loves-knot' because her 'beauty tyed life to [her] house | And brought us saving ayd' ('Knot') is a version of the Incarnation and the Redemption that could border on heresy. The true reason is that Vaughan cannot think of love otherwise than as a response to the attraction of beauty. Stars will only shed their influence when attracted by some 'beauty here below' and 'work all night upon [God's] light and love | As beauteous shapes, we know not why, | Command and guide the eye' ('Starre').

Vaughan is personal in his emphasis on beauty, but he is not singular; he obviously owes allegiance to the tradition of Christian Platonism.[3] In both the 'Discourse' of Anselmus and the Epistle of Eucherius, which he chose to translate, '*Beauty* is a certaine good, which all men naturally desire to have. But in the life to come the beauty of the righteous shall shine equally with the Sunne' (Martin, I. 195). In a passage of *The World Contemned* several of Vaughan's favourite themes are concen-

---

[3] Thomas Vaughan offered an aesthetic view of the creation of the natural world: 'God in love for His own beauty frames a glass, to view it by reflection' (*Works*, ed. A. E. Waite (London, 1919), 5). Aesthetic emotion, however, is not conspicuous in his philosophy.

trated: the ascent from the contemplation of God's works to a meditation on the Creator, the 'boundlesse light' in the state of immortality and the expectation of the 'transcendent beauty' that 'shall be given to all things in that eternall World, seeing this transitory one is so full of Majesty and freshnesse' (Martin, I. 326). In his insistence on observing God in his works for 'Each *Bush* | And *Oak* doth know I AM' ('Rules and Lessons', 13–16, 85–96) and reading the book of nature ('Tempest', 17–40), Vaughan was also in harmony with an age of 'serene contemplators' and 'hortulan saints', to borrow the phrasing of Maren-Sofie Rostvig.[4] Besides, like his brother, he had learnt 'to refer all naturals to their spirituals by the way of secret analogy' and to seek God by walking in groves or by 'clear, active rivers' as 'the mystic poets' had advised.[5] This sharply distinguishes him from Donne and from Crashaw, who never seek the divine in nature. George Herbert knows that all creatures in the 'great chain' of being do 'some good' ('Employment I'), but he never forgets that God's ways are only known to man; beasts, birds, and trees, though they would praise Him, are 'lame and mute' ('Providence I', 5–12). Vaughan insists that 'All things . . . Had their lesson taught them, when first made' and have a voice of their own:

> So hills and valleys into singing break,
> And though poor stones have neither speech nor tongue,
> While active winds and streams both run and speak,
> Yet stones are deep in admiration.
>
> ('The Bird')

Though herbs 'Grow green and gay | *As if* to meet [God] they did know' ('Starre', my italics), Herbert knows it is a mere illusion; Vaughan asserts that 'th'herb [man] treads knows much, much more' ('Constellation', 28).

The perception of a providential order could rest on the objective observation of phenomena and even justify a rational theology, as it did for Lord Herbert.[6] In *The Temple* as in *Silex Scintillans*, God may be contemplated in Nature; to both poets

---

4 In *The Happy Man* (Oslo, 1954), chs. 3 and 4.
5 Thomas Vaughan, *Anima Magica*; Waite, pp. 116–17.
6 See Ch. 14.

'*tree, herb, flowre* | Are shadows of his *wisedome*' ('Rules and Lessons', 85–96), but Vaughan alone prays

> That in these Masques and shadows I may see
> Thy sacred way,
> And by those hid ascents climb to that day
> Which breaks from thee
> Who art in all things, though invisibly.

> ('I walk't the other day', st. viii)

There is an oscillation between the acknowledgement that God's hand 'so shines through all this frame | that by the beauty of the seat, | We plainly see, who made the same' ('Cock-crowing', 20–2), and the realization that we glimpse only 'Some shadows of eternity' ('Retreate', 14) in a world where we see 'darkly in a glasse | But mists, and shadows passe' ('Resurrection and Immortality', 51–2). It creates a duality of feeling towards a sensible world which is an image of the divine, yet awakes a wistful longing for an even diviner world.

This hankering for a 'world beyond' is a characteristic of Vaughan's poetry. Donne sought a fullness of being and expected an 'essential joy' in Heaven (*Second Anniversary*, 383–472), but the preacher reminded his congregation that we can only say about Paradise 'that it is a *Countrey* inhabited with Angells . . . Where it is locally, wee enquire not . . . Of these new heavens and this new earth we must say at last, that we can say nothing' (*Sermons*, VIII. 82). George Herbert and Crashaw yearned for a fullness of divine love; neither of them apparently dreamed of the highest bliss as only attained in some paradisal place: it was, or was to be, an inner experience of the human heart. In the poetry of Henry Vaughan, profane as well as divine, there are so many evocations of Elysium or the Golden Age, of the earthly Paradise and 'the first worlds *Youth*'[7] that his conception of felicity always seems to be linked to some place, which, even when celestial, is reminiscent of an Edenic world, an ideal natural world: 'That shady City of Palme-trees' ('Retreate'), a finer 'Land of flowers and spices' ('Proffer', 47).[8]

---

[7] 'To the River Isca', 19–24; 'Boet. Lib. I, Metrum 5'; 'Retirement'; 'Religion'; 'Isaacs Marriage'; 'Retreate'; 'Rules and Lessons', 25–7; 'Corruption'; 'Ascension-day', 37–48; 'Ascension-Hymn', 19–24; 'Palm-Tree'.

[8] See also 'The Feast', 49–60; 'The Queer'.

Even 'They [who] are gone into the world of light' are compared with birds singing in some unknown 'fair Well, or Grove'. But the most moving expression of the poet's search for a far-off country is linked with his sense of roaming noticed in Chapter 7:

> He knows he hath a home, but scarce knows where,
>   He sayes it is so far
> That he hath quite forgot how to go there.

('Man')

A desire of elevation, however, is inseparable from Vaughan's religious aspirations. His vision of the 'ladder' of Creation, though traditional ('Tempest', 25–40), has a personal intensity, like his images of ascension, whether Christ's or the soul's.[9] He celebrates the eagle's upward flight expressing 'Our souls bold *Heights*' ('Eagle'), compares himself to a 'starv'd Eaglet' ('Favour'), or wishes to be 'some *Bird*, or Star . . . lifted far' above the earth ('CHRISTS Nativity'). His recurrent allusions to hills or mountains are, of course, inspired by the Psalms and the Song of Songs,[10] and the description his brother Thomas Vaughan gave of the 'mystic Horeb' of the alchemists confirms the universal appeal of the mountain symbolism.[11] Yet no 'metaphysical' poet has so insistently evoked the 'holy hill', the 'Everlasting hills', or mountains.[12] Characteristically he turns those '*clear heights*' into *templa serena* by investing them with 'calm' ('Joy', 15). In a pastoral poem he wishes to make the 'Mount of Olives' the poets' hill (Martin, II. 114–15), and he compares the Bible to a 'mount, whose white Ascendents may | Be in conjunction with true light!' ('Agreement', 15–16). His wish is to be removed 'unto that hill, | Where I shall need no glass' ('They are all gone').

Yet his imagination does not soar spontaneously: he has the nostalgia, not the experience, of ascension. In 'The Morning-watch' his prayer is no paradox when he says: 'O let me climbe | When I lye down!' In dreams the soul shines above, freed from

9 'Ascension-day'; 'Ascension-Hymn'; 'Disorder *and* Frailty', st. iv; 'I walkt the other day'; 'Morning-watch', 23, etc.

10 e.g. Psalms 48: 1–2; 50: 2; 68: 15; 87: 1; Song 2: 8, 17; 8: 14.

11 In *Lumen de Lumine*, Waite, p. 261.

12 'Misery', 98; 'Constellation', 3; 'Mans fall', 1; 'Fair and yong light', 50; 'Vanity of Spirit', 18; 'Pilgrimage', 28; 'Sap', 11.

the sleeping body which stays in its 'Curtain'd grave'. But sleep and rest strongly attract the poet's imagination as well. When he mourned a dear one lost the attraction might be momentary: 'I would be | With him I weep | A bed, and sleep | To wake in thee' ('Come, come, what doe I here?'). But the bed is an image of security in 'Joy of my life!' (st. iii) and the tomb may be loved as a bed where you sleep in your 'mothers bosome' ('Death', 28).

A dialogue, 'Resurrection and Immortality', reminds us that the body 'Shall one day rise, and cloath'd with shining light | All pure, and bright | Re-marry to the soule, for 'tis most plaine | Thou only fal'st to be refin'd againe' (47–50). From a theological point of view Vaughan was bound to entertain the same notion of the 'bifold nature' of man as Donne and George Herbert, but he integrated this Christian 'common notion' into a vision of the processes of life inspired by the Hermetic philosophy. His outlook could be described as a 'supernatural naturalism' which, despite the difference in historical context and perspective, has some affinities with the 'natural supernaturalism' of the Romanticists.[13] Though Donne also resorted at times to alchemical images and hyperbolically 'refined' the bodies of the women he praised, he and George Herbert thought of the resurrection as the reconstitution of a person by the reunion of the soul with a body still invested with the particularity and materiality of the earthly body. Vaughan emphasizes the transfiguration that will make the 'refin'd' body 'All pure, and bright'. The refining and transmutation of matter had always been the dream of the alchemists and it rested on an assumption of continuity between matter and spirit.

This continuity, of course, was accepted by all minds before the radical dualism of Descartes,[14] but it could be conceived or

---

[13] Carlyle's term was adopted by M. H. Abrams in his *Natural Supernaturalism* (New York, 1973) to characterize the 'displacement' of inherited Christian ways of thinking 'from a supernatural to a natural frame of reference' in the Romantic age (p. 68). Vaughan had no need to buttress his theological faith, but it was inseparable in his mind from an animistic natural philosophy which had more in common with the later Romantic panpsychism than it had with Aristotelian scholasticism or the new mechanistic philosophy.

[14] Even a theologian like Melanchthon could present it in the crudest way when arguing 'that the organic animal spirits ascend to the brain, where, in a rarefied state, they "mix" with the Holy Ghost', *Liber de Anima*, vol. 13 of *Opera*

emphasized in different ways. Donne only claimed that the blood begets spirits '*as like* soules as it can' ('Extasie', 62; my italics) and George Herbert did not allow them to leap 'the wall that parts | Our souls and fleshly hearts' ('Holy Communion'). Boundaries were blurred in the Hermetic philosophy and in the poetic imagination of Vaughan when 'Resurrection and Immortality' evoked the generation and renewal of all things in nature

> For a preserving spirit doth still passe
>   Untainted through this Masse,
> Which does resolve, produce, and ripen all
>   That to it fall;
> Nor are those births which we
>   Thus suffering see
> Destroy'd at all; But when times restles wave
>   Their substance doth deprave
> And the more noble *Essence* finds his house
>   Sickly, and loose,
>   He, ever young doth wing
>   Unto that spring,
> And source of spirits . . .

This preserving spirit, like the *spiritus vitae* of Paracelsus,[15] animates all beings and survives uncorrupted through all transmutations. It is diffused throughout the cosmos as an emanation of the Neoplatonic World Soul. The 'Masse' which it pervades is the 'confused mass' of matter through which the divine spirit is active in the *Pimander* (IX. 6–8). The *materia prima* of the Hermetists was not the pure potentiality of the Aristotelians, but the 'sperm of the great world, . . . a weak virgin substance', described by Thomas Vaughan as the 'material universal Nature'.[16] The poet, however, avoids the more esoteric notions: his imagination is moved by the cycles of universal life in its 'Phoenix-like' renovations and its upward surge when returning

(Brunswick, 1834–60), 89–90; quoted by D. Shuger, *Habits of Thought in the English Renaissance* (Berkeley, 1991), 10. In the 17th c. the materialization of the spiritual was still perceptible among Platonists like Henry More or empiricists like Walter Charleton in his *Physiologia Epicuro-Gassendo-Charltoniana* (1654) and *Natural History of the Passions* (1674).

[15] *Opera Omnia* (Geneva, 1658), II. 565b ('Naturalis aliquis spiritus rebus omnibus inest') and I. 569a ('Spiritus vitae per se non laeditur').

[16] *Lumen de Lumine*, Waite, pp. 254, 269–70.

to its divine source. His vision, in its very imprecision, reveals a bent of his mind. He does not propose a simple 'analogy' between the incessant renewal of nature and the survival of the soul followed by the body's resurrection. There is a smooth sliding from the sensible to the spiritual when the same term, 'spirit', is first used for the *spiritus vitae*, then for the '*source* of spirits' which is the soul's home.[17] It was agreed that both natural life and the supernatural life of grace had the same origin in the one God, but it is characteristic that Vaughan should choose a cosmic point of view which blurs the distinction between the two, almost confusing them, as he did, too, in 'The Holy Communion' (my italics):

> . . . grace, and blessings came with thee so rife,
> That they have quicken'd even drie stubble;
>   Thus soules their bodies animate,
>   And thus, at first, when things were rude,
>   Dark, void, and Crude
> They, by thy Word, their beauty had, and date;
>   All were by thee,
>   And stil must be,
>   Nothing that is, or lives,
> But hath his Quicknings, and reprieves
>   As thy hand opes, or shuts;
>   Healings, and Cuts,
> Darknes, and day-light, life, and death
> Are but meer leaves turn'd by thy breath.
>   *Spirits without thee die*,
>   And blackness sits
>   On the divinest wits,
>   As on the Sun Ecclipses lie.

With his usual precision Donne had called attention to the different meanings of the term 'spirit', which can apply to the human soul, or to the animal spirits, or to the higher faculties of the soul in regenerate man.[18] Vaughan's use of the term in this poem does not allow such clear distinctions; it applies to all beings. When the dew of grace falls at night on his breast he exclaims: 'O how it *Blouds*, | And *Spirits* all my Earth!'

---

[17] Cf. 'Retirement', 25, where 'spirit' designates the soul.
[18] *Sermons*, V. 60.

('Morning-watch'). Metaphorical though the terms may be, grace seems to have an immediate influence on the animal spirits engendered by the blood; and the blood of Christ proves to be the sap which will 'exalt and rise | And actuate such spirits as are shed' ('Sap', 31–4). This continuity between nature and the supernatural was invited by a Hermetic philosophy which hardly distinguished between the Holy Spirit whose 'sacred Incubation fed | With life this frame' ('I walkt the other day', st. vii), and the 'fire spirit of life', the 'prester of Zoroaster', on which 'the fabric of Nature rests'.[19] God's 'spirit' is a *knowing, glorious spirit* ('Book', my italics), but it is also the 'spirit [that] feeds | All things with life' ('Stone', 25–6).

This dominantly cosmic conception of 'spirit' was alien to the creative imagination of Donne and George Herbert, though the former had dabbled in alchemical notions. Even when he borrowed the image of the 'intrinsique balm' from Paracelsus, the author of the *First Anniversary* explained the dissolution and rebirth of the world by resorting to a distinction between form and matter obnoxious to the Hermetists (ll. 57, 37, 77–8). In Herbert's 'The Holy Communion', as in 'The Extasie', 'spirits' and 'souls', as we have seen in Chapter 12, are of a different nature. These poets are too self-conscious not to be keenly aware that the activity of the mind is irreducible to a life force. Marvell occasionally, Traherne almost constantly, will 'encamp' themselves in their own minds; for introspective poets 'consciousness' characterizes the life of the mind. But we noted in Chapter 3 that Vaughan tends to objectify his thought even in moments of introspection. He thinks of the soul or spirit as a fire or a fluid, substantial though refined, a reality opaque to itself though it can illumine the universe.

Besides, Vaughan's main interest is not in the conjunction effected by the spirits between man's animal and his spiritual nature, but in the ceaseless action of a universal spirit penetrating and transmuting nature, turning a silkworm into a butterfly made up of fire and air ('Resurrection and Immortality', st. i), casting off 'grossness', bringing matter close to immateriality, since 'water's refin'd to *Motion*, Aire to *Light*' ('Tempest', 29–36). Not man alone will be 'brought at last to a celestial,

---

[19] Thomas Vaughan, *Lumen de Lumine*, IX: Waite, pp. 294–9.

immortal constitution', as Thomas Vaughan asserted,[20] but the whole universe, when God's bright self will pass through all His creatures made transparent and 'Fixt by [His] spirit to a state | For evermore immaculate' by a kind of transmutation ('L'Envoy', 9–16).

The poetry of Vaughan thus creates a sense of natural continuity from the mineral to the spiritual, whereas the 'conceits' of Donne and Herbert underlined a discontinuity between matter and spirit even when conjoined in bifold natures. That is the reason why the imagination of the Silurist is so often inclined to present the Resurrection as a universal restoration, in which he only seeks a place for himself, interconnecting his personal destiny and the destiny of all creatures:

> O knowing, glorious spirit! when
> Thou shalt restore trees, beasts and men,
> When thou shalt make all new again,
> Destroying onely death and pain,
> Give him amongst thy works a place,
> Who in them loved and sought thy face![21]

The Resurrection no longer appears as a violence done to nature by the divine power: it seems to be only the crowning of the natural order. When the poet's inspiration obeys the dictates of his sensibility, the Resurrection of Christ as a unique, miraculous event is not the centre of his faith: the spectacle of a constant reviviscence in nature provides 'these *prolusions* and strong *proofs* of our *restoration* laid out in *nature*, besides the promise of the God of nature'.[22] The mention of God's 'promise' after the italicized *proofs* laid out in *nature* almost seems to be an afterthought.

That is why, at the heart of the 'personal' theology of the poet we find a mystic expectation of an inner renovation in each creature rather than the historical, yet transcendent fact of the Incarnation of the Son of God. Vaughan's religious beliefs were perfectly orthodox, but the creative imagination of the different

---

[20] *Lumen de Lumine*, Waite, p. 302. Note that the Hermetists present this change as a gradual purification, as in alchemical processes, not as a sudden and miraculous divine gift.

[21] 'The Book', 25–30; cf. 'Palm-Sunday', 11–17; 'Day of Judgement', 46; 'L'Envoy', 8–22.   [22] *The Mount of Olives*, Martin, I. 177.

'metaphysical' poets had a predilection for different aspects of revealed truth. The Silurist was moved by the suffering of Christ out of human sympathy ('Passion', 'Holy Communion', 33–52), but without the keen awareness of the twofold nature of the God made man displayed in Donne's 'Goodfriday, 1613' or Herbert's 'The Sacrifice'. The union of the divine nature and the human nature in 'The Incarnation, and Passion' stirred his imagination when presented through his favourite contrast between light and darkness:

> To put on Clouds instead of light,
> And cloath the morning-starre with dust,
> Was a translation of such height
> As, but in thee, was ne'r exprest.

This 'translation' creates an aesthetic emotion and is apprehended by the senses rather than the mind. In accordance with his Neoplatonic sympathies, Vaughan emphasizes the 'descent' and the obscuring of the divine splendour.

The love of Christ expressed in *Silex Scintillans* is, however, deeper and more spontaneous than in Donne's Holy Sonnets. Vaughan is not fascinated, as most Baroque poets were, by the bloody spectacle of the Crucifixion; he loves to entertain 'fair thoughts' about the ways in which his Saviour came to dwell in 'his own living works', imagining all the pastoral places his 'deare Lord did often tread'—'What silent paths, what shades, and Cells, | Faire, virgin-flowers, and hallow'd Wells'—in 'the fields of *Bethani*', 'as fresh as Eden' when God used to walk in the earthly paradise at 'the Cool o' th' day'.[23] Among other testimonies of the immanence of the Divine in nature the Incarnation seems to be only a special instance. The 'secret commerce' Christ had with his creatures for forty days after his Resurrection, so 'clear and indisputable' to Vaughan's sight ('Ascension-day', 33–6), was only a prelude to his perpetual though invisible presence in the soul and in the world. This presence in 'The Night' is at once historical and spiritual, for the believer has the same meeting-place with God as Nicodemus with Christ, the nocturnal solitude of nature ('Night').

---

[23] 'The Dwelling-place', 'The Night', 'The Search', 'Ascension-day', 37–8.

The historical birth of the Redeemer in far-off Judaea is celebrated by Vaughan as the assurance of his present mystic birth
in the soul: 'let once more by mystick birth | The Lord of life be
borne in Earth' ('CHRISTS Nativity'). This expectation gives a
personal twist to the dogma of Redemption. From a theological
point of view Vaughan is close to Calvin. He states the doctrine
of imputed merit,[24] fears he may not be among the elect, and
believes in the final perseverance of the saints.[25] In his anxious-
ness for the salvation of his sinful soul he seems to have affinities with Donne, the more so since the latter also relied on
alchemical notions when he called to God to 'purge away | All
vicious tinctures' ('Litanie', st. i), or described the resurrection
of Christ: 'Hee was all gold when he lay downe, but rose | All
tincture' ('Resurrection, imperfect'). Yet the divergences are
noteworthy. Donne focused his attention on the historical fact.
In 'The Crosse' the reader is reminded that crosses must 'take
what hid Christ in [him]', so that he may 'be his image, or not
his, but hee'; yet this identification with Christ through suffering is not presented as a new and 'mystic' birth. Donne did seek
to be 'restored', 'repaired', even 'made new' ('Goodfriday,
1613', 41; Holy Sonnets I, XIV), but he emphasized the divine
violence needed to 'breake, blowe, burn' what was sinful in the
old man rather than the emergence of the new man. Such was
his egotism that he could not wish to lose his self even to be
born again. Imaginatively his mind was set on the Redemption
as a historical fact and a theological concept; Vaughan is pre-
eminently the poet of 'Regeneration'.

Silex Scintillans opens with this record of a spiritual quest,
a poem which calls for an interpretation, but an elucidation of
all the symbols is not necessary here.[26] What is essential is to
note, first, that the poet, like his brother Thomas, makes a
'pilgrimage' which leads him to 'the Temple of Nature', where
he has a vision, though not about the secrets of Creation and

---

[24] In 'The Relapse': 'But he that with his bloud, (a price too deere,) | My scores
did pay, | Bid me, *by vertue from him*, chalenge here | The brightest day' (my ital-
ics).

[25] 'The Agreement', 46–8, 52–4, 59–60. Note the traditional, yet typically
Calvinistic conviction: 'For *I till drawn came not to thee*' (68).

[26] My interpretation (*Poètes métaphysiques*, II. 238–41) and Barbara Lewalski's
in *Protestant Poetics and the Seventeenth-Century Religious Lyric* (Princeton,
1979), 319–21, are reconcilable though the perspective is different.

the first matter as in *Lumen de Lumine*.[27] He reaches the foot of Jacob's ladder, the traditional symbol of 'That busie commerce kept between | God and his Creatures, though unseen' ('Stone', 19–20). To Thomas the Hermetist, Jacob's sleep was the mystical death, *Mors Osculi*, which unites the soul with God.[28] In the poem the quest will end with the expectation of that death, but the pilgrim, greeted by the 'new spring' in a pastoral grove (an image of a conversion[29] by which 'all was chang'd'), is first puzzled by two contrasts. Some of the stones in a Cistern[30] are bright, dancing 'quick as light'; others are dull and 'nailed to the Center'.[31] Among flowers, some are 'fast asleepe, others broad-eyed | And taking in the Ray'. This is obviously a contrast between the faithful and the unbelieving, the elect and the reprobate. A wind of mysterious origin is then heard; though it stirred nothing in the grove, 'It whisper'd; *Where I please*'. The wind is the inner stirring of the spirit of God:

> Lord, then said I, *On me one breath,*
> *And let me dye before my death!*

Whatever his views about predestination may have been, Vaughan prays, not only for the assurance that the eternal decree of God had placed him among the elect, but for a *present experience* of the death of regeneration. Its character is further defined in 'Ascension-Hymn': 'And yet some | That know to die | Before death come, | Walk to the skie | Even in this life; but all such can | Leave behinde them the old Man.' This is different from the death of ecstasy or rapture Crashaw (and occasionally Donne) longed for. It is a 'mystic birth', in Vaughan's own words, which does not mean he achieved truly mystic experiences; he only expressed a longing for them. Indeed, his wish for an awakening to a new life never was a painful straining for it

---

[27] *Lumen de Lumine*, Waite, pp. 244–5, 257.

[28] *Magia Adamica*, Waite, pp. 169–70.

[29] The 'vital gold' shot by the sun is an allusion to the transmutation of metals, an image of conversion: cf. 'I discovered certain pieces of gold' in *Lumen de Lumine*, Waite, p. 257.

[30] Cf. Vaughan's translation of the verses of Paulinus on the baptismal Fount in *Primitive Holiness*, Martin, I. 365.

[31] Cf. Thomas Vaughan's injunction: 'be ye transmuted from dead stones into living philosophical stones'; Waite, p. 100.

was in harmony with an experience of waking at dawn ('The Morning-watch') which he had intensely enjoyed:

> O Joyes! Infinite sweetnes! with what flowres,
> And shoots of glory, my soul breakes, and buds!
>   All the long houres
>   Of night, and Rest
>   Through the still shrouds
>   Of sleep, and Clouds,
> This Dew fell on my Breast.

Around the poet's favourite images and natural emotions, deepened by spiritual longings, Vaughan's religious beliefs crystallize in so perfect agreement that his theology might be defined a theology of dawn:

> *Mornings* are *Mysteries*; the first world's *Youth*,
> Mans *Resurrection*, and the futures *Bud*
> Shrowd in their births: The Crown of life, light, truth
> Is stil'd their *starre*, the *stone*, and *hidden food*.

>   ('Rules *and* Lessons')

'Cock-crowing' reminds us that the 'Father of lights' sends 'dreams of Paradise' all night and calls to the soul to wake at dawn. One who emerges from the unconsciousness of sleep may feel indeed that '*mornings*, new Creations are' ('Day-spring'). Wondering what time the cry 'The *Bridegroome's Comming*' will fill the sky, the poet feels that the best hour would be the time when 'The whole Creation shakes off night, | And for thy shadow looks the light' ('Dawning', 17–18).

We better understand now why Vaughan's gaze is directed at once toward the past and the future. The dawn of Creation and the dawn of the Second Coming become one: the same object of desire.[32] And one who sees 'morning-glories' when he looks back to his 'first, happy age' ('Looking back') may naturally wish for a second birth. A perfect imaginative integration is achieved, fusing sensuous impressions, instinctive emotions, spiritual aspirations, and theological concepts. The poet longed for a paradisal world, akin to the world of vegetation so dear to

---

[32] The prominence given by Vaughan to the expectation of the apocalypse has been acknowledged by Noel Kennedy Thomas in *Henry Vaughan: Poet of Revelation* (Worthing, 1986).

a lover of calm and coolness; the Christian was bound to identify it with Eden. Without an inclination to retrospection, this yearning would not have been expressed as a nostalgic homesickness, contrasting with Traherne's triumphant recapturing of his early intimations as an ever present experience. Vaughan's sense of distance and the slowness of time only allowed a wistful watching in expectation of a second birth, followed by a resurrection which the poet of sympathy conceived as a universal renovation and the poet of Eden as a revival of the first dawn. No one has more deeply felt the secret and sacred character of life: '*A quickness, which my God hath kist*' ('Quickness'). This love of life did not inspire a horror of death: a 'mystic naturalism' will not see it as an extinction, but as a metamorphosis ('Resurrection and Immortality'). The decay of the universe and the approaching end of the world heighten the hopes of the believer, unafraid of Doomsday. Free from the self-centred anguish of Donne, Vaughan can look forward to the rise of 'the new worlds new, quickning Sun! | Ever the same, and never done' ('L'Envoy') and the *Dies Irae* ('The day of Judgement') becomes in his eyes:

> A day of life, of light, of love!
> The onely day dealt from above!
> A day so fresh, so bright, so brave
> Twill shew us each forgotten grave,
> And make the dead, like flowers, arise
> Youthful and fair to see new skies.

A poet more interested in the continuity between nature and the supernatural than in bifold natures, more inclined to reverie than to the dialectics of self-analysis, is unlikely to handle paradoxes and abstractions in the same way as Donne or George Herbert. Even in the observation of his feelings, narrated rather than analysed, he only presents us with an ebb and flow of impressions and a succession of contrasts rather than conceits: 'Misery', with its liquid images, is an illustration of an inner life described as waters 'headlong and loose', or 'wild and waste Infusions | Like waves' beating on his resolutions (9–10, 75–6).

In the celebration of the Virgin Mary as 'the true Loves-knot' the poet's concern is with a spiritual union between God and the faithful who now make up Christ's body, and this universal

inclusion, 'us in him, and him in us', does not call for paradoxical expression. In the 'Incarnation and Passion' the central
paradox—the union of two natures—is not borne in mind. The
'Passion' tells only a 'wofull story' without the ambiguities of
Herbert; to sing Christ's death as a source of life (56) is unoriginal. Vaughan only finds fresh images to suggest the deep identity of life and death when he thinks of the renewal of life on the
pattern of natural phenomena. In an early 'Elegie on the death
of Mr. *R. Hall*', influenced by Donne, the conceit on the identity of West and East seen from different hemispheres had a
paradoxical neatness:

> som *Star*
> Hurl'd in Diurnall motions from far,
> And seen to droop at night, is vainly sed
> To fall, and find an *Occidental bed*,
> Though in that other world what wee judge *West*
> Proves *Elevation* and a new, fresh *East*.

But when life's triumph over death is illustrated by the metamorphosis of a silkworm into a butterfly ('Resurrection and
Immortality'), or the re-emergence of a stream quickened by its
fall in a 'rocky grave' ('Water-fall'), the mind is not struck by a
paradox: the imagination is moved with tranquil wonder.

Vaughan's usual tendency to offer a natural interpretation of
the supernatural is alien to Crashaw's emotive delight in miracles as well as Donne's or Herbert's insistence on the paradoxical aspects of Christian faith. To choose as an argument for a
belief in the Resurrection the principle that 'no thing can to
Nothing fall' ('Resurrection and Immortality', 25) prohibits the
kind of witty play on being and nothingness which attracted the
mind of Donne. As a Christian the poet could not call in question the dogma of a Creation *ex nihilo*, but he refrained from
alluding to it. The pious Anglican who composed several poems
on the Holy Communion and inveighed against Puritan rude-
ness at the Holy Table ('Dressing', 31–42) might have been
expected to show the same sacramental sensibility as his model,
George Herbert. Yet he never meditated on the paradoxes of the
Real Presence. The precepts given in *The Mount of Olives*
(Martin, I. 155–9) only insist on the necessary purification. For
the reality of bread and wine, his imagination constantly substi-
tutes the symbols required by his own sensibility: the 'Well of

living waters'[33] or the 'wind' of the Holy Spirit.[34] In 'Dressing' a 'pure, and whitend soul' calls for a 'clear fire' to prepare it for a 'mysticall *Communion*'. The Real Presence is asserted—'let faith make good | Bread for thy body, and Wine for thy blood'—but the insistence is on 'pitty' and 'love', 'grace' and 'The beams, and brightnes of [God's] face'. 'The Holy Communion' is a welcome to an infusion of spiritual 'life' comparable to the original impregnation of the created universe with natural life: 'Nothing that is, or lives, | But hath his Quicknings'. When the elements of the sacrament are evoked, Christ's blood is described as 'our sap, and Cordial' ('Sap', 27), or as 'quickning showers' that 'make rocks bud | And crown dry hills with wells & flowers' ('Feast', 51–4). Unlike Herbert, Vaughan does not clearly distinguish between the action of the sacrament on the soul and that of the sensible elements on the spirits; he is only alert to the sense of 'secret life, and vertue' exalting at once the 'spirits' and the immortal soul ('Sap', 27–35; 'The Feast', 37–48). Even when he borrows a conceit from the author of 'The Agonie', he turns it into a mere image:

> Most blessed Vine!
> Whose juice so good
> I *feel* as wine,
> But thy fair branches *felt* as bloud.
>
> ('The Passion', my italics)

Herbert had made both actions present, as if Christ, as Pascal thought, would be in agony till the end of the world: 'Love is that liquour . . . | Which my God feels as bloud; but I, as wine.' With the distinction between what Christ *felt* and what the poet now *feels* the paradox is erased. Vaughan is more inclined to echo the ready-made paradoxes on the second birth—'let me dye before my death!' ('Regeneration', 82)—and the freedom found in submission to the Lord: 'let me lye | A Pris'ner to my libertie' ('Misery'). But such paradoxes are purely spiritual, unlike the conceits on bifold natures. Furthermore, in 'Misery', the poet's elaborate justification of the paradox destroys the wonder.

There is, however, a category of paradoxes Vaughan can

[33] *The Mount of Olives*, Martin, I. 155, l. 22; 160, ll. 21–2; 163, ll. 32–3; 165, l. 29   [34] Ibid. I. 155, ll. 38–9.

invest with splendour. They are drawn from unexpected contrasts or equivalences of light and darkness. 'Most blest believer' was Nicodemus 'Who in that land of darkness and blinde eyes . . . Did at mid-night speak with the Sun!' ('Night'). Despite the pun on *Son* and *Sun* this conceit on the nightly encounter appeals to the imagination rather than the intellect. This is true of negative theology when the poet writes: 'There is in God (some say) | A deep, but dazling darkness' ('Night'). Yet this superb oxymoron which anticipates Milton's 'dark with excessive bright' (*Paradise Lost*, III. 380) is followed by a comparison which dulls it by reducing the dazzling to duskiness: 'As men here | Say it is late and dusky, because they | See not all clear'. The wish to live in God 'invisible and dim' is no paradox, but consistent with the sensibility of the Welsh poet, not attuned to an eagle-like contemplation of the divine effulgence.[35]

What is pre-eminent in the poetry of Vaughan is not the search for paradoxes and conceits, but a symbolic imagination which takes us beyond the analogies of Donne and Herbert. With Crashaw fire and light, and flaming hearts, are still most often used as figurative symbols, representing emotional or spiritual realities with which they cannot be identified. With Vaughan the symbol and the reality it discloses tend to be one. Like Crashaw in the 'Epiphanie Hymn', he does contrast the natural light, or sun, with the light that 'shines to eternity',[36] but he only emphasizes a difference in intensity. Such a difference does not require a leap of the mind from one order to another as in Herbert's 'How with their lanterns do they seek the sunne!' ('Sacrifice', 35). In *Silex Scintillans* what characterizes the light symbolism is first the insistence on the substantial nature of light: 'Thy heav'ns (some say) | Are a firie-liquid light' ('Midnight'). In 'Cock-crowing' this substantiality seems to extend from the 'grain' of light enclosed in the bird to the natural light of the sun and, beyond it, to 'the house of light' and the 'Paradise' of a God who is truly the father of all lights:

> Father of lights! What Sunnie seed,
> What glance of day hast thou confin'd

---

[35] This is not in contradiction with Vaughan's longing for light in other poems, for that light is not 'excessive bright', but 'calm' ('World', 3), or a *distant* 'glory', reduced to 'faint beams' when seen from afar ('They are all gone', 5–10).

[36] 'White Sunday'; cf. 'Recovery' and 'The Shepheards', 51–4.

> Into this bird? To all the breed
> This busie Ray thou hast assign'd;
>> Their magnetisme works all night,
>> And dreams of Paradise and light.
>
> Their eyes watch for the morning hue,
> Their little grain, expelling night
> So shines and sings as if it knew
> The path unto the house of light.
>> It seems their candle, howe'r done,
>> Was tinn'd and lighted at the sunne.

Thomas Vaughan's assertion that 'God *essentially* is light'[37] may have favoured this identification of natural and supernatural light in the poet's imagination. No metaphor is intended when he *describes* eternity as a ring of light, Heaven as a world or a sea of light.[38] In the Johannine tradition this view is not unexpected. What is characteristic is the way in which the mind of Vaughan works when he forges analogies between the outer and the inner light. No distinction between the sensible and the spiritual appears either in the antipathy of the soul for darkness or in the identification of thoughts with stars:

It is an observation of some *spirits*, that *the night is the mother of thoughts*. And I shall adde, that those thoughts are *Stars*, the *Scintillations* and *lightnings* of the soul struggling with *darknesse*. This *Antipathy* in her is radical, for being descended from the *house of light*, she hates a contrary *principle* . . . Two great *extremes* there are, which she equally abhors, *Darkness* and *Death*.[39]

In his intense sensitivity to life Vaughan made 'light and life compatriots'.[40] The Son of God is at once 'prince of life' and 'lights living well'; life is a 'fix'd, discerning light', a lamp which God's spirit feeds, and all bodies when 'without *Beames*' are dead.[41] Man in Eden could 'Like the Sun shine | . . . intimate with Heav'n, as light' ('Ascension-Hymn', 19–24) because he was in full possession of natural and supernatural life; though fallen, he still 'shin'd a little' in the early days of the patriarchs ('Corruption').

---

[37] Waite, p. 141; my italics.
[38] 'World', 'They are all gone', 'Water-fall', 18.
[39] *Man in Darkness*, Martin, I. 169.   [40] Ibid. I. 117.
[41] 'Discipline'; 'Quickness', 9; 'Relapse', 15–16; 'Sure, there's a tye of Bodies', 5–6.

This realism of the symbolic imagination extends to all the images that stirred the poet's deeper feelings. Water and air, hills and mountains are not merely 'figures' of lustral purification, God's breath, or spiritual elevation. On the one hand the sensible object, as we noted, can by itself evoke an emotion. On the other hand the spiritual reality it symbolizes takes on the concreteness, the substantiality, the life of the symbolic object. Through the poet's feeling for the growth of plants the parable of 'The Seed Growing Secretly' (Mark 4: 26) illustrates this fusion of the sensible and the spiritual in the apostrophe to the 'Dear, secret *Greenness*! nurst below | Tempests and windes, and winter-nights'.[42] A *Greenness* which retains its sensuousness when transplanted to Heaven and its 'eternal wells': 'A fresh, immortal *green* there dwells, | And spotless *white* is all the wear.' The italics of the text may have been meant to underline the colour symbolism and Vaughan's use of the word 'white' to denote moral or spiritual qualities offers one more opportunity to contrast his mode of imagination with Donne's.

It has been suggested that the Silurist was influenced by the various meanings of the Welsh word *gwynn*: white, beautiful, sacred, holy, blessed. But 'white' has the same connotations in poems of Donne,[43] or Henry King,[44] and in the *OED*. The association of whiteness and purity is constant, but the main literary source in Vaughan's case is the Book of Revelation where the elders round about the throne of God are 'arrayed in white garments' (4: 4; cf. 3: 4–5) and the souls of the elect receive white robes (6: 11, 7: 9). The recurrence of these echoes is striking[45] and the 'angels in white' who stood by the open grave of Christ (John 20: 11–12) are not forgotten.[46] Vaughan's whiteness here, unlike Donne's 'white integritie'

[42] Rudrum finds a parallel in Herbert's 'The Flower'; but when a 'shrivell'd heart' recovers 'greennesse' by going underground 'as flowers depart | To see their mother-root', the mind grasps the significance of the simile, but there is no appeal to the 'symbolic imagination' as I understand it. This is, however, one of the very few instances in which Herbert seems to share to some extent Vaughan's interest in the life of plants.   [43] See Ch. 11, p. 203 and n. 30.

[44] e.g. in 'The Surrender': 'thy purpose fair and white | As thy pure self'.

[45] See 'Ascension-day', 30; 'Proffer', 24; 'Palm-Sunday', 46; 'Men of War', 22; 'Tears', 2; 'Throne', 3; 'L'Envoy', 4. The apocalyptic images recur in *The Mount of Olives* and *Man in Glory* (Martin, I. 156, 159, 180, 193).

[46] 'Ascension-day', 58; 'Obsequies', 19; cf. *The Mount of Olives*, Martin, I. 158, l. 29.

('Funerall Elegie', 75), is obviously something to be visualized. He can, of course, use the epithet apparently in an abstract manner, speak of 'that first white age' of the world, 'those white dayes' of the Biblical patriarchs, or of 'a white, Celestiall thought' in his 'Angell-Infancy' or the 'white designs' of Children'.[47] But whereas the epithet in Donne's 'white truth' or 'white sincerity' brightens the precision of a concept, with Vaughan the idea itself seems to be suffused with the white radiance illuminating the newly created world or the poet's memory. The materiality of this whiteness is heightened when we hear of 'a pure and whitend soul | That feeds[t] among the Lillies' ('Dressing').

When the sensuous or emotional appeal of a symbolic image is uppermost, the poet may find it necessary to set forth its significance in a commentary. Though the author of *Thalia Rediviva* spoke of emblems as 'Bodyed *Idea's*',[48] he seldom showed Herbert's gift for unifying the image and the idea in a single perception. Even when he composed 'The Lampe' on the pattern of Herbert's 'Church-floore' his tendency to disjoin the description and the commentary is noticeable. Vaughan's distinctive mode of figurative expression is a meditation on a symbol, as in 'The Starre', 'Cock-crowing', 'The Palm-tree', 'The Bird', 'The Timber', 'The Water-fall', etc. He does not propose a concrete illustration of a psychological fact as in Donne's 'A Lecture upon the Shadow'. A symbolic object partakes of the spiritual reality evoked, or at least produces by itself impressions of a comparable quality. That is why the very title *Silex Scintillans* has a symbolic impact on the imagination different from *The Temple*. But in Vaughan's poems, unlike Herbert's, the concrete object, star, bird, or palm-tree, first fills our field of consciousness independently of its symbolic significance, which is only perceived subsequently; a comment will universalize a particular truth discovered in the natural order and extend it to the spiritual sphere. Inspiration flags in the second part of 'The Timber' because the meaning is 'stated' in isolation from the initial symbol and emotion. In 'The World',

---

[47] 'Metrum 5'; 'Search', 26; *Isaacs* Marriage', 18; 'Retreate', 6; 'Childhood', 4.
[48] 'To Etesia', Martin, II. 623.

after the striking opening, the visionary imagination awkwardly transposes a moral lesson into emblem-like images. A perfect fusion of image and meaning is only achieved in 'The Waterfall', probably because it conveys a simple idea.

In the modes of thought and expression as in the modes of self-consciousness, or the perception of time and space, Vaughan stands apart from Donne and Herbert as well as from Crashaw. Since he often imitated his predecessors and contemporaries in both his profane and devotional poems, similarities inevitably crop up. He may seem at times very close indeed to the author of *The Temple* when he echoes him and chooses the same poetic form. His 'Son-dayes' has much in common with Herbert's 'Sunday' and 'Prayer I' for, as chains of metaphors, these poems cannot disclose some of the major imaginative differences between the two poets. And yet Vaughan reveals at once his weaknesses and his peculiar power. None of his metaphors have the subtlety and the intellectual density of the conceits I analysed in 'Prayer II' (Chapter 12) and the repetition of the same idea in lines 3 and 23 is awkward. But the image of 'The milky way Chalkt out with Suns' is conjured up by his visionary imagination even if an allusion to the new astronomy is intended.[49] And the most constant and characteristic predilections of the Silurist inspired the beautifully sensuous and soul-stirring Edenic vision he substituted for Herbert's plain 'Heaven in ordinarie':

> Transplanted Paradise; Gods walking houre;
> > The Cool o'th'day;
> The Creatures *Jubile*; Gods parle with dust;
> Heaven here; Man on those hills of Myrrh, and flowres;
> Angels descending . . .

[49] The telescope of Galileo had revealed that the Galaxy was made up of a multitude of stars.

CHAPTER 14

Andrew Marvell and Edward Herbert: The Dualistic Approach

The Christian mysteries—the Incarnation and Resurrection, the Redemption, regeneration, and the Second Coming—are in various ways at the centre of the inspiration of Donne and George Herbert, Crashaw and Vaughan in their religious poetry. Though his Christian faith and Puritan allegiance are undeniable, Marvell shows little interest in those mysteries. His main spiritual concerns are with the overcoming of temptation, the purification or disenthralment of the soul, and the recovery of a paradise, a desire he shares with Vaughan, but his dreams are predominantly Edenic rather than otherworldly.

His 'Dialogue between the Soul and Body' is at first sight in the Christian tradition, but it emphasizes a duality in man's nature in a way which, in fact, calls in question the desirability of this union of body and soul. To present the body as an obstacle to the felicity of the soul was traditional,[1] but why insist that the soul is an obstacle to the felicity of the body? Marvell keeps within the Augustinian tradition when he makes the soul wholly responsible for man's sinfulness (31–42); yet one wonders why he refrains from any allusion to the resurrection of the flesh and the ultimate reconciliation of body and soul. The originality of his point of view lies here in the fact that it is neither purely Platonic nor thoroughly Christian. The duality is almost stressed with a Cartesian definiteness. Borrowing an image from his 'Definition of Love' one may say that body and soul become 'so truly parallel' that they seem at once conjoined and ever unable to converge. Each of them aspires after the felicity of aloneness; to each of them the other is hell. An ideal of pure spirituality and

---

[1] K. S. Datta (*RQ* 1969, 242–54) has shown that Marvell closely follows a Latin poem in Hermann Hugo's *Pia Desideria* (Antwerp, 1624).

a yearning for a purely vegetative existence are set side by side. The soul has fashioned for sin an innocent body:

> What but a Soul could have the wit
> To build me up for Sin so fit?
> So Architects do square and hew
> Green Trees that in the Forest grew.

To give the last word to the body is unusual. Knowing Marvell's attraction to plants and greenness one is even tempted to read the closing lines as a sign that a life freed from the obsession of sin was the secret nostalgia of the Puritan poet. In this impartial dialogue Marvell opposes two points of view and he does not seek either to reconcile them or to set one above the other as he will in 'The Garden'. On the one hand the soul seeks its felicity in the absence of the sensations it owes to the body: 'I feel, that cannot feel, the pain.' On the other hand, the body ascribes its worst pains to the passions of the soul, insinuating that the soul has perverted its natural innocence.

In the opening stanzas of 'The Garden' the poet invites us to renounce 'our Passions heat', at first in favour of the pure sensations supplied by plants and fruits. These sensations, no doubt, are acknowledged to be 'pleasures less' when compared with the happiness enjoyed by the mind in an inward state, which is, however, as earlier shown (Chapter 4), a reflexive contemplation of the mirroring of the scene in the poet's consciousness. This self-reflexive action results in an apparent annihilation of the universe; the soul then can cast 'the Bodies Vest aside'. There is a hierarchy of pleasures, yet their duality is no divorce and the senses are not in abeyance. The pre-eminent sensation—'a green Shade'—has become the very stuff of thought and the poet watches his objectified soul like a bird combing its wings on a bough and waving the light in its plumes. Yet the soul's destiny is to leave the body behind and even the apparent reconciliation of sensuousness and spirituality cannot mask an ambiguity. This new Eden offers pleasures which seem innocent when contrasted with the passions responsible for man's fall, yet they cause the speaker to stumble and fall (39–40). Better be ensnared by fruits and flowers than by women, but 'nature's banquet' is a delay in the more austere 'Dialogue between *The Resolved Soul, and Created Pleasure*' (11–18). Meaning to 'sup above', the soul will not wait to be 'prepar'd for longer flight' ('Garden', 55), but press forward urgently on the way to Heaven. Yet the ascesis of the will does not suppress the duality in man's nature. The world of the senses is not a shadow, the allurement of the *visibilia* is no illusion, but it proves again 'lesser' than the attraction of the *invisibilia*: 'If things of Sight such Heavens be, | What Heavens are those we cannot see?'

The trouble is that Marvell only relies on the resolution of the moral will: no perceptible spiritual reality is opposed to the concrete reality of created pleasure. One wonders whether the poet's quest was not essentially a quest for purity in a pristine Edenic condition. His conception of a paradisiacal state is instinctively pastoral; even when he turns away from an 'enticing' Arcadian scene to sing a greater Pan in 'Clorinda and Damon', his imagination is still haunted by it:

> C. Near this, a Fountaines liquid Bell
>   Tinkles within the concave Shell.
> D. Might a Soul bath there and be clean,
>   Or slake its drought? C. What is't you mean?
> D. These once had been enticing things:
>   *Clorinda*, Pastures, Caves, and Springs.
> C. And what late change? D. The other day
>   *Pan* met me. C. What did great *Pan* say?
> D. Words that transcend poor Shepherds skill,
>   But he ere since my Songs does fill.

This cluster of images and ideas in an idyllic setting is typically Marvellian in its original use of poetic convention. The implied 'conversion' of Damon is ascribed to a meeting with Pan, a figure of Christ for the Renaissance humanists. His query — 'Might a Soul bath there and be clean' — gracefully conveys the notions of baptism and atonement; it apparently denies the Fountain this virtue of purification, yet in this yearning one feels the sensuous appeal of a lustral rite. Marvell apparently was not attracted to the bloody atonement on the Cross. In allegorical interpretations of 'The Nymph complaining' the death of the Fawn (18–24) is supposed to be a reminder of Christ's death, but it is more likely to be only an instance of 'a tacking back and forth between islands of allusive associations'.[2] The only 'crucifixion' his imagination

[2] D. C. Allen, 'Marvell's Nymph', *ELH* 23 (1956), 93. See *Poètes métaphysiques*, II. 164.

willingly lingered on was his own, a fanciful and luxurious one in a green setting, bound by woodbines and nailed by 'courteous Briars' ('Appleton House', lxxii). In 'The Coronet' he does accuse himself of having pierced his Saviour's head with thorns, but hopes to 'redress that Wrong' by weaving a chaplet of flowers, and the serpent he discovers folded in it takes the imagination back to Eden and the Fall.

Marvell seems to feel at once the pull of an Edenic hedonism and an ascetic Christianity coloured by a Platonic idealism. The 'Drop of Dew', 'trembling lest it grow impure', is an image of a Soul eager to exclude the world it disdains and to find its way back 'Into the Glories of th'Almighty Sun'. The comparison with the 'Manna's sacred Dew', 'White, and intire, although congeal'd and chill', is the crystallization of a negative ideal of undefiled purity conceived as unfleshliness, colourlessness, warmthlessness, and utter isolation. But would the poet declare so 'sweet' the 'leaves and blossoms green' if the love of vegetation did not still lurk in his heart? In the 'Dialogue between the Soul and Body' we have seen that the intransigent claim of the Soul to its spiritual nature was counterbalanced by the sense of a native innocence of the Body. From a philosophic point of view one can hardly reconcile the antagonistic attractions, yet a religious perspective opens up a compromise. In 'Bermudas' the Puritan emigrants are safely led by God to a Fortunate Isle where they enjoy the pleasures that were deemed 'lesser' ones in 'The Garden' and were wholly spurned by the Resolved Soul: 'He makes the Figs our mouths to meet; | And throws the Melons at our feet.'[3]

The two tendencies in Marvell's sensibility, though antagonistic, work to the same effect: their common aim is to disjoin the two natures in a *bifold nature* and satisfy each of them separately; to take delight in pure thought or pure sensation. Donne's and George Herbert's sensibility can be said to be

---

[3] The Millenarianism of Marvell has been recently emphasized, from Christopher Hill's 'Milton and Marvell', in *Approaches to Marvell*, ed. Patrides (London, 1978), to Margarita Stocker's *Apocalyptic Marvell* (Brighton, 1986). The expectation of a Millennium is in perfect harmony with a preference of the poet's imagination and sensibility for an Edenic condition rather than the kind of beatitude described in Dante's *Paradiso* or Donne's 'essential joy' in *Second Anniversary*, 383–4.

'unified' inasmuch as their awareness of the complexities of human nature implies no rejection of them. Marvell is conscious of a duality, but he always tends in an almost Cartesian way to separate the components of a complex reality and seek the purity of a *simple nature*.

This distinction has consequences for the poetic handling of the emotions. When Donne and George Herbert write about death they never lose sight of man's twofold nature and remain aware of the future resurrection of the body when they evoke its dissolution: anguish or hope may at one time dominate, but not exclusively. The emotion aroused by death in Marvell's poetry is most often the simple feeling of the brevity and inevitable end of life. In the address 'To His Coy Mistress' the classical theme justifies the focusing on the mere decay of the body in the desert of an eternity with no prospect of resurrection.[4] But when the poet speaks as a Christian and looks forward to the entrance of the soul into immortality, he is silent about the fate of the body.[5] The passage from life to death in 'Thyrsis and Dorinda' is not described after the manner of Donne, as a wrenching apart, but after the manner of Montaigne as a 'sommeil, plein d'insipidité et indolence':[6]

> And thou and I'le pick poppies and them steep
> In wine, and drink on't even till we weep,
> So shall we smoothly pass away in sleep.

The influence of literary conventions must be taken into consideration, but should we ignore the obvious harmony between these aspirations and the epicurean speaker's personality in some of Marvell's poems? Must we ascribe the Platonic idealism of the 'Drop of Dew' or the proud self-denial of the 'Resolved Soul' to a different speaker? Since the latter has to conquer the passions and temptations of the former and, even when so doing, is alive to their allurement, why not consider the alleged *personae* as two facets of the same personality? The

---

4 L. Marcus's suggestion that the ultimate fate of the lovers may be annihilation is justified (*Childhood and Cultural Despair* (Pittsburgh, 1978), 215).

5 In 'On a Drop of Dew', 'Dialogue between the Soul and Body', 'Garden'.

6 *Essais*, III. ix; Pléiade, 1087. It may be objected that the speaker, at least in the profane poems, is not Marvell, but a *persona*. I maintain that a poet writing apparently for his own pleasure is likely to ascribe to a *persona* feelings he can share, or is tempted to share.

religious and moral convictions apparently prevailed, but the dualism may have found an oblique way of associating purity and a sublimated sensuality: the poet allowed his fancy to play on 'Young Love', whose 'fair Blossoms . . . are too green | Yet for Lust, but not for Love'.[7] 'Little T.C.' is painted lying in the green grass, and the poet wishes to 'be laid | Where [he] may see [her] Glories from some shade' before her 'conquering Eyes' can wound hearts. The young daughter of Fairfax is expected to marry, but she gives the Gardens 'That wondrous Beauty which they have' because she is '*yet more Pure*, Sweet, Streight, and Fair | Then Gardens, Woods, Meads, Rivers are' ('Appleton House', lxxxvii; my italics). Marvell's Edenic dreams and his love for fruit and vegetation may be another aspect of this sublimation. His 'Garden' is an earthly Paradise in which he can 'wander solitary' like Adam before the creation of Eve (viii). Yet the first fruit mentioned is an apple, but these apples 'drop' from the tree by themselves (they need not be culled), grapes 'crush their Wine' upon his mouth, the nectarine and peach 'Into [his hands] themselves do reach', offering euphemized sensual pleasures. 'Stumbling on Melons' provokes his fall; the melon is 'a feminine representation in erotic dreams',[8] but the Fall is innocent in this Eden without an Eve. The same transposition of sensuality may occur when the wanderer in Appleton park calls upon the 'gadding Vines' to 'curle [him] about' and bind him, masochistically inviting the Briars to 'nail [him] through' (lxxvii): the play of wit may be guided by secret impulses which were not satisfied or had to be resisted.[9]

The fusion of the spiritual and the sensual created an ambivalence in the poetry of Crashaw. The sensibility of Marvell is at times characterized by a simple duality since opposite tendencies seek different objects; yet his aspiration to the purity of the disincarnate soul as well as his search for a sexless purity in young girls or in nature creates also a kind of ambivalence since he does

---

[7] A theme developed by Michael Long in *Marvell, Nabokov: Childhood and Arcadia* (Oxford, 1984).

[8] Cf. Georges Poulet's comment on the famous dream of Descartes, *Etudes sur le temps humain* (Paris, 1950), 31.

[9] Marvell did not marry and no love affair is known. He was suspected of impotence or homosexuality in his lifetime, but my concern is with the coherence of his poetic inspiration, not with biographical facts.

not appear to be conscious of this repression or sublimation of the sexual drive. This is again different from the ambiguity resulting from Donne's or Herbert's self-consciousness.

The absence of direct allusions to divine grace is surprising.[10] Unlike most Puritans, but like his friend Milton and the Cambridge Platonists, Marvell seems to believe in free will.[11] His 'Resolved Soul' fights and triumphs alone: Heaven only 'views it with delight'.[12] The *'victorious Soul'* (75) seems to 'overcome' all temptations by itself and will be 'crowned' (28–30). In 'A Drop of Dew' the Soul, sprung from the source of eternal light and 'remembering still' its origin in accordance with the Platonic tradition, seems entitled by its very nature to return to Heaven: no redemption, no divine intervention is mentioned.[13] Marvell's belief in Christian dogma is not called in question: he acknowledges his need of a 'Saviour' in 'The Coronet'. What is psychologically and poetically important is the nearly constant emphasis on the preservation or restoration of the soul's natural purity. My concern is with Marvell's spontaneous ways of feeling and modes of imagination which prove different from those of Donne and George Herbert.[14]

[10] C. Raynaud makes a skilful plea for 'Marvell's authentically Protestant vision of grace' in *Andrew Marvell, Poète protestant* (Paris, 1997), 24; cf. 33–5, 165. But she mainly relies on inferences, seeing in Maria a symbol of divine grace (151). In 'Appleton House', 70, and 'Upon the Death of O.C.', 318, 'grace' has no theological meaning and at best a religious connotation. Marvell, no doubt, believed in divine grace, but he defined it in the *Rehearsal Transpros'd* (*Complete Works*, III. 424) as 'an extraordinary work of God's spirit, subduing [men's] wills and heightening men's performances beyond the possibility of our endeavours'. C. Raynaud herself justly points out that this definition is not Calvinistic and 'recalls the position of the Cambridge Platonists' (op. cit. 18).

[11] For Warren L. Chernaik, Marvell 'writes within the overall framework of Puritan belief', yet he 'consistently emphasizes the role of free choice' (*The Poet's Time: Politics and Religion in the Work of Andrew Marvell* (Cambridge, 1983), 129, 143).

[12] The military metaphors borrowed from the Bible (Ephesians 6: 14–17, etc.) were, of course, often used by the Puritans; they have by themselves no theological implication.

[13] For a different view see Raynaud, *Andrew Marvell*, 55, or Joseph Pequigney's article in *Tercentenary Essays in Honor of Andrew Marvell*, ed. K. Friedenreich (Hamden, Conn., 1977), 76–104.

[14] Chernaik has made a strong case for Marvell's 'radical segregation of the orders of nature and grace' in accordance with Milton and 'writers on the Puritan left' (*The Poet's Time*, 136). I agree this may have been Marvell's intellectual position; I only claim that the theological concept was not of primary importance in his poetry.

The poet's apparent lack of interest in the Incarnation, the Redemption, and the Resurrection accounts for Marvell's different use of paradox, in profane as well as in religious poetry. It never is the consequence of Christ's or man's bifold nature, nor the brusque revelation of a surprising truth. The 'green thought' enjoyed in 'The Garden' has been wrongly considered a paradox: the conceit defines a peculiar state of mind, but does not challenge logic, reason, or common sense.[15] The argument in 'To his Coy Mistress' is plainly syllogistic and based on antitheses, even in the final invitation: 'though we cannot make our Sun | Stand still, yet we will make him run'. Sharp antithetical exchanges, rather than paradox, are the natural mode of expression in the dialogues 'Between the Resolved Soul, and Created Pleasure' and 'Clorinda and Damon', which lay stress on mere oppositions. Antitheses again characterize the 'Drop of Dew': 'the World excluding round, | Yet receiving in the Day. | Dark beneath, but bright above: | Here disdaining, there in Love'. The Christian tradition and the contemporary expectation of wit in poetry were bound to produce paradoxes in a 'Dialogue between the Soul and Body', with a Soul 'Here blinded with an Eye; and there | Deaf with the drumming of an Ear', lamenting 'I feel, that cannot feel, the pain', and 'Shipwrackt into Health again', while the Body complains that the Soul 'has made me live to let me dye'. Such conceits are, indeed, as witty as Donne's, but they concern either 'nature' in isolation, not their union in a double nature, and they are embedded in a movement of thought which remains antithetical and expresses a division of sensibility.[16] Donne's paradoxes usually unite contraries; Marvell sets them in opposition.

As a poet of the Baroque age, he was, of course, aware of the taste for paradoxes in the looser sense of wonders, or extraordinary circumstances, and he could play with them though

---

[15]   See Ch. 4, pp. 81–2.

[16]   C. Raynaud has closely studied Marvell's chiastic figures (*Andrew Marvell*, 147–51); to my mind their parallelism or mirroring effect remain dualistic. In 'Eyes and Tears' the line 'These weeping Eyes, those seeing Tears' contrasts the blinding of the eyes by tears and the spiritual sight ascribed to the tears of repentance. R. I. V. Lodge has suggested that Marvell's preference for antithesis was due to his 'basic Ramist training' in rhetoric and stressed a 'mind–matter polarity' in a different way from my own, in *Foreshortened Time. Andrew Marvell & 17th Century Revolutions* (Cambridge, 1978), 7, 15.

affecting to 'Let others tell the *Paradox*, | How Eels now bellow
in the Ox; | . . . How Boats can over Bridges sail; | And Fishes
do the Stables scale' ('Appleton', lx). There is a 'formal' affinity
between these so-called paradoxes and the episodic miracles in
which the imagination of Crashaw revelled. 'Eyes and Tears',
which might have been a companion poem to 'The Weeper',
ends with an antithetical confusion of 'These weeping Eyes'
(certainly not a paradox) and 'these seeing Tears' (a rhetorical
figure requiring a miracle to come true). The 'Unfortunate
Lover' becomes 'Th'*Amphibium* of Life and Death' not by the
union of two natures, as in Sir Thomas Browne's famous definition of man, but only because of a conflict between Hope
and Despair. 'The Definition of Love' claims that this love is 'for
object strange', and its begetting 'by despair | Upon
Impossibility' is a prodigy; for the star-crossed lovers the
coupling of 'a Conjunction of the Mind' with the 'Opposition of
the Stars' is essentially antithetical.

Unsurprisingly, Marvell offers few examples of the interpenetration of the abstract and the concrete, so characteristic of the
poetry of Donne and George Herbert. He often takes a sensuous perception for his poetic object. In Herbert's 'Vertue' the
rose's 'hue angrie and brave' has an emblematic significance and
the perception is transposed into a conceptual image. Marvell
conveys a sense impression directly and sensuously:

> He hangs in shade the Orange bright,
> Like golden Lamps in a green Night.
>
> ('Bermudas')

> While, going home, the Ev'ning sweet
> In cowslip-water bathes my feet.
>
> ('Damon the Mower')

> Then, languishing with ease, I toss
> On Pallets swoln of Velvet Moss;
> While the Wind, cooling thorough the Boughs,
> Flatters with Air my panting Brows.
>
> (Appleton, 593–6)

In his descriptions Marvell, of course, like all Baroque poets,
borrows images from the man-made artificial world, comparing
'Grass, with moister colour dasht' with 'green Silks but newly

washt', or a smoothly mown meadow with 'Clothes for *Lilly* stretcht to stain' ('Appleton House', 627–8, 444). The scenes, we know, are fraught with a historical allusiveness; nevertheless the isolated image is, by itself, the source of a pleasure independent of the larger significance and enjoyed with an almost Keatsian sensuousness.

Marvell's religious feeling or philosophical thought can crystallize round an object carefully described: a drop of dew, tears, a coronet. A comparison of 'Eyes and Tears' with 'The Weeper' is again instructive. After the initial address, 'I mean | Thy fair eyes', Crashaw, lost in his ecstatic contemplation, absents himself from the poem; but he does not 'paint' what he sees; he launches out into a rhapsody in which each sensation is immediately transmuted into an emotion and an idea; the image is surrealistic, as in the claim 'Upwards thou dost weep'. Marvell twice asserts his presence (st. iii and xii–xiiii) and keeps his eye on objects described realistically since the conceit always springs from an exact perception:

> Not full sailes hasting loaden home,
> Nor the chast Ladies pregnant Womb,
> Nor *Cynthia* Teeming show's so fair,
> As two Eyes swoln with weeping are.

The contrast in the art of the two poets is even more striking in a description of uplifted eyes suggestive of Guido Reni's Madonnas:

> Her Eyes confus'd, and doubled ore,
> With Tears suspended ere they flow;
> Seem bending upwards, to restore
> To heaven, whence it came, their Woe.
>
> ('Mourning')

In the poetry of Crashaw images are freely and musically associated; Marvell never loses sight of the *picture* he paints.[17] The very titles disclose this bent: 'The Gallery', 'The Picture of Little T.C. in a Prospect of Flowers', 'The Last Instructions to a Painter'. Though conceits prove a means of loading his descriptions with 'metaphysical' ore and significant allusions in the

---

[17]   Raynaud offers excellent analyses in her *Andrew Marvell*, 74–80.

long poem 'Upon Appleton House', one may regret at times not to have more examples of his gift in apparently artless portrayal:

> A tender Shepherdess, whose Hair
> Hangs loosely playing in the Air,
> Transplanting Flow'rs from the green Hill,
> To crown her Head, and Bosome fill.

('The Gallery')

This pictorial sense is also revealed in the poet's use of colours. Donne played upon moral oppositions between white and red, symbols of purity and sinfulness. Even in his conceits Marvell delights in contrasting colours as a means of conveying and heightening sensations:

> For, in the flaxen Lillies shade,
> It like a bank of Lillies laid;
> Upon the Roses it would feed,
> Until its Lips ev'n seem'd to bleed:
>
> . . . . .
>
> Had it liv'd long, it would have been
> Lillies without, Roses within.

('The Nymph complaining', 81–92)

A correspondence between the impressions of two different senses proceeds from their identical value for the sensibility rather than the mind: white is associated with cold ('Nymph', 90), green with coolness ('Unfortunate Lover', 4). Green, known to be Marvell's favourite colour, is seldom more than a sensation, but it may be, as it were, dematerialized when contemplated isolately:

> I have through every Garden been,
> Amongst the Red, the White, the Green.

('Eyes and Tears')

> No white nor red was ever seen
> So am'rous as this lovely green.

('The Garden')

A Platonizing mind is inclined to rise from the contemplation of objects to the contemplation of essences, but *essential* greenness in Marvell's mind remains a sense impression. No process of

abstraction is required when green is associated with youth or
freshness ('Young Love', 11; 'Appleton House', 496); but the
colour seems to become an attribute of the mind when reduced
to 'a green Thought in a green Shade' in 'The Garden' and in
'The Mower's Song':

> My Mind was once the true survey
> Of all these Medows fresh and gay;
> And in the greenness of the Grass
> Did see its Hopes as in a Glass.

Marvell, of course, was aware of the symbolic meaning (or
meanings) of the colour, but in both poems the concrete sensation of greenness remains predominant: the colour fills the
poet's and the reader's consciousness, as an image fills a
mirror, before the concept of its significance is formed in the
mind. When the drop of dew is described as 'White, and
entire, though congeal'd and chill', 'white' denotes purity, but
the sensation of whiteness is essential. Even in the puzzling
story of 'The Unfortunate Lover' the definitely emblematic
colours—the 'Corm'rants black', the 'Flames' and 'Blood', the
heraldic *Sable* and *Gules*—first vividly impress the imagination and the meaning, perhaps purposely, remains obscurely
allusive.

There are moments, however, when Marvell seems to come
close to Donne in the concrete expression of psychic states. In
the 'Dialogue between the Soul and Body' the 'Cramp of
Hope' and the 'Palsie Shakes of Fear' remind us of the
'cramps of wickednesse | And Apoplexies of fast sin' in 'The
Litanie' (210–11). In 'The Definition of Love' the idea that
the lover lives in the beloved is conveyed through an image of
physical extension as in 'A Valediction: Forbidding
Mourning' (21–4):

> And yet I quickly might arrive
> Where my extended Soul is fixt,
> But Fate does Iron wedges drive,
> And alwaies crouds it self betwixt.

But the metaphor of the 'iron wedges' used to describe the
interposition of Fate has not the imaginative and intellectual
precision of the comparison of the lovers, united in separation,

with a wheeling pair of compasses. The material impression of metallic hardness and hostility creates a sense of insuperable difficulty, but there is no justification for the driving of 'wedges': the correspondence between the image and the idea is *felt*, not intellectually elaborated. In the following stanzas the lovers are placed at the distant poles and the poet assumes that only the cramping of the World into a planisphere could join them, but the cosmic cataclysm cannot represent an actual event that would bring the lovers together, whereas the coming home of the roaming leg in Donne's simile is a precise image of the return of the faithful lover. In the superb and enigmatic 'Unfortunate Lover' the poetic intensity of the visionary imagination is independent of the meaning and even enhanced by the lightning-streaked obscurity of the poem.

A duality between the intellect and the imagination may also account for Marvell's method of composition. At times, particularly in his dialogues, he will build a preconceived construction on neat antitheses, whereas Donne's thought explores a situation, moving sinuously from one problem or paradox to another. When strolling through the Appleton estate, the contemplator follows a chronological order. The various episodes, of course, are contrasted and the historical and political allusions build up to a climax; but in the narrative part of the poem, the conjunctions provide a link of pure succession: to Marvell's 'and when' one could oppose Herbert's 'and so' which marked a cause or consequence in his shorter 'Pilgrimage'.

Structural analogies were discerned between Donne's mind and George Herbert's, despite the obvious dissimilitude of their experiences. Both Crashaw and Vaughan, in different ways, disclose a fundamentally different cast of mind. Marvell's case is more complex. He shows some affinities with Donne in his ironic self-consciousness, his world-awareness and emphasis on the present moment, but resemblances should not mask important divergences. His self-reflexivity is not applied to an analysis of his own thoughts and emotions: it only keeps him aware of the mirroring function of his mind. His dualistic response to the solicitations of the senses and the spirit and his drifting away from the Christian emphasis on bifold natures are also major differences.

Edward Herbert of Cherbury

The dualistic approach and the disinterest in the central mysteries of Christianity had earlier been more obvious in the poetry as well as the philosophy of Lord Herbert.[18] The Incarnation is never evoked. In the poems the only allusion to original sin and the Redemption occurs in a satirical conceit ('State-progress of Ill', 71). Christ is absent and God is very rarely invoked as a person ('Sinner's Lament', 'October 14, 1644'). Divinity is conceived as 'the Eternal Mind', *Mens Divina*, the supreme and invisible 'Power' ('IDEA', 5, 34; '*De Vita Coelesti*', 30; 'Ode upon a Question moved', 80-1). The Creation is never described as the arising of a world *ex nihilo*, the notion which fascinated the imagination of Donne, but as a Platonic world of Ideas, or *rationes*, used by the divine Mind to bring order among the warring elements ('IDEA', 4; '*De Vita Coelesti*', 75-81).

The philosopher acknowledges man's sinfulness, but again espouses a Platonic conception when calling sins errors 'since we commonly sin through no other cause, but that we mistook a true good for that which was only apparent, and so were deceived by making an undue election in the objects proposed to us'.[19] Distress at his own sins is expressed in 'A Sinner's Lament', but this probably early poem is reminiscent of Donne's Holy Sonnet IX in the questioning of God's ways to man.[20] At first sight Lord Herbert and Donne seem again to be agreed in their insistence on the resurrection of the flesh:

> These eyes again then, eyes shall see,
>   And hands again these hands enfold,
>   And all chast pleasures can be told
> Shall with us everlasting be.
>
> ('Ode', 109-12)

---

[18] In his *Edward Lord Herbert of Cherbury* (Boston, Mass., 1987), E. D. Hill has made a strong case for his Deism; his study of the 'natural religion' advocated by the philosopher and my analysis of his modes of thought are mutually supporting. Yet Herbert, I think, did not jettison all Christian ideas but only deflected them.

[19] *Life*, p. 38; cf. *De Veritate*, p. 195: 'it often happens that we hate the good when we mistake it for something that is bad.'

[20] Cf. its close with Donne's 'But who am I, that dare dispute with thee'.

Yet these lines should be interpreted in the light of other texts. The author of *De Veritate* celebrates the soul's escape out of the prison of the body and 'the world's deep and gloomy cavern' (XII. 327). In 'The IDEA' (58–69), as statuaries, when 'th' inward Statua perfectly is cast, | Do throw away the outward Clay at last, | So when that form the Heav'ns at first decreed | Is finished within, Souls do not need | Their Bodies more, but would from them be freed.' Fear shook Donne's every joint at the prospect of the unjointing of his body and soul (Holy Sonnet VI), but Lord Herbert carefully points out that 'It is not our mind which recoils from or is fearful of death . . . It is the body which feels its frame dissolved by the departure of the mind, and finds itself sinking into darkness' (*De Veritate*, XII. 328). Furthermore, in 'A Meditation upon his Wax-Candle burning out', a truly philosophic poem free from the Platonic casuistry of his love poems, Lord Herbert boldly sets forth the Christian and the Platonic conceptions of man's immortality as two possibilities. When our souls 'back unto the Elements dispense | All that built up our frail and earthly frame', these elements will survive 'That so in them we more then once may live'; they may therefore be 'Quick'ned again by the worlds common soul' (a Platonic notion enlisted to make the resurrection of the flesh less miraculous).[21] Second hypothesis: if 'our Souls would all their burdens here devest, | They singly [without their bodies] may that glorious state acquire'. No choice is expressed in the final stanza: to reach 'some immortal state' is Herbert's only concern.

That the lover-poet should have privileged the resurrection of the body in the 'Ode' may be natural. He himself had betrayed sensual longings in several poems.[22] Yet he ambiguously claimed everlastingness only for 'all chast pleasures [that] can be told'. Once again his philosophy may throw light on this distinction. The *De Veritate* (VI. 155–61) institutes a dichotomy

[21] Cf. Plato, *Philebus*, 29–30 and *Timaeus*, 41e, texts mentioned by Nicolas Cusanus, according to whom the Platonists maintain 'that our souls are made of the substance of the world-soul . . . and after death are dissolved in it': *Idiota*, in *Nikolaus von Kues. Werke. Neueausgabe des Strassburger Drucks von 1488*, 2 vols. (Berlin, 1967), I. 269. Gregory of Nyssa had expressed a similar idea in *The Creation of Man*, xxvii (cf. Cyril, *Patrologia Graeca*, XXXIII. 492).

[22] 'Kisses', 'Ditty', and chiefly 'A Description', related to Donne's elegy 'Loves Progress' and Carew's 'Love's Complement'. He ingenuously confessed occasional infidelities to his wife in his *Life*, p. 144.

between two categories of inner apprehension, sharply distinguishing the emotions 'inscribed in the mind' from the impulses
that arise from the body and its humours, among which he
includes envy, melancholy, or hatred as well as hunger, thirst, or
lust. The former, 'commonly called the faculties that hope,
believe, trust, love', give '*assurance of the eternal Blessedness of
the soul*' and will alone survive the death of the body. An ontological division of the affections is substituted for the scholastic
distinction between the various aspects of the same *potestas* or
faculty.[23] When he analyses the concrete data of inner experience Lord Herbert is obliged to admit '*a mixed type of
consciousness*' springing '*from alternatively acting principles*'
(ibid. 178), but it is not easily reconciled with the clear-cut dualism of his initial approach.

A tendency to isolate the mind from the body thus emerges
from Herbert's poetic and philosophic speculations. He was
probably sincere in his celebration of 'a love eternal, which will
yield | All that a pure affection can grant' ('Platonic Love',
'Madam, believe't'). Yet he was obviously unwilling to give up
the pleasures that bring the body into play. His description of
heavenly bliss in the poem '*De Vita Coelesti*' does not present it
as a totally new experience, the 'essential joy' of Donne's *Second
Anniversary*, but as a purified version of our present human
joys. His Platonism is a sublimation of desire, projected into an
ideal world; Marvell, a Platonizing Puritan, will also sublimate
desire by projecting it into the supposedly innocent world of
nature or childhood. In the 'Ode', the lovers' desire called for
the hope that they would again 'hands enfold' (110), but God
must 'this dross of Elements refine' in the Resurrection
('Meditation upon his Wax-Candle', 47). The philosopher first
asserts that after death 'there remains a plastic or motive power,
there remains intact the understanding, the will, all the faculties
which love, hope, trust, believe'. But he makes 'still greater
claims': 'a more amenable matter, consisting of new elements,
will be supplied' to clothe us 'in heavenly glory' (*De Veritate*,
VI. 172). There is a clear contrast between this conception of a
'new' glorious body and Donne's or George Herbert's insistence
on the recovery of their previous individual body.

[23]   See St Thomas, *Summa*, Ia, q. 82, art. 5.

The difference between Donne's and George Herbert's modes of thought, on the one hand, and Edward Herbert's on the other hand may be stated in the following way. For the former, the incarnation of the soul in the body, as well as the Son of God's Incarnation, is the fundamental fact which governs their apprehension of two orders of reality, the sensible and the spiritual, the human and the divine; they apprehend these realities as indissolubly linked at once in the ontological act of incarnation and in each act of the mind that conceives them as clearly distinct yet ultimately inseparable. This type of apprehension cannot be logically justified: it rests on an acceptance of paradox or mystery. Lord Herbert's mind tends first to isolate each order of reality; yet he enters into a process of assimilation when assuming that the higher intellectual and divine order is in some ways a purer replica of the sensible and human.

Unsurprisingly therefore, the typically Christian paradoxes, based on bifold natures or on the Redemption, are absent from Lord Herbert's poems. His belief in immortality allows him to play on man's connection with two worlds, as in the witty and moving 'Epitaph on Sir *Edward Saquevile*'s Child, who dyed in his Birth':

> Reader, here lies a Child that never cry'd,
> And therefore never dy'd,
> 'Twas neither old nor young,
> Born to this and the other world in one:
> Let us then cease to mone,
> Nothing that ever dy'd hath liv'd so long.

In a comparison with Donne's paradoxes on the same theme, e.g. 'When bodies to their graves, soules from their graves remove' ('The Anniversarie'), these conceits, however, seem to play on episodic circumstances.

The philosopher had rationally insisted on the principle of non-contradiction: 'we cannot suppose that any Common Notion has been correctly applied if it contradicts another Notion' (*De Veritate*, V. 138). Some Platonic paradoxes, unlike the Christian paradoxes, did not offend against logic and could be demonstrated. In his 'Elegy for the Prince' Herbert had used the Platonic notion of the world-soul:

Do we then dye in him, only as we
May in the worlds harmonique body see
An universally diffused soul
Move in the parts which moves not in the whole?

He could later frame the hypothesis that his own material elements, after their dispersion, would survive and be 'Quick'ned again by the worlds common soul, | Which in it self and in each part is whole' ('A Meditation', 40–1). In a less serious way he had called the worms that would devour his dead body 'Best framed types of the immortal Soul, | Which in your selves, and in each part are whole' ('To his Mistress for her true Picture', 120–1), remembering perhaps that Aristotle and Plotinus had argued from the segmentation of bodies in their discussions on the nature of the soul.[24]

The idea that the lover's soul lives in the beloved was a commonplace already found in Plutarch and St Augustine[25] and sedulously cultivated by the Renaissance Platonists and poets. Herbert's claim that 'souls be more where they love, then where | They animate' ('Elegy for the Prince', 11) could be supported by the elaborate psycho-physiology of Ficino.[26] Donne, we know, also resorted to these traditional paradoxes, but he usually introduced them as arguments within the analysis of a concrete and singular experience: the paradox was only meant to make the irrational intelligible. Thus in 'The Good-Morrow' and 'The Canonization', the union of the lovers' souls is presented as a *fact* before the speaker explores its mysterious nature and derives from it an assurance of immortality. In Lord Herbert's 'Ode upon a Question moved' Melander argues to give Celinda the rational certainty that their love will continue for ever. In a future world, an ideal world whose laws are a reflection of our desire, no violence is done to nature or reason, whereas Donne wondered at the paradoxical nature of a present experience. The second poem entitled 'Platonick Love' describes the union of the lovers on earth as a communion of thought, which is no miracle, yet claims that 'their exalted fire', when

[24] Aristotle, *De Anima*, I. 4. 15; I. 5. 21; Plotinus, *Enneads*, IV. vii. 8–9. Herbert seems to follow Aristotle here, but he is closer to Plotinus when describing the soul as fully independent from the body in the *De Veritate*.

[25] See the editor's note on 'Elegy for the Prince', l. 11, in *Poems*, p. 150.

[26] *Commentary on Plato's Symposium*, II. 8; ed. Sears R. Jayne (Missouri UP, 1944).

projected into Heaven after their death, will 'Transform and fix them to one Starr at last'. Paradox ironically must turn into a myth in order to survive in Herbert's world of rational Platonism.

The dialectics of contraries was equally alien to the true bent of his mind as revealed in his philosophic works. His new psychology substituted differences in 'degrees' for the scholastic sharp distinction of 'different faculties for heat and for cold', heaviness and lightness, or white and black (*De Veritate*, IV. 110). This conception would condemn the Petrarchan or Baroque conceits based on contraries. It was an early sign of the general evolution in our ways of thinking that destroyed a world picture founded on the interrelations of contrary qualities and put in its place a universe built on mathematical relations. But literary conventions may survive intellectual changes and Lord Herbert as a poet still resorted to antitheses of a Petrarchan type. One may note, however, that he made a sparing and unoriginal use of them, which shows they could not stimulate his imagination. Furthermore, he was not really unfaithful to his principles when he played on 'a living dying' ('Ditty': 'Can I then live to draw that breath'), on 'hate and love' ('Ditty': 'Why dost thou hate return instead of love?'), or on water and fire ('Tears, flow no more'); his philosophy did not deny oppositions of this kind, but he shunned the conventional 'I burn, I freeze' since he assumed that heat and cold only differed in degree.

When praising black, Herbert did not seek the kind of sensuous or symbolic contrast sought by Crashaw in the 'Hymn in the Glorious Epiphanie'; he argued that black 'may be said all colours to infold, | And in that kind to hold | Somewhat of infinite'. The eye must apprehend blackness 'by some other sense, | Then that by which it doth py'd colours see' ('To her Hair'). Herein lies the paradox of a blackness which he saw as 'a spark | Of light inaccessible' ('Sonnet of Black Beauty') and which inspired a 'Sonnet to Black it self':

> Thou Black, wherein all colours are compos'd,
>   And unto which they all at last returne,
> Thou colour of the Sun where it doth burn,
> And shadow where it cools, in thee is clos'd,
>   Whatever nature can, or hath dispos'd
>   In any other Hue . . .

In 'The Brown Beauty' the 'two contraries of Black and White' are said to be so well united 'That they no longer now seem opposite, | Who doubts but love, hath this colour chose, | Since he therein doth both th'extremes compose'. One should not look for a philosophic intention in this witty compliment: the 'Brown Phaie' must be set in the gallery of 'Black', 'Green-Sickness', or 'Sun-burn'd' Beauties celebrated by Lord Herbert and other Caroline poets for the sake of variety. The poem, however, may be the expression, or at least a symbol, of an individual turn of mind: extremes are 'composed' and combined in Herbert's imagination, whereas contraries, though they may be metamorphosed, are offset by each other and never tempered in the baroque imagination of Crashaw.

The dialectical movement of Lord Herbert's thought is different from Donne's in another way. The earlier poet sought to define and understand a complex experience by an analytical process: the arguing clarifies and confirms what was given from the start as an emotional apprehension, e.g. the feeling of immortality of the lovers in several lyrics, or the speaker's sense of annihilation in 'A Nocturnall'. With Lord Herbert a dialectical progress or a deliberation leads to a discovery: the immortality of love and the soul in 'The Ode upon a Question moved', 'A Meditation', and 'Parted Souls'. His mind is not inclined to decompose and dissect, but readily espouses the upward or downward movement of Platonic dialectics, rising from the 'outward sense' to 'the Souls spacious and immortal field' ('Platonic Love': 'Madam, believe't'), or moving from the Ideas 'Conceiv'd above by the Eternal Mind' to Nature, which 'from far th'Idea's views' ('IDEA'). This affinity is even more clearly perceptible in a poem, 'To Her Eyes', which does not set forth a Platonic doctrine but avails itself of it for an amorous conceit, rising from the contemplation of the eyes to the Soul, and thence to the First Cause (15). Lord Herbert's mind moves from one sphere to another through a series of 'connexions' (14), whereas Donne's joined them instantaneously in a single conceit.[27]

This intellectual approach is hardly more favourable to the interpenetration of the concrete and the abstract since Platonists

---

[27] Even in 'The Extasie', influenced by the Neoplatonic philosophy of love, the emphasis is not on the ascent but on the 'subtile knot'.

seek to contemplate forms or ideas abstracted from matter. In Lord Herbert's poetry abstractions have a linear purity and never take on flesh and weight, as even 'dull privations, and leane emptinesse' did in Donne's 'Nocturnall'. Even in 'The Green-Sickness Beauty' where the abstract is a condensation of the concrete, there is no fusion, only a superimposition of a generalizing principle after a series of sense impressions:

> Yet as a rising beam, when first 'tis shown,
>   Points fairer, than when it ascends more red,
> Or as a budding Rose, when first 'tis blown,
>   Smells sweeter far, then when it is more spread,
> As all things best by principles are known . . .

These comparisons, besides, only illustrate the physical traits of a chlorotic young girl. Lord Herbert ratiocinates on appearances as well as ideas, but he seldom explores the psychic experiences which could invite a fusion of the abstract and the concrete when they themselves participate of both the sensible and the intellectual life. He does not resort to allegory like his brother George in order to convey moral or religious truths, but only as a transposition of another concrete 'Vision': a comb gliding on a lady's hair as a barque on a Sea of Gold. Instead of fusing image and concept as in *The Temple*, he indulges in pyrotechnics of conceits sent off from a sensuous image: 'To her Face', 'To her Body', 'The Green-Sickness Beauty', 'The Sun-burn'd Exotic Beauty', etc. When his theme is a psychic state, he offers only a dry, sapless analysis: 'A Sinner's Lament', 'Loves End', 'Parted Souls', 'The Thought'. In a 'Meditation upon his Wax-Candle burning out' he first considers the external fact (1–18), then expounds his philosophic views; conversely, in the 'Ode upon a Question moved', he will first state the soul's immortality abstractly, then support the assertion with several comparisons. In his tendency to dissociate the abstract and the concrete Lord Herbert moves away from Donne and at times comes closer to the philosophic poetry of Sir John Davies.

As all Platonists he is, however, keenly sensitive to aesthetic impressions and capable of conveying a Spenserian sensuous splendour in this wonder-provoking evocation of his mistress 'Combing her hair':

> Breaking from under that thy cloudy Vail,
>> Open and shine yet more, shine out more clear
> Thou glorious golden-beam-darting hair,
> Even till my wonderstrucken Senses fail.

Yet remembering that Donne had found 'Every thy hair for love to work upon | ... much too much', he seeks to elaborate a conceit about 'each hair, | Which if alone had been too great a wonder'. But the conceit here is not a link in a chain of argument as in 'Aire and Angels'. Donne analysed his subjective impression of wonder felt before a fair woman whom he did not describe. Lord Herbert merely grafts a reflection on the contemplation of an object. The final stroke of wit only gives an epigrammatic sharpness to the observation of a change: a gesture, withdrawing the outspread hair, will 'strike out day from thy yet fairer eyes'.

The finest conceit of the philosopher-poet turns out to be the evocation of an attitude:

> This said, in her up-lifted face,
>> Her eyes which did this beauty crown,
>> Were like two starrs, that having faln down,
> Look up again to find their place.

In the 'Ode upon a Question moved' (133–6) this conceit is meaningful; the uplifted eyes, seeking like fallen stars their 'proper place' in the sky, imply that the soul, whose desire the eyes express, would rise to Heaven whence it came. Yet the conceit is not 'metaphysical' after the manner of Donne when compared, for instance, with these lines from 'Loves growth':

> And yet no greater, but more eminent,
>> Love by the Spring is growne;
>> As, in the firmament,
> Starres by the Sunne are not inlargd, but showne.

The analogy between the apparent variations in largeness or intensity observed in the stars and in love is only perceived conceptually—and Donne's lines therefore are not so beauteous. Lord Herbert moves from image to idea insensibly. His contemplation of the face (Donne only evoked a face to read a meaning in it as in 'The Good-Morrow' or 'A Valediction: Of Weeping') is followed by a standard similitude between eyes and stars and a kind of myth, touched with pathetic fallacy: why should not eyes, like fallen stars, aspire to retrieve their place in heaven? Only then is the scholastic idea of 'place' introduced, but a reader unversed in Aristotelian physics would grasp the meaning as well: the soul's aspiration to return to its source. The metaphysical symbol arises here out of the perception of a sensible analogy.

The distinction between a movement of thought progressing from image to concept and the simultaneous apprehension of the concrete and the abstract seems to be structurally identical with the difference between the Platonic ascesis leading from the sensible to the intelligible and the Christian 'incarnational' sensibility which merges the spiritual in the sensible. Lord Herbert's thought is not always, nor fully, Platonic, but I am only trying to oppose two types of mind and explain why similar conceits make a different impression. George Williamson thought he had found the secret of metaphysical expression in the opening stanza of the 'Elegy over a Tomb':[28]

> Must I then see, alas! eternal night
>   Sitting upon those fairest eyes,
> And closing all those beams, which once did rise
>   So radiant and bright,
> That light and heat in them to us did prove
>   Knowledge and Love?

Yet there is only a standard, symbolic and affective correspondence between light and knowledge, heat and love; the reader's mind has not to perceive a complex homology between phenomena belonging to different spheres of experience as in 'Loves Growth'. In the next stanzas the argument is based on the presence of the same sensible qualities—light, waves, colours, smell—in nature and in the woman. The suggestiveness of these lines is not due to a 'metaphysical' conceit but to the genuine aesthetic and cosmic sensibility of the poet investing them with a melancholy splendour:

> Doth the Sun now his light with yours renew?
>   Have waves the curling of your hair?
> Did you restore into the Sky and Air,

---

[28] *The Donne Tradition* (Cambridge, Mass., 1930).

> The red, and white, and blew?
> Have you vouchsafed to flowrs since your death
> That sweetest breath?

This is not the 'world' *conceived* in its *unique* and *absolute* relation with the beloved in Donne's *Songs and Sonets*,[29] but an *imagined* natural world offering multiple and sensuous correspondences.

The Neoplatonic notion of the world-soul appealed to Lord Herbert's mind. It allowed him to hope that the elements of the body, dispersed after death, could be 'Quick'ned again by the worlds common soul, | Which in it self and in each part is whole' ('A Meditation'). Donne had only used the notion as a hyperbole in 'A Feaver', or as a means of suggesting that the lovers made up a world of their own in 'The Canonization'. In the *Second Anniversary* Elizabeth Drury was the 'form' that made the world live (71–2). Donne's apprehension of the world was metaphysical—the totality of existence—or logical—a network of relations and correspondences. He never thought of it as universal life; he had an intuition of being and nothingness, no intuition of cosmic becoming. With Lord Herbert, on the contrary, the Platonic conception of the world is always associated with an interest in the life of nature and its cycles of seasons, deaths and revivals ('Elegy for the Prince', 26–30):

> See we not Autumn give
> Back to the earth again what it receiv'd
> In th'early Spring. And may not we deceiv'd
> Think that those powers are dead, which do but sleep,
> And the world's soul doth reunited keep?

The rational philosophy of Lord Herbert cannot be said to be pantheistic, yet he shows a complacent resignation at the prospect of the dissolution of his elements in the world-soul, for 'who thought Elements unhappy yet, | As long as they were in their stations fix'd?' ('Meditation', 29–30). This, at least, implies that his personal sensibility would not have been disinclined to pantheistic emotions in the Romantic age.[30] His

---

[29]   See Ch. 6, end.

[30]   Jacqueline Lagrée recently ascribed to Lord Herbert 'a philosophy of intuition closer to the pantheism of the German Romantics than to the philosophy of Hobbes and Spinoza', in *Le salut du laïc. Sur Herbert de Cherbury* (Paris, 1989), 32.

Epitaphium in Anagramma nominis sui may be more than a witty transposition: *Reddor ut herbae* suggests a sympathy with the life of vegetation which anticipates Vaughan's. The sonnet 'You well compacted Groves', relating a real experience 'near *Merlow* Castle' (*Poems*, p. 54), shows him enjoying 'A self-renewing vegetable bliss' comparable with Marvell's happiness in 'The Garden' or in the groves of 'Appleton House'. His sensitiveness to heat and coolness in sun or shade has an almost Keatsian keenness here and in 'Another Sonnet to Black it self': 'Thou colour of the sun where it doth burn, | And shadow, where it cools'. Donne's 'Extasie' and Herbert's 'Ode' have a pastoral setting in common, but Donne only evoked it in three conceited lines whereas four stanzas emphasize the correspondence between the 'harmony' reigning in nature and the 'doubling joy' of Melander and Celinda.

The same poem gives an unexpected and bold turn to the Paulinian assertion that 'the invisible things of [God] since the creation of the world are clearly seen, being perceived through the things that are made' (Romans 1: 20):

> . . . for if none can ascend
> Ev'n to the visible degree
> Of things created, how should we
> The invisible comprehend?
>
> Or rather since that Pow'r exprest
> His greatness in his works alone,
> B'ing here best in his Creatures known,
> Why is he not lov'd in them best?

('Ode', 77–84)

From the point of view of Christian theology, and especially Protestant theology,[31] to assert that God is 'best in his Creatures known' rather than in the Bible sounds like heresy. It is at least in sharp contrast with Donne's distrust of the revelation gained

---

[31] Calvin, of course, proclaims with the Psalmist that 'The Knowledge of God Shines Forth in the Fashioning of this Universe' and that God can be contemplated in his works (*Institutes of the Christian Religion*, ed. John T. McNeill (London, 1961), Bk. I, ch. v), but he adds that the manifestation of God in the Creation 'is choked by human superstition and the error of the philosopher' and, though 'the invisible divinity is made manifest in such spectacles', 'we have not the eyes to see this unless they be illumined by the inner revelation of God through faith' (§§11–15, ed. cit., pp. 65–8).

through the Book of Creatures, 'the first, and weakest kinde of proofe', giving 'but a faint knowledge of God' (*Sermons*, VI. 133), for 'it is but an uncertain glimmering which we have of God in the creature' (*Sermons*, I. 290).[32] It was already Donne's position in the *Essays in Divinity* (Simpson, p. 20), but the preacher went further, ultimately as far as Pascal,[33] when he claimed that 'The naturall man had much to do, to conceive God . . . a man does not easily conceive God to be *alone*, to be but *one*' (*Sermons*, VI. 152–3). An inclination to find God in nature is not traceable either in George Herbert. The author of 'Providence' only stressed the transcendent action of the Divine Power, listing its effects in the creatures, but disclaiming the kind of animism later illustrated by Vaughan. God is to be found in man's heart and in Scripture: 'Starres are poor books & oftentimes do misse; | This book of starres lights to eternal blisse' ('Holy Scriptures II'). Lord Herbert, therefore, has more in common with Henry Vaughan than with his own brother,[34] but, since his approach is rational rather than imaginative and therefore devoid of emotional intensity, his rational and natural theology rather forebodes the deistic world view of the classical age.[35]

[32] It does not contradict the poet's earlier assertion that Elizabeth Drury was acquainted with God's presence so 'as to know | His face, in any naturall Stone or Tree' since this is presented as the privilege of her exceptional soul; cf. the complimentary hyperbole in 'To the Countesse of Salisbury', 7–8.

[33] In *Pensées*, IV. 242 (ed. Brunschwig, II. 175–6): 'prouver la Divinité par les ouvrages de la nature' will give the unbeliever 'sujet de croire que les preuves de notre religion sont bien faibles'.

[34] His view of the life led in Heaven by the blessed, roving delightedly in numberless skies ('De Vita Coelesti', 56–61), is also closer to Vaughan's dreams than to Donne's 'essentiall joy'.

[35] In *A Dialogue between a Tutor and his Pupil* (a work ascribed to Lord Herbert) the world is already described as the best of all possible worlds ((London, 1768), 57–9).

CHAPTER 15

Thomas Traherne: Sensuous Idealism

Just as his reflexive awareness of the natural phenomenon of perception turns into a rapturous delight at the possibility of a spiritual possession of the world, ecstasies of divine love at once irradiate and mask the true nature of Traherne's Christianity. Occasional statements, mainly in his early or less inspired works, show that he intended to remain within the bounds of Anglican orthodoxy,[1] but the central dogmas suffered a sea-change in the light of his personal certainties and experiences.

The Divine Philosopher's celebration of man's body and senses disrupts the former balance between disgust and reverence, contempt for the infirmities of the flesh and reverence for a house of clay God himself came to dwell in—a balance preserved by Donne and George Herbert. There were precedents in the Church Fathers for his wonder at the blessings conferred by God on the body, the faculties bestowed on it, but Traherne does not immediately add like Augustine: 'though this body is subject to corruption, to all sorts of ills, and to death'.[2] He commonly seems to screen his gaze from ugliness, disease, and dissolution. He duly acknowledges the pre-eminence of spiritual qualities and pleasures ('Thanksgiving for the Body', 272–3), but what I find characteristic is the way in which sensible enjoyment tends to become self-sufficient either in the exercise of a faculty or by being pervaded with a diffuse spirituality:

Is not Sight a Jewel? Is not Hearing a Treasure? Is not Speech a Glory? (*Centuries*, I. 66)

---

[1] They are more frequent and evident in *Select Meditations*, e.g. III. 25, 58, IV. 44 (on the Church); II. 67, III. 76 (on Christ).

[2] *Soliloquies*, xx. Traherne is closer to Gregory of Nyssa, whose discourse *On the Creation of Man* celebrated the 'preciousness', beauty, and gifts of human nature (iii, vii–ix) and the activity of the spirit through the senses (x), yet rejected 'the vain conjectures of those who enclose the activity of the mind within corporal organs' (xii); cf. *Patrologia Graeca*, XLIV. 665A.

> Such Sacred Treasures are the Lims in Boys,
> In which a Soul doth Dwell.
>
> ('The Salutation', 21-2)

Crashaw used sensations to convey spiritual realities, as God's presence is conveyed by the Eucharistic elements. But Traherne seems to blur the frontier between the sensible and the spiritual, investing the sensation with a glory of its own. Since God has given limbs to man, he had to create the visible world 'for Outward Joys and Pleasures | Are even the Things for which my Lims are Treasures' ('The Estate').[3] Through his very idealization of the body he is one step from an Adamite mysticism and a Blakean apology of nakedness, which in Eden 'had been the Splendor and Ornament of Men, as it will be in Heaven' (*Christian Ethicks*, 33). Traherne's spiritual enjoyment of his senses creates a 'unified sensibility' (though not in the perspective of T. S. Eliot) when he celebrates the fusion of soul and sense in the glorified body:

> Joy shall overflow,
> Affect the Soul, though in the Body grow.
> Return again, and make the Body shine
> Like Jesus Christ, while both in one combine,
> Mysterious Contacts are between the Soul,
> Which touch the Spirits, and by those its Bowl:
> The Marrow, Bowels, Spirits, melt and move,
> Dissolving ravish, teach them how to love.
> He that could bring the heavens thro the Eye,
> And make the World within the Fancy lie,
> By Beams of light that closing meet in one,
>
> .   .   .   .
>
> Can make the Soul by Sense to feel and see,
> And with her Joy the Senses wrap'd to be.
>
> ('Thanksgiving for the Body', 435-51)

This, one may object, will only occur when 'our vile body' will be changed (427). But one line only mentions this vileness in a concession to orthodoxy after a protracted celebration of the glory of 'our earthly Bodies' and their powers of perception

---

[3] In 'Thanksgivings for the Body', 222-4, he claims that God has created the visible world for the human body.

(20–222), clearly prefiguring this final osmosis of soul and sense.

Even when exalting the body, Traherne, however, seems to remain a Platonist when he speaks of the soul as if it were self-sufficient. The felicity of the infant is first described as the felicity of a soul still unconscious of the existence of its body ('The Preparative', st. i). In *Select Meditations* (IV. 37), as in *Christian Ethicks* (p. 104), the body is said to have been 'Superadded' to the soul, as if the soul by itself, not the union of body and soul, as Donne asserted, made up the person.[4] The contradiction is only apparent. To a true Platonist the soul, though animating the body, remains alien to it. But Traherne identifies the soul with consciousness. He curiously argues that 'to make Visible Objects useful it was necessary to enshrine some Spirits in Corporeal Bodies, and therefore to make such creatures as *Men*' (*Christian Ethicks*, 182). Since his consciousness takes in the world and his sensations are felt as present within the soul, there is for him, in fact, no difference between soul and sense in a self-reflexive apprehension. The paradoxical character of the union of body and soul disappears when the soul is made 'by Sense to feel and see, | And with her Joy the Senses wrap'd to be'. Union in indistinction is not a conjunction of distinct realities.

That is why the imagination of the poet does not play with the Christian paradoxes of the Incarnation and the Resurrection. The author of *Christian Ethicks* (p. 34) complacently envisages what religion would have been if Adam had not

---

    4 In *Select Meditations*, III. 94 Traherne admitted that a soul without a body was not 'sufficient to make a Person', but orthodox statements do not fully disclose the bent of his imagination. In his study of *Early Christian Doctrines* (London, 1985) J. N. D. Kelly pointed out that the Eastern Church up to the 4th c. favoured a 'Word–flesh' type interpretation of the Incarnation of the Son of God on the pattern of the Platonic conception of man as a soul animating a body, yet remaining alien to it. The 'Word–man' type of Christology which ultimately triumphed in the Western Church and in medieval scholastic theology conceived the Incarnation as the union of the Word with a complete human entity, comprising a soul and a body, in accordance with the Aristotelian definition of man as a psycho-physical unity. The latter view, as we have seen, dominates Donne's thought. The influence of Platonism and of the pre-Nicene Fathers over Traherne's religious doctrine may be supposed to account for his different conception of the union of soul and body. But, as usual, I assume that his personal mode of thought dictated his preference since he could freely choose among different conceptions.

sinned: 'There would have been no *Faith* in the *Incarnation* of
God, because no occasion for that Incarnation; no Ceremonial
Law of Moses, no *Baptism*, nor *Lords Supper*, because there
were no supernatural Mysteries to be Typified, but the clear
Light of a Diviner Reason, and a free Communion with God.'
He does not add, as George Herbert might have, *Felix culpa!*
One feels such a life was a pleasant prospect for him.[5] He does
celebrate the 'supernatural Mysteries', but in a new perspective.
In 'The Thanksgivings for the Soul' (490) he exclaims: 'Let my
Saviour's Incarnation be my Exaltation'. He does not deny that
a sinful creature had to be redeemed,[6] but points out that only
by giving his Son could God make him understand that he was
'made to inherit all things' (an assurance given in Rom. 8: 32
and Rev. 21: 7). He further claims that this sacrifice was justified because he felt in himself 'a Nature answerable to the
greatness of his [Christ's] Passion' ('Thanksgivings for the
Blessedness of God's Ways', 286–306). But since the soul's
faculties can already ensure our spiritual possession of the
world, the mystery of Redemption is almost reduced to the
wonder of self-reflexive perception. Besides, Traherne's theory
of self-love making him 'prone to desire all that was Profitable
and Delightful to him' is called upon to explain how, after
Christ's sacrifice, man 'was carried now most violently to
the love of GOD' (*Christian Ethicks*, 101–2). Many years before
the publication of Toland's *Christianity not mysterious* (1696)
the Incarnation itself is said to be an 'incredible mystery' only to
those who do not consider 'the love of GOD towards Man'
(ibid. 103)—though Traherne in his rhapsodic way still revels
among mysteries (e.g. in *Centuries*, I. 59), while doing his best
to make them appear natural or rational. The very Passion of
Christ becomes a fulfilment of man's desire 'to possess all the
Things in Heaven and Earth' (*Centuries*, I. 60):

Was He not the Son of GOD and heir of the Whole World? To this poor
Bleeding Naked Man did all the Corn and Wine and Oyl, and Gold
and Silver in the World minister in an Invisible Maner, even as he lay
exposed Lying and Dying upon the Cross.

---

[5] As early as *Select Meditations*, III. 11, 13, 19.
[6] His views on original sin were influenced by the pre-Nicene tradition: see P.
Grant, 'Original Sin and the Fall of Man in Thomas Traherne', *ELH* 38 (1971),
40–61, and his *The Transformation of Sin* (Montreal and London, 1974), 176–95.

This is a paradox, no doubt, but it has little in common with the paradoxes in George Herbert's 'The Sacrifice', though the Crucifixion of the Son of God between two thieves always called for violent contrasts.

Yet Traherne has often been said to delight in paradox.[7] From the beginning he willingly echoed some traditional Neoplatonic paradoxes on God's infinity and the coincidence of contraries (*Select Meditations*, IV. 5). Like Giordano Bruno he felt that all things are one, as Heraclitus had maintained, hence all contradictory propositions true: 'Dunque, l'individuo non è differente dal dividuo, il simplicissimo da l'infinito, il centro de la circonferenza' (Traherne's favourite paradox).[8] He was therefore not insensitive to one aspect of the Incarnational paradox: 'A strang being here upon Earth. . . . Exceeding Great yet very little. Exceeding Rich yet very poor. Exceeding High yet very Low', etc. (*Select Meditations*, II. 64). But the emphasis is on the contrast and the strangeness. A sense of wonder pervades the writings of Traherne. Hyperboles are its most frequent expression in the poems and, unlike Donne's, they are never tinged with a sense of deliberate (and occasionally ironic) excess. He mainly speaks of the divine, in which case 'all Hyperbolies are but little Pygmies, and Diminutive Expressions, in Comparison of the Truth' (*Centuries*, II. 52).

Paradoxes are more frequent in the prose, but their fundamental nature is suggested in the opening statement of the *Centuries* (I. 3): 'I will utter Things that have been kept secret from the foundation of the World. Things strange, yet Common; Incredible, yet Known; most High, yet Plain; infinitly Profitable, but not Esteemed.' Paradox to Traherne will be the *revelation of something long ignored though evident*.[9] It will excite wonder, but not puzzle the mind. Instead of provoking perplexity, it will remove it since the surprising truth is found to be in conformity with reason. For reason is assumed to be 'a transcendent faculty, which extendeth to all

---

[7] Notably by Rosalie Colie in *Paradoxa Epidemica* (Princeton, 1966) and M. M. Day in *SP* 68 (1971), 305–25.

[8] *The Infinite in Giordano Bruno*, by S. Greenberg (New York, 1950), 166; *Opere Italiane* (Bari, 1907), I. 240.

[9] Even 'the Hypostatical union, Divine Lov, or the Passion of our Lord . . . are open and obvious to all': *Select Meditations*, III. 97.

Objects, and penetrates into all mysteries, so far as to enquire what probability may be in them' and 'there is no Repugnance between the Objects offered to our Faith and the Things we already know' through the light of nature (*Christian Ethicks*, 109). When the poet expresses his own experience—present or imaginatively recreated—of enjoying and possessing all things, he usually has no need of paradox for he has not to *prove* what he *feels*. When a paradox emerges—whether evident or demonstrated—it is experienced as a prodigy, for instance when the soul of a little child is discovered to be 'Much wider than the Sky' ('News', 43–56). In his unwearying (though wearisome) accumulation of marvels, Traherne may rush into paradox when straining to outrange himself in the expression of wonder. Thus, having confessed that man, when loving God, can give Him nothing, whereas God's love for His creatures gives man all things, he remarks that God's infinite love sets 'a value infinit' upon man's love for Him. Hence the conclusion, more hyperbolical than paradoxical:

> Let that same Goodness, which is infinit,
> Esteems thy Lov with Infinit Delight,
> Tho less then His, Tho Nothing, always be
>   An Object Infinit to Thee.
>
> ('Another', st. x)

Traherne's mode of apprehension of his own thoughts and sensations does not invite the interpenetration of the concrete and the abstract observed in the poetry of Donne and George Herbert. The poem 'Sight' aims at distinguishing between 'Those Eyes of Sense | That did dispense | Their beams to nat'ral things' and the Eye of the Mind, a 'Looking-Glass' wherein Virtues, Life, Joy, Love, Peace, appeared. Yet the distinction between the sensible and the intelligible is blurred when the mind's longing is to see 'New Regions' and 'In distant Coasts new Glories' 28–32), when this inner Light presents 'Objects' to the 'Sight', and can 'all the Depths descry | That God and Nature do include', 'All Ages' as well as all 'Thoughts' (55–72). In the poet's consciousness all objects seem to be visualized. Several poems deliberately oppose 'things' and 'thoughts' to show the superiority of the latter, and the poet rightly contrasts the inertia of things in comparison with the surging life and

infinite expansion of thoughts ('Thoughts I–IV'). But he indifferently presents as 'thoughts' actual images of the visible sun or
stars, when apprehended as 'representations' within the mind
('Thoughts I', st. iv), or imaginative evocations of distant countries and ages (ibid. vi), as well as concepts of God's 'Attributs,
and Counsels' ('Thoughts III', 52). This indifferentiation, like
the osmosis of soul and sense, is the result of the self-reflexive
apprehension of the world as seated in the consciousness. All
things in it are 'Supersubstancial' ('My Spirit', 113), yet all is
sense: 'There was my Sight, my Life, my Sence, | My Substance
and my Mind' (ibid. 63–4).

That is why transparency is an essential characteristic of
Traherne's style as he himself announced: 'a Simple Light'
discovering 'the naked Truth' through 'transparent words' ('The
Author to the Critical Peruser'). Metaphors are unnecessary for
the apprehension and celebration of either sensible or intellectual objects projected on to the screen of inward consciousness.
The aesthetic rapture awakened by these representations,
however, must be conveyed. Particularly when recording the
awakening consciousness of the child and his intimations of
immortality, the style beats with rapture and burns with beauty
in the best prose of the *Centuries* as in the best poems. Not in
Metaphysical or Baroque conceits, but in the translucence of
plain assertions the purity of the poet's impressions and convictions will shine spontaneously:

> How like an Angel came I down!
>
> Order the Beauty even of Beauty is.
>
> A quiet Silent Person may possess
> All that is Great or High in Blessedness.
>
> This busy, vast, enquiring Soul
> Brooks no Controul. [10]

This perspicuity, of course, was in line with the general evolution of seventeenth-century poetic style; notable in Denham and
in Cowley's later works. Yet its origin and nature were different:
it proceeded from a reliance on imaginative intuition which had
little in common with the rational empiricism of the Royal
Society.

---

[10] 'Wonder'; 'The Vision', 9; 'Silence'; 'Insatiableness II'.

The Divine Philosopher's sense of wonder and illuminated vision likewise transfigure his appeal to reason and nature.[11] 'The NATURAL Doctrines', he asserts, 'are Objects of Divine Faith, only as they are revealed by the Word of God' for with diligent search, those Things can be discerned by the Light of Nature. Among those doctrines we find all the 'common notions' on which, according to Herbert of Cherbury, 'the true Catholic or universal church is built'.[12] Antecedents have been found in the Stoics and in the works of Abelard, Cusanus, Erasmus, Castellio, Acontius, Duplessis-Mornay, Bodin, and Grotius.[13] As early as 1637 Chillingworth wanted men to be governed according to the 'never failing rules of Logick', by 'right reason, grounded on Divine revelation and common notions, written by God in the hearts of all men'.[14] By the middle of the seventeenth century many Anglican theologians thought like Whichcote that 'religion is intelligible, rational, and accountable' and scientists would soon argue that 'nothing can be philosophically true but theo-logically false'.[15] But Traherne adds to the list of common notions 'that the first Estate of the Worlds Creation was pure and perfect' and he alone proclaims the privilege of an intuitive knowledge:

> How easily doth Nature teach the Soul,
> How irresistible is her Infusion!
>
> ('Ease')

[11] That is why he seems at times fairly close to Sir Henry Vane, who also asserted in *The Retired Mans Meditations* (London, 1655) that man 'is capable of associating with Angels, and becoming their equal, even in his natural capacity of a man' (p. 52). They both believed in 'that self-evidencing TRUTH with which all are enlightened more or less', 'making the spirit of man . . . the candle and lamp of the Lord' (ibid. 181).

[12] Cf. *Christian Ethicks*, XVI. 118–19 and the 'five articles' in *De Veritate*, IX. 291–303: 'There is a Supreme God' [which implies 'Infinity, Omnipotence and Liberty']—'This Sovereign Deity ought to be Worshipped'—'The connection of Virtue with Piety is . . . the most important part of religious practice'—'The minds of men have always been filled with horror for their wickedness. Their vices and crimes have been obvious to them. They must be expiated by repentance'—'There is Reward or Punishment after this life' [which implies the immortality of the soul]. In Traherne's Commonplace Book, under 'Theologie' (fo. 93), similar notions are said to have been already asserted by Socrates.

[13] See Jacqueline Lagrée, *Sur Herbert de Cherbury* (Paris, 1989).

[14] *The Religion of Protestants A Safe Way to Salvation*, 'Preface'.

[15] Benjamin Whichcote, *Moral and Religious Aphorisms* (ed. W. R. Inge, 1931), no. 220. Robert Boyle published in 1675 *Some Considerations About the Reconcileableness Of Reason and Religion*.

> The Highest Things are Easiest to be shewn,
> And only capable of being *Known*.
>
> ('The Demonstration')

Certainly Adam in Paradice had not more sweet and Curious Apprehensions of the World, then I when I was a child . . . I knew by Intuition those things which since my Apostasie, I Collected again, by the Highest Reason. (*Centuries*, III. 1-2)

The 'Highest Reason' is kin to the 'holy Sagacity' of Henry More[16] and the intuitive intellect of the Cambridge Platonists, but Traherne does not hesitate to bring into play all the faculties, while respecting their hierarchy, when he declares himself in his maturity instructed 'by Sense, | Experience, Reason, and Intelligence' ('Right Apprehension', 39-40). The highest Truths—Eternity, Infinity, Love, Felicity—'By Instinct *virtualy* were well discernd' and 'did appear: | Not by Reflexion and Distinctly known, | But, by their Efficacy, all mine own' ('Improvment', 77-84). This apology of 'instinct' is an anticipation of the Romantic sensibility and Traherne's sense of the revelation of God to the child through Nature can take on a Wordsworthian solemnity:

> The Heavens were an Orakle, and spake
> *Divinity*: The Earth did undertake
> The office of a Priest . . .
>
> ('Dumnesse', 63-5)

There is, however, no hint of pantheism or animism, nor any Vaughan-like suggestion of sympathy between all living creatures: there are no animals in Traherne's Eden! It may be the consequence of his intense egotism. In his evocations of the natural world he wants all things to be given to him but never gives himself over to the life about him; he always sees himself as the centre and the sovereign of his universe.

That is one of the reasons why, unlike A. L. Clements,[17] I hesitate to declare him a genuine mystic; all depends, of course,

---

[16] Traherne defined 'Sagacitie' in his Commonplace Book as 'a naturall Invention which directs the Reason to find out things wrapt up in nature' (fo. 85ᵛ). Henry More is not mentioned, but the close correspondence with his definition of 'holy Sagacity' in his *Divine Dialogues*, II. xxviii, is obvious (1668 edn., p. 409).

[17] In *The Mystical Poetry of Thomas Traherne* (Cambridge, Mass., 1971).

upon one's conception of mysticism, an elusive notion. In 'Solitude', as in the *Centuries* (III. 23), his account of the horror that fell upon him 'in a Lowering and sad Evening, being alone in the field' betrays an experience of the *numinous*, which he himself perfectly defined in his Commonplace Book when speaking of places, particularly groves, whose strange beauty or horror awakes the impression of touching or perceiving an invisible power.[18] But this would hardly take us beyond the 'natural' or pagan sense of the sacred (Traherne himself refers to Seneca) if the experience had not been also characterized by a 'secret Want':

> Nor could I ghess
> What kind of thing I long'd for: But that I
> Did somwhat lack of Blessedness . . .
>
> ('Solitude')

Like Augustine in the *Confessions* (X. 9) he interrogated Nature, and found natural objects were silent. A want for a thing unknown which exerts a fascination over the mind even before being found and an obstinate quest for a revelation may be a prelude to a mystic experience. This is strongly suggested by the opening of the *Centuries* (I. 2):[19]

. . . Things unknown have a Secret Influence on the Soul: and like the Centre of the Earth unseen, violently Attract it. We lov we know not what: and therfore evry Thing allures us. As Iron at a Distance is drawn by the Loadstone, there being some Invisible Communications between them: So there is in us a World of Lov to somwhat, tho we know not what in the World that should be. There are Invisible Ways of Conveyance by which some Great Thing doth touch our Souls, and by which we tend to it. Do you not feel yourself Drawn with the Expectation and Desire of som Great Thing?

But with the great mystics the intuition of the 'Thing unknown' is the intuition of absolute otherness, as Otto defined it.[20] Traherne undoubtedly had an expectation of

---

[18]   Commonplace Book, fo. 51; cf. Rudolph Otto's remarks on the numinous, the *tremendum, das Ungeheuere*, in *The Idea of the Holy* (*Das Heilige* (1917), trans. J. W. Harvey (London, 1923; Oxford University Press, 1950)), chs. 6 and 9.

[19]   Cf. *The Life of the Servant*, by Henry Suso, trans. J. M. Clark (London, 1952), 'Prologue'.

[20]   Otto, *The Idea of the Holy*.

'Tidings' from 'a foreign Country', a yearning for 'absent Bliss' ('News'), an intense desire which inflamed him 'With restless longing Heavenly Avarice, | That never could be satisfied, | That did incessantly a Paradice | Unknown suggest, and som thing undescried | Discern, and bear me to it' ('Desire'). What is at once singular and disappointing is the way in which this 'desire' was satisfied: simply through the discovery of 'the Liveliness of interior presence' which made the whole World and all Ages 'Accessible to my Understanding, yea with it, yea within it, for without changing Place in my self I could behold and Enjoy all those' (*Centuries*, III. 24). Can a mere self-reflexive awareness of the presence of all things in the mind turn into a mystic revelation?

This discovery of inward presence was probably invested with such a significance only because Traherne had on other occasions enjoyed the kind of illuminated vision of the world recorded by many mystics, mainly the 'nature mystics' studied by William James and Evelyn Underhill. With his vision of a brave new world ascribed to the child—'The Corn was Orient and Immortal Wheat, which never should be reaped, nor was ever sown. . . . Eternity was Manifest in the Light of the Day' (*Centuries*, III. 3)—one may compare the cases of illumination recorded by William James:

The appearance of every thing was altered; there seemed to be, as it were, a calm, sweet cast, or appearance of divine glory, in almost everything . . .

Everything looked new to me, the people, the fields, the cattle, the trees. I was like a new man in a new world.

. . . the glory of God appeared in all his visible creation. I well remember we reaped oats and how every straw and head of the oats seemed, as it were, arrayed in a kind of rainbow glory.[21]

What may be characteristic of the mystic experience is the impression that 'All appeard New, and Strange' (*Centuries*, III. 2), 'Strange all, and New to me' ('Salutation', 40), a feeling also experienced in 1648 by young George Fox, who may have influenced Traherne since he held meetings in Herefordshire in 1663 and 1668:

---

[21]   *The Varieties of Religious Experience* (1901; London, 1971), 247–52.

Now was I come up in spirit through the flaming sword into the paradise of God. All things were new, and all the creation gave another smell unto me than before, beyond what words can utter. I knew nothing but pureness, and innocency, and righteousnes, being renewed up into the image of God by Christ Jesus, so that I was come up to the state of Adam which he was in before he fell. The creation was opened to me.[22]

This is the state described by Evelyn Underhill, quoting Blake's words: 'the doors of perception are cleansed', so that 'everything appears as it *is*, infinite',[23] which was exactly Traherne's impression: 'som thing infinit Behind every thing appeared' (*Centuries*, III. 3). The Divine Philosopher certainly had no experience of the *via negativa*, or the dark night of the soul, nor of a union with God described in erotic terms, but there are many mansions in the house of mysticism and he may be allotted a place in one of them.

Yet the account given in the *Centuries* is now supposed to be a 'late construct' of a conversion achieved conventionally through repentance as stated in the earlier *Select Meditations* (III. 21): 'My Soul was Parched till I knew my God. Confounded and Desolate till I could apprehend his GLORY ... My Soul was never a fountaine of Living waters; till it was fild with fear, and The tears of Repentance.' Sharon Seelig observes that 'the well-known picture of later years is for Traherne a kind of truth, yet the evidence also indicates that that truth was not immediately apparent'.[24] In fact, there is no contradiction, since the recovery of the illumination later ascribed to his childhood was described in the *Centuries* as due to the reading of God's promises in the Scriptures, by which he was 'informed and satisfied' (III. 32–3). What was attained was a conviction that was rational in his eyes: 'Thenceforth I thought the Light of Heaven was in this World: saw it Possible, and very Probable [his requirement in matters of Faith] that I was infinitly belovd of Almighty God' (*Centuries*, III. 35).

An assurance of God's personal love for him was indeed essential for Traherne; this love was reciprocated and ecstatically celebrated. Yet, in the *Select Meditations* (III. 56, IV. 38–40) as well as in the *Centuries* and the *Poems of Felicity*,

---

[22] *The Journal of George Fox* (Cambridge, 1952), 27.
[23] E. Underhill, *Mysticism* (London, 1930), 249; Blake, *The Marriage of Heaven and Hell*, xxii.
[24] In *ELR* 9 (1979), 419–31.

Traherne appears to love God not for Himself, nor for giving him His love, but for giving His child all the riches he craved for. However, the university student apparently lost sight of this revelation (*Centuries*, III. 36–45), or did not avail himself of it until he 'came into the Country' and resolved to spend all his time 'in Search of Happiness, and to Satiat that burning Thirst which Nature had Enkindled, in me from my Youth' (III. 46). This decision was followed, as in the *Select Meditations* (II. 100), by a traditional combat against Satan and his own 'lusts' and sins (*Centuries*, III. 47), which were never completely conquered since they were still deplored in *Commentaries of Heaven* (Nos. 67, 74, 87, 90, 93). His search, probably guided by his reading of Plato and the *Hermetica* as well as by the Bible and the Fathers of the Church (*Centuries*, III. 66), was a rational search for 'Perfect Felicity' (ibid. 54–8), and he found it when discovering that man, being made in God's image, can 'Enjoy the treasures of God in the similitude of God', which meant to him he found himself 'in a World where evry Thing is mine' (ibid. 58–62). Though it is not mentioned here, the reflexive apprehension of the world as seated in the mind, vividly evoked in the poems, must have been to him a confirmation of the Biblical promise. The celebration of 'the Works of God' in the Psalms (ibid. 71–5) was a testimony of the faculty of 'an Enlarged Soul' (ibid. 84) and confirmed his 'sence that God is so Great in Goodnes, and we so Great in Glory, as to be His Sons, and so Rich as to live in Communion with Him' (ibid. 99).

Was this 'Communion' a mystic 'Union'? The word is used in 'Silence' (67–70) about the relationship of the infant with God which may symbolize a later spiritual state; but these lines rather suggest the superimposition of two solipsisms:

> The Union was so Strait between them two
> That all was eithers which my Soul could view.
> His Gifts, and my Possessions, both our Treasures;
> He mine, and I the Ocean of his Pleasures.

What we miss is a previous *deshacimiento*—'stripping'—as in St John of the Cross.[25] There is still, on the contrary, a strong

---

[25] See Jean Baruzzi, *St Jean de la Croix et le problème de l'expérience mystique* (Paris, 1931).

desire of 'Possessions'. And this 'Silence' is not the *altum silen-tium*, the abyss, the night, the desert of the divinity, that the great mystics had to traverse.[26]

According to Salter and Clements 'the doctrines of Christian love found in St Bernard' justified the emphasis on self-love as a necessary stage before coming to the love of God.[27] Bernard does speak of self-love as the first degree of love, but he declares it only a 'natural' instinct of 'animal and carnal man who knew not how to love any one save himself'; far from tending to the love of others, or divine love, it will lead to voluptuousness unless immediately restrained by the command 'love thy neighbour as thyself'. In the second and third degrees of love, man still loves God for his own sake, 'because of deliverance obtained, *quoniam suavis est Dominus*'; when the fourth degree is attained (only in rare 'instants'), 'man loves not even himself except for the sake of God'; God is loved 'only for Himself', and man, *adherens Deo unus cum eo spiritus*, must almost come to self-annihilation—*pene adnullari*.[28] This seems to me at least initially different from Traherne's itinerary. There is no evidence that the Divine Philosopher achieved the theopathic state in which the soul has lost any sense of self and all actions are 'disindividualized', appearing 'exterior and strange'.[29] He rather seeks to take present possession of Paradise. In the state of 'Innocence' (primal or recaptured) 'the anchient light of *Eden*' (st. v) shines over the present world and in the poet's soul ('Thoughts IV', 35–6):

> What hinders then, but we in heav'n may be
> Even here on Earth did we but rightly see?

The poet occasionally seems to rise to a contemplation of the Neoplatonic 'One': 'From One, to one, in one to see *All Things*' ('Vision', 49). But this intuition, with Plotinus as well as the great mystics, implies a 'convergence of the attention of the

---

[26] Otto, *The Idea of the Holy*, ch. ix, 3.

[27] K. W. Salter, *Thomas Traherne* (London, 1964); Clements, *Traherne*, 10.

[28] *De diligendo Deo*, chs. viii–x; *St Bernard on the Love of God*, ed. Gardner (London, n.d.), 89–95. Cf. Bérulle: 'Je veux qu'il n'y ait plus de Moy en moy', *Œuvres* (2nd edn., Paris, 1657), 127. Augustine insisted that man should cease to love himself in order to love God: *Soliloquies*, 8.

[29] Roger Bastide, *Les problèmes de la vie mystique* (Paris, 1948), 110.

mind on an Absolute dialectically assumed to be an extrinsic principle of coordination of scattered forms, but more and more directly apprehended as the unique Being in which all contingent substances are absorbed'.[30] In Traherne's 'Vision' the One ensures the convergence of all the effects of a single Cause in order that all creatures should contribute to the bliss of a single one, that is, the individual consciousness. What is contemplated is not, in fact, the One, but 'All Things', the 'Circulation' (the title and theme of another poem) of 'All the fair Treasures of [God's] Bliss | Which run like Rivers from, into the Main' (82–3).

Traherne repeatedly speaks as if he were 'deified', but only because he declares the infinite capacity of the soul identical with the infinity of God's mind, which looks like wishful thinking. In the same way Henry More celebrated 'the Soul of Man, when the life of God inactuates her, shoots her along with himself through Heaven and Earth; makes her Unite with, and after a Sort feel herself animate, the whole World . . . This is to become Deiform'.[31] This confidence in the natural faculties of the soul (grace is not required) was widespread among the Cambridge Platonists, some of whose works anticipated the writing of the *Centuries* and the Poems.[32] Some of them shared with Traherne a '*restless appetite*' that would not 'be satisfied with any thing less than Infinity itself' and the possession of Heaven here and now.[33]

Traherne's enthusiasm and imagery at times call to mind the

[30] P. J. Maréchal, *Etudes sur la psychologie des mystiques*, 2 vols. (Bruges, 1924), I. 178.

[31] *Second Lash of Alazonomastix* (1651), quoted in *Philosophical Poems*, ed. Geoffrey Bullough (Manchester, 1931), p. xxxvii. Henry More is a more likely influence than Eckhart and Ruysbroeck, mentioned by Clements.

[32] See Culverwell, *An Elegant and Learned Discourse of the Light of Nature* (1652), 'The Worth of Souls', pp. 199–202, on the 'capacity' of the soul; John Smith, *Select Discourses* (1660): 'A Discourse Concerning the Existence and Nature of God', ch. vi (London, 1821, p. 154). As early as 1647 Cudworth said in *A Sermon. . . . Preached at Westminster*: 'No man is truly free, but he that hath his will enlarged to the extent of God's own will by loving whatsoever God loves . . . He injoyes a boundlesse liberty and a boundlesse sweetnesse, according to his boundlesse love. He inclaspeth the whole world within his outstetched arms, his soul is as wide as the whole universe, as big as "yesterday, to day, and forever" ' (p. 60).

[33] J. Smith, *Select Discourses* (1660): 'Men are apt to seek after the Assurance of Heaven as a thing to come, rather than after Heaven it self and the inward possession of it here' (p. 439).

apocalyptic expectations that were widespread at the time,[34] but a reader of Plato and Seneca was protected against their extravagance. Besides he did not need to look forward to a Millennium since the privileges of Eden could be recaptured in the present world. Renaissance humanism was one of the sources of his apology of primitive life. He followed Montaigne and anticipated Rousseau when claiming that 'those Barbarous People that go naked, com nearer to Adam God and Angels in the Simplicity of their Wealth, tho not in Knowledg' (*Centuries*, III. 12). In his pastoral retreat he had discovered that the true goods are universal: natural, not man-made objects. It allowed him to satisfy his wish 'to Enjoy the World', while retaining the traditional Christian contempt for the world (*Centuries*, I. 7):

> Truly there are two Worlds. One was made by God, the other by Men. That made by GOD, was Great and Beautifull. Before the Fall, It was Adams Joy, and the Temple of his Glory. That made by Men is a Babel of Confusions: Invented Riches, Pomps and Vanities, brought in by Sin. Giv all (saith Thomas a Kempis) for all. Leave the one that you may enjoy the other.

In the *Imitation* the world of God was a spiritual world; for the inheritor of Renaissance humanism, it was a sensible world. Not things rare, for the best things are most common: 'Air, Light, Heaven and Earth, Water, the Sun, Trees, Men and Women' (*Centuries*, III. 53). Not ornaments, which are 'Gilded manacles':

> Thy Gifts O God alone Ile prize,
> My Tongue, my Eys,
> My cheeks, my Lips, my Ears, my Hands, my Feet.
>
> ('The Person', st. iv)

These truths were known to the child before he was corrupted by custom ('Wonder', st. vii–viii; 'Eden'; 'Nature'; *Centuries*, III. 7–14). Yet this rejection of civilized life is only a first step in the Gospel of Felicity. In 'A Thanksgiving and Prayer for the NATION' (219–27) the parson calls to the Lord:

---

[34] In his *Revelatio Dei. The Revelation of God and his Great Prophesie* (London, 1649) Hendrich Niclaes spoke of God's gifts in the same language as Traherne: 'by me [God] is all Sweetness, Milk, Honey, Wine, and Oyl, also all Riches' (p. 41). He, too, described his mind as spreading 'so wide that the whole heaven and the universal earth stood comprehended therein' (p. 4).

> . . . give me Eyes
>   To see the beauty of that life and comfort,
>   Wherewith those by their actions
>   Inspire the Nations.

Their Markets, Tillage, Courts of Judicature, Marriages, Feasts and Assemblies, Navies, Armies, Priests and Sabbaths, Trades and Business, the voice of the Bride-groom, Musical Instruments, the light of Candles and the grinding of Mills,
    Are comfortable, O Lord, let them not cease.

This apparent contradiction, one may argue, is found in the mystics whose final vision is optimistic: the world they gave up is given back to them in a new light. But Traherne's itinerary was different. He may have achieved a genuine metamorphosis of self-love into the love of God and his fellow creatures, but the desire of possession, though spiritualized, was never extinguished and his optimism seems facile. The greater mystics finally adhere to the world and often seek to change it.[35] The chaplain of Sir Orlando finally adhered to the society of his time and praised its achievements with a candour which announces the complacency of the Age of Enlightenment:

I know very well that the Age is full of Faults, and lament it: but withal I know it is full of Advantages. As Sin abounds, so does Grace also super-abound. Never so much clear Knowledge in any Age: Learned Ministers, multitude of Sermons, excellent Books, translated Bibles, studious Gentlemen, multitude of Schollers, publick Liberty, Peace and Safety: all great and eminent Blessings.[36]

---

[35] 'St John of the Cross is in the first rank of those mystics who finally adhered to the world' (Baruzzi, *St Jean de la Croix*, 708).
[36] *Christian Ethicks*, 'Appendix', p. 283.

PART IV

Historical Landmarks

CHAPTER 16

The Slow Emergence of Self-Consciousness

The metaphysical poets display various modes of self-awareness, which may, however, be distributed around two poles: the 'self-consciousness' of Donne and George Herbert, in my definition of the term, and the self-reflexive consciousness of Traherne, foreshadowed by some lines of Marvell and the philosophy of Lord Herbert.

Donne's intense self-consciousness is not merely a distinctive feature of his personality. It is a landmark in the history of consciousness from Greek Antiquity to the seventeenth century[1], as clear an illustration of a change and progress as Augustine's *Confessions* or Montaigne's *Essays*, though it cannot be claimed to have been so momentous and influential. I first think it useful to make a sharp distinction between two different ways of using and applying the precept 'Know thyself', so often recalled by philosophers and priests, moralists and poets, whether pagan or Christian, that one might think that the search for one's identity has been a major preoccupation for man at all times. Self-knowledge has been differently understood and practised from Socrates to St Bernard, from Seneca to Erasmus or Montaigne. Originally the Delphic injunction meant: know you are not a God, but a mortal, avoid *hubris*. This meaning prevailed among the Stoics, from Epictetus to Seneca and Marcus Aurelius, and among physicians, notably Galen. Their invitation to self-knowledge was an invitation to test our capacities, control our passions, achieve self-mastery; to the physician self-examination was a remedy to diseases of

---

[1] A collective work I have edited, *Genèse de la conscience moderne* (Publications de la Sorbonne, Paris, 1983), has attempted to trace the emergence and development of self-consciousness from Antiquity to the modern age.

emotional origin.² Even when the field of inquiry widened, there was no search for what is most individual in us. Epictetus invited each one of us to 'discover what he has in common with other men by nature, as a chorist is attentive to the symphony'.³ In his own 'nature' the Stoic always sought to discover an impersonal nature and reason; the individual soul was invited to achieve conformity with the soul of the universe.

Two principles of Stoicism, however, have apparently affected Donne: the call to 'live within oneself' and the recognition that self-knowledge is the hardest achievement. A verse letter to Sir Henry Wotton ('Sir, more then kisses') echoes a phrase of Persius, *tecum habita* ('Satyre I', 5) and expands it: 'Be thou thine own home, and in thy selfe dwell.' The injunction of the Roman satirist had early been Christianized by St Jerome, who called St Augustine's attention to it, and by Gregory I the Great. The twelfth-century mystics later considered it as an invitation to engage in a conversation with oneself, untroubled by concerns for the outer world.⁴ But the invitation of the satirist, *nec te quaesiveris extra*, 'do not seek yourself out of yourself', was only a prelude to a quest that could take different forms. For the Stoics it meant an achievement of self-mastery by an act of the will, not an interest in personality. In Greek and Roman Antiquity men were classified according to types: the distinctive traits of the individual were not the object of attention. The Stoics were mindful of man's experience of the world and the fundamental question for the sage was 'What is my relation to the universe?'⁵ The curiosity of Donne, like Montaigne's, took a different path.

The difficulty of gaining self-knowledge had been acknowledged even by Aristotle: we reprove in others what we do ourselves; we do not notice our own faults since the eye cannot see itself.⁶ Shakespeare resorted to this argument in *Troilus and Cressida* (III. iii. 100–6). Seneca and Persius, following Aesop, introduced another well-known image: man wraps up his

---

² Pierre Courcelle, *Connais-toi toi-même: de Socrate à saint Bernard* (Paris, 1974), 25–62.   ³ *Discourses*, III. 22, 53.
⁴ Courcelle, *Connais-toi toi-même*, 219, 275, 291.
⁵ See Bernard Groethuysen, *Anthropologie philosophique* (Paris, 1953), 88–90.
⁶ *Magna Moralia*, III. 15, 1213a.

defects in a wallet which he carries on his back.[7] Yet the moralists of Antiquity never express that sense of uncertainty about one's own personality which we discover in the *Essays* of Montaigne, some poems of Donne, and some Shakespearean heroes. Aristotle only concluded from our unperceptiveness of our own self that we should take a friend for a mirror since a friend is another self.[8] Horace asked his slave to do the office, tell him his failings, reveal him to himself: a slave to passion, inconstant, incapable of being one hour alone (*Satires*, II. vii; cf. I. iv). One can object that this may be a kind of stage play, that he is only pretending to expect from an observer the revelation of what he himself had observed. Even if it were so, this attitude would be different from our modern inwardness and would still disclose a tendency to objectify the inner life which had been obvious in the Homeric epic and in Greek tragedy.

As many scholars have pointed out, passion was originally felt by man as an exterior and often supernatural force assailing and invading his consciousness.[9] A celebrated line of Racine expressing the passion of Phèdre still conveys this impression: 'C'est Vénus tout entière à sa proie attachée.' When a Homeric hero said 'I was inspired to do this by a god', it literally meant that the suggestion was breathed into him.[10] Like Jean-Pierre Vernant, Suzanne Saïd maintains that the decisions of the Aeschylian hero cannot be interpreted as the result of an inward process.[11] Sophocles first asserted the autonomy of the individual; yet the Sophoclean hero does not illustrate the singularity of the individual but his own 'heroic temper' as opposed to the common sort.[12] Only with Euripides does the word *sunesis* appear, but though the self takes on an individual character, there is yet no evidence of a self-reflexive inwardness. We do not

---

[7] Seneca, *De Ira*, II. 28. 8, and Persius, *Sat.* IV. 24–5. Cf. *Coriolanus*, II. i. 41–4.   [8] Courcelle, *Connais-toi toi-même*, 21.

[9] e.g. C. S. Lewis, *The Allegory of Love* (Oxford, 1936), R. B. Onions, *The Origins of European Thought* (Cambridge, 1951), Bruno Snell, *The Discovery of the Mind* (Harvard UP, 1953).

[10] See A. D. Nuttall, *Openings* (Oxford, 1992), 4.

[11] 'La conscience de soi dans la tragédie grecque', in *Genèse de la conscience moderne*, 31: the terms used, *mel-aitios*, *sun-aitios*, *par-aitios* and *ep-aitios* suggest a kind of co-responsibility for the action.

[12] Saïd, 'La conscience', 38; cf. B. Knox, *The Heroic Temper: Studies in Sophoclean Tragedy* (Berkeley, 1964).

find it either in Greek lyric poetry, though the expression of emotion appears so modern. Not self-consciousness, but a consciousness of the body is disclosed in Sappho's celebrated poem, and in the paraphrase of it by Catullus the absence of first-person pronouns makes it seem almost impersonal:

> lingua sed torpet, tenuis sub artus
> flamma dimanat, sonitu suopte
> tintinnant aures, gemina teguntur
> lumina nocte . . .[13]

Though Roman elegy and satire marked a progress in subjectivity,[14] the description of the emotions usually remained external, behaviouristic.[15] Propertius sees his love frenzy from outside, notes its objective signs—the sleeplessness, the sobbing, the shivering, the frantic language. He will even imagine how his own rival, if repulsed, would experience the same torment, as if he wished to make the contemplation of his own misery more objective (*Elegies*, I). Since Donne was obviously influenced by his Roman predecessors in several elegies[16] it is not surprising that he should adopt their objective point of view in his evocations of outside reality and his own behaviour, as in 'Jealosie' or 'The Perfume', and should still project an outward image of himself in 'His Picture'[17] and 'On his Mistris'. Besides, the elegies were among his earliest poems: inwardness and self-consciousness, though they early appeared in his verse letters, mainly flourished in later works.

Did the Platonists offer a more subjective approach to the ideal of self-knowledge? Their conception of it, traceable to

---

[13] 'my tongue falters, a subtler flame steals down through my limbs, my ears ring with inward humming, my eyes are shrouded in twofold night': trans. F. W. Cornish, in *Catullus, Tibullus and Pervigilium Veneris* (London, 1939).

[14] See *Poètes métaphysiques*, III. 284–99.

[15] Onions, *Origins of European Thought*, 129: 'the Roman conception of the conscious self was virtually identical with that of the Greeks'.

[16] I agree with Stella Revard that Donne had more affinities with Propertius than with the other elegists: 'Donne and Propertius. Love and Death in London and Rome', in *The Eagle and the Dove: Reassessing John Donne*, ed. Claude Summers and Ted Larry Pebworth (Columbia, 1987), 70–9. I maintain, however, the difference in the nature of their self-consciousness. Revard herself notes that three elegies of Propertius 'use the descriptions of *outer scenes* of rage and desolation to depict the state of the poet's *inner* mind' (p. 72; my italics).

[17] His subtle analysis of the motives of love in 'His Picture' hardly required introspection.

Alcibiades I, was the fountainhead of a philosophic and mystic current which ran through the Middle Ages and culminated with the Renaissance Neoplatonists. I think it entirely foreign to Donne's conception of individuality, as well as Montaigne's, since it was claimed that 'to know oneself is not to know one's body, nor the whole made up by body and soul, but the soul alone' (I *Alcib.* 130e). This is antipodean to Donne's emphasis on the union of body and soul which makes up man and the personality of each man. Neoplatonic introversion, instead of reminding man that he is not a god, called upon him to acknowledge himself divine: *Scito te esse deum* was an assertion repeated by Plutarch and Macrobius, Plotinus and Philo.[18] Whereas Aristotle and the Stoics, as we have seen, stressed the difficulty of self-knowledge since the eye cannot see itself, Cicero, Plotinus, and Augustine, following Plato, claimed that the soul, unlike the eye, can apprehend its own activity (*Tusculanes*, 133b). This will be maintained from Plotinus (*Enneads*, VI. 9, 11, 38) to St Augustine (*De Trinitate*, ix), for the proper object of the soul was said to be incorporeal reality. This soul was related to the self, yet it remained supra-personal in its essence. It is in the *Banquet* that Plato probably came nearest to an intuition of individuality, yet his philosophy of love required 'a process of disindividualization'.[19]

The Neoplatonists apparently went no further in Antiquity. When examining the relations between the individual souls and the world-soul Plotinus still called for a purely objective attention to intelligible objects (*Enneads*, IV. iii. 27–8), considering attention to oneself—'a subject examining himself'—as vain and useless, 'a waste of energy' (IV. iv. 25), for in the realm of the intelligible the self is all things and the self and its object are one (IV. iv. 2). Yet the philosopher had noticed that the thinking mind perceives that it is thinking (II. ix. 1): he had had a glimpse of the self-reflexivity of consciousness later extolled by Traherne.[20] With Plotinus, however, this perception was not

---

[18] Courcelle, *Connais-toi toi-même*, 41–4, 87, 114.

[19] Yvon Brès, 'La connaissance de soi chez Platon', in *Psychologie de la connaissance de soi* (Paris, 1975), 18–82. Cf. C. Taylor, *Sources of the Self* (Cambridge, 1994), 174: 'Introspection had no significance for Plato.'

[20] *Enneads*, II. ix. 1: 'For whatever distinction is possible in the Divine between the Intellectual Act and its consciousness of that Act, still all must be one projection not unaware of its own operation . . . The contrary supposition would give us two

presented as an individual experience, a *cogito*, and it was un-attended by an assertion of the self. The Renaissance Neo-platonists, when they followed the Alexandrians, show little progress in self-consciousness. Ficino, after calling to man to 'separate his soul from his body', only invites the soul to seek itself where its aspiration lies, therefore 'seek itself beyond the world'.[21]

Only with Augustine had attention turned to the individual soul as particular to one man. As Groethuysen pointed out, the soul in the *Confessions* is no longer *the* soul within myself, but *my* soul; no longer a cosmic spiritual element, with which I am linked only by participation, but *my own particular soul*.[22] As a Christian Augustine found in the Hebraic heritage an atten-tion to the personal relation between the believer and his God unknown to pagan Antiquity. The first-person pronoun was prominent in the Psalms, in Job, in Ecclesiastes, in the Prophetic books. The Psalms especially came to be considered by Calvin as 'an anatomy of all the parts of the soul, since there is no affection but is here represented as in a glass. Nay, the Holy Spirit has here portrayed in a life-like fashion all the pains, fears, doubts, hopes, cares, and even confused emotions which commonly stir our minds . . . Here the Prophets discover all the inner affections, and call or rather impel each of us to examine himself in order that, out of so many infirmities and vices, noth-ing should remain concealed.'[23] Besides, Augustine was familiar with the portrayal of human passion and inner conflicts offered by the Roman poets.

Though most commentators today tend to emphasize the difference between the saint's God-oriented search for self-

---

beings, one that merely knows, and another—or separate being—that knows of the act of knowing' (trans. G. Stephen Mackenna and R. S. Page, *The Six Enneads*, Chicago, 1952). This assumption concerns the Intellectual Principle; it is, however, extended to human consciousness (and must have been suggested by an awareness of its operation) since 'the question is opened whether our thoughts can entertain a knowing principle so narrowed to its knowing as not to know that it knows'. This, Plotinus adds, would argue 'imbecility even in ourselves', but he keeps arguing objectively and collectively.

[21] In an exhortation to self-knowledge inserted in the first book of his *Correspondence*; trans. André Chastel, *Table Ronde*, 2 (1945), 198–9.

[22] *Anthropologie philosophique*, 127.

[23] From Calvin's *Preface to The Psalmes of David and others*, trans. A. Golding (London, 1571).

knowledge and the curiosity for the self characteristic of the modern age, I still think, as in an early essay,[24] that the *Confessions* really were a landmark in the history of consciousness. Charles Taylor expresses the same view in his monumental study of *The Sources of the Self*,[25] and he seems to be describing what I have observed in the poetry of Donne when he claims that with Augustine 'we become aware of our awareness, try to experience our experiencing, focus on the way the world is for us' (pp. 130–1).

This revolution in the history of consciousness did not directly lead to the kind of self-observation and interrogation about one's own identity which characterized Montaigne's and Donne's self-consciousness. Augustine's quest was God-oriented and led him beyond himself to this inner recess or summit of the soul open only to mystic introspection: *interior intimo meo et superior summo meo* (*Confessions*, III. vi. 11).[26] Yet, before transcending the empirical self, Augustine had explored what Montaigne will call 'les profondeurs opaques de ses replis internes'.[27] Through his self-reflexive attention to the workings of memory he came to a new perception of time, an intuition of inner duration, described as a 'distension' of the soul (XI. xxix). The difficulty of self-knowledge, merely acknowledged by his predecessors, became a harrowing experience and a source of perplexity: 'it is I who remember, and what can be nearer to myself than myself; and yet I cannot understand the power of my memory though I could not name myself without it' (X. xvi. 25).

Augustine discovered the paradoxical elusiveness of the self, unattainable in self-scrutiny: *nec ego ipse capio totum quod sum*, 'I cannot know myself wholly; and thus the mind appears not wide enough to take in itself within itself; and yet where is that part of itself it does not involve? Is it not in itself, not

[24] 'Genèse et dilemme de la conscience moderne', *Revue de la Méditerranée*, 49–51 (1952–3).
[25] Cf. Charles Trinkhaus: 'There is no work like the *Confessions* in entire Antiquity. There the self, Augustine himself, is made manifest as pure subject' (*In Our Image and Likeness: Humanity and Divinity in Italian Humanist Thought* (Chicago, 1970), 18).
[26] Latin text: *Confessions*, ed. J. J. O'Donnell (Oxford, 1992).
[27] *Essais*, II. vi; Florio, 'the thicke-covered depths of these internall winding crankes', Everyman, II. 59.

outside of itself?' (X. viii. 15). Hence his constant interrogations: 'I turned to my self and said "You, who are you?"' (*dixi
mihi, 'tu qui es?'* X. vi. 9); 'Who am I then, O my God?' (*Quis
ergo sum, deus meus?* X. xvii. 26). He even had an intimation
of the unconscious and its secret influence: 'our mind, when
questioning itself about its own powers, must not trust itself too
much for what is inside it often remains concealed from it unless
revealed by experience' (X. xxxii. 48).

There seems to be a close relationship between Augustine's
self-searching and his acute awareness of his own inner conflicts
(VIII. viii. 19) and his wonder at the manifold paradoxes which
made 'made him a great problem' for himself (*Factus eram ipse
mihi magna quaestio*, IV. iv. 9): the pleasurableness of weeping
(IV. v. 10), the commingling of joy and sadness in remembrance
(X. xiv. 21), the concurrence of a horror of life and a fear of
dying (IV. vi. 11), etc. What is surprising and revealing is his
apparent surprise in front of these contradictions though some
of them had already been observed by the Roman poets he had
read: it suggests that little attention had usually been paid so far
to the inner life.

Augustine's insistence on the unity of the self marks a further
progress in subjectivity. This unity was discovered in the very
experience of division, which must be quoted in Latin:

. . . ego eram qui volebam, ego qui nolebam: ego eram. nec plene volebam nec plene nolebam. ideo mecum contendebam et dissipabar a me
ipso, et ipsa dissipatio me invito quidem fiebat, nec tamen ostendebat
naturam mentis alienae sed poenam meam.[28]

Augustine was only refuting here the Manichaean theory about
the presence in each man of *duas naturas duarum mentium* and
asserting the unity of the self. But his rejection of this hypothesis is the token of a revolution in the conception of the inner life.
If an inner conflict was not due to the presence of two 'minds'
or 'souls' of a 'different nature' in one person, if one soul could
balance between contrary impulses (*animam unam diversis
voluntatibus aestuare*), there would be no reason either to
assume the presence of a *daimon* or 'genius' in this one soul.

---

[28] VIII. x. 22; ed. O'Donnell. Other editions print *ego ego eram*, an even
stronger assertion of unity.

Nor could the passions any longer be ascribed to the intrusion of some outer force, though they would still be often so described in literature for many centuries. The newness and inwardness of the Augustinian conception of the divided soul leaps to the eye when compared with the self-questioning of Marcus Aurelius examining on each occasion 'that part of himself which is called the inner guide in order to know whose soul he has at this moment: is it not the soul of a child, a young man, a woman, a tyrant, a packhorse, a wild beast?' (*Meditations, V. 11*). We shall see, however, that the *Confessions* did not inspire a further exploration of the inner life before Petrarch, though they later stimulated Protestant introspection. Donne's quest for his own identity apparently started before his extensive reading of Augustine, mainly for theological purposes; the *Confessions* were not the origin of it.

K. J. Weintraub claimed that 'Augustine's art of confessing became largely identical with self-searching, self-questioning, self-discovery, self-description and self-assessment',[29] but, from the end of Antiquity to the Renaissance, self-knowledge was practically confined to self-examination in order to repent one's sins. An Augustinian inwardness was ensured by the persistent assumption that man could only find God within himself, since man was the image of God and his soul an image of the Trinity.[30] Platonic influences were noticeable in the writings of Bernard of Chartres, but he seemed to reduce self-knowledge to the perception of analogies between the macrocosm and the microcosm. The scholastics 'turned away from Augustine's moral and psychological emphasis to explore the relations of Christian doctrine to ancient conceptions of the cosmos, the physical realm, the problems of logic'.[31] St Thomas appealed to the data of experience, but he always argued from a logical and metaphysical standpoint. To grasp how far we are from the Augustinian living intuition of the workings of the mind we need only compare the investigation of memory in the *Confessions* with the articles devoted to it in the *Summa Theologica* (Ia, q. 79, art. 6–7). The Thomist *quidditas* did not

---

[29] *The Value of the Individual: Self and Circumstance in Autobiography* (Chicago, 1978).
[30] St Bernard, *Patrologia Latina*, Migne, t. 184, cols. 485–90.
[31] Trinkaus, *In Our Image and Likeness*, 21.

invite an exploration of the individual: it assumed the intellect alone apprehends the universal, the particular can only be known by reflection, through phantasms. The Scotists, however, ascribed an intuitive knowledge of the particular to the intellect and asserted that the soul can know its own acts directly, though intuition gives us no immediate knowledge of the essence of the soul; but they did not move beyond these principles into the realm of psychology.[32] Besides, *haecceitas*, like *quidditas*, still implied fixity in each separate nature and the Thomist insistence on *habitus* was bound to reinforce it.

To recover a full sense of inwardness we have to turn to the mystics. St Bernard and St Bonaventura adopted the Augustinian itinerary which leads the soul to God through self-knowledge.[33] In England Walter Hilton, following Augustine and St Bernard, looked upon his soul as a mirror in which he sought to catch the divine image, but he showed little psychological curiosity. The spirituals, as a rule, sought self-absorption in God, which did not prevent some of them from being intensely conscious of their self. Eckhart, like Angelus Silesius, did not hesitate to assert: 'If I were not, God, too, would not be.' But he was thinking of his 'essential being' which had existed from all eternity: 'In the divine Essence I was myself, I wanted myself and knew myself in order to make up the man I am here below.'[34] This intuition of a transcendental subject could not stimulate an exploration of the self in the diversity of its human experiences. In the world below the soul was expected wholly to give up its own self and be drowned in the 'eternal Abyss' of the Deity.[35]

In the domain of literature the allegorical presentation of the

[32] See S. J. Day, *Intuitive Cognition: A Key to the Significance of the Later Scholastics* (New York, 1947). G. Zilboorg's claim that 'Duns Scotus and William of Ockham became interested in feelings, in true human, individual experiences' is questionable (*A History of Medical Psychology* (New York, 1941), 176).

[33] For St Bernard knowledge of God is attained through self-knowledge because man is God's image: *Patrologia*, Migne, t. 184, cols. 485 ff., 494D, 490A.

[34] Sermon *Beati pauperes*, Matt. 5: 3; *Meister Eckharts Predigten*, ed. J. Quint (Stuttgart, 1968), Predigt II, t. 2, p. 504; *Traités et Sermons*, trans. M. de Gandillac (Paris, 1942), 258.

[35] 'den ewigen Abgrund', *Eckharts Predigten*, t. 2, p. 493; Gandillac, p. 256. Heinrich Seuse (Suso), 'the one great mystic prior to Teresa who is accessible as a person' (Weintraub, *The Value of the Individual*, 193) advised man to know himself first as different from God, yet with a view to achieving the divine union.

psychic life was a constant feature from the *Psychomachia* of Prudentius to the *Romaunt of the Rose*. This dominance of an objective projection of inner phenomena was due to the persistence of the mode of consciousness that had long prevailed. There was a wealth of psychological content in medieval allegory. As C. S. Lewis argued in *The Allegory of Love* the personifications were no more arbitrary than the relations between the id, the ego, and the superego would appear if they were acted by characters on a Freudian stage. It is nevertheless indisputable that the inner life was thus frozen, and as it were reified, for centuries.

Throughout the Middle Ages, indeed, society compelled the individual to choose a style of life appropriate to his status. Even in so exceptional an account of oneself as the *Historia Calamitatum* of Abelard, personal experience conforms to type as Weintraub has demonstrated: the heroes 'did not write a script to fit their own lives and personalities; they strove hard to fit their lives and personalities into scripts already written'.[36] The characters in the *Canterbury Tales* have strong and diverse personalities but there is nothing about them that could be said 'ondoyant et divers', as Montaigne defined himself, or as we could describe many Shakespearean characters.

A rough sort of individualism has been discovered in the Latin student songs of the Middle Ages and one may discern at times a keen self-awareness in the lyrical vernacular poetry of the twelfth-century troubadours—particularly Bernard de Ventadour—but their self-analysis hardly extended beyond changing moods of joy and grief.[37] A more elaborate and dialectical presentation of the inner life of the mind and heart was attempted in the thirteenth century by the poets of the *dolce stil novo*, sometimes considered as the forerunners of Metaphysical poetry as they resorted to scholastic and Aristotelian notions.[38] I have shown how superficial the resemblances are in a brief

[36] *The Value of the Individual*, 87. The *Scito te ipsum* was for Abelard a way to the *summum bonum*.

[37] See M. Valency, *In Praise of Love* (London, 1958), 107–204. The lover may reveal a narcissistic tendency when looking at himself in the eyes of the beloved: Bernard, 'Can vei la lauzeta mover' (quoted by Valency p. 137).

[38] F. Figurelli spoke of their effort 'ad esprimere . . . le oscure intricate e talora inesprimibili vicende della coscienza individuale' with scholastic precision: *Il Dolce Stil Novo* (Napoli, 1933), 13; cf. Valency, *In Praise of Love*, 205 ff.

examination of the poetry of Guinizelli and Cavalcanti.[39] Their inwardness and self-allegorization of their states of mind, the monotonous harping upon the same themes and stereotypes of passion cannot reflect a living experience in its complexity. Dante himself in the *Convivio* only comes close to Donne in his 'physiology' of love, not in his self-examination; he even felt it necessary to apologize for speaking about himself (I. ii).[40]

It is not inappropriate to hail Petrarch as the first of the moderns when he asks himself: 'Who am I really?' It is character-istic that his *Secretum* should be a dialogue with Augustine whose *Confessions* even influenced the *Canzoniere*. But the *Secretum* was also strewn with references to Horace and Seneca. Like Augustine and like the Roman poets Petrarch discovers contradictory impulses in his *multivolum pectus*, and acknowledges himself to be *nusquam integer, nusquam totus*.[41] When he calls the soul a mystery, it is the mystery of his own particular soul in his experi-ence of life: he called attention to self-deceit. We come close to Montaigne and Donne, yet with a difference: the exploration of the self, as with Augustine, is meant to bring the self into confor-mity with the universal and unique ideal of Christian perfection.[42]

The author of the *Canzoniere*, however, definitely offers an example of egocentricity comparable with Donne's in his *Songs and Sonets*. The image of Laura we have is essentially its reflec-tion in the sensibility of her lover, who is only moved by his own emotions. In the sonnets on Laura's sickness, his attention and ours is wholly given to his own disquiet and suffering (*Canzoniere*, 184, 231, 233, 241). After her death he makes her shed tears for himself in Heaven (343, 356). Like Donne he indulges in self-pity.[43] Besides, as in the *Songs and Sonets*, attention is often

[39] *Poètes métaphysiques*, III. 203–5. The ancient tendency to project emotions outwardly by referring to their effect on the outward appearance of the speaker is noticeable in the poems of Guinizelli, Cavalcanti, Cino da Pistoia, and even Dante.

[40] See *Poètes métaphysiques*, III. 196–203. Donne owned a copy of *L'Amoroso Convivio* (Vinegia, 1531) and alluded to the *Divine Comedy* in 'Satyre IV', 157–9, but no influence is traceable in his poetry.

[41] An inner conflict to him is no longer a conflict between two souls, but between 'the two men within me' (*Epistolae rerum familiarum*, IV. 1; quoted by Trinkhaus, *In Our Image and Likeness*, 10).

[42] See Weintraub, *The Value of the Individual*, 106–11.

[43] 'I' vo pensando, e nel penser, m'assale | Una pietà si forte di me stesso, | Che mi conduce spesso | Ad altro lagrimar ch'i' non soleva.' *Canzoniere* (Milan, 1954), no. 264.

focused on the present moment. In the more introspective poems he seems to utter his thoughts as they rise in his mind 'Ora, mentre ch'io parlo . . .' (*Canzoniere*, 56). He reproduces the ebb and flow of the stream of consciousness, the succession of conflicting thoughts and feelings with a dramatic vivacity equal to Donne's in a few sonnets.[44] But these dramatic moments are few in the *Canzoniere*. The rhetoric of Petrarch usually sheds little light on the inner life: the expression of passion is stylized and too often confined to the 'bitter-sweet' antithesis traceable to the Roman elegiac poets. We miss Donne's irony directed at himself, the hallmark of his self-consciousness.[45]

The Renaissance and the Reformation in different ways favoured the development of autobiography. Rudolf Gottlieb asserts that autobiography in the modern sense 'hardly exists for Elizabethan literature'[46] and finds only one 'not fully developed' example of it in Thomas Whythorne's 1576 prose and verse life, reminiscent of Menippean satire. Yet Thomas Churchyard's *A Tragicall Discourse of the Unhappy Man's Life* (1575–80) and Thomas Taysser's 'The Authors Life' in *Five Hundred Pointes of Good Husbandry* (1577) disclose a growing 'curiosity about the lives of private men simply as men'[47]—a parallel with the increasing and more sophisticated interest in 'lives' and 'journals' of more illustrious men and women described by Bacon as 'the history of persons' (*Advancement of Learning*, II. ii. 11). On the Continent the study of personality was apparently systematic in Cardano's *De Vita Propria*, which Hugo Friedrich and Weintraub compared to the *Essais* of Montaigne.[48] But this physician only classified features of his

---

44 Notably in *Canzoniere*, 68: 'Ma con questo pensier un altro giostra, | e dice a me:—Perché fuggendo vai? | Se ti rimembra, il tempo passa omai | di tornar a veder la donna nostra.— | I', che' l suo ragionar intendo, allora | m'agghiaccio dentro, in guisa d'uom ch'ascolta | novella che di sùbito l'accora. | Poi torna il primo, e questo dà la volta. | qual vincerà, non so; ma'n fino ad ora | combattuto hanno, e non pur una volta.'

45 For a general comparison with Donne see my *Poètes métaphysiques*, III. 206–13.

46 'Autobiography and Art', in *Literary Criticism and Historical Understanding*, ed. P. Damon (New York, 1967), 110.

47 Wayne Shumaker, *English Autobiography: Its Emergence, Materials, and Form* (Berkeley, 1964).

48 Hugo Friedrich , *Montaigne* (A. Francke Verlag, 1967; trans. R. Rovini, Paris, 1968), 239–40; Weintraub, *The Value of the Individual*, 161.

character placed under the influence of the stars and stressed the part played by exterior forces; dwelling on 'strange occurences and dreams prophetical', he even reintroduced the notion of the *daimon* who conferred on him exceptional gifts.[49] His twenty-line chapter 'De me ipse' is not even concerned with his personality. Nor was Cellini in search of his identity in his autobiography,[50] which could be described, like d'Aubigné's later *Life*, as a 'parade of the self'[51] after the manner of the Burckhardtian type of Renaissance individualism.

Though Burckhardt's views had been severely criticized, Kristeller thought that he had not 'overestimated the individualism of the period or its secularism' and assumed that 'the criticism directed against him on these grounds seems to suffer from a confusion of terminology'.[52] The great figures of the Renaissance usually strove to discover universal norms, not individual peculiarities, yet the Epicurean philosophy of Lorenzo Valla maintained that 'all things are made for the sake of individuals'.[53] The criterion of individualism can be maintained if it is defined as self-assertion in the conduct of one's life, or as a personal quest for truth no longer hemmed in by tradition or authority. Erasmus proved particularly attentive to the individual 'physiognomy of the soul', the *interna species animi* (*Ecclesiastes*, 708) and the personal 'genius' of the orator or writer: 'Nature made us in such sort, attributing his own genius to each of us, that it is difficult to find men endowed with the same faculties and the same tastes.'[54]

A quainter hypothesis about the discovery of self was put forward by Georges Gusdorf: the invention of good mirrors by

---

[49] Cardan, *De Vita Propria Liber* (Paris, 1643), chs. 38, 41, 43, 47.

[50] Cf. Jonathan Goldberg, 'Cellini's *Vita* and the Conventions of Early Autobiography', *MLN* 89 (1974), 82.

[51] Gilbert Schrenck's description of it in his edition of *Sa Vie à ses Enfants* (Paris, 1986).

[52] In *The Renaissance: A Reconsideration of the Theories and Interpretations of the Age*, ed. T. Helton (Madison, 1961), 30. Ernst Cassirer had stressed a growing insistence on individuality in the works of Ficino, Pomponazzi, and Patrizzi, in *L'Individu et le Cosmos dans la philosophie de la Renaissance* (trans., Paris, 1927), 170–91.

[53] *Disputationes Dialecticae* (Cologne, 1541), fo. 221: 'singularum causa facta sunt universa'; fo. 222ᵛ: 'propter te, hoc est propter singulos'.

[54] *Ciceronianus*, p. 165, quoted by Jean Lecointe, *L'idéal et la différence* (Paris, 1993), 439, 451.

the end of the Middle Ages would have been responsible for the proliferation of self-portraits, from Dürer to Rembrandt. The mirror became an 'accessory to introspection'.[55] Donne referred to 'Durer's rules' in 'Satyre IV' (204) and thought 'a hand or eye | By Hilliard drawn . . . worth an history' ('Storme'). He obviously delighted in having several portraits of himself painted: this seems to me to be a testimony of his self-absorption rather than the cause of it, though we have also an evidence of his interest in a Mannerist art more expressive of personality than sixteenth-century English portraiture had been.[56]

In Elizabethan England the early Renaissance had not proved individualistic. The humanist ideal of self-knowledge was Socratic and ethical. William Lily's *Grammar*, revised by Erasmus, taught children that the beginning of wisdom is to know oneself. Sir Thomas Elyot in *The Governor* (1531) argued that self-knowledge was necessary to love one's neighbour and practise justice.[57] In *Toxophilus* (1545) Roger Ascham recommended a study of the capacities of children based on the wise proverb of Apollo, 'Know thyself'.[58] Self-knowledge applied to the active life was no longer a means of attaining the knowledge of God, as it was for St Bernard,[59] but an essential instrument to govern oneself in society.

By the end of Elizabeth's reign the aim of self-knowledge was for Spenser the fashioning of an ideal gentleman; it was expected to lead to self-mastery, but Guyon's allegorical visit to the House of Alma (*Faerie Queene*, II. ix) gave only general information. In the eyes of Sidney 'the highest end' of knowledge stood 'in the knowledge of a mans selfe, in the Ethike and politick consideration, with the end of well dooing and not of well knowing onely'.[60] Philosophical and didactic poetry—the

---

[55] 'Conditions et limites de l'autobiographie', in *Formen des Selbstdarstellung* (Berlin, 1956), quoted by Paul Delany in *British Autobiography in the Seventeenth Century* (London, 1969), 19.

[56] See L. E. Semler, 'John Donne and Early Maniera', *JDJ* 12 (1993), 41–66.

[57] In his treatise *Of the Knowledge Which Maketh a Wise Man* (1533) it was a prerequisite to an understanding of others and of the world (fos. 44–6).

[58] *English Works*, ed. W. A. Wright (Cambridge, 1904), 100.

[59] Bernard's call to self-knowledge, however, was still invoked by the moralists, e.g. in Abraham Fleming's *A monomackhie of motives in the mind of man . . . Hereunto divers golden Sentences of S. Bernard are annexed* (London, 1582).

[60] *Apology for Poetry*, in *Elizabethan Critical Essays*, ed. G. G. Smith (Oxford, 1904), I. 161.

Nosce Teipsum of Sir John Davies (1600), the *Microcosmos* (1603) of John Davies of Hereford—still approached the problem of self-knowledge in an objective and scholastic perspective. The coupling of a psycho-physiological determinism with metaphysical principles was, indeed, characteristic of the psychology of the age as represented by Timothy Bright's *Treatise of Melancholy* (1586), Thomas Wright's *The Passions of the Mind in Generall* (1604), or Huarte Navarro's immensely popular *Examen de Ingenios*, Englished as *The Examination of Mens Wits* (1594).[61] The Elizabethan, Jacobean, and Caroline dramatists relied on this type of psychology when they meant to present the working of the passions in a scientific way. Even after the translation of the *Essais* of Montaigne (1603) and Pierre Charron's *Of Wisdom* (1612) the introspective mode of self-analysis practised or advocated by the French writers did not displace the earlier objective or ethical mode.[62] Bacon himself in *The Advancement of Learning* (1605) spoke of self-knowledge as a means of moral improvement,[63] or only mentioned the general characteristics of the 'league of mind and body' (II. ix. 1). Ralegh, however, was less optimistic and echoed Isabella's description of man as 'Most ignorant of . . . his glassy essence' in *Measure for Measure* (II. ii. 119–20) when he spoke of man as 'ignorant of the essence of his own soul' in his *History of the World*.[64]

Among his many far-flung hypotheses in his 'historical reading' of Donne Thomas Docherty has presented 'the human condition post-Copernicus' as 'forever searching after a centralized stable identity'.[65] But Donne was apparently searching for

---

[61] Juan Vives alone in his *De Anima et Vita* (Basle, 1538) relied on introspection in his analysis of memory and the association of ideas and in a description of the passions which later influenced Descartes (Zilboorg, *History of Medical Psychology*, 191–3).

[62] Charron insisted that self-knowledge was acquired 'par une sérieuse & attentive examination de ses pensées plus secretes (leur naissance, progrez, durée, repetition), de tout ce qui remue en soy, jusques aux songes de la nuict, en s'espiant de pres, en se tastant souvent & à toute heure, pressant & pinssant jusques au vif' (*De la Sagesse* (Paris, 1607), 29).

[63] I. viii. 2: 'For the unlearned man knows not what it is to descend into himself, or to call himself to account, nor the pleasure of that *suavissima vita, indies sentire se fieri meliorem*.'   [64] Ed. 1614, Preface, sig. D3[r].

[65] *John Donne, Undone* (London, 1986), 63; cf. references to 'Copernicus' in the Index. Yet, after Copernicus and Galileo, as Donne himself noted, men went on 'liv[ing] just as they did before' (*Ignatius His Conclave*, 17).

his identity many years before he himself expressed any disquiet about the Copernican hypothesis, which apparently did not perturb his contemporaries. The 'new astronomy' cannot be responsible for the self-questionings of the Elizabethans.

Of greater interest for the development of individualism was the aggressive self-assertiveness which appeared in society and began to parade on the stage. When evoked by the moralists it was condemned as an instance of the Machiavellian spirit, as in the epigram in which Gabriel Harvey made the author of the *Prince* declare 'I alone am wise'.[66] The demonic energy and the limitations of this type of individualism were illustrated by Marlowe's heroes, from Tamburlaine and Faustus to Mortimer, and by Shakespeare's Richard of Gloucester and Edmund.[67] Though still Machiavellian, self-assertion was later invested with Stoic dignity in the characters of Webster who took pride in their isolation and flaunted their identity when facing the finality of death. In *The Duchess of Malfi* (1613?) Bosola claimed 'I'll be mine owne example' (V. iv. 91) and in *The White Devil* (1612) Flamineo, 'in the way to study a long silence', said: 'I doe not looke | Who went before, nor who shall follow mee; | No, at my selfe I will begin and end' (V. vi. 256–8). A purer strain of Stoic self-assertion ran from Chapman to Ford. Inwardness was stressed when Pompey declared 'If ever I be worth a house again | I'll build all inward' and the autonomy of the individual was proclaimed by Cato in *The Tragedy of Caesar and Pompey* (V. ii), but only in opposition to an outward power or influence; it became foolhardiness when Bussy or Byron pretended 'Who to himself is law no law doth need'.[68] Another aspect of Stoicism was the ambition of the individual 'to join himself with the Universe | In his main sway, and make (in all things fit) | One with that All' (*The Revenge of Bussy d'Ambois*, IV. v. 139–41): it had nothing in common with Donne's self-absorption.

Both the Stoic and the Sceptic currents favoured the development of moral autonomy. Yet I am not aware of any Elizabethan

---

[66] In *Gratulationum Valdinenses Libri Quattuor* (1598). Cf. 'The Writers Postscript' (1593) in which Harvey wrote that Machiavel 'nor dreaded Di'vill | Nor ought admired, but his wondrous selfe'.

[67] *3 Henry VI*, V. vi. 82 ('I am myself alone'); *King Lear*, I. ii.

[68] *Bussy d'Ambois*, II. i. 203–4; *The Conspiracy of Byron*, III. iii. 122–45.

precedent for Donne's justification of self-homicide in
Biathanatos: 'For we know that *Some Things are Naturall to the
Species, and other things to the perticular person*, and that the
later may correct the first. And therefore when *Cicero* consulted
the *Oracle* at *Delphos*, he had this answere *Follow your owne
nature*.'[69] Though the argument was buttressed with references
to St Thomas and to Antiquity, it was a bold claim for the
autonomy of the individual; only Marlowe the rebel had been
so audacious. In his Third Satire (89–92) Donne had earlier
daringly asserted the right of the individual to keep the truth he
had found in despite of all authority:

> Keepe the truth which thou hast found; men do not stand
> In so ill case here, that God hath with his hand
> Sign'd Kings blanck-charters to kill whom they hate,
> Nor are they Vicars, but hangmen to Fate.

The satiric outburst at the close of the sixteenth century
disclosed a mood of individual protest and discontent. The pose
of the satirist proved an opportunity for an assertion of the self
against the world[70] and an inflation of the writer's ego. John
Marston dedicated his *Scourge of Villanie* (1599) 'To his most
esteemed, and best beloved Selfe' and proclaimed: 'I am my
selfe, so is my poesie.'[71] The search for originality and singularity studied in Chapter 18 was obviously related to a growing
sense of individuality and self-importance.

At the turn of the century there were undoubtedly in
England social and literary influences favourable to a greater
acuity of self-awareness. They could account for the self-
assertiveness displayed by Donne in his satires and in
Metempsychosis, but not for the persistent egocentricity
detected in all his writings. In the same way, conflicting religious views, together with the dissemination of Sceptic ideas,
favoured the independence of judgement manifested in the
Third Satire and the sense of relativity expressed in the closing

---

[69] *Biathanatos*, 47. Donne's letter to Sir Edward Herbert 'implies that
Biathanatos seriously defends suicide' (Sullivan, p. xxii).

[70] Joseph Hall in *Virgidemiae* will 'chide the world, that did my thoughts
offend' (*Collected Poems*, ed. Davenport (Liverpool, 1949), 10). Cf. 2 *Return from
Parnassus* (*Three Parnassus Plays*, ed. Leishman, 1949), I. iv. 399–400: 'Ile scorne
the world that scorneth me againe.'

[71] *The Scourge of Villanie* (1599), ed. G. B. Harrison (London, 1925), 2.

lines of *Metempsychosis*. But Donne's personal inclination to this mode of thinking must have existed before his encounter with these conflicts and ideas since a vast majority of his contemporaries took sides unhesitatingly and showed no sense of relativity. Very few of them, too, give any evidence of the kind of self-consciousness I have analysed, though a growing number were becoming experts in 'home Cosmographie', to echo William Habington's later advice.[72]

In lyric poetry the 'affections', particularly 'the many moodes and pangs of lovers', were expected 'throughly to be discovered'.[73] Yet among Donne's predecessors there are only glimmers of subjective reflexivity, as in Edward Dyer's often echoed 'My minde to me a Kyngdom is'.[74] Greenblatt admits in his study of the *Penitential Psalms* of Wyatt that 'there is no more insistent expression of the "I" in Tudor literature; . . . of the importance of his identity, Wyatt has no doubt whatever'.[75] But the lyrical poet's self-awareness and inwardness remain superficial, as a comparison of his sonnet 'Unstable dream!' with Donne's elegy 'The Dreame' can show. In the 'Paraphrase of the Penitential Psalms' only brief allusions to his 'instability' and to an 'inward contemplation of his desire' suggest the presence of introspection.[76] Among the sonneteers Sidney alone anticipates the *Songs and Sonets* in dramatic immediacy and in a few flashes of introspective inwardness:

> Griefe, find the words, for thou hast made my braine
> So darke with misty vapors which arise
> From out thy heavy mould that inbent eyes
> Can scarce discerne the shape of mine owne paine.[77]

---

[72] In 'To my honoured friend Sir Ed. P.': 'Direct your eye-sight inward, and you'll find | A thousand regions in your mind, | Yet undiscover'd. Travell then, and be | Expert in home Cosmographie' (*Castara*, 1634–40; ed. K. Allott (1948), 93).

[73] Puttenham, *The Arte of English Poesie* (1589), I. xxii; ed. Arber (Westminster, 1895), 60.

[74] The popularity of the Stoic theme of the contented mind is well known, but Dyer is more introspective in another poem in which he vainly sought to 'appease the discord of [his] minde': 'Oft with my selfe I enter in device'.

[75] *Renaissance Self-Fashioning* (Chicago, 1980), 155. Cf. Anne Ferry, *The 'Inward Image'. Sonnets of Wyatt, Sidney, Shakespeare, Donne* (Chicago, 1983).

[76] Lines 337, 456, 358 in *Complete Poems* (New Haven, 1978).

[77] *Astrophel and Astella*, 94. Only the more 'objective' of Shakespeare's sonnets probably circulated before 1598.

I have traced the evolution of the stage soliloquy from Greene and Marlowe to Shakespeare and shown the slow progress of self-analysis.[78] Jack Donne, as a 'great frequenter of plays', may have heard or even read the self-centred monologue of Richard of Gloucester (*3 Henry VI*, III. ii. 124–95) as early as 1595, and the ruminations of Richard II (V. v) in 1597, but in the first Shakespearean soliloquies the thoughts, desires, or anguish of the hero were still projected outwardly in Protean images, not examined in a truly introspective way.

For a real anticipation of Donne's characteristc self-consciousness one must turn to Montaigne, to whom he made a partly inaccurate allusion in a letter written only in or about 1604.[79] A few parallels between his poems and the *Essays* have been offered, notably by Milgate; but they are only parallels in ideas and there is no evidence of direct or verbal borrowing. I have pointed out similarities in their search for identity and sought to bring out its novelty.[80] It is not a case of influence, but a parallel development. Even if Donne had access to the *Essays* before the publication of Florio's translation in 1603, the reading of Montaigne only stimulated his own tendencies.

If we turn from profane to religious literature, we notice that Donne's self-searchings cannot be due to a direct influence of the *Confessions*[81] since they were already obvious in some of his early Verse Letters and some of the *Songs and Sonets*. The Augustinian influence later traceable in the Holy Sonnets and in *Biathanatos* was theological.[82] In his *Sermons* Donne often alluded to the *Confessions*, but not to the introspective passages I have mentioned.

'Protestant individualism' has been presented as a major influence on the general history of thought in the sixteenth and seventeenth centuries. Luther's *Zwei-Regimente Lehre* had sharply distinguished the sphere of sociopolitical activity and that of private spirituality, a distinction adopted by Perkins in

---

[78] 'Self-consciousness in Montaigne and Shakespeare', *Shakespeare Survey*, 28 (1975), 37–50.   [79] *Letters (1651)*, 106; Hayward, p. 448.

[80] See Ch. 1, pp. 31, 34–5 and n. 17.

[81] This remark could apply to the *Essays* of Montaigne, who never mentioned the *Confessions* and is unlikely to have read them, according to most specialists, from whom, however, I am inclined to dissent.

[82] See Patrick Grant, 'Augustinian Spirituality in the Holy Sonnets of John Donne', *ELH* 38 (1971), 542–61.

his notion of a *duplex persona* of the believer.[83] The great Reformer and the more daring minds of the Renaissance were at one in proclaiming the absoluteness of the individual conscience.[84] Donne followed in their wake when he claimed in *Biathanatos* that 'a man is bound not to doe against his conscience'.[85] Yet, before Donne, in England at least, religious individualism was confined to the creation of a closer relationship between the believer and his God and the anxious search for an inward evidence of election. When recommending self-examination Calvin insisted that 'true self-knowledge . . . leads to self-condemnation and distrust' (*Institutes*, II. i. 3).

Protestant faith invited an appropriation of Scripture by the individual but typological habits tended to impersonalize the self, the believer identifying himself with various Old Testament figures (like George Herbert in 'Aaron'), or with Adam (like Donne in 'Hymn to God my God, in my sicknesse'), or with Christ himself. Barbara Lewalski claimed that this tendency could 'personalize typology'; Barbara Harman objected that 'in Herbert's typological poems persons do not appropriate and rewrite Scripture: Scripture appropriates and rewrites them'.[86] From my point of view it makes little difference, for this kind of typological lyric had not developed before Donne, though Wyatt's intensely personal paraphrases of David's Psalms may be considered as an anticipation of it. In fact, the typological approach may work both ways: either blur the difference between the individual and the type if the writer is not self-conscious, or, if he is, prove a means of heightening a personal drama as in Donne's Hymn. The same remark could apply to the debate whether the Ignatian model of meditation (which may have influenced Donne) or the Salesian (closer to the spirit of Herbert) impeded the expression of individuality: it didn't

---

[83] See Debora Shuger's *Habits of Thought in the English Renaissance* (Berkeley, 1991), 256–7.

[84] Richard Strier showed the convergence of Luther and Castellio on this point in *Resistant Structures: Particularity, Radicalism, and Renaissance Texts* (Berkeley, 1995), 152–4.

[85] *Biathanatos*, 142. He wrote to Goodyere: 'it is a sin to doe against the conscience, though that erre': *Letters* (1651), 76, quoted by Strier in *Resistant Structures*, 154. In so doing, however, Donne was not 'radical': it was the position of Perkins.

[86] Lewalski, 'Typology and Poetry', in *Illustrious Evidence* (Berkeley, 1975), 46; Harman, *Costly Monuments*, 189.

in the case of Donne or Herbert, but with less original writers it could cast the self into a ready-made mould.

A growing interest in cases of conscience calling for individual solutions also became a general characteristic of the age: it brought about the development of both Protestant and Jesuit casuistry. The latter was intended for the confessor; the former was more likely to lead to self-searchings since it was meant to help perplexed and anxious believers. Yet I failed to discover interesting instances of introspective insight in *The Whole Treatise of the Cases of Conscience* of William Perkins (1606), or in William Ames's *Conscience with the Power and Cases thereof* (1639). Ames constantly bases on Biblical texts his call to 'a Proving or examining of our selves, 2 Cor. 13. 5', and his definition of 'that reflex act, which is proper to man, whereby he hath a power, as it were, to enter into, and perceive what is in himself, 1 Cor. 2. 11' by 'a kind of spirituall sense, Luke, 24. 32. Rom. 7. 21, 28'.[87]

The call for constant self-examination accounts for the multiplication of Protestant and Puritan diaries. Donne's *Devotions* in a way illustrate this kind of self-searching as well as the Holy Sonnets. Yet, even in a comparison of the *Devotions* with the diaries, Donne shows a different kind of self-awareness, a more intense self-absorption and a keener interest in psychological complexities. The diaries examined by Elisabeth Bourcier up to the Restoration prove disappointing in their record of the inner life.[88] The religious diarists and autobiographers concentrate on trials and temptations and the daily examination of sins from a purely objective standpoint, multiplying self-accusations. A typical instance is offered by *The Account of Dionysia Fitzherbert* who 'anatomized' her 'own case' in 1608 to comfort

---

[87]   Ames, Bk. I; the 1643 edition, p. 17, reads: 'This *reviewing* is a reflex act of the *understanding*, whereby a man understandeth, and with judgement, weigheth his own actions with their circumstances. It is commonly called *Consideration* or *meditation* on our wayes. It is called in the Scripture, A *respect* or *beholding* by the inside, *Psal.* 119. 15. *Considering*, *Psal.* 50. 22. *Thinking or thinking again*, *Psal.* 119. 59. Laying of the heart, *Hag.* 1. 5 . . . and lastly A *proving* or *examining* of our selves, 2 Cor. 13. 5.'

[88]   *Les journaux privés en Angleterre de 1600 à 1660* (Paris, 1976); see pp. 389, 397. To check this general statement I have perused several diaries, notably those of Richard Rogers (1587–90), Sir Roger Wilbraham (1593–1616), John Rous (1625–42), John Greene (1635–59), Nehemiah Wallington (1641–3), Ralph Josselin (1644–81).

the afflicted and related how a review of her life and failings brought about her conversion.[89] The record of more profane experiences never leads other diarists to closer analyses of their emotions.[90] Some of them prove aware of the danger of self-deceit,[91] though not with the same subtely as Donne, George Herbert, or Marvell. An awareness of this danger was wide-spread after the publication by Daniel Dyke in 1615 of *The Mystery of Selfe-Deceiving*, dedicated to Donne's patroness, Lucy, Countess of Bedford. The book is of particular interest for it illustrates the confluence of the Augustinian and the Stoic concern with self-knowledge:

Here shall they [the readers] finde that dangerous Art of selfe-Sophistry displayed ... And so by seeing their selfe-deceit, shal come to their selfe-knowledge. A knowledge never more neglected. *Ut nemo in sese temptat descendere, nemo, Pers*[ius]. Men care not for knowing themselves, who are oftentimes too too curiously greedy of knowing all things else, being herein like to foolish travellers, that love to travell into, and talke of other strange countries, strangers in the mean time in the rarities, secrets and wonders of their owne.[92]

Dyke repeatedly quotes from Augustine's *Confessions* passages which invite a comparison with Donne's states of mind. Had he not been 'much like to S. Austin that before his conversion prayed to God for chastitie and continency, but yet was afraid, as he writes of himselfe [*Confess*. lib. 8], least God should heare his praier too soone'? Had he not shown the same 'puzzle-mind-edness' and 'sought not God sincerely, but onely for [his] owne ease, to be delivered out of [his] trouble, and so indeed ... sought not God but [himselfe]'? Had not the preacher too

---

[89] Bodleian MS e Musaeo 169; Bourcier, *Les journaux privés*, 356. Richard Rogers comes closer to introspection and may remind us of George Herbert when he speaks of his 'peace of mind' or his 'unsettledness', and of his 'strongue desire to injoy more liberty', but these are brief flashes: *Two Elizabethan Puritan Diaries*, ed. M. M. Knappen (Chicago, 1933), 54–6, 59–60.

[90] Lady Anne Clifford was a remarkable woman who had read Augustine's *City of God*, had Montaigne's *Essays* read to her (Nov. 1616), and heard sermons of 'Dr. Donne' (July 1617); yet she offers no instance of self-analysis: *The Diary of the Lady Anne Clifford, 1616–1619*, ed. V. Sackville-West (London, 1923).

[91] John Beadle, Lady Elizabeth Mordaunt, Nehemiah Wallington: Bourcier, *Les journaux privés*, 359, 368, 386.

[92] *The Mystery of Selfe-Deceiving*, sig. A3ᵛ. Dyke also cites Martial (pp. 324, 404) and Seneca repeatedly (134, 138, 145–6, 172, 181, 239, 244, 295, 322–3). His book, published in London in 1615, was republished in 1628, 1630, 1633, 1634.

bewailed 'that in his most serious meditations of heavenly things his mind was easily distracted by the slightest occasions' (*Confess.* 10. 35)?

When he does not quote Augustine, or the Roman poets and moralists, Dyke himself offers very few interesting observations from a psychological point of view. Yet *The Mystery of Selfe-Deceiving*, translated at Geneva as *La Sonde de la Conscience* in 1634 and *Découverte de la cautèle du cœur de l'homme* in 1664, is supposed to have influenced La Rochefoucauld's analysis of the impure motives of our virtuous actions.[93] But Montaigne had earlier observed that 'we taste nothing purely' and 'vertue . . . hath been able to doe no good without composition' (*Essays*, II. xx), and Marston had echoed him in *The Dutch Curtezan* (1605).[94] A conjunction of the humanistic ethos with the predominantly Augustinian current of faith may account for the full flowering of religious self-examination in seventeenth-century English poetry and in the French Jansenist circles with greater subtlety than in any Puritan diary, just as Augustine's synthesis of the Christian faith with the Greek and Roman heritage had allowed him to penetrate more deeply into the recesses of his own mind.[95] Donne's self-consciousness thus appears to be the culmination of a long historical process, but it remains individually distinctive.

The attention to the reflexive operations of the mind displayed in the writings of Lord Herbert and Thomas Traherne has proved different from the self-consciousness of Donne and George Herbert. The reflex acts of the mind were not unknown to Plotinus and Augustine; they were briefly described by St Thomas in his *Commentary* on Aristotle's *Treatise of the Soul* (I. 1. §3 and III. 8). Donne spoke of the '*Actum reflexum* and *iteratum*' as the faculty which distinguishes the mind of man from the mind of beasts.[96]

---

[93] G. Ascoli, *La Grande-Bretagne devant l'opinion française au XVIIe siècle* (Paris, 1927), t. 2, III. v, §3.

[94] When Freevill says: 'But is this vertue in me? No, not pure, | Nothing extreamely best with us endures . . .' (IV. i); ed. H. H. Wood (Edinburgh and London, 1938). In his own insistent claim to self-knowledge Marston always referred to Seneca and the satirists: see the address 'To my equall Reader' in *The Fawne*.

[95] Patrick Grant has traced an Augustinian influence in the Holy Sonnets of John Donne: *ELH* 38 (1971), 542–61.

[96] To Sir Henry Goodyer (9 Oct. 1607); p. 145 in *John Donne*, ed. Carey.

This act could take the soul as its object in the general manner of ancient philosophy, as in the description of the 'Soules shape' offered by John Davies of Hereford in *Mirum in Modum*: 'the Soule her selfe doth know; | Hir owne effects shee to hir selfe discloseth, | So to herselfe, herselfe, doth shew'.[97] However, the growing interest in psychology (the word was already used in Latin, though not really in the modern sense[98]) must have favoured Lord Herbert's introspective description of the 'faculties'. Whether Descartes was solely responsible for the 'radical twist' given to Augustinian inwardness and 'the idea of the subject as an independent existent', as Charles Taylor apparently assumes,[99] is a question that would deserve investigation: the genius of a philosopher was unlikely to change collective habits of thought if a general evolution had not paved the way for it. The ideas of Descartes, later styled by John Norris the 'great Galileo of the intellectual world', were early discussed, particularly at Cambridge, and undoubtedly created 'a new introspection, a new realization of the individual self'.[100] Cudworth asserted that 'only the Stoicks seemed to have had some hint ... of that peculiar faculty of the soul, the hegemonical', and insisted on the way in which 'the whole Soule redoubled upon it self, which is both conscious of all within it Self and comprehends it Self and houlding it Self as it were in its own hand, turns it Self this way and that way'.[101] In the mid seventeenth century he was one of the many writers who coined compound words with 'self': '*Self-comprehensive, self-reflexive, self-recollective, self-exertive, and therefore lastly self-determinative*'.[102]

---

[97] London, 1602, A4^r. Sir John Davies, too, speaks from a purely objective standpoint in *Nosce Teipsum* (1600). Sir Walter Ralegh only notes that the understanding has a faculty 'by which it knoweth ... and meditates that it knoweth', *Treatise of the Soul*, §5.

[98] In Rudolph Goeckel's *Psychologia. Hoc est de Hominis Perfectione*, 1590, Otto Cassmann's *Psychologia Anthropologica*, 1594, etc.

[99] *Sources of the Self*, 143 and 188.

[100] As Marjorie Nicolson had noted in 'The Early Stages of Cartesianism in England', *SP* 26 (1929), 356–74.

[101] Add. MSS 4480 and 4981; quoted by J.-L. Breteau, in *Ralph Cudworth, le penseur* (Doctorate thesis, Paris 3, 1989), 715–16. Note the capital letter for Self: D. Shuger claims that self 'does not appear as a substantive until the last quarter of the seventeenth century' (*Sacred Rhetoric*, Princeton, 1988), but it seems occasionally to have had this value much earlier, e.g. in 'his wondrous selfe', n. 66 above.

[102] Jean-Louis Breteau, 'La conscience de soi chez les Platoniciens de Cambridge', *Genèse de la conscience moderne*, ed. R. Ellrodt (Paris, 1983), 114.

The Cartesian conception of the ego implied a sharp mind–body dualism reflected in the very title of Sir Kenelm Digby's *Two Treatises: In the one of which, The Nature of Bodies; In the other, The Nature of Mans Soul, is looked into*, and his assertion that 'Reason assureth us that when all body is abstracted in us there still remaineth a substance, a thinker, an Ego, or I.'[103] This conception was resisted by the Platonists and the empiricists alike. Indeed it ran counter to habits of thought which had long been dominant in religion as in philosophy. Spirituality and a materializing tendency of the imagination could be associated when matter could be supposed to be refined to spirit and be invisible. Even for Platonists such as Nicolas of Cusa, thought could be at once a 'substantial form' enveloping all things and a 'power animating the body' and 'transported in the spirit of the arteries'.[104] This view prevailed among the Hermetists and is apparent in the poems of Vaughan. It was dominant in the philosophy and poems of Henry More despite his earlier idolatry of Descartes. In religion the incarnational and sacramental view was displaced by the Protestant emphasis on faith and justification which required no material elements. It resulted in a dichotomy of interests which in a way anticipated Cartesian dualism. This dualistic approach has been traced in the poems of Marvell. Only the ability of their minds to associate opposite realities while maintaining their distinction allowed Donne and George Herbert to straddle the great divide between two worlds in a momentary and paradoxical equilibrium.

Cartesian dualism was bound to lead either to the immaterialism of Berkeley, anticipated by Traherne, or to a materialism divorced from all spirituality. Walter Charleton, eclectically 'interweaving', as he said, 'some threds taken from the webbs of those three excellent men, *Gassendi, Des Cartes*, and our Mr. *Hobbes*', noted that all the Ancients, except Plato, Pythagoras, and perhaps Aristotle, had described the soul as corporeal; he still assumed that the rational soul was created immediately by God, but found its relation with the imagination 'inexplicable'

---

[103] *Two Treatises* (London, 1658), II. 80.
[104] *Idiota III*, trans. Gandillac, in Ernst Cassirer, *Individu et Cosmos* (Paris, 1983), 258–9, 274.

and could not say 'whether or no . . . the Intellect knowes and discerns things by *simple Intuition*', concluding honestly: 'I as little understand how *Intuition* can be ascribed to an *immaterial*, that hath no *Eyes*; as I do how *Feeling* of *strokes* can be ascribed to a thing that cannot be *touched*.'[105] Modern books on the mind or the brain may leave us equally perplexed the other way round: how can physical impressions become conscious? These interrogations arose because of the emergence of new forms of self-awareness in the seventeenth century.

[105] *Natural History of the Passions* (1674), Epistle Prefatory and §iii, art. 15, pp. 65–6. Charleton's book was based on *De l'usage des passions* by J. F. Senault.

CHAPTER 17

New Perceptions of Time and Space?

In his Introduction to his *Etudes sur le temps humain*[1] Georges Poulet defined the various modes of temporal perception that succeeded each other, from the 'medieval architecture of the durations' to 'the Gidian creation of the instant'. The seventeenth century was a period of transition traversed by crosscurrents and I have shown that the originality of the English Metaphysical poets proceeded from the very diversity of their modes of thought. The instant does not offer the same characteristics and does not play the same part in their various works. Alongside new modes of apprehension older modes of perception persisted. Yet a historical continuity underlies the divergences: the intuition of the instant was related to a progression in subjectivity and inwardness.

We have seen in Chapter 6 that Donne was alert to a single moment of experience in a given situation: 'And now good morrow to our waking souls'. This moment is so dense and personal that it has little in common with the bare instant when conceived as a punctual present, a thin limit separating two wide regions. The poet's intuition is in keeping with modern phenomenology since the latter claims that 'experience never gives us a present without any compactness'.[2] Nor is Donne's present the hedonist moment which associates the short spell of enjoyment and the consciousness of its transience. He does not seek to prolong or arrest it like a lover's night—a favourite theme from Ovid to Marlowe, from Shakespeare to John Ford.[3] What he fears is a dissolution, a loss of substance. Whereas phenomenology discerns a becoming—the birth and death of

---

[1] Vol. I, p. xvi; see Introd., n. 63.
[2] Gaston Berger, *Phénoménologie du temps et prospective* (Paris, 1964), 120.
[3] See Erwin Stuerzl, *Der Zeitbegriff in der Elisabethanischen Literatur* (Vienna and Stuttgart, 1965), 420–5.

the phenomena—at the very heart of the present, Donne, closer to the medieval mind in this respect, discovers the subsistence of love and self in a privileged moment. The Christian existential-ism of Kierkegaard will later emphasize this intuition of a full-ness of being when a changeless moment seems to dilate and the instant becomes an atom of eternity.[4] It is a structural parallel to the inclusion of divine infinity within a finite human being through the mystery of the Incarnation. That is why both para-doxes are pre-eminent in the poetry of Donne. In his love lyrics, however, this plenitude of the instant has a purely subjective reality within an individual consciousness. Could it be the distant consequence of an inward apprehension of time first noticeable in the *Confessions* of St Augustine?

The various conceptions of time and eternity that prevailed in Antiquity have been conveniently summed up by Plotinus: their purely objective character is their common feature (*Enneads*, III. vii). As 'the moving image of eternity' time is identified with the motion of the planets in Plato's *Timaeus* (37c). In its spatial and mathematical nature it appears to be a projection of the intelligible into the world of appearances, but the projection is effected outside man's consciousness. In this global time, only divisible as a melody, there can be no privileged instant. Medieval theology readily espoused the Platonic myth since it showed time coming into being, but the *Timaeus* placed no emphasis on the instant of Creation: it dwelt on the coming into existence of a reality which imitates eternity by running in a circle according to number. In Platonic contemplation eternity stands outside time, time runs outside eternity: Vaughan was imaginatively faithful to this fundamental orientation in 'The World'.

In Aristotelian physics time becomes the measure of move-ment, and the measuring implies an operation of the human mind, but it reduces the flow of time to a sequence of moments without extension, or 'nows', analogous to an abstract numeri-cal series.[5] The intervention of the soul is necessary,[6] but only to

---

[4] Jean Wahl, *Etudes Kierkegaardiennes* (Paris, 1938), 241–4, 324–7.
[5] J. S. Callahan, *Four Views of Time in Ancient Philosophy* (Harvard UP, 1948), 194–5.
[6] 'no time without the soul', *Physics*, IV. 223a 26.

discern and number the instants according to the logical distinction between anterior and posterior. Just as the point in space is the beginning of one part and the end of another, the instant at once divides times and ensures its continuity: the *now* (Gk. *to nun*) is a limit, but a moving limit, for time is one in act but infinitely divisible in potentiality.[7] The presence of this *now* cannot be the presence of the eternal: it is at each instant the presence of a new event which displaces an anterior event.[8] It is 'no more a part of time than points are part of a line' (*Physics*, 220a 19–20). Since this movement tends to the realization of form, the Aristotelian notion was later integrated within the Christian conception of the twofold continuity of finite beings: 'sustained by the permanent continuity of substantial forms, the moving continuity of time unrolled itself, so mobile and so fluid that it was impossible to distinguish consecutive moments'.[9] But the Aristotelian structure of time, in fact, allowed no sense of completeness within the instant. Nor did the intervention of the soul invite an inner observation of the succession of impressions in an individual consciousness.

Plotinus showed himself aware of the confusion of time with space or number in earlier theories (*Enneads*, III. vii. 8). He assumed time was produced as an unbroken continuity by an unquiet desire of succession in the world-soul:

Putting forth its energy in act after act, in a constant progress of novelty, the Soul produces succession as well as act; taking up new purposes added to the old it brings thus into being what had not existed . . . the ceaseless forward movement of Life brings with it unending Time.   (III. vii. 11)

As a progressive extension of the world-soul's life (III. vii. 12), time remains independent from the perceiving mind: its existence does not depend on it. It is even conceived as substantial (III. vii. 13). Though the observation of his own inner life may have suggested his description of the successive actions of the universal soul, Plotinus still focused his attention outwardly on conceptual objects as Greek thought had always done. He was

---

[7] Pierre Aubenque, *Le problème de l'être chez Aristote* (Paris, 1962), 436, and 'Note' in *Passion des Formes*, ed. Michèle Porte (Fontenay–St Cloud, 1994), 80–1.

[8] Aubenque, *Aristote*, 436–7.

[9] G. Poulet, *Studies in Human Time* (Baltimore, 1956), 5.

interested in the soul's 'power to turn back and withdraw from the life-course', sinking itself again in the primal unity: time then would disappear (III. vii. 12). This is different from the Christian inrush of the eternal in time. Eternity is defined as 'a Life changelessly motionless and ever holding the Universal content [time, space, and phenomena] in actual presence; not this now and now that other, but always all' (III. vii. 3). Yet with the Greek concept of *being* a sense of *life* is now associated, a 'Life instantaneously entire': essence begins to vibrate with the pulse of existence. Only in the last words of his treatise 'On Eternity and Time' does Plotinus come to the consideration of time in individual souls, simply saying that time, which is in the world-soul, must exist in all souls since all souls are one.[10]

Augustine accomplished the revolution prepared by Plotinus. In the *Confessions* he defined time as an activity of the individual soul, not the world-soul. He did not, however, make time begin with the individual consciousness; he still envisaged it as the process of becoming in the created world. But he anxiously tried to discern its nature in the activity of his own mind and came to define it as a 'distension' of the individual soul by means of memory and anticipation (*Confessions*, XI. xxvi). Time is measured in the mind despite the disorderly flow of impressions (XI. xxvii). Since past and future have no existence, the three modes of time extant in the consciousness are 'the present of the past, the present of the present, the present of the future'. Memory is the present of the past; immediate intuition, the present of the present; expectation, the present of the future (XI. xx). Philosophic reflection, like the Aristotelian analysis, had originally reduced the present or 'now' to a point of time which can 'fly so rapidly from the future to the past that it has no extension' (XI. xv). Yet introspection reveals that the attention of consciousness to the present does last, proposing an object which hastens to exist and ceases to exist: the Augustinian 'now' is the present attention of the soul (XI. xxviii). This seems to be the first intuition of a 'present perceived', not merely 'conceived'. It may also be an anticipation

---

[10]   *Enneads*, III. vii. 13; *Plotinus*, ed. Armstrong, III. 355. In *Enneads*, IV. iii. 7, each individual soul is granted a distinctive character, a 'difference' due to circumstances and 'the temperaments of bodies', but time is not discussed: *Plotinus*, IV. 53.

of this dense moment, this 'outspread' present, which is directed toward a possible perception or momentarily retains a vanishing existence in modern phenomenology.[11] Though different in form and object, Donne's passionate attention directed to the present moment as inwardly apprehended seems to imply a similar inner experience of time. This attention maintains the instant arrested in his consciousness, together with the remembrance of things past, or the anticipation of things to come, in such poems as 'The Good-Morrow' or 'The Nocturnall'.

As a moment of purely human experience this instant is different from the ecstatic instant, *momentum intelligentiae*, when Augustine and Monica were raised to a vision of the eternal Wisdom in which there is no past and no future (*Confessions*, IX. x). This intuition, which can be found in the *Enneads* (III. vii. 12), belongs to the mystic tradition that Christianity and Neoplatonism have in common. Eckhart will maintain that God creates the world in an eternal present and the soul comes into contact with the divine in the present instant. For Nicolas Cusanus 'all time is comprised in the present, or "now" of God', who is the 'infinite present'.[12]

Medieval scholasticism was aware of the eternal instant but St Thomas, following Aristotle, turned away from Augustinian introspection in a purely objective definition of time, which ensured the perpetuation of form.[13] For the Nominalists, who allowed reality only to the existent, the only real time was the present. To live on meant 'to stabilize oneself on the screen of the present among forthcomings and vanishings'.[14] But the logic of being was only superseded by a logic of existence, not by an appeal to psychological investigation, though Ockham practised it occasionally in his insistence on the particular and the individual.[15]

Yet the Christian view of the Creation of the world and its

---

[11] Berger, *Phénoménologie du temps*, 122, 128.

[12] Eckhart, *Predigten*, No. 10; *Maître Eckhart. Traités et Sermons*, trans. M. de Gandillac (Paris, 1942), 167. Nicolas, *Of Learned Ignorance*, II. iii and I. xxvi; trans. Heron (London, 1954), 76, 60.

[13] *Summa*, Ia, q. 10, art. 4.

[14] Georges de Lagarde, *L'individualisme Ockhamiste* (Geneva, 1946), 181.

[15] Ibid. 68.

dissolution as well as the mystery of the Incarnation inevitably conferred a special value on the instant. The Creation took six days, but the first Fiat was an immediate beginning and each of the following ones was an immediate accomplishment. At the end of time the Son of Man would come 'as the lightning cometh forth' (Matthew 24: 27) and 'we shall all be changed in a moment, in the twinkling of an eye' (1 Corinthians 15: 51–2).[16] The Incarnation ensured the junction of transcendence with immanence. Now, 'the contact between these two mutually exclusive realities make up the instant' in a Kierkegaardian interpretation of Christianity and in the wholeness of the instant time is freed from the spatiality which characterized the abstract concept of time.[17]

We have seen the close relation between the individual structures of Donne's mind and these fundamental orientations of Christian thought: it accounts for his obsession with the instant earlier traced in his works in verse and prose alike. This obsession, however, did not merely proceed from the Christian tradition and its Scholastic elaboration, though the instant, supposed always identical with itself, had been used to convey an idea of the simultaneity of divine existence.[18] St Thomas had carefully distinguished the eternal now from the *nunc temporis*.[19] Donne did not mean to efface the distinction when, as a preacher, he insisted that all the sins of the world, accumulated in history, were upon Christ 'in an instant, in a minute; in such a point as admits, and requires a subtile, and a serious consideration; for it is *eternity* . . .' (*Sermons*, II. 139). What is original is the concentration of his attention and his hopes on very special

---

[16] This text was often commented upon by the Fathers: Gregory of Nyssa explained that 'an instant will suffice to transform the creation and the twinkling of an eye expresses an indivisible instant, a limit of time with no part or extension' (*La création de l'homme* (Paris, 1944), 99).

[17] Wahl, *Etudes Kierkegaardiennes*, 326 n. 2, and 243.

[18] e.g. in the *Commentary* of St Thomas on the fourth book of Aristotle's *Physics* (lectio 8).

[19] *Summa*, Ia, q. 10, art. 4, ad. sec.: 'sicut tempus respondet motui, ita nunc temporis respondet mobili; mobile autem est idem subjecto in toto decursu temporis, sed differt ratione, inquantum est hic et ibi. Et ista alternatio ejus est motus. Similiter fluxus ipsius nunc, secundum quod alternatur ratione, est tempus. Aeternitas autem manet eadem et subjecto et ratione. Unde aeternitas non est idem quod nunc temporis.' The objective and logical nature of the argument is obvious: there is no appeal to inward experience.

instants: moments of creation, or conversion, or resurrection and instantaneous entrance into eternal life.[20] He apparently inclined to think of human existence and the Christian mysteries in the same way as Kierkegaard: 'there is an instant of grace, when man is given access to eternal truth; an instant of freedom and decision; an instant—the most paradoxical—when all sins are remitted'.[21]

This religious instant, however, is only evoked and desired: Donne never claims he had a personal experience of it. The claim was only made for the experience of lovers in his profane poetry. Poetry was 'feigning' and we need not assume he ever had more than a wishful experience of it: what matters is the genuine intensity of the imaginative realization of the privileged instant. The poet had the support of another tradition, related to Christianity, courtly love, but he moved beyond the moment of enamoration, immortalized by Dante and Petrarch in the *Convivio* and the *Canzoniere*. In 'The Anniversarie' he did not celebrate 'love at first sight' on the day 'When thou and I first one another saw', but the 'first, last, everlasting day' of an achieved union. Poems like 'The Good-Morrow', 'The Sunne Rising', 'The Canonization' rather call to mind the 'moment one and infinite' and 'the instant made eternity' of some of Browning's love poems,[22] though, unlike the Victorian poet, Donne chooses the moment of actual love-making, but a moment not yet reduced to Hemingway's orgasmic 'now' in *For Whom the Bell Tolls*: 'this was all and always; this was what had been and now and whatever was to come . . . They were having now and before and always and now and now.'[23]

In his intuition of the instant Donne stands at a crossroad. The Christian tradition presented the junction between the temporal and the intemporal in two different ways. Objectively, in the moment of Creation and in the mystery of the Incarnation: Donne here only heightens the sense of immediacy.

---

[20] See Ch. 6, pp. 113–14.
[21] Wahl's interpretation in *Etudes Kierkegaardiennes*, 326.
[22] 'By the Fireside', st. xxxvii; 'The Last Ride Together', 98; cf. 'Two in the Campagna'. The impermanence of the sense of perfect unity is acknowledged by the Victorian poet: 'Already how am I so far | Out of that minute?' ('Two in the Campagna'); Donne need not confess it in a poem supposed to express only the privileged moment, not the moment after love.
[23] (New York, 1943), 379.

Subjectively, as the mystic union transcending time: in the expression of human love Donne creates a moment which is not merely a means of access to a transcendental sphere, it has a human reality, an existential density of its own. It is a moment of intense self-consciousness, not of self-absorption in the divine. This self-consciousness, as in Augustine's exploration of memory, allows a concentration of the attention on the perception of time as in inward reality. From the pure exteriority of Greek time, still dominant in scholastic argument, or the pure negation of time in states of mystic introspection, the mind of Donne, the modern mind, has moved towards an apprehension of the instant in its subjective wholeness and meaningfulness. Despite many divergences and a chronological gap we discover here an anticipation of the Romantic effort to 'incarnate eternity in time' described by Georges Poulet. Like the medieval and Renaissance poets, baroque and classical poets usually sing an eternity they conceive and dream of, but do not experience.[24] Donne gives us at least an impression of personal experience because of his self-conscious absorption in a present moment which becomes the only reality for him.

I have shown in Chapter 7 how this perception of the present is modulated in the poetry of George Herbert through an Augustinian 'distension' of the soul, allowing his attention to embrace a larger space of time. The instant of ecstatic joy is often an instant already fled, yet leaving behind it the prolonged vibration of the chord struck: 'Where is that mightie joy, | Which just now took up all my heart?' ('Temper II'). Barring all differences, this 'just now' is akin to the 'retention'—the outstretched moment of the 'primary memory'—analysed by Husserlian phenomenology: an effort at retaining 'what has just occurred', or 'just disappeared', 'just died'.[25]

When the imagination of Henry Vaughan constantly moves in the universe of retrospection, memory becomes an effort at reviviscence.[26] The author of 'The Retreat' was naturally inclined to the Platonic view of eternity as something left behind, only conceivable though reminiscence. As a Christian,

---

[24] *Mesure de l'instant* (Paris, 1968), 164.
[25] Berger, *Phénoménologie*, 122, 128.
[26] Ibid. 130. On Vaughan, see Ch. 7.

however, he also looked ahead to catch the light of eternity on the distant horizon. The present therefore could only awake the sense of an absence or an expectation, a loss or the hope of a restoration; it was a movement away from the very source of existence, or at best a slow progression towards a recovery. Reality was not in the present, but in the past or the future; attention was focused on the interval and the distance, not on the instant.

Marvell, as we saw in Chapter 9, was an heir of the Renaissance in his apprehension of the flow or rush of time. This Puritan apparently chose to ignore the Christian conception of eternity as a *nunc stans*. He sought, however, to control time in the various ways I have analysed, an effort perhaps indicative of Puritan voluntarism. In Crashaw's baroque and liquid universe a 'musical' time is always oriented towards an expiring finale, when 'A full-mouth'd Diapason swallowes all' ('Musicks Duell', 156). One can hardly look upon the ever-renewed deaths or faintings he celebrates as so many ecstatic instants for they succeed each other like the heave and fall of one wave of emotional intensity.

With Lord Herbert and Traherne, insensitive to the continuous stream of duration,[27] attention is again focused on the isolated and static instant. The former even claims there is a special faculty for the perception of 'the present or instant of time':

It is clear it cannot be derived from movement, for movement is secondary to it, since movement consists of parts which include many items. Therefore the faculty which refers to movement is too sluggish, for everything would have vanished by the time it succeeded in *marking an instant*. There must then be a special analogous faculty in us, and *this is proved by experience*.[28]

From this appeal to inner experience it is obvious that Lord Herbert's perception of the instant proceeds from an act of reflexive consciousness. But this act, unlike the self-conscious

---

[27] The 'incessant Minutes' are ticked off by Lord Herbert's watch in a discontinuous succession of 'short steps' ('To his Watch'). The invention of the watch and its growing use certainly altered the perception of time, which was more continuous with the sun-dial (and the sand glass) and more widely spaced with the church bells and the large clocks.

[28] *De Veritate*, VIII. 273; my italics. See Ch. 9, pp. 160–1.

intuition of a rich moment of experience in the poetry of Donne or George Herbert, is only, we know, an awareness of mental operations: it can only give evidence of an abstract instant devoid of existential density. It is as abstract as the 'vague premonition, which anticipates the actual realization of perception' of any object, an interesting discovery of Lord Herbert's 'careful introspection'.[29] This revelation of the pure exteriority of the object is obviously instantaneous like the reflexive act that reveals its own operation to our consciousness.

This homology between the Herbertian and the Cartesian intuition of consciousness was bound to lead to the same conception of the instant as a limit, the same insistence on the infinite divisibility of time, and the same sense of a precarious existence for, as Descartes put it, 'from the fact that I was a moment before, it does not necessarily follow that I must be now'.[30] But Lord Herbert does not seek support for the permanence of his individual being in the certainty of the existence of God, as Descartes did; nor can he rise like Donne to an immediate intuition of the eternal in a privileged moment. Incapable of 'grasping' eternity 'save through the form of time'[31] he can only offer a dialectical argument for the immortality of the soul.

In a contrary way, closer to Cartesian metaphysics, Traherne, as we saw in Chapter 10, assumed that the intuition of the eternal and the infinite precedes the perception of the temporal and the finite. The self-reflexive consciousness discovers in itself the divine and 'perfect simultaneity', an image of which is offered by the *cogito*. For him, as for Descartes, there is in God 'one single act, wholly simple and pure' and nothing exists unless it is actualized: this 'idealism' is an 'actualism':[32] the eternal instant becomes the only reality. Characteristically, however, the poet of Felicity can only conceive the eternal as the simultaneous presence in the divine mind (therefore in its image, the human mind) of all objects of thought in their infinite multiplicity.

---

[29] *De Veritate*, VII. 208.

[30] Quoted by Jean Wahl in *Du rôle de l'idée de l'instant dans la philosophie de Descartes* (Paris, 1953), 24–5 and 10.

[31] *De Veritate*, III. 104; cf. 91: 'we can only faintly imagine the infinite and eternal after the analogy of the finite and temporal'.

[32] Wahl, *L'instant*, 15, 10.

This rapid exploration of a general evolution in the conception of time and the instant has disclosed at once the slow progress of a subjective perception and the variety prevailing in the modes of time-consciousness throughout the seventeenth century. This diversity allowed each of the seven poets considered to follow his own bent, to choose or even create his own mode of apprehension of the temporal and the eternal. Another general evolution modified the perception of space and also opened the way to various representations of it in close correspondence with the particular structures of each individual mind.

Space

Linguistic usage may reveal habits of thought. The word 'space' was differently used by different poets in the Renaissance and the seventeenth century. When it appears in the poems of Traherne it usually designates the totality of cosmic space or 'endless Space'.[33] Even when used in the plural for particular spaces a total vision is suggested by such phrases as 'Spaces more', 'Spaces fild', 'one Space beyond another still'.[34] The term can also apply to the inward 'unbounded Space' within the mind of man or God.[35]

By the end of the sixteenth century Spenser had used the word 'space' fifty-eight times, but never in the sense of cosmic space. The term commonly indicated a 'space' of time, a short period. When a place or extension was intended, there was no idea of cosmic expansion, of space conceived as the void or as a receptacle. Traherne associated universal concepts when speaking of 'Time and Space', but Spenser only alluded to particular moments or localities when mentioning 'time and place',[36] a phrase also used by Shakespeare in the same sense. The word 'space' appears thirty-three times in Shakespeare's works, but it always stands for a moment, or a definite place, or interval, or

---

[33] Notably in 'Felicity', 4, 16; 'Sight', 3, 39; 'Insatiableness I', 28; 'Consummation', 17; 'Anticipation', 86.

[34] 'Nature', 71, 75; 'Consummation', 35, etc.

[35] 'The Author', 56; 'Felicity', 19.

[36] See the *Concordance* of C. G. Osgood (Gloucester, Mass., 1963).

distance.[37] The allusion to 'the world's large spaces' conveys a sense of vastness, but it concerns a geographic expanse.[38] A comparison of Spenser's and Shakespeare's use of the word 'spacious' shows that the author of the Faerie Queene will use it about a 'court', a castle's 'Chamber', a 'Plain', an 'Island', a river.[39] The dramatist alone offers a vision of a 'spacious world'; yet it is only the world of empire in Richard III (I. ii. 245) and Pericles (IV. ii. 5) or a mirror of it in Antony and Cleopatra (V. i. 34). The context will not even allow us to read an allusion to cosmic infinity in Hamlet's exclamation: 'O God, I could be bounded in a nutshell and count myself a king of infinite space' (II. ii. 256–7).

In the poetry of Donne the word 'space' appears only five times and, despite Empson's famous essay on 'Donne the Space Man', never in a cosmic sense. In 'Obsequies to the Lord Harrington' (76) 'time and space' apply to a particular moment and place. The restricted meaning of the term is less surprising in the poetry and prose of George Herbert. His sense of the relation between man and God may be expressed in images of cosmic amplitude, but only to suggest spiritual proximity or distance: there is no visualization of physical space. Vaughan's gaze, we know, often rests on the distant horizon, yet the word 'space' only appears twice in the poems. It only indicates distance in 'The Retreate' but the idea of a universal (though not endless) receptacle appears when the dissolution of the heavens is evoked: 'And nought must stand of that vast space | Which held up night and day' ('Day of Judgement'). Silex Scintillans was published in 1650. For the astronomical sense of space as 'the immeasurable expanse in which the solar and stellar systems . . . are situated', the first example given in the OED is a line of Paradise Lost: 'Space may produce new worlds . . .' (I. 650). For the metaphysical sense—'continuous, unbounded, or unlimited extension'—there is again no occurrence before Hobbes.

Cosmic themes were present in Renaissance poetry and even

37 See the Concordance of M. Spevack (Hildesheim, 1968–80).
38 Troilus and Cressida, II. ii. 162; cf. Macbeth, IV. iii. 36.
39 Faerie Queene, I. x. 6, 2; III. i. 20, 6 and VI. x. 8, 1; III. i. 31, 7; III. ix. 49, 2; IV. xi. 41, 3.

in Ptolemaic astronomy the immensity of the distance between
the earth and the outermost sphere was well known. In painting
as in poetry distant prospects solicited the gazer's attention. Yet
there was no current English word to denote boundless extension.[40] No French word either: I checked it in the *Thrésor de la
Langue Française* of Jean Nicot in its 1616 edition and in the
Thrésor des Trois Langues published at Geneva in 1627. The
late appearance of the modern meaning of the word may indi-
cate a change in the modes of thought and imagination. Many
learned studies have been devoted to the concept or the use of
space in the history of science and philosophy and in the history
of the figurative arts. They may shed light on the representation
of space in literary works. At the present time I can only offer
hypotheses; other scholars may one day come to conclusions.

At first sight the views of some pre-Socratic philosophers,
revived in the Renaissance, seem closer to the modern conception of space than the Aristotelian notion of 'place' which had
been long dominant. Yet the 'infinite void' of the atomists[41] has
little in common with the unbounded space of the seventeenth
century. A superficial resemblance is suggested by a fragment
from Aristotle's lost monograph 'On Democritus':

Democritus is of the opinion that the nature of the eternal things is:
small beings [atoms] which are infinite in number. He assumes that,
underlying these, there is another thing, place/space (*topos*) which is
infinite in extent. And he calls place/space by the following names:
'void', 'nothing', and 'infinite'.[42]

Yet historians are agreed on the ambiguity of Greek spatial
terms: 'the Greek language did not have a one-word equivalent
of our "space" '.[43] Epicurus spoke of an 'intangible substance'
(*anaphes phusis*) which he called 'void' (*kenon*) when empty of
all body, 'place' (*topos*) when occupied by a body, and 'room'

---

[40] *Spatium* was available in Latin and it may have been used in its Lucretian
sense earlier than 'space'; I have not checked it, but a time-lag would not be surprising in the vernacular.

[41] See Max Jammer, *Concepts of Space* (Cambridge, Mass., 1954), 7–10; Millic
Capek, *The Philosophical Impact of Contemporary Physics* (New York, 1961), 7–8;
Keimpe Algra, *Concepts of Space in Greek Thought* (Leiden and New York, 1995),
passim.

[42] Simplicius, *In Cael.* (p. 294, 33 Heiberg), quoted by Algra, *Concepts*, 47.

[43] Algra, *Concepts*, 70.

(*chora*) when bodies roam through it.[44] Different conceptions of this void or *kenon* can be traced. The Stoics, who conceived the cosmos as a *plenum* with no empty space within it, came to use this word for the infinite extracosmic extension surrounding the cosmos. But this extension was declared infinite only because it was supposed to be incorporeal and 'the incorporeal, *qua talis*, has no limit'.[45] This concept, I think, could make no visual appeal to the imagination,[46] but could later be reconciled with the Christian view of a finite cosmos and an infinite Heaven.

For the atomists the void separated the atoms within the cosmos itself: 'Epicurus tries to show that the universe, *to pan*, is infinite, both in respect of the *number* of its atoms and in respect of the *extent* of the *kenon*.'[47] Hence the attraction of the atomist philosophy for a thinker obsessed by the notion of infinity as Traherne was throughout his life. Lucretius' version of his argument, using the word *spatium* for *kenon* (*De Rerum Natura*, I. 364–9, 425–8), was probably most influential for Renaissance poets. His evocation of an infinite space extending beyond our cosmos may seem to anticipate Traherne's or Henry More's rapturous flights of imagination (ibid. I. 1044–7). Yet, though he invites us to notice the absence of any limitation about us, his allusion to the 'walls of the universe', *moenia mundi*, tends to close the horizon for the imagination if not for the mind. Furthermore, he describes this world lit by the sun as geocentric (V. 344) and assumes that the disc of the sun can be no larger than it appears to our sight (V. 564–5)!

One may therefore incline to think that the early notion of the infinite did not proceed from an imaginative intuition of unlimited space, but from the intellectual realization that you can always prolong a straight line (the second postulate of Euclid) or a series of numbers, and that a movement can always continue beyond the point reached. This concept was illustrated by the throwing of a dart from the extreme border of the

---

44 Sextus M., 10, 2; quoted by Algra, *Concepts*, 53.
45 Algra, *Concepts*, ch. 6, *passim*, and pp. 317–18.
46 In the *Hermetica*, a major influence on Traherne, it is however indirectly associated with cosmic flights of the imagination, though the principle is maintained; we read in the *Pymander* (trans. Everard, 1650, IX. 55–6): 'what shall we call the place in which the whole Universe is moved?—Herm. Call it incorporeal.'
47 Algra, *Concepts*, 56.

universe: it will either follow its course or meet with an obstacle (*De Rerum Natura*, I. 968–76).

This was the argument Aristotle had refuted, arguing there can be no void beyond a finite universe. The world picture he built needs no description. Less familiar is his 'reified conception of place' (*topos*) as the adjacent boundary of a surrounding body. Neither the outer sphere of the heavens nor the whole cosmos could be said to be in a place since they had no surrounding body.[48] Within the cosmos itself, limited by the ultimate sphere, there was no continuous and homogeneous space, only a collection of places held together by a binding force. Aristotelian space, therefore medieval space, was a mosaic with no empty interval, as well as a kind of field of force in which bodies continually sought to regain their natural position.[49]

Aristotle criticized Plato's notion of the 'receptacle', which was avowedly 'difficult and obscure' (*Timaeus*, 49a). Modern exegetes still quarrel about it. This receptacle is 'the nurse of becoming'; it gives birth to all things by receiving 'imprints', and functions like a sieve to separate the elements (49a–52d): it has obviously nothing in common with our modern conception of space. Plato, in fact, made no clear distinction between *physical* and *metaphysical* space—a distinction later made by Plotinus and the Neoplatonists. The latter, however, came to build a 'stratification of hypostases'; in the fifth century Syrianus distinguished (1) physical place, (2) a place of 'enmattered' forms, e.g. matter, (3) a place of mathematical bodies, viz. imagination, and (4) a place of transcendent Ideas, the intellect or *nous*.[50] Such speculations ignored the immediate apprehension of unlimited space. The Judaeo-Christian Neoplatonists came to associate the ubiquity of God with the notion of infinite space, but their notion of infinity too was transcendental.

Despite the controversy over the existence of the void, one may surmise that the Ancients had no conception of a continuous and homogeneous space. Erwin Panofsky came to the same conclusion concerning the art of Antiquity. He described the

---

[48] Algra, *Concepts*, 223–4 and 193.
[49] Léon Robin, *Aristote* (Paris, 1944), 142.
[50] Algra, *Concepts*, 119–20.

representation of objects as 'aggregative', not systematic; when there is a suggestion of perspective it never leads to the construction of space.[51] An evolution, however, seems to have taken place in the Hellenistic representation of landscape and an extension in depth became characteristic of Roman art.[52] A similar evolution is perceptible from the abstract infinite of the Greek atomists to the Lucretian visual evocation of the course of lightning through a limitless space (*De Rerum Natura*, 1002–7).

The image of the closed world prevailed throughout the Middle Ages because the cosmogony of the atomists could not be reconciled with Christian faith. Furthermore the Aristotelian conception of space, freed from its logical framework, is close to our spontaneous perception of the space about us when analysed either by Piaget or by Merleau-Ponty. What is first revealed to our consciousness is not the empty expansion of space but the places occupied by the various objects perceived.[53] Merleau-Ponty wondered 'why it was so difficult for so many great minds to understand that this vault was only an appearance bound to recede indefinitely for someone who would rise up into the sky, just as the horizon recedes before us when we sail'. His philosophic answer was that 'the simple possibility of a simple geometric interpretation of the celestial motions' seemed to prove that rationality was present in the universe.[54] But this image of the world was also satisfying for the uneducated, since children, according to Piaget, would not discover that the sky is not a solid vault if they did not ask questions. Besides, the explanations framed by children to account for the origin of the world are close to the theories of the pre-Socratic philosophers.[55] Reasons for the preference for a closed world may also be found in psychoanalysis or in the play of imagination in states of reverie.[56]

[51] *La perspective comme forme symbolique* (Paris, 1975), 82, 91–3.

[52] Ibid. 87–9.

[53] J. Piaget and P. Inkhelder, *La représentation de l'espace chez l'enfant* (Paris, 1948), III. ix, §1, p. 554; J. Merleau-Ponty, *Phénoménologie de la perception* (Paris, 1946), Part 2, ii, 'L'espace'.

[54] J. Merleau-Ponty and B. Morando, *Les trois étapes de la cosmologie* (Paris, 1971).

[55] J. Piaget, *La représentation du monde chez l'enfant*, IX, §1 (Paris, 1938 edn.), 296–9.

[56] See Hélène Tuzet, *Le cosmos et l'imagination* (Paris, 1965), ch. i.

The fifteenth century was marked by a revival of the hypothesis of infinity and by the invention of perspective; though there is no obvious link between the two, the parallel is interesting. In medieval art 'the graphic construction of groups of figures took precedence of the graphic construction of space'. A progress is noticeable in the Quattrocento, but there is no unification of the total space: its continuity and possible infinity are first perceptible in the paintings of Jan Van Eyck. The priority of space over isolated objects deepened through the sixteenth century. Panofsky himself suspected a correspondence between the evolution of figurative space and the dismantlement of Aristotelian cosmogony from Nicolas of Cusa to Copernicus and Giordano Bruno.[57]

The notion of an infinite world, however, was developed in stages which must, I think, be clearly marked out. With Nicolas of Cusa the infinite is first a mathematical concept derived from 'the absolute infinite line' and the 'analogy between the infinite circle and unity' (*Of Learned Ignorance*, I. xiii, xxi). That the universe is 'limitless' can be logically 'inferred' (II. i)—not 'imagined', nor observed—from the conception of God as the Absolute Maximum and the analogy between God and the 'infinite sphere' (I. xxi), but it is only called 'infinite' because nothing greater than the universe 'is able actually to exist' (II. i, end). The 'spirit intermediary between matter and form' diffused in the universe is 'finite' (II. x). In the Neoplatonic *Zodiacus Vitae* (1534) of Palingenius immaterial creatures people supracelestial regions extending beyond a material universe still enclosed within its nine spheres:[58] this was the image still presented in Spenser's *Hymn to Celestial Beauty* (ll. 51–98). The Copernican hypothesis (still unverifiable) 'extended the volume of the sphere of the fixed stars indefinitely upwards', yet the visible world was described as *immensum*, not declared infinite: the sphere of fixed stars was arrested, not dissolved in boundless space.[59] According to Cassirer[60] a cosmic feeling, in the modern

---

[57] Panofsky, *Perspective*, 123–35, 158.
[58] Alexandre Koyré (trans.), *From the Closed World to the Infinite Universe* (Baltimore, 1952), 25–7.
[59] Ibid. 30–3.
[60] Ernst Cassirer, *Individuum und Kosmos* (Berlin, 1927); *Individu et cosmos dans la philosophie de la Renaissance* (Paris, 1983), 237.

sense, first appeared in Giordano Bruno's *De l'infinito universo e mondi* (1584), but his boundless universe still seems to be born from a metaphysical and mystic impulse in which the direct intuition of space apparently played little part. In a general way, I doubt whether a living intuition of spatiality can be discovered in a world still conceived throughout the Renaissance as a network of closely interwoven correspondences in which influences operated magically and substantially.

In Renaissance England Thomas Digges, though a pioneer in astronomic observation, extended the ultimate sphere indefinitely like Copernicus, and yet, like Palingenius, he still merged the celestial bodies in an empyrean sky of theology, as the physicist William Gilbert complained.[61] From Telesio's *De Natura Rerum* (1565) to Gilbert, who defined space as *nihil*—the Non-Being of Democritus—the conception of space as the immaterial receptor of all beings progressed, but hardly affected the literary imagination.

Elizabethan descriptive poetry shows no distinct awareness of the continuity of space and the possibilities of systematic construction of it offered by Continental Renaissance painting.[62] Marlowe's 'imaginative preoccupation with the dazzling heights and vast spaces of the universe' is not an intuition of spatial infinity. He was uplifted by the 'pathos of the immense' (Hélène Tuzet's phrase), but the immensity is often geographic: circles of conquest widening on the surface of the globe (*Tamburlaine*, 4519–51). The vertical movement—'Affecting thoughts coequal with the clouds', scaling mountain tops, or 'climbing after knowledge infinite'—is still an élan toward supremacy, a search for an exaltation, an aspiration to a celestial throne, when it is not bathetically reduced to 'the sweet fruition of an earthly crowne' (*Tamburlaine*, 261, 296, 875, 432, 880). Comets and blazings stars 'reach down to the earth' (4202) and do not lose themselves in space. The hero, in his 'Giantly presumption', may threaten to 'shiver all the starry firmament' (813, 3074), but the 'frame' or 'towers' of heaven are always a solid boundary (3072, 3877) and the world of Faustus, like Tamburlaine's, is still enclosed in spheres. Donne's

---

[61] Koyré, *Closed World*, 38–9.
[62] See Panofsky, *Perspective*, 138, 157.

'titanic management of space' (in John Carey's phrase) seems to cast an even wider net over the universe, but it is woven of abstractions, 'Meridians and Parallels' (*First Anniversary*, 278). Despite the poet's awareness of astronomical discoveries this net, unlike Galileo's telescope, will bring us no miraculous haul of shining stars and planets. The difference between Donne's concept of infinitude in number or in intensity, and Traherne's imagining of a spatial infinity has been discussed in Chapter 10.

The new perception of space was due to telescopic observation. In his *Sidereus Nuncius* (1610) Galileo expressed his wonder at and delight in 'the sensible certainty'—*sensata certitudine*—which now superseded mathematical speculation. He called attention to the beauty of the 'spectacle', *pulcherrimum atque visu iocundissimum*. By revealing new phenomena to the senses, not to the intellect only—*sensui nedum intellectui*—the telescope had put an end to endless 'verbal controversies'.[63] Strangely enough, despite the numerous allusions to the new astronomy in seventeenth-century English poetry, their full imaginative impact can only be traced in *Paradise Lost*. Milton, who had visited Galileo, 'the Tuscan artist', in Italy, had certainly wondered like him at the spectacle of the moon seen 'through optic glass' (I. 287–91). Unlike Donne's bullet-like trajectories from earth to heaven, the voyages of Satan and the angels evoke the sensation of travelling through an open space, not the compartmentalized world of the older cosmogony. The 'camera eye' of the epic poet creates constant cinematic 'travellings' on the screen of the poet's and the reader's imagination.[64] The impression conveyed is still one of immensity, not infinity, but Milton gives us for the first time the 'feel' of space—perhaps on account of his very blindness—in his descriptions of flights (III. 561–74, IV. 555–60, V. 261–74), and particularly in the conjuring of the 'silent course' of the rotating Earth 'that spinning sleeps | On her soft Axle, while she paces Eev'n, | And bears thee soft with the smooth Air along' (VIII. 163–6).

Different is the space of Traherne. Pure motionless extension,

---

[63] *Sydereus Nuncius*, in *Opere* (Bononiae, 1655), II. 7–25.
[64] *Paradise Lost*, I. 283–91, 331–50, II. 642. At times the effect is comparable to the focusing and adjusting of a telescope, bringing the image closer: VI. 768

unencumbered by the warring elements of Milton's chaos, free from any breath of air, a luminous and insubstantial 'capacity'. The identification of space with light may be traced to Neoplatonism.[65] The implicit parallel between the attributes of God and the attributes of space became explicit with Henry More.[66] Traherne's originality was to fuse in a single vision his spontaneous intuition of boundlessness (supposed to be inherited from childhood), Neoplatonic and perhaps Cartesian concepts of infinity, and the new cosmogony. There is no certain link, however, between his passion for infinity and the new astronomy. The scientific discoveries were not unknown to him: he mentioned the observations of Galileo and Hevelius in his *Centuries* (III. 41). Yet, while welcoming the notion of an infinity of worlds, he still inclined to see the Earth as 'Heavens Center', probably on account of his egocentricity and his conception of man's greatness (*Commentaries*, No. 42). Besides, as I pointed out in Chapter 10, Traherne argued like Descartes for a primary inner intuition of infinity though he was himself primarily concerned with the concrete sense of surrounding space (*Centuries*, II. 81). Particular too, and related to his 'insatiableness', was his desire to absorb all outer space into his soul: 'When Souls spread forth to Omnipresent space | Their Willing Bosoms that they might embrace | It all and take it in' (*Commentaries*, 44). Traherne's space is not necessarily homogeneous: just as he often conceived eternity as a numberless plurality of 'ages', from the beginning he came to speak of infinite space as a countless multiplicity of 'spaces' (*Select Meditations*, IV. 3). He even seems to make the void only a part of space ('Nature', 77). In his evocations his tendency to rapturous enumeration rather than contemplative description precluded any construction of space and he showed no sense of perspective.

The perception of space and the intuition of infinity are not of major importance for the other writers studied in this book. Crashaw's poetry only suggests baroque ascensions in crowded

---

[65] Jammer, *Concepts of Space*, 55–8.

[66] 'Unum, Simplex, Immobile, Aeternum, Completum, ... Immensum, Increatum, Incircumscriptum, Incomprehensibile, Omnipresens, Incorporeum, Omnia permeans et completans, Ens per essentiam, Ens actu, Purus Actus': *Enchiridon Metaphysicum* (London, 1671), vii.

skies. George Herbert at times had doubts about the existence of solid spheres,[67] but his concern was with his own spiritual distance from or nearness to God ('Temper I', 'Search'). The stars that 'have us to bed' ('Man', 31) are no occasion for cosmic contemplation as they were for Henry Vaughan.[68] The Silurist, however, hardly goes beyond Boethius and Palingenius in his evocation of 'the Zodiacks firie way'.[69] He was acquainted with the telescope, but proclaimed it ineffectual to reach 'that glorious pitch' where man can be 'in a conjunction with Divinity'.[70] Marvell was aware of both the telescopic and the microscopic vision ('Last Instructions to a Painter', 949–54; 'Appleton House', 462), but unconcerned by infinity. A sky described as a 'liquid Region' ('Last Instruction', 553) and a flight through 'viscous air' ('Appleton', 673) hardly give us a sense of space. Yet Marvell seems to give more attention than earlier poets to the spatiality of a landscape, opening up prospects from a commanding position ('Upon the Hill and Grove at Bilborough', 25; 'Appleton', 73–80, 441–60). In the eyes of Lord Herbert the 'infinity of God is proved by the infinity of position or space' (*De Veritate*, IX. 292) and man's desire of a happiness 'infinite in its extent and eternal in its duration' is supposed to be a guarantee of the soul's immortality,[71] arguments that would have been congenial to Traherne. He makes 'suitable distance' a condition of 'truth of appearance' (ibid. III. 95) but he enters into no discussion of space and finds no 'satisfactory answer' to 'the great problem' of perception (ibid. VII. 214). The poet only plays with the notion of the infinity of black ('To her Hair', 24); neither his celebration of the world's 'universally diffused soul', nor his evocation of 'numberless heavens'[72] convey a sense of infinite space.

---

[67] In 'Divinitie', 1–4, but 'the fleet Astronomer' can still 'thred the spheres' in 'Vanitie (I)'.

[68] Herbert's 'The Starre' centres on its action on the poet's heart; contrast Vaughan's 'Constellation', 1–16 and his translations from Boethius, *Lib. I. Metrum*, 5, 7.

[69] Boethius, *Lib. I. Metrum*, 5; *In Zodiacum Marcelli Palingenii*.

[70] *To the ingenious Author of* Thalia Rediviva, 13, *In Zodiacum*; cf. 'They are all gone', 40.

[71] In *A Dialogue between a Tutor and Pupil* (London edn., 1768, p. 114), which I assume to be a genuine work of Lord Herbert.

[72] Elegie for the Prince, 21; 'Meditation upon his Wax-Candle', 40.

We come again to the conclusion that each poet (including here Milton) responded in a personal way to an evolution in the history of ideas. Taylor, like Panofsky, assumes that the discovery of perspective and the new perception of space favoured the development of subjectivity by introducing an individual factor.[73] The parallel evolution is, indeed, noteworthy, but no cause-and-effect relationship should be presumed in individual cases: Donne could be highly self-conscious though his poetry displays little sense of perspective.

[73] Panofsky, *Perspective*, 159, 174; *Renaissance and Renascence* (London, 1970), 120; Taylor, *Sources of the Self*, 201. Modern phenomenology insists on the intervention of the perceiving subject in the spontaneous perception of space, but this activity is not self-conscious perception.

CHAPTER 18

Change and the Donne Generation

New attitudes and a new style undoubtedly characterized the poetry of John Donne from the very beginning in his satires, his verse letters, and his *Songs and Sonets*. The third volume of my *Poètes métaphysiques* was devoted to a study of the social, psychological, and literary origins of new trends in the closing years of the reign of Elizabeth. I came to the conclusion that Donne himself often took the lead in innovation and distinctly expressed his own personality as well as the temper and dominant inclinations of his own generation. I can here only present the main points of the argument; for a fuller illustration the reader will have to consult the earlier book.[1]

The significance of the period has always been acknowledged and was well defined in Elaine Scarry's collection of essays on *Fins de Siècle*: 'The end of the sixteeth century . . . has become an important turning-point in these coordinate histories (of early capitalism, subjectivity, and authorial genius), possessing both the synchronic coherence and the diachronic telos that nineteenth-century historiography requires.'[2] From a literary point of view real coherence, however, is chiefly to be found in a fairly narrow group of writers in the Inns of Court circle. Their influence hardly calls for further comment.[3] I must, however, again call attention to the list of young men admitted

---

[1] Relevant passages will be easily found in the detailed table of contents. Unlike the first two volumes, the third one has not been reprinted and is only available in libraries.

[2] *Fins de Siècle. English Poetry in 1590, 1690, 1790, 1890, 1990* (Baltimore, 1995, Introduction).

[3] In *John Donne, Coterie Poet* (Madison, 1980) Arthur Marotti kindly sent readers to my *Poètes métaphysiques* 'for a good discussion of the Inns as a literary milieu' (232 n. 26), referring to pp. 13–42, 185–92 and 284–91 in vol. III. See also L. Martines, *Society and History in English Renaissance Verse* (Oxford, 1985) and the studies mentioned; the views developed on pp. 26–69 are very close to mine.

to the Inns of Court from 1578 to 1600 for they were mainly responsible for the cultivation and popularity of all the literary genres that became fashionable in the 1590s: satire with Lodge, Donne, Marston, and Guilpin; the epigram with Campion, Donne, Sir John Harington, Sir John Davies, and Stradling; the verse epistle with Donne and his several correspondents; the Ovidian or burlesque elegy with Donne and Francis Beaumont; the philosophical poem with Fulke Greville and Sir John Davies; lyrics in the 'metaphysical style' with Donne, Hoskyns, Sir Henry Wotton, Benjamin Rudyerd, and William Herbert. Their innovative influence was no less remarkable in prose, with the paradoxes or essays of Donne, Cornwallis, and Bacon (another inmate of the Inns), and with the characters of Donne and Thomas Overbury. The recurrence of Donne's name is striking: he had, indeed, an oar in every boat newly launched.

It is essential to note that this was not, in fact, a 'literary milieu' though Ben Jonson came to be associated with it; none of these men made literature his profession. L. C. Knights was the first critic to suggest that the diversity of interests in the social group concerned was responsible for the variety of images and allusions found in metaphysical poetry.[4] This is true, but what is really distinctive is not the variety, which can be found in Spenser, but the quickness and deftness of association that allowed a simultaneous awareness of the many facets of life. This ability was developed in circles like the Mermaid club which brought together men of very different interests and responsibilities. It was displayed in the *Convivium Philosophicum* (ascribed to Hopkins) or in the fifth satire of Guilpin's *Skialetheia* as well as in Donne's poems: attention could swiftly veer from love to law, from the theatre to Court, from politics to theology or science. Whether or not written for male readers, as the satires and Donne's early verse letters undoubtedly were, love poetry in such a circle would not be confined to a self-enclosed world of gallantry or Platonic idealism, but integrated to the wider world of daily experience which included war, travel, and discovery as well as the affairs of the city. Even when passion eclipses the outer world in the *Songs*

---

[4] 'On the Social Background of Metaphysical Poetry', *Scrutiny*, 13 (1945), 37–52.

and Sonets the imagery reminds us of all the other aspects of life transcended by, yet enclosed, in the lovers' world.

This is only one of the reasons why the urban environment deeply affected the evolution of literature in this period. Donne was a London poet,[5] not only because many of his poems reflect the bustling life of London, but because his writings denote a lively and varied curiosity and a quickened pace and rhythm of thought usually absent in more academic works: this is one of the differences between Joseph Hall's satires and the urban satirists.[6] The contrast is a matter of tempo as well as temper. Spenser, too, had been occasionally satirical, but in the more leisurely way of the preceding generation, more concerned with decorative rhetorical elaboration than sprightliness of wit. With Donne, besides, the vivid awareness of the urban environment, even in his satires and elegies, mostly served the expression of his intense subjectivity. The close links between these urban poets in a narrow circle also favoured the exchange of letters and verse epistles that lent themselves to the expression of identity.[7]

In tracing the reasons for new attitudes and new literary trends by the end of the century the advent of a new generation proves no less important than the urban milieu or the social group. The amateur writers of Donne's circle were joined in their mood and taste by slightly older writers, but only after an evolution illustrated by Drayton's revision of his sonnets and the changes in Shakespeare's style; definitely older men, like Chapman, though apparently in harmony with some of the new concerns, remained closer to the generation of Spenser in their conception of poetry.[8]

The prevailing tendencies of a new generation are usually best defined by negatives: by what young people, angry or not,

[5] See *Poètes métaphysiques*, III, ch. I: 'Le réalisme urbain et les "Inns of Court"'; and Barbara Everett, *Donne: A London Poet* (British Academy Lecture, 1972). In *John Marston of the Middle Temple* (Cambridge, Mass., 1969), 30, P. J. Finkelpearl also pointed out the connection with Donne's 'highly original, virtually revolutionary poetry in the 1590's'.

[6] See *Poètes métaphysiques*, III. 284–5.

[7] See *Poètes métaphysiques*, III. 292–5.

[8] On the differences between Chapman and Donne see *Poètes métaphysiques*, III. 135–46.

reject in their teens or their twenties. After leaving the trodden road, each of them is likely to choose a different path.[9] The poets of the Donne generation rejected the floridness, mellifluousness, and melodiousness of 'golden' verse and 'sugared' sonnets. One of the reasons for the rejection—perhaps the main one—was that a 'sweet society' inevitably palls upon the taste and calls for 'the remedie of contraries', as Nashe put it.[10] Satirists and epigrammatists—Harington, Weever, Guilpin, etc.—call for salt or bile, absinthe, camphor or saltpetre. Disssonance—tolerated when intermittent by Elizabethan rhetoric—becomes the rule for those who, like Marston, 'crave no Syrens of our Halcyon times, | To grace the accents of [their] rough-hew'd rimes'.[11] This preference, of course, was in keeping with the conventions of the satiric 'genre' and the vogue of satire can be accounted for by the discontent of scholars and other well-known social or political circumstances by the end of the century. Donne, however, did not obey a convention when he wrote in a verse letter 'I sing not Siren like to tempt | For I am harsh',[12] and his use of dissonance in the *Songs and Sonets*[13] is far more subtle than the harshness of the satirists. The rejection of Lydian airs for Doric accents advocated by Guilpin[14] only implied the 'manlie style fitted to manlie ears' recommended even by 'honey-dropping Daniel' in his repentance for his earlier 'dainties' (*Musophilus*, ll. 506–13). When condemning both extremes Jonson also contrasted manliness with the effeminacy of the 'poets for women' who only sought a melodious cadence for the mere sake of sound.[15]

The search for manly attitudes and the 'manly style', related

---

[9] The role of the generations was stressed by Sainte-Beuve (*Nouveaux Lundis*, III. 21–2) and Henri Peyre, *Les générations littéraires* (Paris, 1948), 48.

[10] When he reminded his readers that the Sabaeans 'overcloyd with such odoriferous savours as the natural increase of their country (Balsamum, Amomum, with Myrrhe and Frankincense) sends forth, refresh their nosthrilles with the unsavourie sent of the pitchy slime that Euphrates casts up, & the contagious fumes of Goats beards burned': Nashe's Preface to Greene's *Menaphon* (1589), in *Works*, ed. Ronald B. McKerrow (London, 1904), III. 313–14.

[11] See *Poètes métaphysiques*, III. 76–7 for more examples and references.

[12] 'To Mr S.B.'; cf. 'To Mr T.W.', 'Hast thee harsh verse'.

[13] See *Poètes métaphysiques*, I. 196–201.

[14] In *Skialetheia*, 'Satyre Preludium'.

[15] *Discoveries: Ben Jonson*, ed. C. H. Herford and P. and E. Simpson (Oxford, 1925–52), VIII. 585.

to a search for truth and meaning, was, indeed, the dominant
trend in the Donne generation. It accounts for the change of
mood and expression in love poetry. Donne's anti-Petrarchism
has sometimes been denied in recent criticism. Justly in a way:
I have pointed out affinities in egotism and self-searching
while maintaining that the English poet's conceits are not
Petrarchan.[16] The erotic elegies—some of them Ovidian, others
merely Bernesque[17]—and the more cynical lyrics are only one
aspect, and the more superficial, of a general reaction against
the conventions and hypocrisy of love-making in the courtly
way, the obdurate mistress and the submissive lover. The type of
the rough wooer had always been more congenial to the
English, witness Wyatt and Shakespeare's Henry V. The satirists
heaped scorn upon the Italianate *inamorato* or *amoroso*, and Sir
John Davies, refusing to 'dally, caper, daunce and sing', made a
crude promise to his mistress.[18] Donne more courteously wrote:
'The honesties of love with ease I doe, | But am no porter for a
tedious woo' ('That unripe side of earth'). The first part of this
epistle to the Countess of Huntington is a forthright and splen-
didly balanced expression of a conception of love which bears
the imprint of his personality. It is different from (and perhaps
earlier than) the love celebrated in his more passionate lyrics,
yet it contrasts strongly with the current forms of 'anti-
Petrarchism'.

Donne can avail himself of Petrarchan themes, as several critics have pointed out,[19] but, when so doing, he only borrows a
language which suits his design. His intention may be satirical
or libertine as in 'The broken heart' or 'The Dampe'. The
convention of the murdered lover is a starting-point for a thoroughly realistic and sardonic poem, 'The Apparition'. In the
'Legacie' the sending of his heart is an occasion for playful teas-
ing. In 'Twicknam Garden' and 'The Funerall', through a play
of dissonances, a modulation of hyperbole, and the intrusion of

---

[16] *Poètes métaphysiques*, III. 87–9, 206–14.

[17] Burlesque love-making is already found in Heywood's *Epigrams* ('Fifth
hundred', no. 23) and Sidney's *Arcadia*, in *Complete Works*, ed. Albert Feuillerat
(Cambridge, 1922), I. 21, II. 18.

[18] 'Hark in thine eare, Zounds, I can (   ) thee soundly': so printed by
Grosart, *The Works in Verse and Prose* (London, 1969–76), 59–60.

[19] See Silvia Ruffo-Fiori, *Donne's Petrarchism* (Florence, 1976); cf. *Poètes métaphysiques*, III. 84–6.

irony directed at himself, the genuine or pretended emotion of the speaker takes on an original colouring: this blend of seriousness and levity, tenderness and sarcasm is never found in Petrarch himself nor in the Elizabethan sonneteers.

In his 'anti-Platonism' too, Donne is distinctive. I cannot again enter into the controversies over the interpretation of poems obviously influenced by Renaissance Neoplatonism; to my mind, his position is original both when he reconciles the claims of body and soul (triumphantly at times, ironically perhaps at other times), and when he sincerely acknowledges the value of a love that can 'forget the He and She', ungrudgingly in 'The Undertaking' though regretfully in 'The Relique'.[20] He also parts company with the Platonists when he refuses to aestheticize passion. Beauty can arouse physical desire in 'Going to Bed', but it is never the original or deeper cause of the poet's love,[21] not even in 'Aire and Angels' when he first contemplates 'Some lovely glorious nothing'. His praise of an 'Autumnall' beauty was not a mere paradox. In the elegy 'His Picture' the rejoinder of the woman taunted for loving a weather-beaten lover is characteristic of his attitude:

> That which in him was faire and delicate,
> Was but the milke, which in loves childish state
> Did nurse it: who now is growne strong enough
> To feed on that, which to disused tasts seemes tough.[22]

In literary expression a desire of change for the sake of change (a desire paraded in Donne's elegy so entitled) was a prominent feature of this generation, akin to the general eagerness for 'news' and new fashions, which propagate more rapidly and are sooner displaced by other news and fashions in an urban environment.[23] John Hoskyns confessed: 'I have used & outworne 6 several styles since I was first fellowe of newe Colledge.'[24] Change had never been so rapid; the Ciceronianism

---

[20] See *Poètes métaphysiques*, III. 89–93 and 401–10.

[21] In 'Valediction: Of the Booke' beauty is only 'a convenient type to figure' the 'heaven, where love doth sit': the idea is Platonic, but with no Platonic sense of the transcendence of beauty.

[22] When Donne had his portraits painted he obviously sought to strike an attitude rather than offer a mere image of handsomeness.

[23] See *Poètes métaphysiques*, III. 99.

[24] *Life, Letters, and Writings*, ed. L. B. Osborn (New Haven, 1937), 152.

of Ascham still prevailed in Spenser's time; Euphuism and Arcadianism, born almost simultaneously, had a shorter yet still fairly spacious reign. In 1599 John Weever published *Epigrammes in the oldest cut and newest fashion . . . No longer (like the fashion) not unlike to continue.* Sir John Davies said his Muse and 'the black feather | Grew both together fresh in estimation' and were soon 'cast away together' (Epigram 48) and Drayton declared his Muse 'rightly of the *English* straine | That cannot long one fashion entertaine'.[25] In Sonnet lxxvi Shakespeare half-sincerely described his verse as 'far from variation or quick change', failing to 'glance aside to new-found methods'. This reign of fashion was largely due to the urban setting and the fast-increasing literary production which created a spirit of emulation, criticism, and parody. It was attended by a preference for 'an extemporall vaine' challenging 'the prowdest Rhetoritian to the contention of like perfection with like expedition'.[26] It favoured the composition of occasional verse in a conversational language.

The desire for change implied a rejection of imitation, further sharpened by a search for self-assertion and singularity. The Humanist principle of *imitatio*, however tempered by Erasmus, Politian, and Vives,[27] had so far been admitted by all Renaissance poets from Wyatt to Spenser. The satirists of the Donne generation wanted 'that no man would challenge [them] with servile imitation'; they condemned Daniel and Drayton for making 'use of others wit' and derided the sonneteers for 'filching whole pages from honest Petrarch'.[28] Marston was particularly vociferous in

---

[25] *Works*, ed. Hebel, II. 310.

[26] Nashe, *Works*, III. 312. Hall pretended to serve poetry 'with the broken Messes of our twelve-a-cloke houres' (Joseph Hall, *Collected Poems*, ed. A. Davenport (Liverpool, 1949), 97–8) and when industrious Jonson thought fit to state that he had spent only fifteen weeks on *The Poetaster* he was derided for his slowness of wit: Dekker, *Satiromastix*, l. 640; cf. 2 *Return from Parnassus*, I. ii. 296–7.

[27] See J. W. H. Atkins, *English Literary Criticism: The Renaissance* (London, 1947), 23, 46, 214, 312. Imitation had also been criticized by Petrarch himself, Leonardo, and Montaigne, though they practised it: Thomas M. Greene, *The Light in Troy* (New Haven, 1982), 44.

[28] Lodge, *A Fig for Momus* (1595), sig. A3[v]; 2 *Return from Parnassus*, I. ii. 235–40; Guilpin, *Skialetheia* (1598), sig. E1[v]; Hall (1598), *Virgidemiae*, VI. i. 251–2.

this respect.[29] Before them Donne had declared 'worst, who (beggarly) doth chaw | Others wits fruits, and . . . | doth those things out-spue, | As his own things'.[30] But Marston himself was only a 'servile imitating spirit' to Jonson,[31] and Guilpin imitated Donne, who seems alone entitled to declare: 'Now when I beginne this booke, I have no purpose to come into any mans debt . . . if I doe borrow any thing of Antiquitie, besides that I make account that I pay it to posterity, with as much and as good: You shall still finde mee to acknowledge it' (*Metempsychosis*; Epistle). What he owed to the Roman satirists and elegists in his poems, he did not, and hardly could, acknowledge, but he did pay with as much and as good.

In an elaborate comparison with Italian, Spanish, and French poets I have shown that the characteristics of Donne's poetry cannot be due to their influence, though he had in his closet 'Giddie fantastique Poëts of each land' ('Satyre I'). This discussion cannot be summarized since it was based on analyses of poems and figures.[32] It is interesting, however, to note that the poets of his generation ceased to imitate Italian and French poets as their predecessors had done from Surrey to Spenser. They turned for inspiration from the *Aeneid* or the *Metamorphoses* to the Roman Satires and Elegies, from pastoral and idyllic themes to Georgic realism and the country-house poem.[33] Donne's 'Baite' was no mere parody of Marlowe's 'Come live with mee and bee my love': he would 'some *new* pleasures prove' (my italics) and surpass his model, but he did it in such a self-conscious fashion that he seems to be satirizing the worn-out Arcadian themes as well as mocking himself in the closing exclamation.

[29] Marston, *The Scourge of Villanie* (1598), ed. G. B. Harrison (London, 1925), 'Satyre IX'; *Jack Drum's Entertainment*, IV. i. 47–8.

[30] 'Satyre II', 25–30. Puttenham had already criticized those who pilfered 'other mens devises': *Arte of English Poesie*, III. xxii (ed. Arber, p. 260) and Sidney claimed he was 'no pick-purse of another's wit' (*Astrophel and Stella*, 74), but they did not call in question the general principle of imitation.

[31] *Every Man out of his Humour*, Induction. Jonson clearly manifests the link between the rejection of servile imitation (he himself could imitate creatively) and the expression of individuality: 'we so insist on imitating others, as we cannot (when it is necessary) returne to our selves' (*Ben Jonson*, VIII. 597).

[32] *Poètes métaphysiques*, III, ch. 5.

[33] Ibid. 167–73; see the whole chapter for the rejection of the complaint, of allegory, of chivalric themes.

The general rejection of imitation by the Donne generation was an attitude of youthful bravado. An elder poet, Chapman, had a different purpose when he exalted Homer's original genius over Virgil's imitative talent ('To the Earl Marshal' in *Seven Books of the Iliads*) for he had a different conception of the uses and dignity of poetry, still based, like Spenser's, on the highest pretension of Renaissance Humanism.[34] The poets of the Donne generation gave up the notion of 'heroic furor' spread by the Neoplatonists and Giordano Bruno. When Donne speaks lightly of 'giddie fantastique Poëts' ('Satyre I', 10), or contemptuously of poetry and of those 'who write to Lords, rewards to get' ('Satyre II', 5–22), he obviously takes the pose expected from a gentleman who will never condescend to print. He is probably more sincere in his short verse letters to friends, admitting that 'to use, and love Poëtrie, to mee, | Betroth'd to no'one Art, be no' adulterie' ('To Mr Rowland Woodward'); but even when he exclaims 'All haile sweet Poët, more full of strong fire | Then hath or shall enkindle any spirit' ('To Mr T. W.'), he does not allude to a supernatural inspiration; he admires what 'nature' gave him, 'this merit | Of wit and Art'— a combination Jonson would have approved of. The love poet will only 'build in sonnets pretty roomes' and fashion 'a well-wrought urne' ('Canonization'), a modest claim for immortality when compared with the proud *monumentum aere perennius* of Horace (*Odes*, III. xxx) or Shakespeare. In fact, as I have shown in Chapter 1, he is interested in building a 'legend' or securing the attention of posterity ('Valediction: Of the Booke') in order to achieve an immediate sense of his own identity *sub specie aeternitatis*. When he writes that 'Verse the Fame enroules' (*First Anniversary*, 474) or 'embalmes' the virtue of the Countess of Bedford ('This twilight of two yeares', 13), he is in the humanistic tradition, but in a Jonsonian way, not in the Orphic or Platonic current of it.

That is why the 'difficulty' of Donne's poetry has nothing in common with the 'obscurity' Chapman cultivated as a majestic shrine for mysterious truths in his *Hymnus in Noctem*. He is close to the satirists of his generation who proclaimed that to be 'obscure' was 'yong mens Rhetoricke' and 'now a schollers

---

[34] This was amply discussed in *Poètes métaphysiques*, III. 106–26.

vaine';[35] yet, though harsh and at times 'crabbed', he is not really 'murky' and 'gloomy' as Juvenal and Persius were said to be.[36] Hall and Marston themselves sought to temper what they considered a requirement of the literary genre and mocked the eagerness of some readers for verse they could not understand.[37] Donne derided 'an obscure writer' in an epigram. He wrote for the 'understander' and meant to be understood: the difficulty of his poetry proceeds from his taste for the surprising simile, the singular illustration (which may even be mythological if uncommon),[38] and the subtlety of his argument. I hope I have shown that his generation had a cult for originality, not for obscurity.[39]

In their cult of wit the poets of the Donne generation were at one with their predecessors in England and abroad, but they were interested in new forms of wit, displayed in the epigram, the paradox, and the rhetorical figures that create surprise and call for a quick apprehension of thought.

The epigram was acknowledged to be the 'wittiest' of all poems: *argutia* (*argutezza* in Italian) was said by Thomas Correa to be its soul, nerve, and blood.[40] William Drummond's opinion that Donne was the best English epigrammatist is unexpected since the 'monarch of wit' wrote few and rather uninteresting epigrams;[41] but Drummond probably had in mind some of his lyrics and satirical elegies. The Renaissance epigram could belong to any of the eight categories distinguished in Correa's treatise: they ranged from the 'descriptive epigram' to the 'elegiac poem', from the epitaph and the epicedium to the threnos. The Latin epigrams of Campion (1595), influenced by

---

[35] Weever, *Epigrammes* (1599), Epig. 8, p. 54.

[36] Hall, *Virgidemiae*, 'Postscript'; Marston, *Scourge*, Preface and 'Satyre VI'.

[37] *Virgidemiae*, 'Postscript'; *Scourge*, ed. Harrison, p. 9.

[38] On the attitude to mythology of the Donne generation, see *Poètes métaphysiques*, III. 155–65.

[39] *Poètes métaphysiques*, III, ch. 3, §3.

[40] John Heath, *Two Centuries of Epigrammes* (London, 1610), fo. A3; Thomas Correa, *De toto eo poematis genere quod epigramma dicitur* (Venetiis), p. 38 in the 1590 edition.

[41] *Critical Essays of the Seventeenth Century*, ed. J. E. Spingarn (Oxford, 1957), I. 216–17. Thomas Hester's praise of Donne's 'ability to suggest the wondrous mysteries of human motivation' in his epigrams has not fully convinced me (in *The Eagle and the Dove*, ed. Claude Summers and Ted Larry Pebworth (Columbia, 1987), 80–91).

Catullus as well as Martial, included encomia, epitaphs, and short love poems close to the amatory elegy. The links with satire, however, were closest: John Owen claimed that the epigram in order to please had to savour of satire and satire had to borrow wit from the epigram.[42] Occasional verse, like Donne's early verse letters to male friends, would also be looked upon as epigrams. Dowland, Robert Jones, and Campion published their 'books of songs and airs' in that period (1597–1601) and the air, unlike the polyphonic madrigal, could claim kinship with the epigram.[43] Donne's song 'Goe, and catch a falling starre' has an epigrammatic close. The sudden profusion of epigrammatic poems at the end of the sixteenth century denotes a fashion, but the Latin epigram, cultivated at Winchester and Oxford, came to maturity before its counterpart in the vernacular. Owen, Stradling, the Michelborne brothers only wrote in Latin; the Latin epigrams of Hoskyns and Charles Fitzgeffrey outweigh the English ones. Donne proved resolutely more 'modern'. Uninfluenced by the Greek Anthology which had attracted Spenser, he sought to achieve the kind of dramatic surprise and comic effect noticeable in the epigrams of Martial and innovated in introducing this comic element in the ironic close of some of his *Songs and Sonets*.[44]

In Donne's composition of prose paradoxes, as well as in his use of the paradox in poetry, the bent of his mind is also disclosed.[45] The *paradoxon* of the Sophists was meant to show that one could argue indifferently for or against any opinion, which implied scepticism or bad faith. Plato used sophistry to discredit the Sophists: the argument of Thrasymachus in Book I of the *Republic* was often included in Renaissance collections of paradoxes. Yet Socrates resorted to paradox in order to lead the mind to a higher truth. So did the Stoics, but without his subtlety and irony: they demonstrated with unrelieved seriousness that their moral precepts, though contrary to the common opinion, were rational. Cicero and Plutarch followed suit, but the latter insisted on *mirabilia* in his *Quaestiones Naturales*.

---

[42] *Epigrammatum Liber II* (1607), 181; fo. D7ᵛ. Yet the epigrams he addressed to his mistress resembled short elegies.

[43] *Campion's Works*, ed. Percival Vivian (Oxford, 1909), 4.

[44] See *Poètes métaphysiques*, III. 322–9.

[45] See ibid. 330–51.

With the Stoics, indeed, whatever provoked wonder had become paradoxical; Philostephanos had even listed 'paradoxical rivers'. The rhetoricians of late Antiquity also came to use the term paradox for a figure of style meant to create surprise. The comic effect was emphasized and the name of *paradoxi* was even given to mimes. This may explain why the paradox was confused with the mock-encomium which had originated in the rhetoric, not the philosophy of Antiquity. In the Middle Ages it was the form of paradox mainly cultivated by rhetoricians; theologians did not use the term paradox, though the *Quaestiones logicales impossibiles* of Siger had much in common with the dialectical paradox. The Renaissance usually made no distinction between the paradox, the mock encomium, and the *mirabilia*.[46] Gaspar Dornau's jumbling of philosophical paradoxes, Erasmus' *Praise of Folly*, and More's *Utopia*, with Claudian's *De Magnete* and innumerable burlesque encomia, is typical.[47] In Renaissance literature at large as in Donne's poems, rather than separate jest from earnestness, one should admit a playful seriousness and the presence of a serious meaning in jest.

Donne, however, chose the type of paradox that suited his mind. Lyly had drawn on the *Paradoxa Stoicorum*, which he ignored, and the translation of Castiglione's *Cortegiano* had called attention to the mock encomium, which proved unattractive to him, with the exception of the more intellectual attempts, like Edward Daunce's *Prayse of Nothing*[48] or Jean Passerat's *Nihil*, imitated in a galaxy of poems based on philosophical, alchemical, theological notions as Donne's often are.[49] Yet Donne's play on 'all' and 'nothing', as I have shown (see p. 37), is not an idle game, but an expression of a personal aspiration or disquiet. Nor did the author of *The Flea* choose to write one more praise of an animal, an exercise derided in Hall's *Virgidemiae* (VI. i. 153), in *The Return from Parnassus* (1, III. i. 889–96), and in Shakespeare's *Henry V* (III. vii. 32–43): even

---

[46]   R. Colie, who presented the 'siren' as a paradox, apparently shared this conception in her brilliant but to my mind confusing survey of *Paradoxa Epidemica*.

[47]   *Amphitheatrum Sapientiae Socraticae Joco-Seriae*, 2 vols. (Hanoviae, 1619).

[48]   London, 1585; originally attributed to Edward Dyer.

[49]   *Nihil* (Paris, 1585) was followed by *Rien. Traduit du latin de Jean Passerat . . . Quelque Chose. Tout* (Paris, 1597). Cf. Dornau, *Amphitheatrum*, I. 723–39, 757–71.

when playful he wanted to make his readers think. The kind of wit that pleased him and pleased his generation is found in the more intellectual paradoxes of Ortensio Landi.[50] Like Cicero, Landi took ideas, not objects, for his themes, often Stoic or Christian. Donne apologetically described his own paradoxes as 'rather alarums to truth to arme her then enemies',[51] yet he often found in them opportunities to state truths.[52] He even condemned 'Extreames' for being 'equally removed from the meane' (Paradox v). In some manuscripts 'The Autumnall' was entitled 'A paradox of an ould Woman', but it was no mock-encomium: the paradox here has suffered a sea-change into something rich and strange. Donne's inmost preoccupations were expressed in *Biathanatos*, presented as a *Paradox*. His playful *Problems* were also studded with shrewd observations. Characteristically, though riddles were popular,[53] he did not indulge in this artificial game but applied the word seriously to the enigmas of the human heart and his own 'riddling soul'.[54]

Rosemond Tuve's assumption that Ramism influenced both Elizabethan and Metaphysical imagery blurred important differences between the two.[55] I refuted the argument at length in 1960; it may be sufficient here to point out that Ramistic logic, based on the self-evident axiom and dichotomy, was obviously alien to the subtlety of Donne's dialectics. By transferring invention and composition from rhetoric to logic Ramus was also responsible for the reduction of rhetoric to a storehouse of figures considered as an 'ornament added' to the thought.[56] In 1588 the *Arcadian Rhetoricke* of Abraham Fraunce followed Ramus and fetched its illustrations from Sidney's romance. A comparison of it with the *Directions for Speech and Style* of John Hoskyns, probably written about 1599, clearly shows an evolution of taste in the younger

---

[50] Translated into English in 1593; they were imitated by William Cornwallis in his *Essayes of certaine Paradoxes* (1600).

[51] Letter to Wotton (1600?); in *Paradoxes and Problems*, xxvi.

[52] For instance about old men exclaiming against the times who 'betray themselves. For yf the tymes be chang'd, ther manners have chang'd them' (Paradox viii).

[53] e.g. *The Riddles of Heraclitus and Democritus* (1598).

[54] *Sermons*, VIII. 332, l. 740; 'Canonization', 23; 'Lovers infinitenesse', 29; Holy Sonnet XIX, etc.

[55] *Elizabethan and Metaphysical Imagery* (Chicago, 1947).

[56] *P. Rami Dialecticae Libri Duo* (Paris, 1560), Lib. I, q. 61.

generation.[57] By 1598 Guilpin knew that 'wits Caesar, Sidney' could be 'censur'd for affectation' (*Skialetheia*, Sat. Sexta) and Sir John Roe, born in 1581, parodied the figures commended by Fraunce.[58] Hoskyns sought to temper the use of exclamations, also derided in Hall's *Virgidemiae* (IV. i. 153); as a lawyer he privileged interrogation for its vivacity (*Directions*, 146–7). Rhetoricians distinguished between 'figures of words', said to be 'delicate' or 'feminine', and 'figures of thought' or 'figures of sentences', 'more forcible and apt to perswade'.[59] Hoskyns, like all the poets of the Donne generation, obviously preferred the latter. Repetitions of words or sounds, praised by Fraunce in *complexio* or *symploce*, are discountenanced.[60] Repetition, however, is permissible in the polyptoton when it serves the meaning and Hoskyns would not have disapproved of Donne's 'all formes, uniforme deformity | Doth cover' in 'The Storme'. Epanodos and epizeuxis are also admitted for they are 'freest from the oppinion of affectacon' (128). The criticism of affectation had earlier been directed only against inkhorn terms.

Copia and 'wittie invention' were linked in Thomas Wilson's *Arte of Rhetorique* (1560) and Richard Rainolde's *Foundacion of Rhetorike* (1563)[61] and amplification long remained a favourite figure. Hoskyns tolerated it only as a process of thought: mere litanies of synonyms should be left to schoolmasters (138). Comparison, division, and progression are preferable to accumulation (131–42). Division begets other figures, which are modes of reasoning: induction, dilemma, and 'prosopoesis', 'that over throweth noe pte of the Division, but returneth some reason to each' (160): this was Donne's way of arguing in 'Lovers Infinitenesse'. Hoskyns, trained on law, gave instances of suppositions advanced 'without intangling a mans self' (163), a method suited to Donne's examination of problematic 'cases'.

Puttenham and Hoskyns were agreed on the importance of

---

[57] Included in *The Life, Letters and Writings of John Hoskyns*, ed. L. B. Osborn (New Haven, 1937).

[58] 'O dire Mischance! And, O vile verse! And yet your Abraham France | Writes thus, and jests not': included in *Donne's Poetical Works*, p. 374.

[59] *The Arcadian Rhetoricke*, ed. Ethel Seaton (Oxford, 1950), 63.

[60] Contrast *Arcadian Rhetoricke*, 50, 53, and *Hoskyns*, ed. Osborn, 127.

[61] Wilson, *Arte of Rhetorique*, ed. G. H. Mair (Oxford, 1909), 120, 190; Rainolde, *Foundacion of Rhetorike*, fo. 1ᵛ.

irony, but the examples given by the former—the 'drie mock', the 'bitter taunt', the 'fleering frump', etc.—rather recalled Touchstone's blunt flouting than Donne's irony; Hoskyns was subtler in his attention to the ironic use of understatement (144). When reviewing figures 'of quick conceit' (as Puttenham designated them), he called attention to the union of contraries (*Synoeceosis*), as in 'wittie ignorance', adding however that this 'musicke made of cunning discords' 'was an easie figure now in fashion not like ever to be soe usuall' (150). Like Jonson he was diffident about violent metaphors, particularly *Catachresis*, which was also 'now growne in fashion' (125). He was here in line with Jonson, who criticized mixed metaphors,[62] but not in opposition to Donne, who relied on similes. And in the search for witty similitudes he did not recommend joining things of 'proud compare' but 'inventing matter of agreem^t in things most unlike' (132), a characteristic feature of the 'metaphysical' style.

The fields of imagery were not discussed by Fraunce and Hoskyns, though the latter at times mocked mathematical images (*Directions*, 100, 152). I have argued that scientific or theological imagery is not by itself a distinctive feature either of Donne's style or of the new taste.[63] Much more importance should be attached to the link with the anti-Ciceronian movement and the Senecan style. The writers who called for things, not words (*res non verba*) were not averse from the subtleties of language (as the fellows of the Royal Society later proved) when they were used to convey pith and sense like the prose of Seneca, or Bacon's *Essays*, or the poetry of Donne. I have tried to show that the monarch of wit, the lover of the *Songs and Sonets*, like the author of the *Satires*, was entitled to apostrophize Truth as '[his] mistress'.[64] In this allegiance he was in harmony with his generation in his Inns of Court environment, but he did speak with his own voice and singular accent in a social and literary milieu favourable to innovation and originality.

---

[62] In *Discoveries: Ben Jonson*, VIII. 624–5.

[63] *Poètes métaphysiques*, III. 383–6.

[64] 'Satyre IV', 163; Ellrodt, 'Poésie et vérité chez John Donne', *EA* 40 (1987), 1–14. He even made a truthful use of the fabulous: see my 'Le fabuleux et l'imagination poétique dans l'œuvre de John Donne', *De Shakespeare à T. S. Eliot: Mélanges Fluchère* (Paris, 1976).

Conclusion

Examined from a structural point of view the modes of thought, imagination, and sensibility of the seven authors studied in this volume evidence a formal coherence reflected in the composition and style of their poems. I cannot offer a unified conception of each personality based on a single dominant feature, or a single existential project, or a fundamental experience; but three systems of interrelated traits have been brought to light. A summary will inevitably appear abstract and jejune unless the reader keeps in mind the many nuances disclosed in the previous analyses.

A first set of correlations centres on the poet's modes of self-awareness and its consequences for the affections.

With Donne, self-centredness is the starting-point, but what I call self-consciousness is a more complex structure: it implies an immediate reflexivity in the very moment of experience. With George Herbert as with Donne, self-consciousness invites at once self-analysis and irony directed at oneself, hence ambiguity. It sharpens Donne's egotistic desire of achieving self-knowledge and a permanent identity, but Herbert's constant apprehension of his self in relation with God creates a different approach in self-analysis. Crashaw, whom I contrasted with Herbert though they seem to have much in common in their love of God, obeys ambivalent impulses and proves self-conscious only in his desire to lose himself in the object of his love. Vaughan's emotional subjectivity, or 'sentiment de soi', overflows into a diffuse sympathy with natural objects. Closer to Donne's is Marvell's self-consciousness, responsible for his elusiveness and ironical detachment; yet he seems to shrink from self-questionings and tends to become a contemplator of the world or his own experience as mirrored in his mind. Entirely different is the epistemological curiosity of Lord Herbert, bent on an introspective, yet impersonal survey of the operations of the mind. Traherne's point of view is initially solipsistic, like the child's, and his self-consciousness has more in common with Lord Herbert's than with Donne's; it does not invite self-analysis, ambiguity, and irony, but engenders his wonder at the phenomenon of reflexivity which places the world in his mind.

The nature of their self-awareness affected in different ways Donne's and Marvell's attitude to human love. The reaction of each poet at the prospect of death (ignored in Traherne's emphasis on his sense of immortality) also proves individual and distinctive. Their deeper wish—a stable 'essential joy' (Donne), a permanent love relationship with God (George Herbert), access to a paradisiac world (Vaughan and, in a different way, Marvell), the certainty of the soul's immortality (Lord Herbert), the desire to possess all things (Traherne)—was also discussed in Part I and occasionally in Part III.

In the second system of correlations presentness was found to be dominant among six poets, but with important variations:

- Donne's and George Herbert's present: concrete, dense, dynamic, an instant filled with life and substantiality (more spacious with Herbert, who seeks at times to recapitulate his experience);
- Crashaw's and Marvell's fluid or slippery present, on which they seek to impose a rhythm;
- Lord Herbert's intemporal present, a succession of empty instants;
- Traherne's infinite stasis.

It appeared that Vaughan alone (here contrasted with George Herbert) was predominantly engaged in retrospection or long-distance expectation.

These primary distinctions led to further differences between:

- Donne's and George Herbert's living intuition of a concrete eternity, embodied in a privileged moment with Donne, underlying the course of a whole life with George Herbert;
- Vaughan's contemplation of an eternity beyond time, preceding or following it, therefore creating a twofold orientation toward the past and toward the future;
- Crashaw's and Marvell's experience of time as a flow only; with Crashaw, an irresistible rush toward a closing ecstasy in

death, or the death of rapture; with Marvell, an unceasing
motion which the poet seeks to control by accelerating or
slowing it down;

- Lord Herbert's eternity, imagined only 'after the analogy of
the finite and the temporal' with no certainty of the persistence of being, hence his own persistent preoccupation with
immortality;
- Traherne's firm and constant assurance of a stable eternity,
conceived as an infinite extension, hence without the sense of
transcendence always associated by Donne and George
Herbert with the experience of immanence.

We also noticed that the distinctive features in each poet's
apprehension of time, and occasionally in his dominant mode of
self-awareness, could be correlated with other traits concerning:

- the modes of motion: discontinuous and brusque (Donne,
George Herbert), continuous and slow (Vaughan), continuous and swift (Crashaw), interspersed with pauses or frozen
(Marvell), at a standstill (Traherne);
- the perception of space by a consciousness with a wide or
narrow field: attention foregrounded on a near object within
an enclosure (Donne, George Herbert), or ranging to the
distant horizon (Vaughan), or quite uncircumscribed
(Traherne); a procession of distinct images (Marvell), or fleet-
ing metamorphoses (Crashaw);
- a 'formal' (as distinguished from Bachelard's 'elemental')
imagination of matter, with a predominance of the solid and
tangible (Donne, George Herbert) or the fluid and liquid
(Crashaw, Marvell), of images of living growth (Vaughan), or
visual images only (Traherne);
- particular modes of thinking: analytical division and definition (Donne, George Herbert); rumination and vagueness
(Vaughan); mere succession or a surface logical frame
(Crashaw and Marvell), dialectical movement (Lord Herbert);
straightforward statements of general views (Traherne);
- particular modes of literary composition: a preference for
dramatic immediacy (Donne, George Herbert), for lyrical
élan (Crashaw), for narration (Vaughan), for tableaux
(Marvell), for description (Lord Herbert), for enumeration
and rhapsody (Traherne).

In a third and last group of correlations Donne's and George Herbert's vivid and simultaneous awareness of two orders of reality appeared to be responsible for their emphasis on 'double natures', on the necessary conjunction of body and soul, and on the mysteries of the Incarnation and the Resurrection. It also accounts for the nature of their paradoxes, and the various ways in which their styles, however different, are characterized by a constant interpenetration of the concrete and the abstract. In his handling of the same Christian themes, Crashaw mainly gives his attention to the 'spectacle' of the Nativity or the Passion; he turns paradoxes into miracles and merges the spiritual in the sensible. Vaughan's approach privileges regeneration and an Edenic restoration; his 'supernatural naturalism' acknowledges a cosmic continuity between matter and spirit; yet image and idea are often disjoined in his poetry; he is at his best when he can rely on the symbolic imagination. Marvell, poetically uninterested in the Christian mysteries and only intent on purity, also tends to dissociate the abstract and the concrete in a parallel consideration of body and soul, or pure sensation and pure thought. Lord Herbert only seeks a Platonic sublimation and moves from image to concept in his philosophical paradoxes. Traherne abolishes all duality in his anticipation of Berkeleyan idealism, his rational 'mysticism' achieves a metamorphosis of the Christian spirit and, in fact, foreshadows the optimism of the Enlightenment.

The exploration of the minds of these seventeenth-century poets has not only disclosed an inner coherence; it has, I hope, established the permanence of their essential modes of thought and consciousness in all their works despite changes in allegiance, themes, or moods, or supposed 'conversions'.

By tracing the progress of self-awareness in its different aspects from Antiquity to the Renaissance and the seventeenth century I intended to assess its significance for the history of the European mind and the literary expression of identity. I tried to discriminate between successive and various modes of apprehension of the self, and demonstrate that there were very few and imperfect precedents (with the exception of Montaigne) for the modern type of self-consciousness displayed by Donne, or for Traherne's solipsistic delight in his self-reflexive perception of the world.

A historical account of a general evolution in the intuition of time and the conception of space was also meant to make a deep change in habits of thought more perceptible in the seventeenth century. The change opened up various possibilities for the imagination in each domain and each author availed himself of them in accordance with the bent of his own mind.

The last chapter showed that, by the end of the sixteenth century, poets belonging to the same generation, living in the same environment, were agreed in their rejection of the themes, literary genres, and rhetorical figures favoured by their immediate predecessors. It appeared, however, that Donne was free and fully able to impress his own personality upon the new attitudes, the fashionable genres, and the new forms of wit cultivated by his contemporaries.[1]

Cowley had been included in the volumes published in 1960. Why was he left out here? Partly for reasons of space. Mainly because his poetry is not an apt illustration of an 'unchanging mind'. This is not in contradiction with my general thesis, but I can only give an outline of the argument I developed in a chapter.[2] Cowley was a 'littérateur' who constantly transposed life in literary terms. Poetry to him was an end in itself, yet not the highest end. He changed his models, moved from a late Elizabethan lyricism in *Sylva* to a 'metaphysical' style in *The Mistress*; but he only borrowed its trappings. His later poems became vehicles for the objective expression of religious, philosophical, or scientific truths studiously adorned. Yet he ultimately revealed his true bent, long concealed by imitativeness, in the pre-classical eloquence of his Odes and the simplicity of his poems on gardens.

Close imitation of earlier literary models is always unsuccessful when it does not allow the free play of the writer's own

---

[1] Several of my previously published essays had also called attention to the individual and diverse views of the Metaphysical poets in various fields in which one might have thought that their cultural milieu in a particular period would have been determinant: e.g. the notion of miracle and angelology. They reinforce my general thesis; see esp.: 'Miracle et nature de saint Augustin à la poésie métaphysique anglaise', *Réseaux, Revue interdisciplinaire de philosophie morale et politique*, 24–5 (1975), 1–36; 'Angels and the Poetic Imagination from Donne to Traherne', *English Renaissance Studies Presented to Dame Helen Gardner* (Oxford, 1980), 164–79.

[2] See *Poètes métaphysiques*, II, ch. ii.

tendencies and individual modes of imagination. With greater poets than Cowley, however, the permanence of essential elements of their personality may be observed in all their works even when they tried several styles in succession. In a brief article I have shown that some structures of Milton's mind were discernible in his earliest compositions, Latin and English, though these poems were highly different in spirit and style from the later ones.[3] I have traced the same type of unbroken imaginative continuity in the poetry of Keats over a much shorter period of evolution.[4] Notwithstanding the postmodernist dismissal of personal inspiration,[5] I am convinced that some minds are truly creative: the contrary assumption makes innovation unexplainable, and innovation is a fact. I have always endeavoured to show that the creator is visible in his creation, not face to face, after the manner of the more naive autobiographical interpretations, nor only 'through a glass, darkly', but through the characteristic interplay of his personal modes of thought, imagination, and sensibility. The constancy of these individual traits justifies the seemingly paradoxical assertion of Proust about the 'monotony' of the truly original works: by projecting out of themselves 'a world that is unique', great writers create 'a single work, or rather refract through various objects the selfsame beauty they bring to the world'.[6]

[3] See 'Milton's Unchanging Mind and the Early Poems', *Milton Quarterly*, 22 (1988), 59–62.

[4] In my Introduction to *John Keats. Poésie* (a bilingual edition) (Paris, 2000).

[5] The problem of inspiration is discussed in my article 'Origines et contraintes de l'inspiration poétique', in *L'Acte créateur*, ed. G. Gadoffre (Paris, 1997).

[6] *La prisonnière*, in *A la recherche du temps perdu*, III (Paris, 1988), 877.

Index of Topics

Since the main topics are apparent in chapter headings attention is only called to some subsidiary topics.

Index of Names

This index includes all authors and scholars whose works are studied, quoted from or commented upon, not merely mentioned. The figures are in italics when I quote, however briefly.